AGE OF PROPAGANDA

AGE OF
PROPAGANDA

The Everyday Use and Abuse of Persuasion

REVISED EDITION

ANTHONY R. PRATKANIS and
ELLIOT ARONSON
University of California, Santa Cruz

W. H. FREEMAN AND COMPANY
NEW YORK

Portions of this book first appeared in *The Social Animal*.
Cartoons © 2000, 1991 by Sidney Harris

Library of Congress Cataloging-in-Publication Data

Pratkanis, Anthony R.
   Age of Propaganda : The everyday use and abuse of persuasion / Anthony R.
Pratkanis and Elliot Aronson – Rev. ed.
         p.   cm.
   Includes bibliographical references and index.
   ISBN 0-7167-3108-8 (pbk.)
   1. Propaganda. 2. Persuasion (Psychology) 3. Public opinion.
   4. Advertising. 5. Television in propaganda. I. Aronson, Elliot.
   II. Title.
HM263.P715   2001
303.3'75—dc21   97-008615

Printed in the United States of America

First printing 2001

**To the memory of my parents, Harry Aronson
(1903–1950) and Dorothy Aronson (1901–1989)**

*They had a wonderfully innocent, childlike trust that, in this
country, almost everything they read (especially if it was between
the covers of a book) was absolutely true.*

E. A.

To my son, Tony T. Pratkanis (born 1991)

*Chances are, he will grow up with a healthy skepticism but a
regrettable cynicism about the truth of everything he reads, hears,
and sees.*

A. R. P.

CONTENTS

COUNTERACTING THE TACTICS OF PROPAGANDA

WHY WE WROTE |||||||||||||||||||||
THIS BOOK

We are of different generations. One of us (E. A.) was born in 1932 and grew up during World War II. "At that time, I fervently believed just about everything I was exposed to in school and in the media. For example, I knew that all Germans were evil and that all Japanese were sneaky and treacherous, while all white Americans were clean-cut, honest, fair-minded, and trusting. Perhaps you had to be eleven years old to take seriously the racial and national caricatures presented in the war movies of the early 1940s. But in those days, most grown-ups—including my parents (to whom this book is dedicated)—certainly wanted to believe in the basic message of the war movies and did, in fact, have a childlike trust in the media. They hung on every word President Roosevelt said in his famous fireside chats and never dreamed of questioning the nobility of the motives behind our national policy. They thought (and so did I) that the purpose of commercial advertising was to inform the consumer."

The world has taken a few turns since then. A. R. P. grew up during the Vietnam war and was witness to the blatant lying by public officials of that era. "At the time, I sat riveted to my television screen, scared to death by the images of death and destruction beamed into my living room from Vietnam, all the while learning that politicians only lie when their lips move. I came of age during the Watergate era when a sitting president, Richard Nixon, was forced to resign when faced with incontrovertible evidence (some of it supplied by his own tape recordings) of the lying, dirty tricks, and attempted cover-up that he and his cronies had perpetrated on the American people. For me, commercials, whether for different brands of products or different brands of politicians, were entertainment designed to make someone rich or more powerful."

In the first edition of this book, we lamented the fact that there was no White House tape recorder in use during the 1980s—so that President Reagan escaped the consequences of deceiving the American people (and the world) by subverting the Constitution through the covert sale of arms to Iran and the diversion of the profits from that sale to support the Nicaraguan Contras.[1] We felt (and continue to feel) it to be a sad commentary on our times that, although the majority of the American people were furious at Nixon and his cronies, by the time of the Iran-Contra scandal most Americans seemed to have developed a more cynical attitude about being deceived and did not seem displeased when Oliver North, John Poindexter, and President Reagan himself succeeded, for the most part, in "beating the rap." And now, ho hum, other investigations come along—the savings and loan debacle, the BCCI crisis, Ruby Ridge, and various shady campaign contributions given to U.S. politicians of every stripe. Who cares? Business as usual. Such cynicism carries a price. A cynical electorate is a lackadaisical electorate, as evidenced by the fact that fewer than 50% of eligible Americans now bother to vote.

And then there was the world-famous slow-speed chase, the media circus of the century—the trial of O. J. Simpson.[2] An international audience sat riveted to their TV sets as an army of more than 1,000 credentialed reporters plus untold media pundits went over and over and over every excruciating detail of the case and the story—from the cost of the trial to the menu at the Mezzaluna Restaurant to Marcia Clark's topless vacation on the French Riviera. CNN alone employed 70 correspondents and 250 legal experts to produce 1,530 hours of O. J. trial coverage and commentary. O. J. trinket vendors made more than $1 billion selling such treasures as novelty Simpson wristwatches, T-shirts, orange-scented O. J. air fresheners, and Judge Ito Jell-O molds. From January 1, 1995, until the week after the verdict, television network news spent twenty-six hours and fifty minutes, or 13.6% of the available airtime, covering the O. J. story. That is more time than was devoted to Bosnia (thirteen hours and one minute), the bombing in Oklahoma City (eight hours and fifty-three minutes), and the U.S. budget (three hours and thirty-nine minutes)—the other top three "news" stories—combined.

And after the O. J. verdict was rendered, what was the news media to do? The trial had been a cash cow. The coverage was relatively cheap to produce, garnered great ratings, and brought in top advertising revenues. For example, the television networks charged advertisers ten times their normal rate for thirty seconds of commercial time during the O. J. verdict. What would top a juicy, intriguing trial of a prominent athlete? What would keep the advertising revenue flowing? How about an impeachment trial of a U.S. president for sex crimes?

And that is what we watched next. Beginning in January of 1998, the nation's mass media, particularly its news programming, launched around-the-clock coverage of stories and speculation about then-President Clinton's sexual misconduct, especially with a White House intern named Monica Lewinsky.[3] The number of jokes told about Bill Clinton on late-night TV soared a whopping 111.3 % during the year of the saga. An estimated 67.6 million Americans watched Clinton's televised speech on August 17, 1998, in which he admitted an inappropriate relationship with Monica Lewinsky. In the month just before this announcement, the network morning news shows devoted 179 segments to the Clinton sex scandal and only 56 segments to any other news about the Clinton administration. Much of this coverage bordered on the hysterical, with rumor chasing gossip chasing innuendo—much like the coverage of the O. J. trial. For example, a panelist on CNBC stated that the president had had sex with four other interns besides Lewinsky, ABC News reported that Clinton and Lewinsky had been caught in the act, possibly by Secret Service agents, and then the *Dallas Morning News* followed up with news that an agent was ready to testify that he saw the president and Lewinsky engage in a sex act. Of course, these still unsubstantiated rumors were repeated over and over again by the news media, giving them an air of respectability. Amidst this media roar, President Clinton infamously shook his finger at the American public and denied having sex with "that woman."

What were the reactions of Americans to having their news shows turned into the "All Monica, All the Time" network? Bill Clinton's approval ratings soared during the period. Newt Gingrich and others who led the impeachment charge lost favor with the American public (with some being forced to leave government because of their own revealed sexual indiscretions). Opinion polls showed that Americans had lost respect for the news media and did not like the way the saga was covered. We think the most telling statistic of all is this: QVC, the "All

Shopping, All the Time" TV network posted the second-highest sales week in its history immediately after the August 17 admission by Clinton. Apparently, many of those 67.6 million Americans who tuned in to hear Clinton went channel surfing without delay after the pronouncement and settled on QVC as an alternative to the "news" coverage. It was as if American citizens were saying, *"I am sick and tired of the blather. I am going shopping."*

Something needs to change. The mass media respond to our itch for entertainment and spectacle and create "news" coverage of the ilk found in the O. J. Simpson trial and the Monica Lewinsky saga. Such "news" coverage feeds our cynicism about government and the state of our nation. For example, consider the media coverage of the 2000 U.S. presidential election. The campaign was marked by a lack of interest from both citizens and the news media. However, as soon as a possibly entertaining spectacle emerged—the recount of votes in Florida—then the networks launched around-the-clock coverage—coverage that feeds our cynicism that things seem to be out of control.

The losers are those of us who respect democracy. For while we sat glued to the trial and the saga, we didn't sit glued to stories covering investigations of campaign finance violations or providing in-depth analysis of issues of great importance to our country, such as spiraling health care costs, the continued proliferation of nuclear weapons at the international level, the shrinking middle class, the expanding number of children in poverty, and the continued consolidation of mass media power into the hands of a few large firms. This itch for entertainment carries a price—the information we need to participate in a democracy is replaced by trivial entertainment, thus making it harder and harder for us to carry out our responsibilities as citizens.

We wrote this book because we passionately believe that there are more than two choices: naive acceptance of the fruits of propaganda on the one hand and total cynicism combined with a lust for entertainment on the other. During an age characterized by ever more sophisticated uses of propaganda techniques, it is important, especially in a democracy, that citizens become informed about these devices, the psychological dynamics of what makes them effective, and how to counteract their effectiveness without withdrawing into abject cynicism. That's what this book is about. We are researchers who have been studying the nuts and bolts of persuasion techniques for a combined total of more than fifty years—and we believe we know something about what works and what doesn't work and why. Moreover, we believe we know something about how to guard against the abuse of these techniques by unscrupulous communicators—including (especially) those unscrupulous communicators who might be running for the highest political offices in the land.

In addition, our experience has led us to understand the difference between persuasion and propaganda. Thus, this book also contains advice for those of you who might want to be effective communicators in ways that are honest and above-board. We believe that, in an age of propaganda, the most important thing for the survival of democracy is the existence of communicators who know how to present their message clearly and fairly, coupled with an informed electorate that knows the difference between a fair presentation and a con job. It is toward achieving these ends that we wrote this book.

As with any effort of this size, there are a number of people who should be thanked. First, we would like to thank all the readers of the first edition of this book who bothered to mail us their opinions or who corresponded with us via interactive media such as talk radio and the Internet. In this revision, we sought to respond to your comments by clarifying a misleading or inaccurate point or even revising our opinion. In addition to these changes, we have also updated the research (where appropriate), added new chapters on issues of concern to readers (e.g., the use of hypocrisy in persuasion, what to do about propaganda), and updated our examples of propaganda.

Some people deserve special thanks. Vera Aronson, Mahzarin Banaji, Susan Brennan, Jonathan Cobb, Peter Farquhar, Erika Goldman, Craig Leve, Nathan Maccoby, Richard Petty and the Ohio State Research Group on Attitudes and Persuasion, Rosemarie Pratkanis, Michael Santos, Carol Tavris, and our students at the University of California, Santa Cruz, provided helpful comments. Marlene Turner provided continuous, invaluable feedback as the book was being written.

▮▮▮▮▮▮▮▮▮▮▮▮▮▮▮▮▮▮

Our Age of Propaganda

In the early 1990s, seventeen-year-old Demetrick James Walker was sentenced to life in prison for killing a sixteen-year-old. The reason for the slaying: Demetrick so badly wanted a pair of $125 Nike Air Jordans like the ones he had seen on TV that he put a .22-caliber pistol to the head of Johnny Bates, pulled the trigger, and walked off with a new pair of high-tops. During the trial, Houston prosecutor Mark Vinson placed some of the blame on the images created by advertising. Said Vinson, "It's bad when we create an image of luxury about athletic gear that it forces people to kill over it."[1]

The 1990 North Carolina U.S. Senate race was one of the most heated—and expensive—political contests in recent years. Going into the last weeks of the campaign, the black Democratic challenger, Harvey Gantt, held a slight lead in the polls over the white Republican incumbent, Jesse Helms. Eight days before the election, Helms broadcast an ad dubbed "White Hands." The spot, created by political consultant Alex Castellanos, showed a pair of white hands crumpling a letter of rejection. The voice-over: "You needed that job, but they had to give it to a minority because of racial quotas. Is that really fair?" Although Gantt was on record as opposed to quotas, the spot appears to have had its intended effect: Helms squeaked through and by a slim margin was reelected to the Senate, supported by a huge majority in white precincts. The tactic worked so well that Helms did it again in his 1996 rematch with Gantt; this time Helms accused Gantt of being the recipient of preferential treatment in the awarding of contracts.[2] In the 2000 U.S. presidential election, Alex Castellanos again achieved notoriety when he produced a 30-second ad for the Republican National Committee. This ad contained the word RATS subliminally flashed across the television screen.

Some years ago, CBS aired the film *Cry Rape*. Essentially, the story made it clear that a rape victim who chooses to press charges against her attacker runs the risk of undergoing an ordeal that may be as harrowing as the rape itself. In this case the rapist, exuding boyish innocence, presented a convincing argument to the effect that he had been seduced by the woman. During the next few weeks, there was a sharp decrease in the number of rapes reported by victims to the police—apparently because victims, taking their cue from the television movie, feared the police would not believe them.

In October 1982, when seven people in the Chicago area died after taking Tylenol headache capsules laced with cyanide, the event was widely publicized by the national news media. Indeed, for several days it was difficult to turn on the TV or radio, or pick up a newspaper, without encountering the Tylenol poisonings. The effects of this prominent coverage were immediate: Similar poisonings were reported in cities across the country, involving the contamination of mouthwash, eyedrops, nasal spray, soda pop, even hot dogs. Dramatically billed as "copycat poisonings," these incidents, in turn, received widespread media attention. The public reaction spiralled: Many people panicked, seeking medical aid for burns and poisonings when they suffered from no more than common sore

throats and stomachaches. False alarms outnumbered
actual cases of product tampering by 7 to 1.

What do Demetrick James Walker, the voters of North Carolina,
rape victims, and, indeed, anyone who has ever watched television or read a newspaper or magazine have in common? Every
time we turn on the radio or television, every time we open a
book, magazine, or newspaper, someone is trying to educate us,
to convince us to buy a product, to persuade us to vote for a
candidate or to subscribe to some version of what is right, true,
or beautiful. This aim is most obvious in advertising: Manufacturers of nearly identical products (aspirins, for example, or
toothpastes, or detergents, or political candidates) spend vast
amounts of money to persuade us to buy the product in their
package. Influence need not be so blatant—the impact of television news shows and programs such as *Cry Rape*, for instance,
extends far beyond their most obvious effects as documentaries
or dramatizations. This influence can be very subtle indeed,
even unintentional. As the response to the movie about rape
aptly illustrates, even when communicators are not directly
attempting to sell us something, they can succeed in influencing
the way we look at the world and the way we respond to important events in our lives. The purpose of this book is to look at
the nature of persuasion in our everyday life—to understand
how it influences our behavior, how we can protect ourselves
from unwanted propaganda, and how we can ultimately come
to use persuasion wisely.

A Glut of Influence

The primary vehicle for many persuasive appeals is the mass
media. The statistics on the pervasiveness of the mass media are
startling.[3] Communications is a $400-billion-plus industry with
$206 billion spent on mass communications, that is, communi-
cations produced and distributed in identical form to people in
different locations. In the United States, there are 1,449 television stations and four major networks, 10,379 radio stations,
1,509 daily newspapers and 7,047 weekly newspapers, more than
17,000 magazines and newsletters, and nine major film studios.
Americans have ample opportunity to consume mass media
messages, and consume they do. Each year the typical American

" We limit him to an hour a day. He's up to March 29, 2014."

watches 1,550 hours of TV, listens to 1,160 hours of radio on one of 530 million radio sets, and spends 180 hours reading 94 pounds of newspapers and 110 hours reading magazines. Each year an American has the opportunity to read more than 50,000 new books in print. More than half of our waking hours are spent with the mass media.

If you watch thirty hours of TV per week (as does the typical American), you will view roughly 38,000 commercials per year. The average prime-time hour of TV contains more than 11 minutes of advertising. That works out to more than 100 TV ads per day. You are likely to hear or see another 100 to 300 ads per day through the other mass media of radio, newspapers, and magazines.

And the advertising glut does not stop there. More than 100 million orders will be placed after home viewers watch continuous advertising on networks such as QVC and the Home Shopping Network—resulting in sales of more than $2.5 billion. This year you will receive, on average, 252 pieces of direct-mail advertising (a $144.5-billion industry and still growing) and about fifty phone calls from telemarketers, who contact 7 million persons a day. Americans purchase $600 billion worth of goods and services over the phone each year. Today advertisers are developing new ways of delivering their message using the Internet and World Wide Web. Each day more than 257 million Internet users worldwide check more than 11.1 million available Web sites featuring a range of information, propaganda, and, of course, merchandise for sale. Each year, American businesses spend $150 billion to hire more than 6.4 million sales agents. Approximately one in every twelve American families has a member working in sales. This force of millions attempts to persuade others to purchase everything from cars to shoes to small and large appliances, to contribute vast sums to needy charities, to enlist in the military, or to enroll in a specific college.

If you walk down just about any city street in America, you will encounter countless billboards, posters, bumper stickers, and bus and cab displays, each with a separate advertising appeal. Your kitchen cupboard is probably full of product packages and labels, each containing at least one sales message. It seems that no place is free of advertising. Go to the racetrack and you will see 200-mile-an-hour race cars carry advertising worth $75 million per year. Go to a tennis tournament, a jazz festival, or a golf match and you will find corporate sponsors, such as the makers of Virginia Slims, Kool, and Doral cigarettes. Go to a movie and you will find that marketers have paid a handsome sum (roughly $50 million per year) to have your favorite stars use their products in the film. Even 007's famous martini dictum, "shaken, not stirred," is not sacred, as James Bond orders a "Smirnoff Black, neat" in *Goldeneye* thanks to a pricey product-placement fee paid to the movie's producers. Look at just about anyone in America and you will see human bodies turned into walking billboards with brand names appearing on T-shirts and ballcaps, not to mention the ubiquitous designer labels.

On any given day, Americans are exposed to 18 billion magazine and newspaper ads, 2.6 million radio commercials, 300,000 TV commercials, 500,000 billboards, and 40 million pieces of direct mail. With 6% of the world's population, the United States consumes 57% of the world's advertising. Manufacturers spend more than $165 billion a year on advertising and more than $115 billion a year on product promotions (coupons, free samples, rebates, premiums, and the like). This corresponds to spending 2.2% of the U.S. gross national product on advertising (compared to 0.95% in Japan and 0.9% in Germany), or more than $1,000 per year per American—a sum larger than the yearly income of a typical citizen of a third world nation.

But persuasion is not just the specialty of advertisers and marketers. The U.S. government spends more than $400 million per year to employ more than 8,000 workers to create propaganda favorable to the United States. The result: ninety films per year, twelve magazines in twenty-two languages, and 800 hours of Voice of America programming in thirty-seven languages with an estimated audience of 75 million listeners—all describing the virtues of the American way.

Persuasion shows up in almost every walk of life. Nearly every major politician hires media consultants and political pundits to provide advice on how to persuade the public and how to get elected (and then how to stay elected). For example, in the 2000 U.S. presidential election, George W. Bush raised more than $184 million to support his campaign, with Al Gore collecting more than $133 million in his bid for the White House. Once elected, the typical U.S. president is likely to spend millions of dollars to hire personal pollsters and political consultants in an attempt to keep those positive approval ratings.

Virtually every major business and special-interest group has hired a lobbyist to take its concerns to Congress or to state and local governments. Today, such political action committees serve as a primary source of funds for most political campaigns. Is it any wonder that Congress is loath to instigate serious curbs on major lobbyists such as the NRA, AARP, or AMA? In nearly every community, activists try to persuade their fellow citizens on important policy issues.

The workplace, too, has always been fertile ground for office politics and persuasion. One study estimates that general managers spend upwards of 80% of their time in verbal communication—most of it with the intent of cajoling and persuading their fellow employees. With the advent of the photocopying machine, a whole new medium for office persuasion was invented—the photocopied memo. The Pentagon alone copies an average of 350,000 pages a day, the equivalent of 1,000 novels. Sunday may be a day of rest, but not from persuasion, as an army of preachers takes to the pulpits to convince us of the true moral course of action. They also take to the airwaves, with 14% of all radio stations airing programs extolling the virtues of Christianity.

And should you need assistance in preparing your persuasive message, millions stand ready in the wings to help (for a fee). Today there are 675,000 lawyers actively arguing and persuading in courts of law—and in the courts of public opinion when their high-profile clients so require. More than 300 companies (at billings of $130 million per year) provide "image consulting"—advice on how to make your personal image more appealing. Public relations firms can be hired to deal with any public opinion problem. There are more than 500 major marketing research and opinion-polling firms ready to find out what Americans think about any conceivable issue. These firms query more than 72 million Americans a year. The top 100 marketing research firms alone have combined revenues of more than $5 billion.

Every day we are bombarded with one persuasive communication after another. These appeals persuade not through the give-and-take of argument and debate but through the manipulation of symbols and of our most basic human emotions. For better or worse, ours is an age of propaganda.

The Growth of Postindustrial Propaganda

Every society requires a mechanism for making decisions, resolving disputes, and coordinating activities. Our society has opted for persuasion. In the former Soviet Union, during the heyday of Communist party rule, a bureaucratic Politburo attempted to regulate consumer tastes and choices. In our culture, we assign that function to the persuasive skills of the advertiser. In traditional societies, marriages are arranged by parental authority according to rules and customs. In modern Western societies, love is left to the social-influence devices of the two potential lovebirds and their friends and families. During the Middle Ages in Europe, most disputes were settled by the decree of feudal lords or by the papacy or by a joust. Today lawyers attempt to solve disputes by negotiating out-of-court settlements and, if that fails, arguing the merits of the case before a complex system of judges. In many of the world's cultures, rulers come to power either by the use of force or by family inheritance. The populace of the United States selects its rulers by a persuasion ritual known as the election campaign.

The roots of American persuasion practices go back to the founding of the nation.[4] The United States was then, as it is today, a diverse society populated by native Americans and people from England, Spain, Africa, Holland, and France, among other places. Each possessed his or her own beliefs and values. Although violence and threats of violence were frequently used to secure compliance, the bulk of the work of forging a new consensus from this diversity of opinion and perspective fell to persuasion. Early promoters induced settlers to the New World with promises of vast riches, cheap land, religious freedom, and a strange new world. Catholic priests and Protestant ministers preached to the converted and attempted to win over the unconverted, mostly native Americans, to the cause of Christ. The establishment of printing presses in America made possible the wide distribution of tracts, pamphlets, and newspapers designed to persuade fellow colonists. When the colonists ratified the U.S. Constitution, they ensured that persuasion would be at the heart of decision making by guaranteeing freedom of speech, freedom of the press, and the rights of assembly and of petitioning the government. The U.S. government, with its three branches (including two legislative houses), is a system of checks and balances that demands debate, argument, and compromise. The U.S. legal system is adversarial and requires the government to prove by strength of fact and argument, beyond a reasonable doubt, that a citizen committed a crime.

Few places symbolize this early American fascination with persuasion as vividly as Faneuil Hall and Quincy Market in Boston.[5] The hall, built in 1742 by Peter Faneuil, was originally intended to be a market "to Encourage and accommodate the Countrey People who bring Provisions into this Town." However, consumerism then, as now, was somewhat controversial, and to encourage the town of Boston to accept his gift, Faneuil added a meeting hall on the second floor, above the market stalls. Faneuil Hall has witnessed debate on nearly every major issue that has confronted the United States, including the decisions for independence, slavery, temperance, and women's rights, as well as debate on every American war from 1812 to the Persian Gulf. The market, expanded eighty-four years later and renamed Quincy for the then-mayor of Boston, is still in use today as one of America's oldest shopping malls. Not far away stand such monuments to persuasion as the Old State House and the Old North Church, the location of many of the first speeches and acts of the independence movement. Is it any wonder that the government these colonists helped to establish in the late eighteenth century had at its heart the art of persuasion?

However, it was not until the full force of the Industrial Revolution was felt in the nineteenth century that interest in, and organization of, persuasion emerged in earnest on a mass scale. The Industrial Revolution saw the invention of many new devices—steam engines, cotton gins, power looms, railroads, telegraphs, and assembly lines—resulting in the manufacture of more and more material goods for the mass market. Within a few generations, goods that could once be possessed only by the rich became the aspiration of almost everyone. An ever increasing supply of products meant that items were purchased not solely because of need, but because of the dictates of fashion and style as well.

Consumers did not always buy the offered goods, however. There are a number of possible reasons for this. Potential customers might not know about the advantages of a certain product, or they might distrust the manufacturer, or they might consider the product to be frivolous. They may not have had enough money to purchase the offered goods immediately. Out of necessity, manufacturers increasingly turned to sales and marketing to persuade people to purchase their products on a mass scale. With the rise of each of the mass media—printing presses in the seventeenth century, mass market magazines in the 1880s, radio in the 1930s, television in the 1950s, direct-mail advertising and telemarketing in the 1980s, and the World Wide Web as we entered the new millennium—manufacturers found an increasingly convenient way to do just that.

If we were to pick a specific date for the beginnings of our age of propaganda, however, we would select an obscure event that is not covered in most textbooks of American history. The modern age of propaganda began in Philadelphia in 1843 when a young man named Volney Palmer opened the first advertising agency. The shop was primitive by today's standards, serving only to broker advertising space between newspaper publishers and advertisers.[6] Soon thereafter, full-service advertising agencies offering a wide range of client services, such as media planning and the creation and preparation of ad copy, appeared, along with a host of marketing research firms, publicity agencies, and opinion pollsters—all in the service of persuasion.

Academics were quick to get in on the act as well. In the early 1890s, new courses with titles such as "Principles of Advertising," "Salesmanship," and "Wholesaling and Retailing" began appearing at universities. Academic textbooks with titles such as *Advertising and Its Mental Laws* and *Psychology in Advertising* were being published, all promising to teach the art of persuasion—at least as applied to advertising and sales.[7] Just after the turn of the century, the basic institutions of American propaganda became firmly established. The evolution of humankind from hunter-gatherers to shopper-disposers was complete.

It did not take long for the principles of advertising and marketing developed to sell consumer goods to be applied to the "sale" of political ideas and candidates. One of the first such applications came in the selling of World War I. In a book first published in 1920 and entitled *How We Advertised America*, George Creel, a publisher and head of the Committee on Public Information, proudly divulged how he and his committee used the principles of advertising to convince Americans to go to war with Germany.[8] Creel's success inspired others, most notably Adolf Hitler, to use and develop these techniques on a grand scale. The apparent success of such ventures has caused considerable concern—to say the least; modern critics have referred to persuasion as mind-control, brainwashing, and hidden seduction and have called attention to the damaging effects of propaganda.

The Distinction Between Propaganda and Persuasion

The forms of persuasion that have come to dominate our twentieth-century lifestyle are much different from those seen in any other age of persuasion, certainly much different from those experienced by colonial Americans. For this reason, we use the term *propaganda* to refer to the techniques of mass persuasion that have come to characterize our postindustrial society. The word *propaganda* is of relatively recent origin. Its first documented use occurred in 1622, when Pope Gregory XV established the Sacra Congregatio de Propaganda Fide. At the time, in the wake of the Protestant Reformation, the Roman Catholic Church was engaged in mostly unsuccessful holy wars to reestablish the faith by force of arms. Realizing that this was a losing effort, Pope Gregory established the papal propaganda office as a means of coordinating efforts to bring men and women to the "voluntary" acceptance of church doctrines. The word *propaganda* thus took on a negative connotation in Protestant countries but a positive one (similar to that of *education* or *preaching*) in Catholic areas.

The term *propaganda* did not see widespread use until the beginning of the twentieth century, when it was used to describe the persuasion tactics employed during World War I and those later used by totalitarian regimes. *Propaganda* was originally defined as the dissemination of biased ideas and opinions, often through the use of lies and deception. However, as scholars began to study the topic in more detail, many came to realize that propaganda was not the sole property of "evil" and totalitarian regimes and that it often consists of more than just clever deceptions. The word *propaganda* has since evolved to mean mass "suggestion" or "influence" through the manipulation of symbols and the psychology of the individual. Propaganda involves the dextrous use of images, slogans, and symbols that play on our prejudices and emotions; it is the communication of a point of view with the ultimate goal of having the recipient of the appeal come to "voluntarily" accept this position as if it were his or her own.[9]

The use of propaganda goes back to the birth of human civilization itself. For example, the early hieroglyphic writings of Egyptian and Mesoamerican (Aztec, Mixtec, Zapotec, and Maya) cultures consisted of symbols and images describing a "history" that favored the ruling class.[10] As just one case in point, Mayan texts and monuments often manipulated historic dates, life spans of rulers, astronomical cycles, and real events to place a current ruler in a favorable light—for example, aligning the birth date of a current leader with the birth date of a stronger leader of the past to suggest the old leader's reincarnation, or depicting slain enemies and captives in an exaggerated way to make a leader appear strong and to strike fear into the masses. Given that only leaders and their priests could decipher and create hieroglyphic images and symbols, the nature of persuasion in these cultures was unidirectional—from the ruler to the masses.

However, not all persuasion is propaganda. The classical rhetorical techniques of the ancient Greeks and Romans—which were avidly studied by those responsible for crafting the governments of Western Europe and America—were aimed at creating discourse that could illuminate the issue at hand. Such persuasion could take the form of an argument, a debate, a discussion, or just a well-argued speech presenting the case for or against a given proposition. The end result was an education for both the audience and the speakers.

In the city-states of ancient Greece, all citizens were considered equal and everyone was expected to be able to speak on his own behalf.[11] For example, the Greek court system did not allow lawyers or individuals hired to plead a case; citizens were required to plead their own cases in the courts or, more exactly, before a jury of their neighbors. Similarly, the citizen of Greece was also expected to speak on the issues of the day in political assemblies. This task was not left to elected representatives. Needless to say, the average Greek citizen was interested in learning how to argue, lest he lose his possessions or be banished from his community on the basis of a frivolous lawsuit.

To help him learn about persuasion, the Greek citizen could hire a Sophist to provide instruction on how to argue. The Sophists were itinerant teachers who gave lectures and wrote the first books on persuasion, similar in nature to the how-to books that can be found in bookstores today. These handbooks, most of which are now lost to antiquity, described "commonplaces"—general arguments and techniques that could be adapted for a variety of persuasive purposes. One famous handbook, the *Dissoi Logoi*, consisted of a series of pro and con arguments on a number of topics—ready for use by a speaker at a moment's notice.

The Sophists are perhaps best known for their "dangerous" views about the role of persuasion in society—hence the negative connotations of the word *sophistry*, meaning "trickery" or "fallacious argumentation." The Sophist viewpoint is expressed in two seemingly innocent maxims attributed to Protagoras: "Humans are the measure of all things" and "There are two sides to every issue." For the Sophist there is no absolute truth and no surefire means, whether through divine inspiration or human intuition, for finding this truth. The only standards are human ones, and these are always debatable. How, then, does one decide what to do? The Sophists believed that persuasion is necessary to discover the "best" course of action; by arguing and debating, many facets of an issue can be laid bare and the advantages and disadvantages of a course of action can be more plainly seen.

Foreshadowing much modern commentary on persuasion, Plato was outraged by the Sophist position. Plato believed in an absolute truth that could be appreciated only through the study of philosophy. The "word tricks" of the Sophists, in Plato's mind, merely confused the youth of Athens and clouded the understanding of what he saw as truth.

Around 323 B.C., Aristotle reconciled the view of the Sophists and the position of his teacher, Plato, in the *Rhetoric*—the first comprehensive theory of persuasion. For Aristotle, the purpose of persuasion was the communication of a point of view or position. Although the Sophists believed that persuasion was needed to discover important facts, Aristotle believed that knowledge could be gained only by logic and reason. Unfortunately, according to Aristotle, not everyone was capable of reasoning clearly about every issue. For these denser souls, the art of persuasion was needed to communicate the truth to them in such a manner that they might come to a *right* conclusion.

The tradition of "decision by persuasion" was kept alive by the early Romans. The political and court system of the Roman Republic, much like that of the Greeks, encouraged debate and political speechmaking. However, unlike the Greeks, the Romans employed professional persuaders—politicians and lawyers who made a career of arguing. The role of persuasion in Roman society was aptly expressed by one of the most famous of the Roman professional persuaders, the lawyer Cicero (106 to 43 B.C.). When asked "Has rhetoric produced more harm than good?" Cicero gave an answer that would have satisfied even

Aristotle: "Wisdom without eloquence has been of little help to the states, but eloquence without wisdom has often been a great obstacle and never an advantage."[12]

The eloquent rhetoric of ancient Greek and Roman, as well as colonial American, is a far cry from the typical communication of today, with its emphasis on the use of simple slogans and images. Increasingly, the goal of modern propaganda is not to inform and enlighten but rather to move the masses toward a desired position or point of view. The persuasion landscape of today differs vastly from those of the past in some very important ways.

We live in a message-dense environment. The advertisers Al Ries and Jack Trout call ours an "overcommunicated" society.[13] The average American will see or hear more than 7 million advertisements in his or her lifetime. In contrast, the average pious Puritan attending church once a week in seventeenth-century New England would hear about 3,000 sermons in a lifetime. This message-dense environment places a burden on both the communicator and the recipient of a message intended to persuade. The communicator must design a message that will not only be appealing but will also attract special notice in this cluttered environment. On the other hand, the recipient is so deluged by messages that it becomes difficult to devote the mental energy necessary to make sense of many of the important issues of the day.

Our age of propaganda differs in another way as well. Puritan sermons could last as long as two hours. Roman orators of the second century took courses to improve their memory so that they could remember all that they had to say. Early American patriots spent the entire summer of 1787 debating the U.S. Constitution and then produced, for the newspapers of the day, eighty-five articles totaling nearly 600 pages in its defense. Today, a televised political advertisement typically runs for thirty seconds or less. Magazine ads often consist of little more than a picture and a phrase. News of the day comes in short "sound-bites" and "news snippets." For example, 70% of all local TV news stories are a minute or less in length. As the columnist George Will once put it, if Lincoln were to issue the Emancipation Proclamation today, he would probably say: "Read my lips. No more slavery." Our age of persuasion is populated with short, catchy, and often visually oriented messages. Although such persuasive images are frequently successful in capturing our attention in the message-dense environment, they substitute slogans and images for well-reasoned arguments and can turn complex issues into vulgar black-and-white caricatures of reason.

Persuasion in modern times is also much more immediate. The Puritan would wait all week for a sermon and months for news from England. Since the launch of *Telstar 1* in July 1962, any event happening almost anywhere in the world can be covered immediately. For example, despite efforts by the Chinese government to the contrary, CNN's coverage of the Tian'anmen Square massacre consisted of journalists telephoning detailed reports of the violence as well as play-by-play descriptions of government action and student reaction, which were then quickly broadcast to an eagerly waiting but stunned world. In a similar vein, a week before the Allied bombing of Iraq in 1991, Tariq Aziz, foreign minister of Iraq, claimed to understand American politics because he got his news from CNN. Over 1 billion people in 108 nations tuned in to CNN to watch its live and on-line coverage of the Persian Gulf war. After the nation was entertained by O. J. Simpson's slow-speed chase, CNN, E!, Court TV, and others offered continuous coverage and immediate "analysis" of the trial. More than 150 million Americans watched the delivery of the verdict on TV. Such intense coverage was repeated again only a short time later—but this time it was the president of the United States, Bill Clinton, on trial for lying about his affair with a young intern.

In the 2000 U.S. presidential election, this itch for immediacy created a bizarre situation in which the news media first claimed that Al Gore had won in the state of Florida (before some polls even closed in the state) and then later in the same evening stated that the vote in Florida was too close to call and then finally reported that George W. Bush had won the state. This news prompted Gore to telephone Bush conceding the election. However, before announcing his concession to the nation, Gore found out that the election was once again too close to call and retracted his statement. The news media's rush to call the election and then recall it sent the candidates and the nation on an emotional roller coaster, creating confusion and anger on all sides.

And the immediacy of today's persuasion is getting even more immediate. As just one indicator: The first TV movie about the 1978 mass suicide in Jonestown took 513 days to produce; only 34 days elapsed between the fire at the Branch Davidian compound in Waco, Texas, and the first TV movie about it. The result is timely information—but often, perhaps, too timely. Whereas the Puritan could spend all week mulling over the implications of last Sunday's sermon, today's TV viewer and magazine reader has little time to think about one persuasive image before another one quickly takes its place: The trees are replacing the forest.

Perhaps the major difference between our own and past eras is the way in which we instruct our citizens about persuasion. If you were a citizen of a Greek city-state in the third century B.C., your education would include four years of rhetoric designed to teach you how to understand persuasive arguments and to construct your own. Should you miss your lessons, a Sophist could be hired to provide further instruction. Roman students of the first century took courses in persuasion from perhaps the greatest professor of rhetoric of all times, Quintilian, whose textbook on the subject was used for almost 1,000 years. Students at Harvard College in seventeenth-century America also had many opportunities to learn about persuasion. Every Friday afternoon for four years, the students would study how to argue; at least once a month they were required to demonstrate what they had learned by taking a stand, defending it, and attacking the views of others.

These cultures, unlike our own, considered an understanding of persuasion to be an essential skill needed by every citizen in order to participate fully in the affairs of state. The teaching of persuasion was a basic component of their education. In contrast, few Americans have taken a formal course on social influence. "Pop" books on the subject typically present exaggerated warnings of the dire consequences of persuasion and the mass media or simplistic "how-to-get-ahead" instructions. Although we are bombarded daily with persuasive messages, we have little opportunity to learn about the techniques of persuasion and to understand how they work. Sadly, such a state of affairs can lead to a sense of alienation and cynicism, as many Americans become bewildered by the basic decision-making processes of their society.

The Goals of This Book

For the last six decades, social psychologists such as ourselves have been studying the everyday use and abuse of persuasion.[14] They have conducted thousands of experiments to test countless hypotheses concerning the effects of a persuasive communication. Their labors have resulted in the discovery of which persuasion techniques are effective and an understanding of what makes a persuasive message so persuasive. One purpose of this book is to share this information.

In the next section, we provide an overview of what social psychologists and other investigators have discovered about how we are persuaded: What factors determine when we will be influenced? How do we respond, in general, to a persuasion attempt? The next four sections, the heart of the book, present an in-depth analysis of propaganda tactics commonly used today, along with a discussion of why these tactics are so effective in securing our compliance. Then, investigating the techniques of the propagandist, we look at how these tactics can be put together to create a campaign of persuasion. We conclude by discussing what we can do to limit the effects of propaganda in our lives and to insure that deliberative persuasion remains at the heart of democracy.

This book has a second purpose as well. The persuasive appeals directed at Demetrick James Walker, the voters of North Carolina, rape victims, and every television viewer and magazine reader take advantage of our basic human psychology; they often appeal to our deepest fears and most irrational hopes, all the while playing to our most simplistic beliefs; they come to paint a picture of the world—distorted as it may be—in which we must live. It is our hope that by discussing the ways of persuasion, we can all better understand our world of propaganda and deal with it sensibly and effectively.

The Psychology of
Everyday Persuasion

Mysterious Influence

The Manchurian Candidate, produced in 1962, has become something of a cult classic. The movie, starring Angela Lansbury, Frank Sinatra, and Laurence Harvey, tells the story of an American soldier captured during the Korean War and brainwashed by the Chinese Communists. The POW is programmed to go into a hypnotic trance and to assassinate U.S. political leaders on command. The plot thickens when the Chinese Communists are able to mastermind the nomination of their own candidate for U.S. vice-president and the brainwashed ex-soldier is commanded to kill the presidential nominee.

The Manchurian Candidate is certainly a thriller. But we wonder if its popularity is not based, at least in part, on the image it presents of social influence. Persuasion is presented as a mysterious and powerful force. In the hands of those "in the know," it can be used to bring us to perform some strange and often despicable acts for no apparent good reason.

People indeed do strange things for seemingly no good reason. Many mysterious causes have been invented throughout history to help explain why we humans are influenced and persuaded. For example, the ancients believed that a person's fate is determined by the position of distant stars. During the Middle

Ages, there was a widespread belief that a person could be possessed by demons or that behavior could be controlled by witches who cast spells over the unsuspecting.

Centuries later, in the 1770s, Franz Anton Mesmer (whose name gave us the word *mesmerize*) created a secular version of witchcraft that still influences our thinking today.[1] According to Mesmer, we are not possessed by spirits or demons, but each of us possesses an "animal fluid" that serves as a major determinant of our behavior—as well as of our health and well-being. (Interestingly, the word *influence* comes from the word *fluid* and literally means "to affect fluid.") Mesmer claimed he could control human behavior and promote human potentials by passing a magnet over the body to redirect the flow of this animal fluid.

Therapy sessions inspired by Mesmer's ideas created quite a stir in eighteenth-century Europe and America. At a typical session, a leader would "mesmerize" a few faithful souls either by placing magnets at key locations around their bodies, or by manually massaging their bodies to stimulate the flow of the animal fluid, or, later, simply by a voice command. Those in the mesmerized state would report seeing bright lights or feeling the animal magnetism tingle their bodies or would report no pain from pinpricks, pinches, or other pain inducers. Loud clapping and ammonia passed under the nose would not wake them from the trance. Some claimed to be cured of disease. A blue-ribbon panel of the leading scientists of the day—including Antoine Lavoisier and Benjamin Franklin—was commissioned to investigate Mesmer's practices. They concluded that "there is no proof of the existence of Animal Magnetism; that this fluid, having no existence, has in consequence no utility." The panel dismissed the claims for physical cures as "the mere product of the patient's own imaginations."[2] Indeed, Mesmer used many common influence tactics—making himself into an authority, manipulating expectations for a cure, playing on people's hopes and self-esteem—to promote his "therapy."

Mesmer's successors were undaunted by the commission's report. They began a search for new and improved techniques, leading to the abandonment of magnetism and the discovery of the hypnotic trance as a technique for controlling our animal nature.[3] The first popular self-help movements in America, the Society of Harmony of the 1830s and the New Thought movement of the 1890s, made extensive use of Mesmer's theories of human nature. Thousands of Americans sought relief from all sorts of ailments—psychological and physical—by taking the "cure," which could involve anything from being placed in a hypnotic trance, to receiving treatment from a magnet, to the spiritual healing of Mary Baker Eddy. Similarly, today's New Age healers seek to influence behavior by rechanneling the inner self, sometimes called *chi*, by means of hypnotic trances, subliminal commands, or the power not of magnets but of crystals.

In nearly every age and nearly every culture, humans wonder just how they come to be influenced by others. Our culture is no different. With the coming of the Industrial Revolution, much of this reflection has centered on the influence of the mass media and on the power of strong individuals such as demagogues, politicians, sales agents, and cult leaders. Opinion on the power of mass media influence is divided. Some people believe that the mass media are all-powerful and capable of influencing and duping the masses on just about any issue. In other words, they believe that the mass media are today's functional equivalent of Mesmer, inducing us into a trancelike acceptance of all that we see and hear. Others believe that the mass media have little influence, especially when they think of the impact on their own lives: *"I am smart enough and rational enough to see through the cheap ploys of advertisers and politicians"*—or so we think. Wherein lies the truth? As with most great debates, the answer is "somewhere in-between." But we get ahead of ourselves. Let's look at each of these beliefs—that the mass media are mysteriously all-powerful versus that they have little effect—so that we will be in a better position to understand when we are most likely to be influenced by the propagandist.

Myth #1: Magic Bullets

By the beginning of the twentieth century, the Industrial Revolution had brought about dramatic changes in American society. As we saw in the last chapter, the development of industry led to a rise of the mass media, which some feared would come to dominate and control a mass public. Sociologists of the day observed that Western societies were experiencing a change in the nature of social relationships—from small, cohesive communities emphasizing personal relationships to a web of impersonal, secondary relationships in which the individual was socially isolated and in tension with others.[4] Cut off from their social roots, individuals, it was feared, would be dependent on the mass media and select leaders for all their information and thus would be defenseless against propaganda. As some claimed, the mass media could fire *magic bullets* of information capable of shaping public opinion and swaying the masses toward any point of view advocated by the communicator.[5]

Proponents of this view cited many examples of the power of propagandists, especially those who had the means to use the mass media—for example, the dissemination of atrocity stories by British and American governments to mobilize their citizens for World War I; the rise of demagogues, such as Pitchfork Ben Tillman, Aimee Semple McPherson, Father Divine, Father Coughlin, and Joseph McCarthy, capable of captivating crowds as well as radio and TV audiences; the increasing use of advertising to sell consumer goods and, subsequently, politicians; and, of course, the systematic use of propaganda in Nazi and other totalitarian regimes.

The two dominant psychological theories of the early twentieth century—behaviorism and psychoanalysis—also lent support to the magic bullet thesis. According to the boast of behaviorist John Watson, he could take any infant at birth and, through the systematic application of behavioral principles, create any sort of human being he desired. What Watson had in mind was the systematic application of the principles of classical conditioning developed by Ivan Pavlov.[6] According to Pavlov, we learn by the repeated pairing of an unconditioned stimulus (say, a shock that elicits the unconditioned response of pain) with a neutral stimulus (say, a picture of a foreign leader or a political point of view). Eventually, mere exposure to the neutral stimulus—the foreign leader or the political point of view—would come to elicit pain. The mass media could fire magic bullets, according to the behaviorist, simply by repeatedly associating stimuli—for example, a brand of car with an attractive woman—and thus come to control the thoughts of the masses.

Such claims obviously attracted the attention of advertisers. Early advertising textbooks spelled out how behavioral principles such as *repetition, intensity* (use bright and loud ads), *asso-*

ciation (link content to the recipient's experiences), and *ingenuity* (make the ad distinctive) can be used to improve the effectiveness of a message.[7] Indeed, after he was asked to leave his faculty position at Johns Hopkins University because he was having an affair with one of his students, Watson was quickly hired by the advertising agency of J. Walter Thompson. The behaviorist's vision of society also inspired its share of critics, as evidenced by books such as Aldous Huxley's *Brave New World* and Anthony Burgess's *A Clockwork Orange*—both of which provide a futuristic glimpse of a bleak and scary world completely guided by behavioristic principles.

Although often seen as antagonists, behaviorists and psychoanalysts do agree on the power of the mass media to fire magic bullets of influence. The two theories differ, however, on the nature of those bullets. In many respects, the psychoanalytic theory of persuasion can be seen as a descendant of mesmerism. Animal magnetism is replaced by the psychic energy of the unconscious; magnets as a means of influence are replaced by appeals to the hidden world of the unconscious through the use of hypnotism, subliminal commands, or symbolic messages.

As early as the 1890s, the concept of hypnotic suggestion was used to explain the reaction of the masses to demagogues and other assorted scoundrels. The French sociologist Gustave Le Bon argued that crowds transformed individuals into mindless, anonymous entities through a form of hypnotic suggestion and a dissociation of higher mental processes. Others quickly applied this metaphor to suggest that the mass media hypnotized their audiences.[8]

However, it wasn't until the 1950s that the psychoanalytic approach to persuasion was brought to the public's attention in Vance Packard's highly popular exposé, *The Hidden Persuaders*.[9] According to Packard, advertising agencies were secretly using the principles of psychoanalysis to create ads that were amazingly powerful and successful. To produce such ads, marketers were busily engaged in finding the hidden meaning of things. One handbook on the subject, prepared by Ernest Dichter, actually listed common objects and what they mean, in theory, to the unconscious—for example, he claimed rice means fertility, removing one's gloves is erotic and intimate, soup is the magic elixir of life, and eggs mean growth and fertility.[10] Once the unconscious meaning of a thing was uncovered, an advertiser could design a campaign, at least according to psychoanalytic theory, that appealed to our deepest motivations and thus was capable of overwhelming our defenses.

Myth #2: The Rational Citizen

If true, these claims about the power of the mass media and other agents of influence—whether through classical conditioning or hidden persuasion—are quite frightening and, for the most part, mysterious. However, beginning in the 1940s, researchers found it difficult to document the power of the mass media. This research led some to conclude that the mass media have a minimal effect and that citizens use the information distributed by the mass media in a rational manner to determine the best course of action.

One of the first studies to question the belief that the mass media are all-powerful was conducted by the famed communications researcher Paul Lazarsfeld and his colleagues during the 1940 presidential campaign.[11] At the beginning and end of the campaign, the voters of Erie County, Ohio, were interviewed about their preferences, party affiliation, media habits, and so on. The results showed that the mass media had little impact on whom a citizen voted for; much better predictors were the voter's political party (Republican or Democratic) and the preferences of friends—the beliefs of those the voter worked, played, and prayed with. Other studies followed showing that the mass media had limited, if any, effects on behavior. For example, early studies of advertising found that the amount a firm spends on advertising has little or no effect on either sales or growth in market share. Experimental investigations of single exposures to ads found that few people pay attention to any specific exposure and what little effects are created usually dissipate quickly.[12]

The psychological underpinnings of the magic bullet theory also did not fare well. Although many of the basic findings of behaviorism have been supported, subsequent research found that many of its effects are often limited in nature; for example, it was found that some associations are very difficult to learn and that rewards can often backfire and lead to the opposite of the intended results.[13]

Similarly, attempts to use psychoanalysis to guide propaganda efforts failed. For example, in the 1950s and early 1960s, the U.S. Central Intelligence Agency (CIA) did indeed attempt to create the "Manchurian Candidate"—that is, the CIA experimented with a variety of "magic bullets," such as hypnosis, drugs, and subliminal implants, in an attempt to control human behavior.[14] The experiments failed to achieve their goal, prompting one CIA official to conclude that it would be far easier just to hire a professional killer to perform assassinations than to attempt to engineer one using psychological techniques. During the 1950s, advertisers also employed consultants and others trained in psychoanalysis to help create advertising, just as Vance Packard claimed. Every agency had its "depth man." However, by the mid-1960s most agencies had abandoned this approach, because, quite simply, it did not work. Advertisers found psychoanalytic theory to be too vague to guide their applications; the techniques used for assessing the psychoanalytic meaning of a persuasive communication—analysis of inkblots, free associations, dreams, hypnosis—were notoriously unreliable.[15] The sensational claims of effectiveness made during the 1950s were never realized. Nevertheless, the psychoanalytic theory of persuasion continues to garner much popular attention, as evidenced by the storylines of movies such as *The Manchurian Candidate* and many television crime dramas, as well as by the marketing success of books and tapes touting the power of subliminal influence. As we will see in Chapter 34, there is yet to be a reliable demonstration that a subliminal message can influence motivation or behavior.

As evidence appeared to accumulate that the mass media produced minimal effects, an information-processing model (sometimes called a learning model) replaced behaviorism and psychoanalytic theory as the primary explanation of mass media effects. According to the information-processing model, a persuasive message must successfully pass through a series of stages.[16] First, the message must attract the recipient's attention; ignored messages will have little persuasive impact. Second, the arguments in the message must be understood and comprehended. Third, the recipient must learn the arguments contained in the message and come to accept them as true; the task of the advertiser and other persuaders is to teach arguments supportive of the cause, so that these arguments will come easily to mind at the appropriate time and place. Finally, the recipient of the messages acts on this learned knowledge when there is an incentive to do so; a persuasive message is learned, accepted, and acted upon if it is rewarding to do so. Given that later stages of the persuasion process are dependent on the completion of earlier stages, the chances of any given persuasive communication passing to the final stage are quite low and thus the effects are minimal. The recipient of the message, according to the information-processing model, is quite rational, deciding on how much information to accept from each communication depending on how that information satisfies and rewards.

The Law of Cognitive Response

Of course, if that were the end of the story and the mass media were truly watched by rational citizens with minimal effects, then there would be no need for this book. We would tell you, "Go ahead and watch TV; let the advertisers pay for it; it won't have any effect on you." But that is *not* the end of the story. In the last decade, researchers have found that the mass media can have strong effects under certain identifiable conditions, which, in turn, has led to a new understanding of how persuasion works. Let's look at some of this research.

First, investigators have found that the mass media can produce many subtle, or "indirect," effects—in other words, the mass media may not tell you what to think, but they do tell you what to think *about* and *how to do it.*[17] Consider someone who watches TV and repeatedly sees competing ads extolling the virtues of Chevys and of Fords. It is unlikely (in most cases) that any given ad will cause that person to switch her or his preference for one car over the other. However, it is very likely that this heavy dose of car ads will lead that person to want a car and to give little consideration to alternative modes of transportation, such as mass transit or walking. Many of us dream of that special car—the feeling of independence of the open road, listening to the ooohs and ahhhs from our neighbors and members of the opposite sex as they see our new car. Few of us have such fantasies about taking the subway. Further, that massive dose of car advertising will suggest what factors are important to consider in making our purchase—namely, those attributes that appear in the advertising, such as sportiness, luxury, or high performance, as opposed to others that might be considered in selecting a mode of transportation, such as the vehicle's impact on the environment or the ability to work, socialize, or just enjoy the passing scenery as you ride to your destination. We will have more to say about this in the section on pre-persuasion, and especially in Chapter 7.

Second, researchers have also found evidence for the direct effects of the mass media—that is, changes in attitudes consistent with the content of the mass media message. The Chevy-versus-Ford advertising illustrates the difficulty of detecting such effects, however. With massive doses of influence from each side, there is little reason to expect the average consumer to prefer one car over the other. However, what about the case when a consumer sees more ads from one brand as opposed to its competitor?

Such cases can be identified using what has been termed "single-source" data—that is, data that result from tracking the TV ads watched by a household and the brands of products that household subsequently purchases. Using such data, advertising researcher John Philip Jones found that, on average, watching an ad for a brand at least once during a seven-day period increased the brand's share of purchases by 6%.[18] However, these effects varied considerably, with strong ads (those that communicated a benefit and that consumers found likable and visually appealing) tripling sales and weak ads actually cutting purchase rates in half.

The political scientist John Zaller has found similar results for the effects of news and political advertising.[19] Zaller identified U.S. House of Representatives elections in which there were what he called "reception gaps"—that is, voters were likely to receive the campaign message of one candidate but not the other. In such cases, he found that voters often defected from their own party to vote for the candidate who received more exposure in the mass media. This defection rate could be as high as 70%. But in elections in which voters were likely to receive information from and about both candidates (say, in a heavily covered presidential contest), exposure to the mass media produced minimal effects because the effect of a message from one candidate was canceled by the message from the other candidate.

Sometimes the mass media carry only one side of an issue. Such was the case in 1990 when then-president George Bush decided to send troops to the Persian Gulf. His decision was also supported by members of Congress, none of whom issued a statement opposing the decision. The mass media reflected this consensus among Washington policy makers and carried news stories describing the arguments for sending troops to the Gulf. The effect of watching this one-sided coverage is clear. According to Zaller, only 23% of those Americans who watched very little news in August of 1990 supported the decision to send troops to the Persian Gulf. However, among those who habitually kept track of the news, 76% favored the invasion of Iraq—a gain of 53%!

But that wasn't the only way the media affected our attitudes about the Persian Gulf crisis. Although both conservatives and liberals agreed on the need for intervention, they differed on *how* this should be done, with conservatives taking a tougher stand (for example, favoring immediate military action) than liberals (who wanted to give economic sanctions more time to work)—a difference of opinion that was also reflected in the mass media. In this case, watching the news merely reinforced one's original beliefs. Those conservatives who habitually attended to their TV sets took a tougher stand on intervention than those conservatives who watched little news, whereas liberals showed the opposite pattern.

Clearly, then, the mass media do affect some of our most fundamental beliefs and opinions and can even lead us to purchase an advertised brand of product or to support the destruction of other human beings. It is true that sometimes we can act as rational beings—for example, when the mass media carry a full debate on an issue and we are motivated to think about that issue. However, this is not always the case. Sometimes we may hear only one side of the issue and not take the time to explore alternatives; in such circumstances, we are likely to adhere mindlessly to what we have been told. In other cases, the mass media may present viewpoints that oppose our own and we either attempt to avoid them or rationalize them away, in the process becoming more entrenched in our own beliefs.

To understand how the mass media (and other influence agents, for that matter) persuade, we need to understand our cognitive responses to what is communicated—that is, the thoughts running through our head as we see and hear the message. In other words, influence depends on how a message is interpreted and responded to by the recipient—which could vary depending on the individual, the situation, and the appeal. For example, sometimes we think carefully about what is said; at other times we think very little and follow our initial prejudices; at still other times we may be overcome with emotions— our fears, our hopes, our insecurities—to such an extent that it clouds our judgment.

The cognitive response approach to persuasion began in the late 1960s at Ohio State University in response to some findings that could not be explained by the information-processing model.[20] Research accumulated showing that a communication can be persuasive even if it fails in a few of the information-processing stages. Sometimes a message can be persuasive even if its arguments are *not* fully understood or comprehended. For example, in his autobiography the onetime Watergate burglar and current talk-show host G. Gordon Liddy reports that in his youth he would often be persuaded by the speeches of Adolf Hitler, which he heard in German on the radio, even though he knew only a few German phrases.[21] Sometimes a message can be persuasive even if the key arguments are *not* learned or remembered. For example, children are often influenced by toy ads even though they recall very little of the content of the communication. Similarly, much research shows that there is little relationship between what someone recalls of a message and whether he or she will be persuaded by that message.

The cognitive response approach has given us one of the most important laws for determining the effectiveness of a persuasive tactic: *The successful persuasion tactic is one that directs and channels thoughts so that the target thinks in a manner agreeable to the communicator's point of view; the successful tactic disrupts any negative thoughts and promotes positive thoughts about the proposed course of action.*

To say that persuasion is dependent on the thoughts running through one's head as a persuasive message is received seems straightforward. But it begs an important question: What determines the thoughts running through one's head? Where do our cognitive responses come from? What determines the way we think about a persuasive communication? This book seeks to answer these questions. In the next three chapters of this section we will look at some overarching principles that describe our cognitive responses to persuasive communications. In Chapter 3, we will find that we humans often seek to conserve our cognitive energy by taking mental shortcuts whenever we can. We will explore when we are most likely to do this and examine some of the consequences. In Chapter 4, we will explore a human tendency to rationalize our thoughts and behaviors so that they appear reasonable to ourselves and others. In Chapter 5, we will look at four goals that propagandists must achieve if they hope to be effective. To do so, propagandists attempt to take advantage of our two basic human tendencies—to take mental shortcuts and to rationalize our behavior—by constructing various tactics that play on our prejudices and emotions.[22] We look at those tactics in the next four sections.

As we journey through this book, the reader should note a constant theme: Persuasion is no more mysterious than a household lamp. For those who do not understand the principles of electricity, a modern lamp can be a magical, often frightening device. Imagine for a moment that you know nothing about electricity and a woman comes into your home and plugs in a lamp—and suddenly the room becomes brighter. What would you think? You would probably wonder in awe: *"Who is this all-powerful goddess of light? What magical fluid or spirit resides in the lamp, hidden from view? Can this goddess with her magical fluid cure my insomnia, too?"* If you happen to touch the lamp and receive a shock, your reverence may turn quickly to fear. In many ways, your reactions to the lamp would not be much different from the feelings of those who first saw Mesmer and his magnets or watched *The Manchurian Candidate* in fear and amazement. Suppose we told you that we were going to equip every home in a faraway land with electricity and modern electrical devices but that we were going to keep the populace of that country ignorant of how electricity works. You would no doubt call us irresponsible and perhaps evil. How much more irresponsible would it then be to equip every home with modern propaganda and not provide instructions concerning the ways of persuasion?

3

IIIIIIIIIIIIIIIIIIIIIII

Mindless Propaganda, Thoughtful Persuasion

Here are six facts that professional persuaders have learned about modern propaganda:[1]

Ads that contain the words *new, quick, easy, improved, now, suddenly, amazing,* and *introducing* sell more products.

In supermarkets, merchandise placed on shelves at eye level sells best. Indeed, one study found that sales for products at waist level were only 74% as great and sales for products at floor level were only 57% as great as for those products placed at eye level.

Ads that use animals, babies, or sex appeal are more likely to sell the product than those that use cartoon characters and historical figures.

Merchandise placed at the end of a supermarket aisle or near the checkout aisle is more likely to be purchased.

Bundle pricing—for example, selling items at two for $1 instead of 50¢ each—often increases the customer's perception of product "value."

In solicitations and sales calls, asking the target "How are you feeling?" and then acknowledging the response can double the rate of compliance with the request.

Why do these six techniques work? When you think about it, it makes little sense to purchase an item because it happens to be placed at the end of a supermarket aisle or on a shelf at eye level. You may not really need this conveniently located product, or the item you really want may be located on a top shelf. It makes little sense to be convinced by an ad because it uses a baby or contains certain words; such "information" is of little value in determining the quality of the product. A subtle rewording of the price does not add any value to the product.

Merely asking us how we feel does not make the charity or product any better. But that is the point—we consumers often don't think about the reasons we make the decisions we do. Studies show that about half of purchases in a supermarket are impulse buys and that upwards of 62% of all shoppers in discount stores buy at least one item on an unplanned basis.[2]

We often respond to propaganda with little thought and in a mindless fashion. Consider the experiments on mindlessness conducted by Ellen Langer and her colleagues.[3] Langer's collaborators walked up to persons busily using a university copy machine and said: "Excuse me: May I use the Xerox machine?" What would you do in such a situation? If you are like most people, it would depend on your mood. On some occasions you might think: *"Sure, why not? I'm a helpful person."* At other times, you might say to yourself: *"Is this person nuts or what? I got here first and have lots of work to do."* Indeed, Langer's results indicate that both types of thinking were going on—a little more than half of the people complied with this request.

Now, here's the interesting part. Langer found that she could get almost everyone to agree to let another person cut in front of them at the copy machine by adding one detail to the request—a *reason* for why the machine was needed. This makes sense. It takes a cold heart to deny someone, perhaps panic-stricken with an urgent need, the simple use of a copy machine. The odd thing about Langer's study is that although some of the reasons given made no sense at all, nearly everyone let the person cut in. For example, on some occasions Langer's collaborators would say, "Excuse me: May I use the Xerox machine, because I have to make copies." When you think about it, this is a pretty silly thing to say: Why would you need a copy machine if you were not planning to make copies? It is the same as no reason at all. But that is the point. Most of the people in the study did not think about it and mindlessly complied with the request. Any reason will do!

Advertisers understand that often any reason will do. The communications expert Ivan Preston made a catalog of typical claims made in mass media advertising.[4] He notes that many ads trumpet trivial differences as if they were important (e.g., Camel Wides, which are two millimeters wider than usual), state nonfacts that make the brand appear impressive (e.g., "Coke is it!"—whatever "it" may mean), and exude meaningless puffery or meaningless superlatives (e.g., "Bayer—the world's best aspirin" when all aspirin are alike). In other words, just about any reason apparently will do.

We can also be influenced when we are being thoughtful. For example, most of us, at one time or another, have been panhandled, that is, stopped on the street by a passerby who asks for a quarter or any spare change. A common response is to ignore the request and continue to walk *mindlessly* down the street. Recently, we were panhandled in a novel manner. The panhandler asked, "Excuse me, do you have 17¢ that I could have?" What thoughts would run through your head in this situation? When this happened to us, our immediate thought was: *"Why does this person need exactly 17¢? Is it for bus fare? Is it for a specific food purchase? Maybe the person came up short at the market."* Suddenly the panhandler was a real individual with real needs, not someone we could mindlessly pass by. We were persuaded to part with a handful of change. Intrigued, we later sent our students out on the streets to panhandle for a local charity. They found that almost 60% more people contributed when asked for 17¢ or 37¢ compared to those who were asked for a quarter or any spare change.[5]

People can be persuaded both when they are in a mindless state *and* when they are thoughtful, but exactly how they are influenced in either of these two states differs considerably. Richard Petty and John Cacioppo argue that there are two routes to persuasion—*peripheral* and *central*.[6] In the peripheral route, a message recipient devotes little attention and effort to processing a communication. Some examples might include watching television while doing something else or listening to a debate on an issue that you don't care much about. In the peripheral route, persuasion is determined by simple cues, such as the attractiveness of the communicator, whether or not the people around you agree with the position presented, the pleasure or pain associated with agreeing with the position, or whether a reason is given (no matter how bogus) for complying with a request. In the central route, a message recipient engages in a careful and thoughtful consideration of the true merits of the information presented. For example, in the central route the person may actively argue against the message, may want to know the answer to additional questions, or may seek out new information. The persuasiveness of the message is determined by how well it can stand up to this scrutiny.

Let's see how the two routes to persuasion could be used to process one of the most influential and controversial television ads in the history of presidential elections. It was 1988; George Bush was running against Michael Dukakis. This ad, prepared by the Bush campaign, told the story of Willie Horton, a black man who had been sent to prison for murder. During the time when Dukakis was governor of Massachusetts, Horton was released on a prison furlough program. While on furlough, Horton fled to Maryland, where he raped a white woman after stabbing her male companion.

The ad was influential because it required little thought for a person in the peripheral route to get the point. A typical response elicited by the ad went something like this: *"Dukakis let Horton out of prison to rape and kill. Dukakis is weak on crime, especially those committed by bad black guys."* The ad follows the classic propaganda formula: a simple image (Willie Horton) that plays on prejudices (white Americans' stereotypes of black Americans) and emotions (fear of crime) to produce a simple, but nonetheless effective, response (in favor of George Bush). Michael Dukakis was painted as a weak leader who was soft on crime; by comparison, George Bush looked strong and tough, capable of protecting us from the likes of Willie Horton.

However, no one was forced to think about this ad in the peripheral route. For example, in the central route to persuasion, the viewer might have asked: "Just how unusual is the Massachusetts prison furlough program? Do other states have similar programs? What is the success rate of such programs? Have instances like the Horton case happened in other states and with other governors? Can Dukakis really be held personally responsible for the decision to release Horton? How many prisoners were furloughed in Massachusetts without incident? Given that the cost in 1988 of imprisoning someone for four years was approximately $88,000, or equal to the cost of four years of tuition for a student at Harvard with enough left over to buy the student a BMW upon graduation, is the prison furlough program worth trying?"* In the central route, the Horton ad is potentially less effective (and might even have had the potential to damage the Bush campaign). The ad addressed few questions that a thoughtful viewer might raise.

This raises a crucial question: What determines which route to persuasion will be adopted? One factor identified by Petty and Cacioppo is the recipient's motivation to think about the message. In one experiment, Petty and Cacioppo, along with their student Rachel Goldman,[8] investigated the role of personal involvement in determining how we think about a message. Students at the University of Missouri heard a message advocating that their university adopt an exam that all students would need to pass in their senior year in order to graduate. Half of the students were told that their university's chancellor was considering adopting the comprehensive exam the following year, thereby making the issue of adopting the exam personally relevant for these students. The other half were told that the changes would not take effect for ten years and thus would not affect them personally.

To see how the personal relevance of an issue influenced thinking about a communication, Petty, Cacioppo, and Goldman prepared four different versions of the comprehensive exam message. Half of the messages were attributed to a source low in

---

* Some facts about Dukakis and the furlough program did emerge a few years after the election.[7] Some of these facts include: Four other convicted murderers who were participants in the furlough program escaped—all white; selecting the one black man for the ad emphasized the racial motives. The furlough program was begun in Massachusetts by Dukakis's Republican predecessor; during ten years of the Dukakis administration, 275 furlough participants escaped compared with 269 in just three years of the preceding Republican administration. After the Horton escape (and before the 1988 election), Dukakis strengthened the program requirements created by his Republican predecessor. Similar crimes had been committed by participants in the federal and California furlough programs under Bush and Reagan. The creator of some of Bush's negative campaign ads, Dennis Frankenberry, was himself a beneficiary of a work-release program, serving 250 hours of community service as opposed to going to prison for severely injuring two young men in a hit-and-run accident that occurred when he was driving under the influence of alcohol. Ironically, it was the public service announcements that Frankenberry created while on work-release that brought him to the attention of the Bush campaign.

⋆ Refer to past Social Psy notes for other possible studies on the.

expertise—a local high school class. The other half of the messages were attributed to a source high in expertise—the Carnegie Commission on Higher Education. The researchers also varied the quality of arguments in the message, with half of the messages containing weak arguments (personal opinions and anecdotes) and the other half consisting of strong arguments (statistics and other data about the value of the exam).

○ This simple study can tell us a lot about the way people think about a persuasive message. Suppose someone was operating in the central route to persuasion and was carefully scrutinizing the communication. When would that person be most persuaded? Given that the person was thinking carefully, he or she would not be persuaded by weak arguments and the source of the communication would not matter much; however, a strong message that stood up to close examination would be very effective. In contrast, the content of the message would not matter much to someone who was not thinking too much about the issue; instead, someone using the peripheral route would be most persuaded by a simple device such as attributing the communication to an apparently expert source.

What did Petty, Cacioppo, and Goldman find? The personal relevance of the issue determined the route to persuasion. For those students for whom the issue of comprehensive exams was personally relevant, the strength of the message's argument was the most important factor determining whether or not they were persuaded. In contrast, for those students for whom the issue of the comprehensive exam was not personally relevant, the source of the communication mattered—the source high in expertise convinced; the one from the high school class failed to do so.

Petty and Cacioppo's two routes to persuasion should alert us to two important points—one about ourselves as human beings and one about propaganda in our modern world. In many ways, we are *cognitive misers*, forever trying to conserve our cognitive energy.[9] Given our finite ability to process information, we often adopt the strategies of the peripheral route for simplifying complex problems; we mindlessly accept a conclusion or proposition not for any good reason but because it is accompanied by a simplistic persuasion device.

Modern propaganda promotes the use of the peripheral route to persuasion and is designed to take advantage of the

limited processing capabilities of the cognitive miser. The characteristics of modern persuasion—the message-dense environment, the thirty-second ad, the immediacy of persuasion—make
it increasingly more difficult to think deeply about important
issues and decisions. Given that we often operate in the peripheral route, professional propagandists have free rein to use the
type of tactics described at the beginning of this chapter and
throughout this book to achieve, with impunity, whatever goal
they may have in mind.

We have a state of affairs that may be called the *essential
dilemma of modern democracy*. On the one hand, we, as a society, value persuasion; our government is based on the belief that
free speech and discussion and exchange of ideas can lead to
fairer and better decision making. On the other hand, as cognitive misers we often do not participate fully in this discussion,
instead relying not on careful thought and scrutiny of a message
but on simplistic persuasion devices and limited reasoning.
Mindless propaganda, not thoughtful persuasion, flourishes.

The antidote to the dilemma of modern democracy is not a
simple one. It requires each of us to take steps to minimize the

likelihood of our processing important information in the peripheral route. This might include increasing our ability to think about an issue through education or improving our ability to detect and understand propaganda by learning more about persuasion. It could involve restructuring the way information is presented in our society so that we have the time as well as the ability to think before we decide. It may mean alerting others to the personal importance of an issue so that many more citizens are encouraged to think deeply about a proposition. The dilemma of modern democracy is one that we will face throughout this volume. Given the stakes, it behooves each of us to think carefully about how this dilemma can best be resolved.

---

4 |||||||||||||||||||||

The Rationalizing Animal

We humans like to think of ourselves as rational animals. However, it is more true that we are *rationalizing* animals, that, no matter how irrationally we might actually behave, we attempt to appear reasonable to ourselves and to others. According to the existentialist philosopher Albert Camus, we humans are creatures who spend our entire lives in an attempt to convince ourselves that our lives are not absurd. How do we demonstrate that our lives are not absurd? By finding ways to justify our actions, as the following example illustrates.

Marian Keech was a charismatic, middle-aged woman living in a large midwestern city who, in the early 1950s, claimed to be receiving messages from outer space.[1] One evening in September, she received a message from the planet Clarion informing her that on December 21, the world would be destroyed by a great flood. The message went on to say that a fleet of flying saucers would come from Clarion to rescue her and those close to her.

Mrs. Keech attracted a small but loyal group of followers who fervently believed in her prophecy and made a great many sacrifices consistent with this belief—they quit their jobs; gave away their money, houses, and possessions (who needs money and possessions on the planet Clarion?); and withdrew from their friends. A few even left their spouses.

Mrs. Keech also attracted a small group of social psychologists who infiltrated the movement, pretending to be believers, because they wanted to get a precise, close-up view of what these people would do after December 21 when they discovered that their prophecy had failed—*if*, indeed, it *did* fail! The social psychologists noted that Mrs. Keech and her followers were a gentle, benign, reclusive group. One of the most interesting things about them was that they shunned publicity and discouraged converts; they were content to stick to themselves. They treated the "newcomers" politely, but they made it clear that it was of no consequence to them whether or not the newcomers chose to remain a part of the group. They were confident in their beliefs, but it was a quiet, nonflamboyant confidence. Mrs. Keech and her followers refused to grant interviews to reporters and declined to publicize their beliefs in any way.

On the morning of December 20, Mrs. Keech received a message from the planet Clarion instructing her group to be prepared to be picked up precisely at midnight. They were also told to remove all metal from their clothing. The group complied; zippers and clasps were dutifully removed from trousers, skirts, and blouses. When midnight passed and the spaceship did not arrive, the group became increasingly engulfed by feelings of anxiety and despair. By 4:00 A.M. the group was sitting in stunned silence. But then, at 4:45 A.M., Mrs. Keech's face suddenly took on a radiant glow; she had just received a message from Clarion to the effect that there was no longer any need for the flying saucers to descend—the world had been spared a cataclysm because of the unflagging faith of this small group of believers! The message went on to say that the little group, sitting all night long, had spread so much light that the God of Earth had decided to save the world from destruction. As you might imagine, the group was relieved and elated to hear this news.

What the group did next aroused the curiosity of the social psychologists even more. Within twenty-four hours, the true believers—this group of quiet, reclusive, shy people—began calling newspapers and TV stations to talk about their prophecy and why it had failed. They made speeches at the drop of a hat and stood on street corners handing out leaflets trying very hard to attract followers. Apparently, the group suddenly found it of urgent importance to spread its message to as broad an audience as possible. Why?

We would suggest that, after the initial elation, the group experienced some doubts; they had given up a great deal because of their belief in the imminent end of the world. The world had not ended, and they were now devoid of their homes, jobs, and possessions—even, a few of them, their spouses. How could they be certain that they had done the right thing? How could they convince themselves that their behavior had not been absurd? By convincing others, of course! After their original prophecy failed, the group felt motivated to attract followers as a way of convincing *themselves* that the sacrifices they had made were not in vain; if they could somehow persuade *others* that their belief had saved the world, then they could allay their own doubts. In the process, they transformed themselves from believers into zealots.

In 1957, Leon Festinger, one of social psychology's most important theorists and a member of the team of social psychologists who had infiltrated Mrs. Keech's group, proposed his theory of *cognitive dissonance*, which describes and predicts how we humans rationalize behavior.[2] Dissonance occurs whenever a person simultaneously holds two inconsistent cognitions (ideas, beliefs, opinions). For example, the belief that the world will end on a certain day is dissonant with the awareness, when the day breaks, that the world has not ended. Festinger maintained that this state of inconsistency is so uncomfortable that people strive to reduce the conflict in the easiest way possible. They will change one or both cognitions so that they will "fit together" better. This is especially true in situations (such as the one just described) in which a person's self-esteem is at risk.[3] In these circumstances, individuals will go to great lengths of distortion, denial, and self-persuasion in order to justify their past behavior. When our self-esteem has been threatened by our own past behavior, we all have a powerful tendency to become rationalizing animals.

The fact that we are rationalizing animals has important implications for how we receive and react to propaganda. Consider what happens when Frank, a smoker, is confronted with evidence that smoking causes cancer. Frank will be motivated to change either his attitudes about smoking or his behavior. And as anyone who has tried to quit knows, the former alternative is easier. Frank may decide that the studies are lousy. He may point to friends—"If Sam, Jack, and Kate smoke, cigarettes can't be all that dangerous." He may conclude that filters trap all the cancer-producing materials or he may try a low-tar, low-nicotine brand of cigarette. Or he may argue that he would rather live a short and happy life with cigarettes than a long and miserable life without them. The more a person is committed to a course of action, the more resistant that person will be to information that threatens that course. Psychologists have reported that the people who are least likely to believe in the dangers of smoking are those who tried to quit and failed. They have become more committed to smoking.

By reducing dissonance, a person defends the ego and retains a positive self-image. But self-justification can reach startling extremes; people will ignore danger in order to avoid dissonance, even when that ignorance can cause their deaths and the deaths of loved ones. We mean that literally.

California is earthquake country.[4] On May 2, 1983, an earthquake of magnitude 6.5 struck the quiet farming town of Colinga, California. Although the quake caused considerable damage and destruction to the town, there was one positive result: The state of California mandated that all cities and towns assess how local buildings would fare in a large earthquake and begin to take steps to minimize that damage. In the city of Santa Cruz (where we live), Dave Steeves, a respected engineer, was charged with the task of preparing such an earthquake audit. Steeves identified 175 buildings that would suffer severe damage in a large earthquake, many of which were located in the Pacific Garden Mall area, the picturesque downtown shopping area of Santa Cruz. This area was particularly vulnerable to earthquake damage because many of the buildings were constructed of unreinforced masonry and, in addition, were built on sandy landfill, which tends to magnify the effects of a quake.

What was the reaction of the Santa Cruz city council to Steeves's report? A rational response would have been to evaluate carefully what he had to say. Did his arguments about unreinforced masonry and sandy landfill make sense? Did he do a complete inspection of the town? Once satisfied that Steeves's argument was sound, a rational person would then have turned to a search for solutions—perhaps asking state and federal agencies for aid, alerting citizens to the danger, identifying immediate but low-cost ways of improving safety, marshaling local citizens to help with the situation, and so on. Indeed, Steeves identified at least one such low-cost solution.

But this was not the reaction of the town to Steeves's news. Instead, his report was dismissed by the city council, which voted unanimously in 1987 to wait for the state of California to clarify the "nature of the state law, its options and their legal circumstances regarding the state law" and to convene a new committee to look at the issue. Steeves was called an alarmist and was charged with threatening the town with financial ruin. Many denied that a large earthquake was imminent or would even come at all. In short, Steeves's report set off an attempt at collective dissonance reduction among town leaders.

On October 17, 1989, an earthquake of magnitude 7.1 hit Loma Prieta, a mountain area just outside Santa Cruz. Five people were killed and about 2,000 were injured in Santa Cruz County; 300 homes were destroyed and 5,000 more were seriously damaged. The Pacific Garden Mall lay in ruins. If anything, Steeves's report had erred on the side of optimism. As further testimony to the powerful need to reduce dissonance, one city official blamed Steeves for the lack of earthquake preparedness because his report "succeeded in having the whole issue put off by scaring people."

Dissonance reduction can lead to more than just attempts to avoid disagreeable information, as in the case of the smoker and the city of Santa Cruz. The reduction of dissonance is a part of everyday life; this is used to advantage by propagandists in what we call the *rationalization trap*. The trap goes like this. First, the propagandist intentionally arouses feelings of dissonance by threatening self-esteem—for example, by making the person feel guilty about something, by arousing feelings of shame or inadequacy, or by making the person look like a hypocrite or someone who does not honor his or her word. Next, the propagandist offers one solution, one way of reducing this dissonance—by complying with whatever request the propagandist has in mind. The way to reduce that guilt, eliminate that shame, honor that commitment, and restore your feelings of adequacy is to give to that charity, buy that car, hate that enemy, or vote for that leader.

Throughout this book, we will see many variations of the rationalization trap, especially when we talk about the use of emotions in propaganda. But for now, to provide a flavor of what we mean, let's look at two examples of the trap: one involving a subtle request to give to a charity and the other dealing with the more serious issue of war propaganda.

Suppose you are at home and someone knocks at your door, asking you to contribute to a worthy charity. If you don't want to contribute, you probably wouldn't find it too difficult to come up with reasons for declining—you don't have the money, your contribution probably won't help much anyway, and so on. But suppose that, after delivering a standard plea for a donation, the fund-raiser adds one simple phrase—"even a penny will help." There goes your easy excuse. Refusing to donate after hearing this statement would undoubtedly stir up some dissonance by challenging your self-concept. After all, what kind of person is it who is too mean or stingy to come up with a penny? Your previous justifications would no longer apply. The rationalization trap is set. The request threatens your self-esteem, and there is only one way to reduce this negative feeling—give to the charity.

Such a scenario was tested experimentally by Robert Cialdini and David Schroeder.[5] Students acting as fund-raisers went door to door asking for donations. Their appeal was identical except that half of the time they added the phrase "even a penny will help." The residents who were approached with the "even-a-penny" request gave contributions more often, donating almost twice as frequently as those getting just the standard plea. Furthermore, on average, the "even-a-penny" contributors were likely to give as much money as the others; that is, the statement legitimizing the small donation did not reduce the size of the contributions. Why? Apparently, not only does the lack of external justification for refusing to donate encourage people to give money, but, after they have decided *whether* to contribute, the desire to avoid appearing stingy or cheap affects their decision about *how much* to give. Once people reach into their pockets, emerging with a mere penny is self-demeaning; a larger donation is consistent with their self-perception of being reasonably kind and generous.

One of the most pernicious functions of war propaganda is to make it easier for members of one nation to destroy members of another nation with psychological impunity. War causes a great deal of harm and destruction, often to innocent bystanders and children. The cognition *"I and my country are decent, fair, and reasonable"* is dissonant with the cognition *"I and my country have hurt innocent people."* If the harm is clear, then you cannot reduce your dissonance by claiming that it wasn't done or it wasn't really violence. In this situation, the most effective way to reduce dissonance is to minimize the humanity or maximize the culpability of the victim of your action—to convince yourself the victims deserved what they got.

How else can we account for the following phenomenon? Near the end of World War II, American planes dropped nuclear bombs on Hiroshima and Nagasaki. More than 100,000 civilians (including women and children) were killed, and countless thousands suffered severe injuries. It is currently fashionable for most Americans to decry that decision. But a week after the bombs were dropped, a public opinion poll indicated that less than 5% of the American population felt we should not have used those weapons, and an astonishing 23% felt we should have used many more of them before allowing Japan the opportunity to surrender.[6]

Some of our readers might consider these events ancient history. But, more recently, during the Persian Gulf war, the people of Iraq were depicted as the unfortunate followers of Saddam Hussein, "the butcher of Baghdad." In the aftermath of the war, amidst the legitimate celebration of a stunning victory, very few Americans paused to express much regret about the killing of tens of thousands of Iraqi noncombatants by our "surgical" bombing raids—which also destroyed the infrastructure of Baghdad (including the water supply), resulting in the suffering of hundreds of thousands of innocent civilians. Almost every war in modern times has been accompanied by characterizations of the enemy as less than human.

Dehumanization succeeds in resolving any disso
may be aroused by our cruelty toward our enemies
watch out; the more we justify our cruelty, the easier it becomes.
The rationalization trap becomes an escalating spiral: *"I committed an act of cruelty; I justify this act by believing that the victim
deserved it. If the victim deserved that cruelty, well maybe they
deserve more and maybe I am just the one to give it to them."*
Today's "ethnic cleansing" in places such as Bosnia, Rwanda,
and Kosovo are yet other cruel examples of this cruel trap.

In this chapter, we have seen that the tendency to justify our
past behavior can lead us into an escalation of rationalizations
that can be disastrous. The irony, of course, is that, in order
to avoid thinking of ourselves as stupid or immoral, we set
the stage for increasing our acts of stupidity or immorality. Is
there any antidote to the rationalization trap? Although it is
clear that most of us will go to great lengths to justify our
actions, it is just as clear that, if that were all we did, we would
never learn from our experience; human beings cannot live by
consonance alone.[7]

In our everyday experience, we have seen people break out
of the rationalization trap by courageously admitting to their
mistakes and learning from their errors. How? Under what conditions? Ideally, when we make a mistake, it would be useful for
us to be able to interrupt the ego-protective tendency to deny,
distort, and to justify it; to bring ourselves to say, in effect, "OK,
I blew it. What can I learn from the experience so I will not end
up in this position again?" This can come about, first, through
an understanding of our defensiveness and dissonance-reducing
tendencies and, second, through the development of enough ego
strength to recognize and face up to errors in past behavior that
require correction—not justification.

We are well aware of the fact that this is easier said than
done. We live in a culture where mistakes are not easily tolerated
and failure is considered sinful—where children who flunk an
exam are sometimes held up to ridicule and where skillful major
league baseball managers are fired after one losing season.[20] Perhaps, if we could bring ourselves to be more tolerant of the failure of others, we might be able to tolerate our own shortcomings
and thereby short-circuit the knee-jerk tendency to justify whatever it is that we have done.

5   IIIIIIIIIIIIIIIIIIIII

The Four Stratagems of Influence

In the fall of 1863, Abraham Lincoln was perhaps one of the least popular and most despised presidents in U.S. history. Elected in 1860 with less than 40% of the popular vote, Lincoln presided over a divided nation. He faced a hostile press that accused him of everything from being a drunkard to exchanging pardons for votes to warmongering to being a cowardly tyrant and dictator to advocating "free love, free land, and free Negroes." His Union soldiers were called "Lincolnpoop."

Immediately after Lincoln assumed the presidency, rebel forces took control of Fort Sumter in South Carolina, forcing a bloody civil war. The war was unpopular from the start, and support ebbed further as the citizens of the northern states, never fully convinced of why slavery should be abolished, witnessed one bloody battle after another and mourned the loss of their war dead. By 1863, anti-war sentiment had coalesced into draft riots, with mobs raging through the streets of New York City looting, burning, and killing until federal troops could be brought from the battlefield to quell the violence. One of the bloodiest battles of the Civil War occurred at Gettysburg, Pennsylvania, where both sides suffered casualties of more than 50,000 dead or wounded. The bodies were buried by a local contractor in a new seventeen-acre cemetery at a cost of $1.59 per corpse. To dedicate the cemetery, Edward Everett, a politician, orator, and former president of Harvard College, gave a two-hour address recounting the events of the battle. President Lincoln was also invited to attend the dedication and to deliver "a few appropriate remarks." He required only three minutes to speak his 272 words at Gettysburg; however, when he finished, Abraham Lincoln had given the citizens of his country a vision of what they were building—a nation based on the principles that all are created equal and that government should be of the people, by the people, for the people.[1]

During the early 1970s, Jeff Christy was a little-known disc jockey working in the Pittsburgh, Pennsylvania, area. However, Christy's stint ended in 1974, when radio station KQV fired him for being a "no-talent bum." After landing a job on Kansas City's KFIX, Christy was fired again, this time because of "personality clashes." To make a living, Rush Limbaugh (Christy's real name) took a job in the sales department of the Kansas City Royals baseball team until he got his big break—his own radio talk show with KFBK in Sacramento, California. Today, Rush Limbaugh is heard (on almost 600 radio stations) at least two times a week by 11% of the U.S. adult population. And his influence doesn't stop there. During the 1992 presidential election, Limbaugh was invited to spend the night at the White House; President Bush personally carried Limbaugh's luggage to the Lincoln bedroom. In 1994, Supreme Court Justice Clarence Thomas took time from his busy schedule to officiate at the wedding of Limbaugh to his third wife, Marta. Justice Thomas hosted the wedding at his own home. Mary Matalin, Bush's deputy campaign manager in 1992 and co-host of a cable TV talk show, told one reporter, "Senators and congressmen all across the board on the Republican side call [Limbaugh] all morning long before he goes on the air."[2]

Paul Ingram was a pillar of his Olympia, Washington, community. At age forty-three, he was the chief civil deputy of the sheriff's department and active in both local politics and his Church of Living Water. All that changed on November 28, 1988, when Ingram was arrested for sexually molesting his two daughters—Ericka (then twenty-two years old) and Julie (then eighteen years old). After a series of interrogations led by police detectives Joe Vukich and Brian Schoening, clinical psychologist Richard Peterson, and Pastor John Bratun, Ingram confessed to these heinous crimes. According to the confession, he and his wife, Sandy, had been sexually abusing their daughters for seventeen years. Ingram admitted that he was the leader of a satanic cult engaged in ritual slaughter of infants and animals on his farm. He admitted further that he had impregnated one of his daughters and then forced her to have an abortion. He stated that his home served as headquarters for a ring of pedophiles (including two members of the local police) who would regularly get drunk and rape Julie.

What makes this story even more remarkable is that there is no evidence that what Ingram admitted to ever occurred and much evidence that, at the very least, parts of it never could have happened. For example, after massive police investigations, including large-scale excavations of Ingram's farm, no physical evidence of murdered infants and animals was ever found. Despite an extensive search, the doctor who allegedly performed the abortion was never located. The Ingram family doctor found no physical evidence of abuse when he examined the daughters. Nighttime aircraft patrols never spotted the bonfires supposedly at the center of ongoing satanic rituals in the area (although these patrols did lead to busts of a few fraternity beer parties). The two police officers alleged to be members of the ring of pedophiles denied abusing the daughters. Julie Ingram did claim to have received a threatening letter from her father; however, the letter was later shown to be written in Julie's own handwriting. Court-ordered examinations failed to find scars on the bodies of Ericka and Julie—scars that they claimed were the result of repeated satanic tortures. Ericka still publicly claims that she carries these scars and has denounced the sheriff's office for refusing to arrest thirty doctors, lawyers, and judges who she identified as part of the satanic conspiracy and who she claims continue to murder innocent babies. Other than Ingram's confession, there is no evidence to corroborate the allegations of sexual abuse made by Ericka and Julie. Paul Ingram is now serving a twenty-one-year sentence for a crime most experts agree was never committed.[3]

Although Abraham Lincoln, Rush Limbaugh, and the interrogation team of Vukich, Schoening, Peterson, and Bratun appear to be as different from each other as different can be, they all have at least one thing in common—each provides us with an example of extremely effective persuasion. Abraham Lincoln's Gettysburg Address defined what it means to be an "American"; it continues to be taught in American schools and influences us yet today, some six score and seventeen years later. Through entertainment and persuasion, Rush Limbaugh has captured the attention of presidents, congressional leaders, Supreme Court justices, key political operatives, and more than 20 million regular listeners. The interrogation team convinced Paul Ingram to do something many people think is impossible—to change the memory of his life—and to believe (almost certainly falsely) that he committed a crime that is perhaps the worst a father could commit. How did these brokers of persuasion do it? What makes someone an effective influence agent?

The successful persuasion agent can use any number of influence tactics capable of inducing the target to think positively about an issue or course of action. However, maximum influence is most likely to occur when four main stratagems of influence or general maneuvers for obtaining compliance are accomplished.

What are these four stratagems of influence? The first is to take control of the situation and establish a favorable climate for your message, a process we call *pre-persuasion*. Pre-persuasion refers to how the issue is structured and how the decision is framed. If fully successful, pre-persuasion establishes "what everyone knows" and "what everyone takes for granted" (even if it shouldn't be and should, instead, be taken as a point of discussion). By cleverly establishing how an issue is defined and discussed, however, a communicator can influence cognitive responses and obtain consent without even appearing to be attempting to persuade us. Next, the communicator needs to establish a favorable image in the eyes of the audience. We call this stratagem *source credibility*. In other words, the communicator needs to appear likable or authoritative or trustworthy or possessed of any other attribute that would facilitate persuasion. The third stratagem is to construct and deliver a *message* that focuses the targets' attention and thoughts on exactly what the communicator wants them to think about—for example, by distracting the targets from arguing against the proposal, or by focusing targets' attention on a vivid and powerful image, or even by inducing the targets to persuade themselves. Finally, effective influence controls the *emotions* of the target and follows a simple rule: Arouse an emotion and then offer the target a way of responding to that emotion that just happens to be the desired course of action. In such situations, the target becomes preoccupied with dealing with the emotions, complying with the request in hopes of escaping a negative emotion or maintaining a positive one.

The four stratagems of influence go back to ancient times. As we noted in Chapter 1, Aristotle was the first to develop a comprehensive theory of persuasion.[4] His theory recognized three facets of persuasion—the source (*ethos*), the message (*logos*), and the emotions of the audience (*pathos*). For each facet, Aristotle provided recommendations to the would-be communicator. For example, he recommended that the orator present himself as a good person and as one who could be trusted; he advised that speech writers, in constructing a persuasive message, use arguments that appear to follow the rules of logic and that they use vivid historical and imaginary examples to illustrate points. The message should be tailored to fit the preexisting beliefs of the audience. Aristotle considered an understanding of the feelings of the audience to be essential. An angry person will act differently from one who is pleased. The orator must be able to direct these emotions to good use. To this end, Aristotle described how to evoke emotions in an audience—anger, friendship, fear, envy, shame—and discussed how to put such emotions to effective persuasive use.

Aristotle also recognized one other factor influencing persuasion, which he called *atechnoi*—facts and events outside the immediate control of the speaker. In a court of law, for example, he identified certain circumstances—the way the law is written, the content of a contract, the testimony of a witness—that set the stage for persuasive argument; in a sense, these circumstances establish the playing field on which argument takes place. They serve to focus the issue and to constrain the range of tactics that might be used. As such, they are important determinants of the outcome of a case. Aristotle suggested a number of ways for dealing with these factors—challenging the validity of a law, discrediting a witness—that we might today call "putting the right spin" on the matter.

The Roman lawyer Cicero agreed with much of what Aristotle said about persuasion. Cicero, who achieved fame in ancient Rome for his successful courtroom defense of some of Rome's most notorious villains and murderers, established what he called the *officia oratoris*, the duties of the orator—to charm (establish the credibility of the orator), to teach (present a message with sound arguments), and to move (fill an audience with emotions).

One of Cicero's most important contributions was the further development of Aristotle's concept of *atechnoi* into a theory of *statis*, or status of the issue—what we term *pre-persuasion*. The task of an orator or a lawyer is to provide a definition of the situation that is most advantageous for her or his own point of view. For example, suppose your client has been accused of murder. The first line of defense is to deny the facts—"No, my client didn't do it." If that is not possible, then challenge the definition of the action—"Sure, she killed him, but it wasn't murder." If that fails, then question the quality of the deed—"Yes, it was murder, but it was murder with good intent and performed under extenuating circumstances." When all else fails, question the right of the tribunal to try the case in the first place—"This court has no authority to judge a queen." Readers will probably see parallels between Cicero's recommendations and the conduct of many modern legal cases.

Let's turn our attention now to the three effective influence agents described at the beginning of this chapter and see how each accomplished the four stratagems of influence.

Abraham Lincoln's persuasion task at Gettysburg was a multifaceted one, to say the least. First, he had to justify the war effort. For what purpose had these soldiers died at Gettysburg? Why was the continuation of the war worth the continued loss of life? Next, Lincoln had to justify an action he had taken a few months earlier—the issuance of the Emancipation Proclamation, which freed the enslaved population of the South. The Emancipation Proclamation represented a shift in Lincoln's policy from containment of slavery to the southern states to its elimination. Had he lived today, Lincoln would have been labeled a "waffler" or a "liberal masquerading as a conservative," depending on your position on slavery. Finally, and most importantly, Lincoln had to heal the nation, preserve the Union, and unite the rebels to the rest of the nation. Notice that this complex of objectives limited the rhetoric that Lincoln could use. For example, one common way of justifying war is to use the atrocity story—in this case, to vilify the southern rebels through graphic depictions of the pain of slavery or incidents of slaughter. Such a tactic would have made it harder, however, for the rebels to later embrace the Union. At the end of this chapter, we reprint how Lincoln addressed these issues at Gettysburg.

In his Gettysburg Address, Lincoln employed a standard pre-persuasion tactic used by just about every politician worth his or her salt—define the issue in such a way that you can't help but win. What is remarkable about the speech is that it failed to mention any of the major issues of the day—slavery, the Emancipation Proclamation, a policy for treatment of the former slaves, or how the war would be waged to achieve victory. It was not a speech for policy wonks—those seeking a detailed analysis of why we should embark on a given course of action. Instead, Lincoln defined the issues in a way that everyone could agree with, using glittering generalities and purr words (see Chapter 6)—for example, Lincoln called for the nation to support the "unfinished work" of those who died and to usher in a "new birth of freedom." These are issues that just about any one could endorse.

Perhaps Lincoln's most effective pre-persuasion tactic, however, occurred in the first six words of the address—the ones learned and often parodied by schoolchildren: "Four score and seven years ago." How so? With these six words, Lincoln identified the birth of the United States with the signing of the Declaration of Independence in 1776, not the ratification of the U.S. Constitution in 1789. The fact that Americans now universally accept 1776 as the birth of the nation, not 1789 (witness the celebration of the bicentennial in 1976 compared to the near neglect of the Constitution's bicentennial in 1989), is a testament to the power of Lincoln's message. Such acceptance was not the case in 1863. The first government established by the colonists was based on the Articles of Confederation, and, for the most part, it failed. The founders tried again with a new Constitution, adopted in 1789. Proponents of slavery argued for the primacy of the U.S. Constitution, which at the time did not outlaw slavery. On the other hand, those who opposed slavery took solace in the Declaration's proposition "that all men are created equal."[5] So without so much as mentioning the abolition of slavery, the Emancipation Proclamation, or the war, Lincoln justified them all with six little words that identified the birth of the nation with the Declaration of Independence and the guiding principle of equality. Interestingly, Lincoln's sleight of hand was not accepted by everyone in the North at the time. An editorial in the *Chicago Times* expressed outrage that Lincoln would betray the Constitution (by giving priority to the Declaration) and defame those who wrote it and died for it at Gettysburg—"men with too much self-respect to declare that Negroes were their equals."[6]

When it came to establishing and using source credibility, Lincoln had a major problem: His authority as president was not accepted by large portions of his audience—most obviously by southerners in rebellion, but also by many northerners who disliked his policy of war and felt that slavery should be contained but not necessarily eliminated, and even by abolitionists who distrusted him because of the slow pace of change. What could Honest Abe do? He adopted a tactic commonly used today by advertisers (who are not much trusted either): Get someone else to be the source of the message. Although Lincoln delivered the speech (the voice-over, if you will), the source of the message was the nation's founders and the soldiers who died in battle for a nation conceived in liberty. Lincoln built their credibility by calling them brave and honored, and calling their cause nobly advanced; he even questioned his own and his audience's worthiness to dedicate the ground in which they were buried. Note how this redirection of source enhances the effectiveness of the message. If Lincoln had implied that he was asking the nation to unite in his name, he would have been scoffed at by all who opposed him and found him untrustworthy. But who can argue with the nation's founders and those who died in battle to protect their vision?

Surprisingly, the Gettysburg Address does not employ many of the message tactics commonly used today; for example, the speech contains no vivid, searing images of battle and no repetition of a catchphrase. Lincoln, however, did package his message around a theme that appears throughout the speech—conception, birth, dedication, and consecration of a new nation. For the nineteenth-century audience, well versed in the Bible, this packaging conveyed a special, spiritual nature to American democracy. To turn one's back on this special nation would be to turn one's back on God's will.

At Gettysburg, Lincoln masterfully played on the emotions of Americans. First, he summoned the pride in being an American (by making use of what we call in Chapter 25 the granfalloon tactic). Interestingly, he never mentioned the sides that fought in the battle at Gettysburg, nor did he divide Americans into southerner versus northerner or black versus white or slave versus free. Instead, he talked about all Americans, even the southerners in rebellion, as special and engaged in a great experiment of self-government and liberty. Next, he aroused fear—fear that a nation conceived in liberty and dedicated to that proposition of equality could forever perish from the earth. Finally, he evoked feelings of obligation and commitment to those who brought forth this special nation and who had given their lives to preserve it. Note how each of these emotions requires one concerted action: To maintain our pride as Americans, to eliminate the fear that this special nation will be no more, and to repay our debt, we must continue to fight for the Union, work for liberty, and join with all Americans to fulfill this special mission.

It is Lincoln's evoking of the emotion of hypocrisy that perhaps did the most to change the course of American history. As Garry Wills puts it: "Americans at that time were reverent toward (prejudiced in favor of) the Declaration of Independence; yet many of them were also prejudiced in favor of slavery. Lincoln kept arguing, in ingenious ways, that they must, in consistency, give up one or the other prejudice."[7] At that time, the typical way to resolve this inconsistency was to claim that, regardless of how one felt about slavery, the U.S. Constitution gave Americans the right to self-govern—and if some states wanted slavery, so be it. Even Lincoln had accepted this compromise for some time. However, at Gettysburg he would have none of this. He reminded his audience of their hypocrisy in his first line—a nation "dedicated to the proposition that all men are created equal." How could there be government of the people, by the people, and for the people if some Americans could be excluded against their will? He offered his audience no choice but to confront their prejudice and decide whether a nation "so conceived and dedicated, can long endure." Within seven years of the Gettysburg Address, the United States had adopted the Thirteenth, Fourteenth, and Fifteenth Amendments to the Constitution—amendments that forever secured the nation's commitment to equality by outlawing slavery, ensuring equal protection under the law for all citizens, and guaranteeing the right to vote regardless of race or color.

In contrast to the complexity of Lincoln's mission, Rush Limbaugh needs to perform only two simpler tasks of influence. First, he has to secure an audience. As he puts it, "A turning point in my career came when I realized that the sole purpose for all of us in radio is to sell advertising"[8]—that is, to secure ratings. Limbaugh's second task, which he often denies or downplays, is to win support for his political views. His show is replete with calls to write Congress regarding issues Limbaugh feels are important and to vote for his preferred candidates. He accomplishes the first task by being engaging, entertaining, and fun to listen to, especially if you agree with him. He accomplishes the second task by executing the four stratagems of influence.

One pre-persuasion tactic Limbaugh frequently uses is labeling a person or issue in such a way that few would be inclined to like the person or endorse the issue. For example, he cautions his audience to look out for environmental wackos, feminazis, liberal Democrats, the spaced-out Hollywood Left, long-haired maggot-infested dope-smoking peace pansies, faggots, commie libs, and uglo-Americans. On the other hand, he defines his program as "excellence in broadcasting." Who can be for Nazis of any stripe, and who can oppose "excellence"? Limbaugh also distorts positions to make them easy to refute. For example, during the Clinton years, Limbaugh took Bill Clinton to task for his proposed income tax increase on families making less than $50,000 and his plan to unilaterally disarm the United States. Pretty frightening, huh? Clinton, of course, had neither advocated nor attempted to implement either policy.

Next, Limbaugh maintains complete control of the information on his show. To participate, callers must go through a screening process ensuring that what they have to say fits with what Limbaugh wants. Should an unwanted point of view happen to make it through the screen, Limbaugh can cut off the audio to the caller so that he or she can't hear the program and thus sounds stupid for not responding to the issues; if the caller is particularly troublesome, Limbaugh can simply hang up. For example, when a conversation with an African-American caller wasn't going the way he wanted, Limbaugh hung up and told the caller to "take that bone out of your nose and call me back." The caller, of course, couldn't do the same to Limbaugh or answer his charge. Limbaugh wins by default.

Limbaugh's stock-in-trade pre-persuasion tactic is rumor and innuendo—a distortion, half-truth, outright falsity, or unsupported claim presented as the truth. Rumor and innuendo pre-persuade by setting a context for later argument. For example, suppose I wanted you to believe that government is too liberal and wasteful and that this "liberal" government was failing in areas such as civil rights, energy, education, and tobacco regulation. One way, adopted by Limbaugh, is to repeat rumors and innuendoes such as the following:

"The Supreme Court has become the refuge of liberalism." (At the time of the statement, eight of the nine Supreme Court members had been appointed by Republican presidents, with four appointed by Reagan.)

"I remember those long gas lines of the 1970s resulting from Jimmy Carter." (The lines occurred in 1973 during the Nixon administration.)

"Kansas City now has more people working for the government than they have working in the private sector." (Roughly 5% of the workers in Kansas City work for the government.)

"Supreme Court Justice Clarence Thomas is a man who escaped the bonds of poverty by methods other than those prescribed by civil rights organizations." (Thomas was admitted in 1971 to Yale's law school under an affirmative action program with a goal of admitting 10% minority students—a fact acknowledged by Thomas.)

"We are providing enough money per classroom today to provide chauffeured limousines to teachers and kids." (In Santa Cruz, California, it costs $55 per hour plus tax and tip, with a three-hour minimum, to hire 5-Star Limo Service; this works out to $512 per eight-hour day, or $102,400 per forty-week year for each kid and teacher—tip not included. For each class of twenty students and a teacher, the school board would need to spend more than $2.1 million per year—perhaps they can car-pool.)

"There is no conclusive proof that nicotine's addictive. And the same thing with cigarettes causing emphysema, lung cancer, heart disease." (Virtually all scientists agree that there is abundant evidence to justify government alarm.)

To establish source credibility, Limbaugh presents an image of a "regular guy just like his audience members." For example, Limbaugh stated on his TV show: "All of these rich guys—like the Kennedy family and Perot—pretending to live just like we do and pretending to understand our trials and tribulations and pretending to represent us, and they get away with this." Notice how this image facilitates influence: We usually don't argue with our friends. (We should also note that when he said this,

Limbaugh was earning an estimated $20 million a year—a salary far above that of the average American.)

Rush Limbaugh employs a number of tactics to ensure that his audience thinks about his message in the way he desires. For example, he uses vivid images to focus attention on his arguments: "Watermelons are environmentalist. They're green on the outside but red on the inside." "Ralph Nader is a human handkerchief." Limbaugh distracts his audience members from thinking deeply about what is said with disparaging humor: "Governor Ann Richards was born needing her face ironed." "Hillary Clinton looks like a Pontiac hood ornament." His arguments are packaged in racism, making them more persuasive to listeners who are racially prejudiced: In arguing for NAFTA, he said, "Let the unskilled jobs, let the kinds of jobs that take absolutely no knowledge whatsoever to do—let stupid and unskilled Mexicans do that work." Finally, he repeats his arguments over and over; for example, he will pick a theme for the day and keep repeating his point of view in different ways. In Chapter 20 we discuss how repetition alone can increase the effectiveness of a communication.

Limbaugh frequently plays on two sets of emotions. First, he arouses fear of what might happen if his preferred course of action is not granted. Some examples: "There is a law coming down which says if you have a Bible at your desk at work, then you are guilty of religious harassment." He relabeled an attempt to reinstate the Fairness Doctrine (a requirement that broadcasters cover some controversial issues in their community with balancing views) as "the Hush Rush Bill," intended to get him personally off the airwaves. He also claimed, "The First Amendment has been used to forcibly remove religion from not just our classrooms but all government institutions."

Second, similar to Abraham Lincoln, Rush Limbaugh employs the granfalloon (group-pride) tactic, but with some important twists. Whereas Lincoln aroused feelings of pride in being an American, Limbaugh trumpets the superiority of being a "dittohead"—an avid listener to Limbaugh who agrees with whatever Limbaugh just said. Whereas Lincoln meant the term *American* to be inclusive, Limbaugh enhances the prestige of being a dittohead by contrasting it with out-groups such as liberals ("You are morally superior to those liberal compassion

fascists; you have a real job—they must beg for a living"),
minorities ("Have you noticed how all newspaper composite
pictures of wanted criminals resemble Jesse Jackson?"), and
his political rivals ("Those of you who want to take off the
Clinton/Gore bumper stickers, just go get a handicapped parking sticker instead, and people will know why you voted that
way"). Feelings of superiority among dittoheads are strengthened by ridiculing others. In 1993, on his TV show, Limbaugh
put up a picture of Socks, the Clintons' cat, and asked, "Did you
know there is a White House dog?" He then proceeded to show
a picture of Chelsea Clinton, then thirteen years old. How can
you get these feelings of superiority for yourself? Simple. Listen
in (thereby increasing Limbaugh's ratings) and just say, "Ditto."

Finally, let's see how Paul Ingram came to believe that he
raped and molested his daughters. This involves two persuasion
tasks—convincing first the daughters and then the father.

The evidence for how Ericka and Julie came to believe their
father molested them is spotty. What is known is that they
attended an annual retreat for teenage girls, called Heart to
Heart, sponsored by their church. Apparently, child abuse was
often discussed at the camp. During earlier retreats, both
Ericka and Julie had lodged independent complaints alleging
sexual abuse by two different neighbors. Police follow-ups
determined that there was no basis to press charges in either
case. During the 1988 retreat, Karla Franko, a born-again
Christian claiming the gift of healing, made a prophecy—someone in the room had been molested as a young girl by a relative. Immediately, one girl ran out of the room, claiming abuse.
Other girls joined in stating that they, too, had been abused. By
late afternoon of the last day of the retreat, Ericka had come
forward as well with the realization that she, too, had been sexually abused by her father.

Although this description is incomplete, we can begin to see
some of the influence factors that produced the charge—a situation in which claiming sexual abuse was not only appropriate
but also rewarded with attention, affection, and a sense of
belonging. Unfortunately, the Ingram case is not an isolated
incident; there has been a nationwide epidemic of parents being
accused of sexually abusing their children. Needless to say, sexual abuse does occur within families, with tragic consequences.

At the same time, there is growing evidence that many of these claims of sexual abuse are based on constructed memories that do not reflect reality.[9] A close examination of these cases reveals parallels to the Ingram incident and the consistent use of the four stratagems of influence.

Therapy sessions that elicit false memories of sexual abuse use a number of pre-persuasion tactics. First, a context for sexual abuse claims is created by promoting—through interpersonal influence, stories in the mass media, and books such as *The Courage to Heal, Repressed Memories,* and *Michelle Remembers*[10]—three interrelated assumptions: (1) incest is much more common than people think and can include nonphysical abuse such as seeing your father in the bathroom or hearing an uncle making a suggestive remark; (2) satanic cults are operating in secret across the nation and have ritually abused children and animals; and (3) survivors of incest repress the memory of their abuse for many years after the fact, with 60% of all incest victims not remembering their abuse. (Actually, careful research shows the opposite—that it is extremely difficult for trauma victims to forget.) Next, a jargon is promoted for interpreting events—terms such as *in denial, violated boundaries, emotional incest, codependency,* and *in recovery.* Note how these terms can be used to put a spin on virtually any given event. When the client raises an argument against the abuse hypothesis, she is in denial. The mother who will not back the daughter's story of dad's rape is a codependent. Ambiguous behavior and even acts of love can be cast in a sinister mold by claiming that the fatherly hug violated boundaries and was really emotional rape. Clients who behave in a manner acceptable to the therapist are in recovery. Finally, the expectation is established that the client was probably sexually abused. For example, Franko made a prophecy that someone in the audience had been abused; therapists often ask about abuse directly ("Were you sexually abused as a child?") or indirectly ("You sound to me like the sort of person who might have been sexually abused").

The source of the abuse message is typically a therapist or counselor. We expect therapists to be professional, to have specialized training in their area of expertise, and to have our best interests at heart. In addition to these characteristics, Ericka and Julie accepted Karla Franko's claims of the gift of healing and prophecy. As such, the therapist is accepted as an authority figure who ultimately knows what is best for us.

The therapy session is conducive to the use of one of the most powerful message tactics: self-generated persuasion or prompting and guiding the target to generate a message that is consistent with a diagnosis of sexual abuse. How is this done? One way to have a client convince herself that she was sexually abused is to provide her with a long checklist of symptoms supposedly indicating abuse: Do you have trouble knowing what you want? Are you afraid to try new experiences? Are you fearful of being alone in the dark? Do you feel different from other people? The problem is that most normal people experience some of these symptoms from time to time. By answering "yes" to a few of these questions, the client is on the road to convincing herself that she is a victim of abuse. Next, the client needs to develop an understanding of how the abuse occurred. Here the therapist may use "imagistic work" (taking a negative scene from childhood—say, a bad dream or being afraid in bed—and then attempting to add as much detail to the image as possible); hypnotize the client (age-regressing her in an attempt to remember the past); administer a drug such as sodium amytal, which is inaccurately called a "truth serum," and then guide her recall of sexual abuse; or ask the client to maintain a journal in which she free-associates to fleeting images from the past. The result is often a set of vivid "memories" of sexual abuse—"memories" that are highly believable because they were self-generated.

The therapy session is often an emotional one; after all, people enter therapy because they feel they have problems that need to be solved. In therapy sessions that create false memories of abuse, hope is raised by promising the client that "you'll feel better once you bring out the memories of abuse." The alleged abuse becomes a psychological crutch, a means for justifying failure; any problem—failure in school, a poor love life, being overweight—is attributable to the abusive parent, not to anything for which the client herself might be responsible. A new identity is given to the client—that of victim and survivor. The client is rewarded for adopting this new identity by the therapist and in group sessions where reporting of abuse is encouraged. And this new identity feels good. As Robert Lynd once put it: "There is nothing that makes us feel so good as the idea that someone else is an evildoer."[11] Finally, the client is encouraged to confront the parent with the charge of sexual abuse. Once the confrontation takes place, the client becomes committed to a course of action that is hard to reverse, and the family is almost always torn apart by the turmoil caused by these allegations.

In his interrogation, Paul Ingram faced many of the same tactics that created false memories in "survivors." For example, his interrogators reminded Ingram of the reality of the devil (an entity he believed in) and told him that it was common to repress memories of crimes of this nature. He was pressed to agree that his daughters would not lie about something like this, thus forcing Ingram to either admit the crime or accuse his daughters of lying (as opposed to another possibility—that his daughters had succumbed to influence tactics at the summer camp). Everyone in Ingram's immediate environment—police, ministers, family, counselors, friends—behaved as if the accusations were true. Not only were these people authorities and experts who should know about such matters, but they were also trusted friends who would not knowingly lie and deceive. Ingram was reminded of certain ambiguous events (such as Julie's and Ericka's aloofness over the past few years) and asked to generate an explanation for it. With his best friends and the experts convinced that he had committed the crime, Ingram's confidence in his own memories was undermined. He felt guilty as a parent for what his daughters were experiencing and felt fear that something worse could happen. He was offered the same hope as Julie and Ericka—confession would begin the healing process and allow the family to face what had happened.

The power of these techniques can be seen in an interview of Paul Ingram by the social psychologist Richard Ofshe—an expert on cults who was called in by the prosecution for some advice on how to investigate the case. From the beginning, Ofshe was skeptical of the story and decided to test his suspicions by seeing if Ingram would accept as true an incident that was entirely fabricated—that Ingram had forced his son and daughters to have sex together while he watched. At first Ingram could not remember the event. Ofshe instructed him to attempt to remember the scene. Ingram complied with the request and the next day returned with a detailed account of how, on a Saturday or Sunday afternoon, he told his children to undress and ordered Ericka to kneel and have oral sex with his son.

Ofshe's demonstration is remarkable on at least two accounts. First, it clearly illustrates a finding consistent with much research in psychology—that human memory is a constructive process. For example, in her research on human memory, cognitive psychologist Elizabeth Loftus frequently demonstrates that memories of, say, an accident or a crime scene can be modified and changed simply through the questions asked about the incident (see Chapter 9).[12] In one study, Loftus took it a step further by demonstrating that it is possible to implant childhood memories simply by having a parent or family member ask leading questions about a fictitious event (in this case, being lost in a shopping mall as a child). Second, Ofshe's questioning of Paul Ingram shows in no uncertain terms how some common but nonetheless powerful persuasion tactics are capable of changing something that most people hold as quite precious—their own memories.

We had two purposes for describing these three successful sources of influence in detail. First, we wanted to present an overview of what lies ahead. In the next four sections of the book we will describe various tactics for accomplishing the four stratagems of influence—to see what works and why. Second, we juxtaposed these three sources of influence to raise some questions: When does persuasion turn into propaganda? What forms of persuasion serve our interests the best?

One way commonly suggested to identify propaganda is by how likable or agreeable it is. We suspect that readers' reaction to the previous passages varied, depending on how much they admire Abraham Lincoln, respect Rush Limbaugh, and believe in the value of certain therapies. If you find Lincoln or Limbaugh attractive or believe that traumatic memories are commonly repressed and recovered, then you probably cringed as you read this chapter (if you indeed continued to read it) and probably labeled us as "biased" and "propagandist." On the other hand, if you think Lincoln is overrated, hate Limbaugh, or think psychotherapy is all bunk, you probably cheered and exclaimed, "Finally someone who exposed those charlatans for what they are." But there is a problem here. The use of "likable" and "agreeable" makes it seem arbitrary as to just what propaganda is. For example, in the 1860s Abraham Lincoln would have been labeled a propagandist; today, he is an American hero. And there is an irony. The primary purpose of propaganda is to get you to like the communicator and to agree with the message. So, if you find yourself readily liking and agreeing with a communicator, this could be a sign that the message was not the truth you thought it was, but just some very effective propaganda.

We would like to suggest two sets of questions, based on the theories presented in the last two chapters, for distinguishing propaganda from fair and deliberative persuasion.

First, does the communication induce thought about the issues at hand? Or does it truncate thought and play on prejudices? (In other words, is the message processed in the central or peripheral route described in Chapter 3?) For example, as we prepared the material on the Gettysburg Address, we were surprised by just how much we learned about American history, the issues of the time, the way government does and should work, the range of options open to a leader, why the U.S. Constitution was amended three times in the decade after the Gettysburg Address, precisely why safeguarding of minority opinions and rights is important in a democracy, and what the traditional values of America are. Contrast this with the innuendo that Hillary Clinton looks like a Pontiac hood ornament or the rumor that Paul Ingram led a satanic ring of pedophiles. Thought stops. There is no reason to discuss further an opinion of Hillary Clinton's—say, on health care or on parenting— because she is nothing more than a silly hood ornament not worthy of our attention. Far from encouraging deliberation, such disparaging humor results in what is known as *jeer pressure:* It induces conformity to others' opinions out of a fear that we, too, can be the subject of ridicule.[13] Similarly, once we become committed to the notion that Paul Ingram is satanic, there is no reason to investigate further or to consider alternative explanations—but there are plenty of reasons to overlook any evidence that happens to be inconsistent with our position.

Second, how does the communicator use emotions? It is absurd to think that we can respond without feelings to the issues of the day; indeed, it would be a sorry world if we did not feel anger at injustice or sorrow at the pain of another or pride in what we have accomplished. But how we feel these emotions can make all the difference. Lincoln used our sense of pride to ask us to explore what it meant to be an American and to be consistent with that ideal. A good therapist can do the same—using feelings of, say, dissatisfaction to motivate the exploration of how one should live and to stimulate the development of skills for living.[14] Contrast this with a cheap joke designed to make fun of a teenager's looks just because she happens to be the daughter of a president. What purpose does this serve? Does it advance our understanding of policy issues? Does it encourage the deliberative persuasion so vital to a democracy? It is nothing more than a cheap attempt to make us feel superior at the expense of another. Such humor can also serve to increase prejudices against those who are disparaged.[15] When a propagandist unscrupulously plays on our feelings of insecurity, or exploits our darkest fears, or offers fake hope, exploration and inquiry stop. We become snared in the rationalization trap described in the previous chapter. The goal becomes to prove yourself superior and right no matter what. We become dependent on those who will support our masquerade. Our emotions overwhelm our critical abilities. And we take actions that we might not otherwise consider wise to take—developing false memories of the past or treating an innocent person cruelly.

At a party, Tom Milewski—chief operating officer of Greater Media, a network of highly successful radio stations—once quipped, "The formula for a successful talk show these days is to find out what your audience's bigotry is and play to it."[16] His statement is worthy taking seriously and is a challenge to us all.

Abraham Lincoln's Gettysburg Address

Four score and seven years ago our fathers brought forth on this continent a new nation, conceived in Liberty, and dedicated to the proposition that all men are created equal.

Now we are engaged in a great civil war, testing whether that nation or any nation so conceived and so dedicated can long endure. We are met on a great battle-field of that war. We have come to dedicate a portion of that field as a final resting place for those who here gave their lives that that nation might live. It is altogether fitting and proper that we should do this.

But, in a larger sense, we cannot dedicate—we cannot consecrate—we cannot hallow—this ground. The brave men, living and dead, who struggled here have consecrated it, far above our poor power to add or detract. The world will little note, nor long remember what we say here, but it can never forget what they did here. It is for us, the living, rather, to be dedicated here to the unfinished work which they who fought here have thus far so nobly advanced. It is rather for us to be here dedicated to the great task remaining before us—that from these honored dead we take increased devotion to that cause for which they gave the last full measure of devotion—that we here highly resolve that these dead shall not have died in vain—that this nation, under God, shall have a new birth of freedom—and that government of the people, by the people, for the people shall not perish from the earth.

Pre-Persuasion:
Setting the Stage
for Effective Influence

Words of Influence

The popular comedienne Roseanne tells a joke that goes something like this. "I have a great new recipe for trail mix—two scoops of Reese's Pieces to one scoop of Peanut M&M's. The kids love it. You know it's nutritional because it's trail mix." The joke is funny because we all know that candy cannot be turned into a nutritional foodstuff simply by calling it by a different name. Yet this is what advertisers and political pundits do every day for their products with great success. They know that the language allows for much latitude in usage and interpretation—latitude that can be used for persuasive purposes. In such cases, *their* joke may be on us.

The social psychologist Daryl Bem provides us with an interesting analysis of how words and slogans are used in television commercials.[1] According to Bem, a well-known brand of aspirin (which we will call "Brand A") is advertised as 100% pure aspirin; the commercial goes on to say that government tests have shown that no other pain remedy is stronger or more effective than Brand A. What the maker does not bother to mention is that the tests actually showed that no brand was any weaker or less effective than any of the others. In other words, aspirin is aspirin; all tested brands are equal—except in price, that is. For the privilege of gulping down Brand A, consumers must pay approximately three times the price of an equally effective but unadvertised brand.

Or perhaps you prefer an aspirin proclaimed to be "unsurpassed in speed—no other brand works faster" and buffered so that "none is gentler to your stomach." The same government tests showed that this buffered brand works no faster than regular aspirin, nor is there any difference between the two in the frequency of stomach upset. Thus it is truly unsurpassed—but, of course, it doesn't surpass any other brand, either. This well-known brand sells briskly at five times the price of equally effective products with less familiar brand names.

Another product is touted as using the ingredient "that doctors recommend." By reading the label, we discover the "magic" ingredient to be good old inexpensive aspirin. Several pharmaceutical companies also market "extra-strength" varieties of "arthritic pain" formulations. You will pay a premium price for these products, although their extra strength comes only from extra aspirin (or acetaminophen, an aspirin substitute), along with a dose of caffeine. Taking additional aspirin would be less expensive, but the product sounds great in the ads: "Not one, but a combination of medically proven ingredients in an extra-strength formula."

Such blatant attempts at mass persuasion seem pitifully obvious when we are mindful and scrutinize them closely. But most of us are not always mindful and are, therefore, vulnerable to being unwittingly influenced. Thus the cash registers ring, and in tremendous numbers we line up and buy the advertised product as if we really believed that there is a major difference among brands of aspirin.

How, then, do words gain their power, their ability to influence and persuade? Briefly put, the way an object is described and the manner in which a course of action is presented direct our thoughts and channel our cognitive responses concerning the communication. Through the labels we use to describe an object or event, we can define it in such a way that the recipient of our message accepts our definition of the situation and is thus pre-persuaded even before we seriously begin to argue. This simple rule of persuasion was recognized by Cicero more than two millennia ago. Cicero claimed that one of the factors in his success at establishing the innocence of some of Rome's most notorious murderers was his ability to argue that their heinous crimes were not "crimes" at all, but virtuous deeds—that the victims were villains who deserved to be killed.

Psychologically, the aspirin commercials work because by saying that no other remedy is stronger, faster, gentler, or more effective, they lead us to draw, almost automatically, the (incorrect) inference that no other pain reliever is *as* strong, *as* fast, *as* gentle, *as* effective as Brand A. The product description creates the illusion that Brand A is the best, not that Brand A is just like all the rest.

In a telling experiment, two consumer psychologists demonstrated the effectiveness of message wording in the formation of consumers' attitudes toward ground beef.[2] They found that consumers' evaluations were more favorable toward a beef labeled "75% lean" than one labeled "25% fat." Is it any wonder that gasoline stations (who charge a bit more if you use a credit card) call the price of gas purchased by cash "a cash discount," that grocery stores refer to frozen fish for sale in the fresh meats department as "fresh frozen," that hawkers of health care insurance for the elderly call their sales brochure "a free Medicare supplementary guide," and that small-appliance makers describe their battery-run products as "cordless electric"? The word *lean* is more attractive than the word *fat*; the word *fresh* tends to obscure the fact that the fish is frozen; a *free guide* is much more useful than another piece of advertising; *cordless electric* sounds much more powerful than "runs on two D-cell batteries."

Often the full meaning of the inference is left to the imagination of the audience. In the late 1930s, the Institute for Propaganda Analysis, a group of leading intellectuals of the day who shared the common goal of lessening the effects of propaganda, identified this tactic as the use of *glittering generalities*.[3] In such cases, the propagandist uses "purr" words—words that have positive connotations but are usually ambiguous in the context in which they are used. Some examples include: "A *kinder, gentler* America"; "Let's make America *strong* again"; "The *best* that money can buy"; "We must support our *valiant freedom fighters*." Few would disagree that kindness, gentleness, strength, the best, and fighting for freedom are good things; in most concrete situations, however, even fewer would agree on the meaning of each of these words.

Take, for example, Richard Nixon's 1968 campaign pledge to secure an "honorable peace" in Vietnam. What did this really mean? For some, an honorable peace meant immediate withdrawal and an end to an unjust war. For others it meant fighting until the United States had achieved an unconditional victory. What Richard Nixon meant by an honorable peace was left to each listener's imagination, but it was made perfectly clear that Nixon had the "right" objective regarding the Vietnam war.

Words can also be used to define problems and thus create personal and societal needs. In his history of American advertising, Stephen Fox argues that advertising had its greatest influence during the 1920s.[4] At that time, advertisers gave names to many of the "consumer needs" that we seek to satisfy even today. For example, the Lambert Company, makers of Listerine, popularized the term *halitosis* to refer to bad breath; most Americans didn't know they *had* halitosis until the Lambert Company made us all aware of the possibility of offense by informing us that "even your best friends won't tell you." Arthur Kudner, a copywriter at Erwin, Wasey, & Jefferson, invented the phrase *athlete's foot* (to refer to a fungus infection) and then linked it to a product, Absorbine Jr., that would presumably cure it. Everett Grady of Ruthrauff & Ryan advertised Lifebuoy soap as a cure for that dreaded disease, B.O. (body odor)!

More recently, advertisers have invented new product categories (needs) and brands to fill them, such as NyQuil, the nighttime cold medicine; 7-Up, the uncola; Miller, the "lite" beer; various brands of vaginal deodorants; and Bill Clinton, the new-style, centrist Democrat. A good brand name can be worth more than the factory that makes it. For example, Philip Morris purchased Kraft for more than six times its book value. When asked why, the CEO of Philip Morris, Hamish Maxwell, put it bluntly: Kraft is a trusted name with the consumer and could be used to sell other products. Perhaps one of the most revealing episodes in the "name is the same" game involved an ad for Procter & Gamble's Rely tampons. You might remember this product; it was removed from the market after being associated with toxic shock syndrome. The advertising proudly stated: "Remember, they named it Rely," as if the name made it so. From our perspective, perhaps we should all remember that they named it

Rely—and that is all they did. A weed by any other name should still be a weed.

Advertisers, of course, are not the only ones to invent new labels as a means of propaganda.[5] Early American patriots were able to increase revolutionary fervor by terming a minor skirmish with the British the *Boston massacre*. Adolf Hitler used the same technique to mobilize the German people by explaining Germany's economic troubles in terms of the *Red menace* and the *Jewish problem*. Those opposed to abortion call their position *pro-life* (who could be against life?), whereas those supporting a woman's right to elect an abortion call themselves *pro-choice* (who could be against choice?). The Defense Department (formerly called the War Department) uses the term *low-intensity conflict* to refer to wars the United States supported in Nicaragua and El Salvador during the 1980s; this is a curious term when one considers that these conflicts have been very intense experiences for those innocent civilians caught in the crossfire—estimated at 50,000 in Nicaragua and 70,000 in El Salvador. Similarly, those opposed to the war with Iraq talked about "bringing home our sons and daughters in body bags," whereas the military used more sanitized terms, such as *collateral damage* and *BDA* (bomb-damage assessment).

Politicians interpret social problems and invent the national agenda by using such phrases as *the Cold War, the domino theory of creeping communism, perestroika and glasnost, the war against drugs, Japanese protectionism, the new world order*, and *a bridge to the twenty-first century*. A self-conscious example: a memo entitled "Language: A key mechanism of control" circulated by Newt Gingrich to other conservative Republicans on how to "speak like Newt." The memo lists two sets of words for spicing up any speech: "optimistic positive governing" words such as "empowering, workfare, choice, initiative, and eliminate good-time in prison," which are useful for describing one's own position, and "contrasting" words such as "decay, liberal, they/them, radical, unionized, and betray" for defining an opponent. Indeed, the use of words in such a manner is so common that William Lutz has amassed a volume of what he calls "doublespeak" and annually presents an award for the most deceptive and self-contradictory use of language by a public figure.[6]

And the power of a name was clearly understood by one Vernon Howell. Upon assuming leadership of a small religious group in Waco, Texas, called the Branch Davidians, Howell sought to define himself as a prophet linked to religious leaders of the past. He took as his last name "Koresh," which is Hebrew for "Cyrus"—a Persian king who defeated the Babylonians and who is viewed as a messiah, or one anointed to carry out a special mission for God. Howell took "David" as his first name, thereby establishing himself as a spiritual descendant of King David. "David Koresh" thus means a descendant of David and a messiah destined to carry out a divine mission.[7] As a messiah, David Koresh believed it was his responsibility to sow his seed and create a new generation of the elect. Koresh attempted to impregnate many of his women followers, including both the wives of other men and children—an activity that was often approved by their husbands and, in the case of twelve- and fourteen-year-old girls, by their parents. And why not approve such liaisons? After all, David Koresh was a prophet; his name told you so.

The propaganda power of words is dramatically portrayed in George Orwell's novel *1984*, in which history is continually rewritten in the language of the day—Newspeak—to conform to the needs and desires of government leaders. As Orwell put it:

> The purpose of Newspeak was not only to provide a medium of expression for the world-view and mental habits proper to the devotees of Ingsoc, but to make all other modes of thought impossible. It was intended that when Newspeak had been adopted once and for all and Oldspeak forgotten, a heretical thought—that is, a thought diverging from the principles of Ingsoc—should be literally unthinkable, at least so far as thought is dependent on words.[8]

This novel takes on even more chilling dimensions when one realizes that Orwell's job during World War II was to write pro-British propaganda for broadcast to India.

The psychologist Gordon Allport pointed out that it is the nature of language to divide up and categorize the buzzing boom of information that comes our way every second of the day.[9] It is this inherent nature of language that gives it the power to persuade. By labeling someone a "man," a "woman," a "philanthropist," an "attractive Chinese," a "physician," an "athlete," we emphasize some particular feature of the object "human being" over many other possible ones. We then respond to these features, organizing our realities around the label. Nouns that "cut slices"—such as we–they, black–white, rich–poor, free–Soviet, male–female—serve to divide up the world into neat little packages and to imply the range of appropriate courses of action to take. As just one example, researchers have found that job announcements using the generic *he* (a pronoun that supposedly applies to both males and females) produced considerably fewer female applicants than those that use more inclusive terms.[10] Advertisers know the power of naming and so select brand names for their products—such as Head & Shoulders shampoo, DieHard battery, Close-Up toothpaste—that draw attention to the brand's major selling point.[11]

The history of advertising and political movements attests to the fact that people tend to act on the names and labels that are used to describe an event or situation. But the power of words and labels to influence how we conceive of the world extends to other contexts as well. One of social psychology's best documented phenomena is the *self-fulfilling prophecy*—the tendency for a definition of a situation to evoke behavior that makes the definition come true. Dozens of experiments have shown that students who are randomly labeled "smarter" tend to *act* smarter; sane people identified as "insane" are treated as if they *are* insane and may begin to act that way; and women labeled "beautiful" behave as if they *are* beautiful.

The research of Richard Miller, Phillip Brickman, and Diana Bolin, for example, illustrates the persuasive power of a label in an educational setting.[12] In one of their studies, Miller and his colleagues attempted to persuade fifth-grade students in Chicago to be neat and tidy and not to litter—a task that most parents will recognize as quite formidable. Some of the students received lectures on the importance of being neat and tidy. These included lectures on ecology and the dangers of pollution, on why it is important to throw away lunchroom trash, and a plea from the janitor to keep things clean. Other students did not receive a lecture but were repeatedly told that they were a neat and tidy class. For example, these students were told by the janitor that they were one of the neatest classes in the school, and they were encouraged by their teacher to think about why they were so tidy.

What did the results show? Those students who received lectures did *not* improve their littering behavior. In contrast, the fifth-graders who were randomly labeled "neat and tidy" became neater and tidier, dropping three times more litter in the trash cans than did their classmates. In a second study, Miller and his colleagues repeated their results, finding that average second-graders who were labeled "math achievers" subsequently improved in math to a greater extent than their classmates who were merely exhorted to do better at math.[13] In both cases, the *name* made the *thing*; a weed by any other name may be a rose.

How do these effects come about? It's not magic. A study by Mark Snyder, Ellen Decker Tanke, and Ellen Berscheid illustrates how our labels and conceptions of reality can actually come to create and change that reality.[14] Put yourself in the place of a typical male in their experiment: You have volunteered to participate in an investigation of "how people become acquainted with each other," and you have been paired with a female who is located in another room, ostensibly because the two of you are assigned to the "no nonverbal communication" condition of the study. You will communicate with her on a telephone. Although you have not seen your partner, you have been given a packet of information that contains a snapshot. For half of the subjects, the snapshot was of a very attractive woman; for the others, it was of a relatively unattractive woman.

How did the label "attractive female" influence the males' behavior? The males who thought they were talking with an attractive partner rated her as more poised, humorous, and socially adept than did those who thought they were talking with a less attractive woman. This is not very surprising. But what *was* startling is this: When independent observers were allowed to listen to a tape recording of only the woman's half of the conversation (without looking at the photograph), they were far more impressed by the woman whose male partner thought she was physically attractive. Why? Since the male partner thought he was talking to an attractive woman, he spoke to her in a way that brought out her best and most sparkling qualities. When these independent observers listened to her conversation, they rated her as more attractive, more confident, more animated, and warmer than the woman whose partner thought her to be less beautiful. In other words, expectations had created reality.

Throughout this chapter, we have emphasized the propaganda value of words and labels—how they can be used to persuade and create social reality. But words do not have to be used to cloak reality in deception. The ability to manipulate words and concepts in our head—that is, the ability to think—is a uniquely human characteristic. It allows us to solve problems creatively without requiring the manipulation of the actual thing itself in a trial-and-error fashion. Given the flexibility of the human mind, there are many ways to label any given event. This flexibility provides the key to overcoming the propagandist's intent: When presented with a definition of the world, we can always ask, "Why this label? What other definitions of the situation would shed more light on the issue?" By looking at any given event from many different perspectives, we can gain new insights to guide our decision making.

At the same time, it is important to remember that words have the power to pre-persuade. The words and labels we use come to define and create our social world. This definition of reality directs our thoughts, our feelings, our imagination and thus influences our behavior. Perhaps Joseph Goebbels, Hitler's minister of propaganda, best described the power of words:

> It would not be impossible to prove with sufficient repetition and psychological understanding of the people concerned that a square is in fact a circle. What after all are a square and a circle? They are mere words and words can be moulded until they clothe ideas in disguise.[15]

7 ||||||||||||||||||||||

Pictures in Our Heads

In *Public Opinion*, the distinguished political analyst Walter Lippmann tells the story of a young girl, brought up in a small mining town, who one day went from cheerfulness into a deep spasm of grief.[1] A gust of wind had suddenly cracked a kitchen windowpane. The young girl was inconsolable and spoke incomprehensibly for hours. When she finally was able to speak intelligibly, she explained that a broken pane of glass meant that a close relative had died. She was therefore mourning her father, who she felt certain had just passed away. The young girl remained disconsolate until, days later, a telegram arrived verifying that her father was still alive. It appears that the girl had constructed a complete fiction based on a simple external fact (a broken window), a superstition (broken window means death), fear, and love for her father.

The point of Lippmann's story was not to explore the inner workings of an abnormal personality but to ask a question about ourselves: To what extent do we, like the young girl, let our fictions guide our thoughts and actions? Lippmann believed that we are much more similar to that young girl than we might readily admit. He contended that the mass media paint an imagined world and that the "pictures in our heads" derived from the media influence what men and women will do and say at any particular moment. Lippmann made these observations in 1922. More than seven decades later, we can ask: What is the evidence for his claim? To what extent do the pictures we see on television and in other mass media influence how we see the world and set the agenda for what we view as most important in our lives?

Let's look at the world we see on television. George Gerbner and his colleagues have conducted the most extensive analysis of television to date.[2] Since the late 1960s, these researchers have been videotaping and carefully analyzing thousands of prime-time television programs and characters. Their findings, taken as a whole, indicate that the world portrayed on television is grossly misleading as a representation of reality. Their research further suggests that, to a surprising extent, we take what we see on television as a reflection of reality.

In prime-time programming, males outnumber females by 3 to 1, and the women portrayed are younger than the men they encounter. Nonwhites (especially Hispanics), young children, and the elderly are underrepresented; and members of minority groups are disproportionately cast in minor roles. Moreover, most prime-time characters are portrayed as professional or

" . . . No, he can't really fly . . . no, the bad guys don't really have
a ray gun . . . no, this cereal really isn't the best food in the whole
world . . . no, it won't make you as strong as a giant . . . "

managerial workers: Although 67% of the work force in the
United States are employed in blue-collar or service jobs, only
25% of TV characters hold such jobs. Prime-time scientists are
portrayed as dangerous, mad, and out of control; although in
real life scientists do not frequently commit homicide, no other
occupational group is more likely to kill on prime-time television. Finally, crime on television is ten times more prevalent
than it is in real life.

The average fifteen-year-old has viewed more than 13,000 TV
killings. More than half of TV's characters are involved in a violent confrontation each week; in reality, less than 1% of people in
the nation are victims of criminal violence in any given year,
according to FBI statistics. Indeed, although violence in the
United States has been declining over the past decade, violence
on TV has not. David Rintels, a television writer and former
president of the Writers' Guild of America, summed it up best
when he said, "From 8 to 11 o'clock each night, television is one
long lie."[3]

To gain an understanding of the relationship between television watching and the pictures in our heads, Gerbner and his colleagues compared the attitudes and beliefs of heavy viewers

(those who watch more than four hours a day) and light viewers (those who watch less than two hours a day). They found that heavy viewers (1) express more racially prejudiced attitudes; (2) overestimate the number of people employed as physicians, lawyers, and athletes; (3) perceive women as having more limited abilities and interests than men; (4) believe that science is dangerous and that scientists are odd and peculiar people; (5) hold exaggerated views of the prevalence of violence in society; and (6) believe old people are fewer in number and less healthy today than they were thirty years ago, even though the opposite is true. What is more, heavy viewers tend to see the world as a more sinister place than do light viewers; they are more likely to agree that most people are just looking out for themselves and would take advantage of you if they had a chance. Gerbner and his colleagues conclude that these attitudes and beliefs reflect the inaccurate portrayals of American life provided to us by television.

Let's examine the relationship between television watching and our images of the world by looking more closely at how we picture criminal activity. In an analysis of "television criminology," Craig Haney and John Manzolati point out that crime shows dispense remarkably consistent images of both the police and criminals.[4] For example, they found that television police officers are amazingly effective, solving almost every crime, and are absolutely infallible in one regard: The wrong person is never in jail at the end of a show. Television fosters an illusion of certainty in crime-fighting. Television criminals generally turn to crime because of psychopathology or insatiable (and unnecessary) greed. Television emphasizes criminals' personal responsibility for their actions and largely ignores situational pressures correlated with crime, such as poverty and unemployment.

Haney and Manzolati go on to suggest that this portrayal of the criminal justice system has important social consequences. People who watch a lot of television tend to share this belief system, which affects their expectations and can cause them to take a hard-line stance when serving on juries. Heavy viewers are likely to reverse the presumption of innocence, believing that defendants must be guilty of something, because otherwise they wouldn't be brought to trial.

A similar tale can be told about other "pictures painted in our heads." For example, heavy readers of newspaper accounts of sensational and random crimes report higher levels of fear of crime. Repeated viewing of R-rated violent "slasher" films is associated with less sympathy and empathy for victims of rape. A heavy dose of ads portraying women as sex objects induces females to believe that their current bodies are too large. When television is introduced into an area, the incidence of theft increases, perhaps due partly to television's promotion of consumerism, which may frustrate and anger economically deprived viewers who compare their lifestyles with those portrayed on television.[5]

It should be noted, however, that the research just described—that done by Gerbner and colleagues and by others—is correlational; that is, it shows merely an association, not a causal relation, between television viewing and beliefs. It is therefore impossible to determine from this research whether heavy viewing actually causes prejudiced attitudes and inaccurate beliefs or whether people already holding such attitudes and beliefs simply tend to watch more television. In order to be certain that watching TV causes such attitudes and beliefs, it would be necessary to perform a controlled experiment in which people are randomly assigned to conditions. Fortunately, some recent experiments do allow us to be fairly certain that heavy viewing does indeed determine the pictures we form of the world.

In a set of ingenious experiments, the political psychologists Shanto Iyengar and Donald Kinder varied the contents of evening news shows watched by their research participants.[6] In their studies, Iyengar and Kinder edited the evening news so that participants received a steady dose of news about a specific problem facing the United States. For example, in one of their experiments, some participants heard about the weaknesses of U.S. defense capabilities; a second group watched shows emphasizing pollution concerns; a third group heard about inflation and economic matters.

The results were clear. After a week of viewing the specially edited programs, participants emerged from the study more convinced than they were before viewing the shows that the target problem—the one receiving extensive coverage in the shows they had watched—was a very important one for the country to solve. What is more, the participants acted on their newfound perceptions, evaluating the current president's performance on the basis of how he handled the target issue and evaluating more positively than their competitors those candidates who took strong positions on the target issue.

Iyengar and Kinder's findings are not a fluke. Communications researchers repeatedly find a link between what stories the mass media cover and what viewers consider to be the most important issues of the day.[7] The content of the mass media sets the public's political and social agenda. As just one example, in a pioneering study of an election in North Carolina, researchers found that the issues that voters came to consider to be most important in the campaign coincided with the amount of coverage those issues received in the local media.[8] Similarly, the problems of racism and the police, international terrorism, NASA incompetence, and nuclear energy were catapulted into the nation's consciousness by the coverage of such dramatic events as the beating of Rodney King by Los Angeles police, the explosion of a Pan American jet over Lockerbie, Scotland, the *Challenger* explosion, and the nuclear-reactor accidents at Three Mile Island and Chernobyl. Former Secretary of State Henry Kissinger clearly understood the power of the news media in setting agendas. He once noted that he never watched the content of the evening news but was only interested in "what they covered and for what length of time, to learn what the country was getting."[9]

Even subtle ways in which a story is told can have a dramatic impact on the pictures in our head. In later research, Shanto Iyengar explored the effects of how TV news frames a story as either *episodic* (depicting a single concrete, specific event such as an attempted murder, terrorist bombing, illegal drug bust, etc.) or *thematic* (an abstract report about a general topic such as crime, terrorism, or drug abuse).[10] Not surprisingly, TV news coverage is primarily episodic: Between 1981 and 1986, 89% of reports on crime focused on a specific perpetrator or victim and 74% of all terrorism stories focused on a single act. Some stories do receive more thematic coverage—for example, coverage of unemployment tends to be thematic.

What is the impact of how TV news is framed on our pictures of the world? To find out, Iyengar created news stories that were either episodic or thematic in nature. For example, a story could tell about a person who recently lost his job or could discuss the nature of unemployment in general. The results showed that those viewers who were exposed to a story with a concrete episode were more likely to attribute responsibility for a problem to private motives and the actions of an individual; those viewers who saw a more thematic presentation held society and government officials accountable for any wrongdoing and responsible for fixing the problem. The implication is clear: How a story is told determines our picture of the world and how we will act on such basic issues as crime, terrorism, poverty, and unemployment.

Of course, each of us has had extensive personal contact with many people in a myriad of social contexts; the media are just one source of our knowledge about political affairs and different ethnic, gender, and occupational groups. The information and impressions we receive through the media are relatively less influential when we can also rely on firsthand experience. Thus those of us who have been in close contact with several women who work outside the home are probably less susceptible to the stereotypes of women portrayed on television. On the other hand, when it comes to issues with which most of us have had limited or no personal experience, such as crime and violence, television and the other mass media are virtually the only vivid sources of information for constructing our image of the world.

The propaganda value of the mass media in painting a picture of the world has not been overlooked by would-be leaders. A social policy such as a "get tough on crime" program, for example, can be easily sold by relating it to the prime-time picture of crime as acts committed by the psychopathic and the greedy, rather than dealing with situational determinants such as poverty and unemployment. In a similar vein, it is easier to sell a "war on drugs" after the drug-related death of a prominent basketball star or to promote an end to nuclear power after a fatal tragedy at a nuclear reactor.

It is even more important for a would-be leader to propagate his or her own picture of the world. The political scientist Roderick Hart notes that since the early 1960s, U.S. presidents have averaged more than twenty-five speeches per month—a very large amount of public speaking.[11] By speaking frequently on certain issues (and thus gaining access to the nightly news), a president can create a political agenda—a picture of the world that is favorable to his social policies. For example, during the

1992 U.S. presidential election, a sign hung in Clinton's Little Rock campaign headquarters that read "The economy, stupid"— a not so subtle reminder to Clinton operatives to keep the campaign focused on the economy.[12] The Clinton forces (with help from Ross Perot) focused mass media coverage of the campaign on the economy (a weak spot for George Bush) by linking every other issue to this one concern. For example, civil rights were portrayed in terms of national productivity ("We don't have a person to waste"); education and welfare reform were termed "investment"; affordable health care was presented as a means of reducing the budget deficit; environmental protection was linked to creating business opportunities; change was said to be needed because trickle-down economics doesn't work. In other words, Clinton set the mass media agenda in a way that put him at an advantage over his opponent, George Bush. In the 1996 presidential election, Clinton once again controlled the political agenda by taking a "middle-of-the-road" position on any issue that might have won votes for his opponent, Bob Dole (such as welfare reform, school prayer, or family values), and thus removed those issues from discussion in the campaign. The 2000 U.S. presidential election can be seen as a battle to control the agenda, with Al Gore seeking to keep the discussion centered on the economy and George W. Bush attempting to focus media coverage on problems such as a declining military.

Agenda setting is of great importance in maintaining power. According to Jeffrey Pfeffer, an expert on business organizations, one of the most important sources of power for a chief executive officer is the ability to set the organization's agenda by determining what issues will be discussed and when, what criteria will be used to resolve disputes, who will sit on what committees, and, perhaps most importantly, which information will be widely disseminated and which will be selectively ignored.[13]

Why are the pictures of the world painted by the mass media so persuasive? For one thing, we rarely question the picture that is shown. We seldom ask ourselves, for example, "Why are they showing me this story on the evening news rather than some other one? Do the police really operate in this manner? Is the world really this violent and crime-ridden?" The pictures that television beams into our homes are almost always simply taken for granted as representing reality. As the Nazi propagandist

Joseph Goebbels once noted: "This is the secret of propaganda: Those who are to be persuaded by it should be completely immersed in the ideas of the propaganda, without ever noticing that they are being immersed in it."[14]

Once accepted, the pictures we form in our heads serve as fictions to guide our thoughts and actions. The images serve as primitive social theories—providing us with the "facts" of the matter, determining which issues are most pressing, and decreeing the terms in which we think about our social world. As the political scientist Bernard Cohen observed, the mass media

> may not be successful much of the time in telling people *what to think*, but it is stunningly successful in telling its readers *what to think about*. . . . The world will look different to different people, depending . . . on the map that is drawn for them by writers, editors, and publishers of the papers they read.[15]

8

Saddam Hussein: The Hitler of Baghdad?

The most recent major war our nation engaged in was the Persian Gulf war of 1991. Before entering that war, the Americans debated the positive and negative consequences of that action. Those who supported the war described Saddam Hussein as the new Hitler: They emphasized the parallels between Saddam's gassing of the Kurds and Hitler's gassing of the Jews, Iraq's invasion of Kuwait and Germany's invasion of Czechoslovakia and Poland, and Saddam's and Hitler's build-up of armaments.[1] Those who opposed the war saw the situation in Iraq as paralleling that in Vietnam: They saw both incidents as civil wars—a fight among various Arab factions and between North and South Vietnam; they worried about the U.S. military's ability to fight in difficult foreign terrain consisting of deserts and swamps; they characterized the war effort as being in support of "big business" and "big oil."

The debate over war with Iraq was really a debate over whose definition of ambiguous events was "correct." And with good reason: Once it is decided how an event or person should be categorized, it becomes clear what course of action should be taken. If Saddam was truly a new Hitler, then a policy of appeasement and letting him have Kuwait would only bring additional threats to peace and ultimately a much worse war. If Iraq was another Vietnam, then U.S. intervention would lead to a long and divisive war and the country would become stuck in a quagmire with no clear victors and losers.

We "debate" how to define persons and events thousands of times a day, and, although we usually do not go to war as a result, the consequences of how we interpret and define events can be quite significant. For example, we may see a political candidate as "presidential" simply because he or she shares some irrelevant mannerisms with one of our favorite politicians from the past; a college athlete may be viewed as "pro" material because he fits the mold of past successes—he's a Lynn Swann type or he reminds us of the old-style Steeler linebackers of a previous era; we like the inexpensive new car we purchased because it is similar in style to a high-priced, sporty model we cannot afford.

Ten years before the Persian Gulf war, Thomas Gilovich published a set of experiments looking at how irrelevant associations to the past can influence decision making.[2] In one of his studies, students majoring in political science were asked to resolve a hypothetical international crisis. In this crisis, a small democratic country was being threatened by an aggressive, totalitarian neighbor that was conducting subversive activities against the democratic regime as well as massing troops along a shared border. Embedded in the information about the crisis were irrelevant phrases designed to highlight the similarities in the hypothetical crisis to either the war against Nazi Germany or that against North Vietnam. For example, the political science majors were told either that minorities were fleeing the democratic country via boxcars on freight trains or via small boats; the impending invasion was referred to as a Blitzkrieg or a Quick-strike; the current U.S. president was from the state of New York (as was FDR) or from Texas (as was LBJ); the briefing concerning the crisis was held in Winston Churchill Hall or Dean Rusk Hall. Did these irrelevant "similarities" influence judgments about what should be done about the crisis? Amazingly, they did. Gilovich found that the students who were primed to see the crisis as like the one involving Nazi Germany were more likely to recommend U.S. military intervention than were those primed to see it as another Vietnam.

How do analogies and metaphors persuade?[3] In a nutshell, an analogy or metaphor pre-persuades by highlighting some comparisons while hiding others and by providing a theme or structure for making sense of potentially ambiguous information. For example, consider these common metaphors of love— love is war (his conquest; she fought for his love), love is magic (she cast a spell), love is a patient (this is a sick relationship), love is a physical force (I was drawn to her; the relationship lost momentum), and love is madness (I'm crazy about her). Each metaphor highlights certain aspects of the love relationship (e.g., trickery is OK, a problem needs to be solved, love is beyond my control), specifies exactly what to do (e.g., trick her into love, try to heal the relationship, just let things take their course), and provides a way of making sense of behavior (e.g., boys will be boys, love grows).

Consider the metaphor of "propaganda is invasion" (i.e., an attacker is trying to conquer your mind and beliefs), which we developed in the first chapter. It draws your attention to certain factors: Propagandists such as politicians and advertisers are the enemy; propaganda tactics are like military maneuvers and armaments that must be disassembled if they are to be stopped; your mind and emotions need to be fortified against attack. If you accepted our metaphor of propaganda, we suspect that you are probably enjoying this book right now. But we could have selected other metaphors. For example, in the former Soviet Union, propaganda was seen as education (indoctrination). If we had chosen this metaphor, this would be quite a different book. We would be discussing "students" who have an easy or difficult time learning (being persuaded) and how to use persuasion tactics to open young minds to the truth. On the other hand, we could have explored the metaphor endorsed by the founders of this country—persuasion as a building (laying a foundation for argument) and as a journey (a trip to discover something new). This, too, would be a different book, but probably one still worth writing.

In the end, however, debates on a course of action must come down to which definition of the situation is perceived to be *correct:* Is Saddam more like Hitler or is Iraq more like Vietnam? Of course, we should entertain the hypotheses that both analogies are true, that neither is true, or that perhaps other analogies also fit the situation. For example, the historian Paul Kennedy saw the U.S. military involvement in the Persian Gulf as reminiscent of Spain's foreign wars of the 1630s and 1640s.[4] One argument given by supporters of U.S. participation in the war was that the success of the war would help restore American self-confidence and break the mood of self-doubt and defeatism that had purportedly prevailed in the country since the 1960s—in other words, overcome the "Vietnam syndrome." The great Spanish minister the Count-Duke de Olivares made a similar argument in favor of Spain's intervention on the side of the Hapsburgs in the Thirty Years' War. Upon hearing of Spain's first battlefield success, Olivares declared it to be "the greatest victory of our times," one that proved Spain's domestic and foreign detractors wrong; because of military prowess, Spain was still number one on the international scene. Domestically, however, Spain's industries lacked competitiveness, its streets were filled with the unemployed and the homeless, and the nation's debts were increasing at a rapid clip. A generation later, Spain was no longer a world power.

Classical theories of rhetoric look with disdain upon analogy as a form of persuasion; any given analogy is vulnerable to the attack that it is based on faulty comparisons—that the points of similarity presented in the analogy are irrelevant and inconsequential. According to classical theory, analogies should be evaluated using two rules:

1. The similarities between two things must concern pertinent, significant aspects of the two things.

2. The analogy must not ignore pertinent dissimilarities between the two things being compared.[5]

Notice what happens if we use these two classical rules to evaluate any of the three proposed perspectives on the Persian

Gulf war. We immediately desire more information and facts about the present and the past: What are the economic and social conditions of the nations involved? What happened to the Hapsburg Empire, Germany, and Vietnam after each respective war was over? What were the economic and social costs of each war? In answering such questions, we can develop a more complete understanding of the situation at hand—an analysis that can inform such important decisions as whether or not to go to war.

There is another way to evaluate the validity of a communicator's definition of the situation—by the sincerity of the communicator. In other words, does the advocate of a given view of the world really believe that is the way things are, or has he or she merely adopted this viewpoint for expedient, propaganda purposes? For example, shortly before the onset of the Persian Gulf war on October 15, 1990, President Bush stated:

> Every day now, new word filters out [of Kuwait] about the ghastly atrocities perpetrated by Saddam's forces . . . of a systematic assault on the soul of a nation, summary executions, routine torture . . . newborn babies thrown out of incubators . . . dialysis patients ripped from their machines . . . Hitler revisited. But remember, when Hitler's war ended there were the Nuremberg trials.[6]

Was he serious? Perhaps so. But given the fact that, just a short time earlier, our government was staunchly supporting Saddam in his war against Iran, it is at least conceivable that Bush was exaggerating. In addition, reports of babies being thrown from incubators and similar atrocity stories were later found to be rumors started by pro-Kuwaiti sources and reported uncritically by the news media.

If the president was engaging in hyperbole, some people believe that it is forgivable. After all, he was intent on mobilizing the nation for what might have been a long and costly war and on gaining the approval of his fellow citizens for putting hundreds of thousands of young American men and women in harm's way in order to come to the aid of a nondemocratic nation. And it worked; support for the war soared and George Bush's popularity soon reached an all-time high. During and immediately after the war, Bush's approval rating hovered around 90%.

But the use of such propaganda devices carries a price—for the communicator as well as the audience. In this case, once the American people recovered from their euphoria after the war came to a quick and (in terms of U.S. casualties) relatively bloodless end, a great many Americans began to wonder why, after having achieved total military dominance, we had allowed Saddam to remain in power with a large part of his military force intact—a force that he promptly began to use with impunity against his own civilian population.[7] Indeed, even the commander of the United Nations forces in the Persian Gulf, General Norman Schwarzkopf, was bold enough to wonder about this out loud on network television. Can you imagine the president of the United States in 1945, having won a smashing victory over Adolf Hitler, allowing Hitler to continue to govern the German people? Can you imagine the Allied forces stopping just inside the border of Germany and then turning back? Utterly impossible. If Hitler had survived he would certainly have been tried, convicted, and executed as a war criminal.

Why, then, did George Bush allow Saddam Hussein free rein in Iraq? It was confusing. In a *Newsweek* poll taken on May 1, 1991, 55% of those questioned did not view the Persian Gulf war as a victory because Saddam was still in power. President Bush's popularity began to fade. Ironically, Bush's use of the "Saddam is Hitler" metaphor was so successful that it contributed to his own decline as a weak leader who could not finish the job he started—an image that encouraged others in his party to challenge his leadership in the presidential primaries and helped set the stage for his eventual defeat in the 1992 election. This is a common occurrence with the use of metaphor and analogy to pre-persuade; they often take on a life of their own, trapping the creator in the web of the creation.[8]

We think that a good case can be made that George Bush never really believed that Saddam Hussein was another Hitler. His use of the analogy was a cynical attempt to strike fear and loathing into the hearts of the American people. Saddam Hussein is certainly an unsavory villain. But an unsavory villain capable of achieving stability in Iraq—a stability that President Bush and his advisors obviously considered worth the price of allowing him to remain in office. An unsavory villain whom we could live with comfortably—one we had lived with and supported in the past and not unlike a great many other unsavory villains around the world whom the United States continues to support.

The cynicism evinced by President Bush is more than merely unfortunate. As citizens of a democracy, we have the right to look closely at the facts so that we may arrive at our own rational conclusions about whether or not we should go to war and whether or not it is appropriate to bring Saddam to trial as a war criminal—based not on the hyperbole of a president but on the facts of the matter. We have a right to be angry at being manipulated by a president if he depicts our enemy as another Hitler one month and as a difficult but stabilizing force the next.

It is not our intention to single out George Bush for special criticism. Unfortunately, pulling the wool over the eyes of the people has been a common practice in the White House; from Lyndon Johnson's false statements of optimism during the Vietnam war ("There is light at the end of the tunnel") to Richard Nixon's stonewalling of the Watergate affair ("I am not a crook") to Ronald Reagan's statements about the Iran-Contra scandal ("I think I don't remember") to Bill Clinton's outright lies regarding his sexual improprieties ("I did not have sexual relations with that woman"), American presidents have been denying citizens the information necessary to properly analyze a situation and to act rationally. The truly unfortunate aspect of this is that most Americans have rather cynically come to take it for granted that they will be misled. Is it any wonder that in this country, the cradle of modern democracy, less than 50% of the people now bother to vote?

9 ||||||||||||||||||||||||

A Questionable Persuasion

Imagine that you are the president of the United States and the country is bracing itself for the outbreak of an unusual epidemic expected to kill 600 people. Your top advisors have prepared two alternative programs to combat the disease and have estimated, to the best of their abilities, the likely consequences of each program.

If Program A is adopted, 200 people will be saved.

If Program B is adopted, there is a one-third probability that 600 people will be saved and a two-thirds probability that no people will be saved.

Mr. or Ms. President, which program do you favor?

If you are like most of the participants in an experiment performed by Daniel Kahneman and Amos Tversky, you would select Program A[1] (seventy-two percent of their subjects selected this option). You might think to yourself, "Program A guarantees that 200 people will be saved, while Program B gambles the lives of these people for only a 1 in 3 chance that more lives could be saved."

But suppose your advisors had presented the epidemic problem this way instead: .

If Program A is adopted, 400 people will die.

If Program B is adopted, there is a one-third probability that nobody will die and a two-thirds probability that 600 people will die.

Which program would you now favor?

The two sets of options are the same. Program A means that 200 people will live and 400 will die. Program B results in a one-third chance that no one will die and 600 people will live and a two-thirds chance that no one will be saved and 600 people will die.

But for most people, their thinking about the epidemic is quite different. *"If I go with Program A, 400 people will surely die; I might as well gamble on B."* When asked in this second manner, 78% of Kahneman and Tversky's subjects favored Program B.

Why did such a simple rewording of the options produce such a drastic switch in answers? Kahneman and Tversky (as well as others) have noted that people dislike losses and seek to avoid them. It is more painful to give up $20 than it is pleasurable to gain $20. The first policy decision was worded so that Program B looked like the bigger loss; the second version was phrased so that Program A looked like a sure loss. It's all in how the question is *framed.*

This is, of course, just a hypothetical situation. What happens when requests are reworded in real life? Let's look at the prevention of breast cancer, which is a serious health threat for many women. Fortunately, early detection and diagnosis of breast cancer can greatly improve a woman's chances of surviving the disease. Unfortunately, one of the best methods for detecting breast cancer, a monthly breast self-examination, is not performed regularly by most women.

Beth Meyerowitz and Shelly Chaiken developed and distributed three pamphlets asking women to perform a routine breast self-examination regularly.[2] One pamphlet contained only instructions on how to perform a breast self-examination. The second pamphlet contained these instructions and asked women to perform the exam and emphasized the positive consequences of self-examination (i.e., women who perform such examinations have an *increased* chance of finding a tumor at a treatable stage). The third pamphlet contained the instructions and stressed the negative consequences of failing to perform a self-examination (i.e., women who do *not* perform such examinations have a *decreased* chance of finding a tumor at a treatable stage). Meyerowitz and Chaiken found that, four months after reading the pamphlet, those women who were asked to perform the breast exam and were informed of the negative consequences of failing to do so were significantly more likely to perform a self-examination. How you ask can make a significant difference in a real life-and-death situation.

In both of the above examples—the epidemic decision and the communication about breast self-exams—the way the question was put influenced the way the issue was defined. In both cases, defining the issue as "losing something" was more persuasive than stating it in terms of a gain.

Question-asking can be a subtle form of pre-persuasion—a carefully crafted question can be used to define the issue at hand, to suggest subtly what the "right" answer may be, and to organize the way we think about the issue. Let's look at some of the ways that an artfully worded question can produce the results we seek.

Opinion pollsters have long known that subtle changes in the wording of a question can produce dramatically different responses. For example, the percentage of Americans supporting aid for the Contras in Nicaragua from 1983 to 1986 varied from 13% to 42%, depending on how the question was worded.[3] If the question mentioned Ronald Reagan or the Contras explicitly, or used ideological labels to identify the opposing forces in Nicaragua, more Americans supported the aid. If the question mentioned a dollar amount of aid or presented both sides of the issue, fewer Americans wanted to give aid to the Contra rebels. Or consider this polling inconsistency: Within days of each other, a Fox News opinion poll reported that 54% of Americans believed that Bill Clinton had sexually assaulted and raped Juanita Broaddrick in 1978, whereas a CNN/Gallup/*USA Today* poll found that only 34% of Americans believed the charges. Why the discrepancy? It appears that the Fox News poll prefaced the question with another loaded and highly charged question that presumed Clinton's guilt in the matter. Other pollsters using more neutral wording found results consistent with the CNN/Gallup/*USA Today* poll.[4] Legitimate pollsters who seek accurate responses will go to great lengths to avoid bias in the wording of questions. Those who seek to use polls for their own advantage—to convince people that everyone else supports their policy or their political candidacy—will not be so careful.

Lawyers also know the importance of a carefully phrased question. Textbooks describing how to cross-examine a witness stress the maxim, "Never ask a question for which you don't already know the answer." Or, put more accurately, "Never ask a question that doesn't get the answer you want." Several years ago, in a murder trial that held our collective attention for months, the world witnessed a vivid demonstration of the significance of this textbook maxim. Los Angeles County prosecutor Christopher Darden asked O. J. Simpson to try on a pair of bloody gloves. Darden got an answer he neither anticipated nor wanted—an O. J. Simpson seemingly struggling to put on a pair of gloves allegedly worn by the killer of Nicole Brown Simpson and Ronald Goldman. The incident was one of the deciding moments of the trial. The gloves seemed too small

The famed trial attorney Gerry Spence takes the issue one step further, claiming that a well-phrased question may contain more persuasive information than the answer to that question. In a case in which he and his client sued *Penthouse* magazine for libel, Spence asked *Penthouse* publisher Bob Guccione a series of questions about the nature of the contents of his magazines. The questions were designed to show that *Penthouse* was little more than obscene pornography disguised as literature. The judge sus-

"Of course you agree, don't you—only a fool would disagree— that a question can be worded to get a positive answer."

tained most of Guccione's attorney's objections to the questions. Spence was unfazed. As he put it, the objections merely annoyed the jury and "the information I wanted to convey to the jury was sometimes better contained in my questions than any answers I might hope to get from Guccione."[5]

Elizabeth Loftus has conducted a program of research looking at how leading questions can influence eyewitness testimony.[6] In one of her studies, Loftus showed subjects a film depicting a multiple-car accident. After the film, some of the subjects were asked, "About how fast were the cars going when they *smashed* into each other?" Other subjects were asked the same question, but the word *smashed* was replaced by the word *hit*. Subjects who were asked about *smashing* cars, as opposed to *hitting* cars, estimated that the cars were going significantly faster and, a week after seeing the film, were more likely to state that there was broken glass at the accident scene (even though no broken glass was shown in the film).

Leading questions can influence not only judgment of facts but also actual memory of what has happened. In another study, Loftus showed subjects a series of slides depicting an auto–pedestrian accident. In a critical slide, a *green* car drove past the accident. Immediately after viewing the slides, half of the subjects were asked, "Did the *blue* car that drove past the accident have a ski rack on the roof?" The remaining subjects were asked this same question but with the word *blue* deleted. The results showed that those subjects who were asked about the "blue" car were more likely to claim incorrectly that they had seen a blue car (even though in the slide it was green). A simple question had distorted their memory.

It is not only what is asked but also the order in which it is asked that influence our decisions and choices. Suppose your head is throbbing and your stomach is acting up. You need a strong pain reliever that will not adversely affect your stomach. Displayed below are your available options and how they rate on various attributes of a pain reliever:

	Special-Grip Bottle	Easy on the Stomach	Pain-Relief Strength
Brand W	yes	good	very good
Brand X	yes	good	good
Brand Y	yes	poor	excellent
Brand Z	no	excellent	excellent

Before you rush out to the store, you see the following ad for Brand W on television: All four pain relievers are lined up in a row. The announcer asks, "Which of these pain relievers gives you a special-grip bottle?" Brand Z is removed before your eyes. "Which of these brands won't upset your stomach?" Out goes Brand Y. "Which brand gives you the most pain relief?" Brand X is forcefully removed. "The choice is—Brand W."

Or is it? Suppose only the last two questions were asked, and in reverse order? Our choice would be much different—Brand Z would be our *best* buy and Brand W the *worst*. Given your throbbing head and your upset stomach, you may wish to give more weight to these two attributes than the special-grip bottle. Again, Brand Z is your pain reliever.

With all of the information on the different pain relievers conveniently displayed, it is easy to see how the order in which questions are asked and the order in which information is received can distort and bias the decision-making process. The propagandist has employed the technique of *card-stacking*, or the deceptive manipulation of information and facts.[7] Unfortunately, we rarely have all the information at once for many of our decisions—either it is unavailable, or we do not have the time or energy to secure it, or the critical pieces of information are purposefully hidden and distorted. In such cases, the order in which we seek and obtain information can influence our decisions in subtle but important ways.

Question-asking can be a powerful persuasion device because questions structure our decision-making process.[8] They do this by directing our thoughts about the issues at hand and by implicitly specifying the range of possible answers. Consider the question, "Do you support the constitutional right to bear arms?" The question directs our thoughts and attention to the constitutionality of gun ownership as opposed to other concerns, such as the right to a safe neighborhood. The question also implicitly defines the issue as guns versus no guns and excludes middle-of-the road proposals such as gun registration, waiting periods, and restricted access to certain types of arms (such as Saturday-night specials, automatic assault weapons, or nuclear arms). The Constitution also guarantees free speech—but not the right to yell *fire* in a crowded movie house.

If you doubt the power of a question to pre-persuade, observe how politicians handle themselves at press conferences and on public affairs programs. They know that questions can direct attention and change public opinion. That is why, when a question is not to a politician's liking, he or she will try to dodge it. Suppose a politician is on record as favoring gun control. The stinging question about supporting the Constitution can be avoided by rephrasing it ("It's a good question; just what will I do about the crime in our streets?"), by postponing it ("Let's first clear up a few important issues"), by glossing over it in a way that appears to answer the question ("You know I support the Constitution of the United States and the people's right to live in safety as they see fit"), or by diverting attention by asking yet another question ("But do you believe in the right of every American to live in safety?").

So far in this section, we have seen how the definition of an issue—whether it be through choice of words, images, analogies, or just by asking the "right question"—serves as a form of prepersuasion. In the next chapter, we look at how context—the "other" issues and objects that we can consider—influences perception and, thus, our subsequent behavior.

10

The Power of Decoys

An outing with your local real estate agent can illustrate the powerful impact of a decoy. At the realtor's office, you are shown pictures and given descriptions of many homes—beautiful split-levels, roomy ranches, an old Victorian. After determining your needs, the agent drives you to some homes "you might find of interest." The first stop is a tiny two-bedroom house sitting on a narrow lot. The house needs a new coat of paint; the interior is in disarray; the linoleum in the kitchen is buckling; the living room carpet is worn; the master bedroom is so small that an average-sized bedroom suite just won't fit. When the realtor tells you the asking price, you exclaim, "Holy cow! Who'd be dumb enough to pay so much for this shack?" Probably not you, and probably not anyone else. But that dilapidated house may influence you to buy another house more readily and to buy it at a much higher price than you might normally have been willing to pay.

How can this come about? We can clarify the process by looking at an experiment we conducted with our colleagues Peter Farquhar, Sarah Silbert, and Jennifer Hearst.[1] In our study, students were asked to make decisions such as the following:

Which would you select (a or b)?
a. *Nutri-burger:* a tofu burger that is very good on nutrition but only average on taste
b. *Tasti-burger:* a hamburger that is very good on taste but only average on nutrition.

For some decisions, a *decoy* was given as an additional option. A decoy is an alternative that is inferior to other possible selections. For example:

Which would you prefer (a, b, or c)?
a. *Nutri-burger:* the tofu burger described above
b. *Tasti-burger:* the hamburger described above
c. *Bummer-burger:* a hamburger that is only good on taste and only average on nutrition.

In this case, the decoy is option c—the hamburger that is only *good* on taste (as opposed to very good). No reasonable person would select this inferior burger. If you wanted a lunch that tasted great, you would select option b, the very-good-tasting Tasti-burger. If you wanted nutrition, you would go for the Nutri-burger. Indeed, in our study the decoy was almost never selected.

But that doesn't mean that its presence as an option wasn't influential. Our study investigated decisions about nine common consumer products; we found that, on average, including a decoy increased the probability of people's selecting the products that were similar but superior to the decoy, such as the Tasti-burger over the Nutri-burger, by 6.7%. Does 6.7% seem like a small amount? To put this in perspective, a 1% change in market share for a small brand manufactured by a company like Procter & Gamble or General Motors could mean an annual increase in sales of more than $10 million. In short, extrapolating into the real world, our decoys might have produced a $67-million effect!

How did this relatively worthless decoy change our students' choices? The answer in a nutshell: contrast effects. To contrast means to make differences apparent. When an object is contrasted with something similar but not as good, or not as pretty, or not as tall, it is judged to be better, prettier, taller than would normally be the case. If a man of normal height (say 5 feet, 11 inches) is in the company of midgets, he seems very tall. If he is a member of a professional basketball team, he seems very short. Such was the case with "Tiny" Archibald, who played basketball for the Boston Celtics. "Tiny" stood 6 feet, 1 inch tall. In Jonathan Swift's classic novel *Gulliver's Travels*, the hero, a man of normal height, was considered a giant when traveling among the residents of Lilliput and a dwarf when traveling among the residents of Brobdingnag.

As a scientific example of contrast effects, let's look at an experiment by Douglass Kenrick and Sara Gutierres, who asked males to rate the attractiveness of a potential blind date before or after watching the television show "Charlie's Angels."[2] The males rated the woman as less attractive after they saw the show than before. Presumably, the gorgeous Angels provided a stringent context for rating attractiveness; the blind date appeared to be far less physically attractive when compared to the Angels than to women in general.

In our study on consumer decision making, two contrast effects occurred that made the Tasti-burger look more attractive. The presence of a decoy made the very-good-tasting Tasti-burger appear to be even better-tasting and the average-tasting Nutri-burger to be even worse-tasting. In other words, the decoy "spread apart" the Tasti- and Nutri-burgers on the dimension of taste. With this change in the perception of tastiness, the choice became much clearer for our subjects.

Decoys don't influence just the brands of products we choose. They can also affect whom we would like to date. In a recent experiment conducted by Constantine Sedikides and his colleagues,[3] students were asked to make dating choices such as the following:

Who would you most like to date (a or b)?
a. *Chris*, who is very handsome but rather inarticulate
b. *Tory*, who is not really handsome but is very articulate.

This is a tough decision that requires a trade-off: Is it better to spend the evening with someone who looks great but isn't much of a conversationalist or someone who's a great conversationalist but who doesn't look so great? The choice becomes much easier when a decoy is added. Some of the subjects also received information about a third potential date: *Jackie*, who is fairly handsome (just slightly less so than Chris) and rather inarticulate (just like Chris). When Jackie enters the dating scene, Chris increases in popularity and becomes the dating partner of choice. Poor Tory and Jackie! They spend the evening alone at home.

Now we can see how that visit to the dilapidated house can influence our purchase. Perhaps the next house we look at is *not* really ideal. But compared to that last one—what an improvement! The yard and the master bedroom are bigger. The interior is in good shape. We won't need to paint it for at least three years. And the price is only slightly higher than what they were asking for that old shack. What a deal! We'll take it right away— before the owners have a chance to change their mind!

Decoys come in a variety of shapes and sizes. A used-car dealer may place an old clunker on the lot to "improve the appearance" of the other autos. A presidential candidate may select a vice-presidential running mate of lesser stature to enhance the positive perception of his or her own presidential qualities. That blind date looks a lot better compared to the loser your uncle is trying to fix you up with. The taking of seven hostages in Beirut doesn't seem so bad compared to the taking of an entire embassy in Iran.

The lesson to be learned from research on decoys is that the *context* makes a difference. Judgment is relative, not absolute. Depending on the context, objects and alternatives can be made to look better or worse. Often we do not pay much attention to the influence of context, much less question the validity of the alternatives presented. This greatly enhances the power of "context-makers," such as politicians, advertisers, journalists, and sales agents. The context they set can pre-persuade us by influencing our perceptions and judgments; we are thus lulled into decisions that we would not normally make.

11

The Psychology of Factoids

On September 1, 1944, the *Daily Journal-Gazette* carried a startling story of a "gas attack" on the citizens of Mattoon, Illinois. The headline read: ANESTHETIC PROWLER ON LOOSE. The story described how a local woman and her daughter had been gassed by an intruder. Apparently, a sickish, sweet-smelling gas had been sprayed into their open bedroom window. The gas made both the woman and her daughter ill and paralyzed their legs for a couple of hours. Although police found no sign of the intruder, when the woman's husband arrived home from work a few hours after the incident, he saw a man run from the window.[1]

This would not be the gasser's last strike. A short time later, Mattoon's at-large anesthetist attacked another couple, with the husband becoming sick to his stomach and the woman unable to walk. Four days later, another woman reported finding a cloth on her porch, which, when she smelled it, burned her mouth and lips so badly that they bled. In the week that followed, twenty-one more incidents were reported to the police. All the victims reported symptoms such as nausea and vomiting, paralysis of the legs, dryness of the mouth and throat, and burns about the mouth.

The local police were stymied. They beefed up patrols. The state police were called in as reinforcements. Analysis of the crime scenes and cloths that carried the gas turned up nothing. Physicians, after examining the victims, were unable to isolate the chemicals used in the attack.

To this day, the gasser of Mattoon remains at large. He or she has never been captured or brought to justice for one simple reason—the elusive anesthetist never existed except in the minds of the citizens of Mattoon. The gasser was a factoid.

The novelist Norman Mailer, who coined the term *factoid*,* defines it as "facts which have no existence before appearing in a magazine or newspaper."[2] We define *factoid* as an assertion of fact that is not backed up by evidence, usually because the fact is false or because evidence in support of the assertion cannot be obtained. Factoids are presented in such a manner that they become widely treated as true. In our workplaces and neighborhoods, they are known as rumors, gossip, and urban legends. In courts of law, factoids are called hearsay and inadmissible evidence. In the mass media, they are called libel, slander, innuendo, and the reporting of currently circulating rumors, gossip, and hearsay as news.

---

* *CNN uses the term* factoid *to mean little fact, a usage quite different from ours and Mailer's.*

Factoids are common.[3] On October 30, 1938, Orson Welles presented a radio dramatization of *The War of the Worlds*, the H. G. Wells classic that describes the takeover of Earth by invaders from Mars. The broadcast, coming during a time of concern over the events in Europe, set off a panic—people all over the United States were praying, crying, and fleeing frantically from what they thought was an invasion from Mars. Some tried to rescue loved ones; others telephoned friends with the news and to say their last good-byes. A year later, a Spanish version was broadcast in Ecuador. Panic resulted. When the public found out it was a hoax, a riot broke out, resulting in the burning of a radio station and the death of twenty-one people.

In the 1960s, rumors circulated that the Beatle Paul McCartney was dead. Music fans around the world scoured album covers and music lyrics (forward and backward) looking for (and finding!) clues of Paul's death—a fascination that still continues.[4] Since the late 1970s, consumers have boycotted Procter & Gamble's products because of a rumor that the thirteen stars in the company's logo were a tribute to the devil. In the late 1980s, the nation's attention was riveted on a hunt by Boston police for the black man who murdered Carol Stuart, a white woman. The search, which eventually resulted in the jailing of a prime suspect, was instigated by a 911 call placed by Charles Stuart from his car phone reporting that his wife, Carol, had just been killed by a black youth. A recording of the phone call was repeatedly played on national television news shows. It was subsequently discovered that Charles had killed his own wife. The use of race to spread a rumor was so successful that less than a decade later Susan Smith tried the same factoid by accusing an unknown black man of abducting her two children. Susan Smith was later convicted of murdering her own children by trapping them in a car and then pushing that car to the bottom of a lake. Prejudice played a key role again in the spread of rumors as CNN, CBS, ABC, the *New York Times*, and others initially reported (without hard evidence) that the tragic bombing of a federal building in Oklahoma City was most likely the result of a jihad masterminded by Middle Eastern terrorists.

The modern contemporary version of the gasser of Mattoon is the alien abduction story.[5] Books such as *Communion* by Whitley Striever and *Intruders* by Budd Hopkins tell the tale of hundreds of people who have been kidnapped by extraterrestrial visitors, often for purposes of bizarre sexual and genetic experiments. The story of Barney and Betty Hill—perhaps the first case of alien abduction—is typical. Driving home on a lonely New England road in September 1961, they thought their car was being followed by a bright object in the sky (which, based on their later description of its location, seems to be the planet Jupiter). Several days afterward, Betty began to have a recurring nightmare that she and Barney had been abducted aboard a flying saucer. She told her story to friends, who noted that the Hills had been two hours late in coming home that night; perhaps, they conjectured, these nightmares were true and the "abduction" could account for the "missing time." The Hills sought the advice of a therapist, who used hypnotic regression to get to the "truth" of the matter. Under hypnosis, Betty gave a detailed account of the "abduction," whereas Barney told a much more limited tale. However, their stories did not match on many important details (such as the looks of the aliens, the language spoken by the aliens, and the aliens' knowledge of earth's customs), causing the therapist to conclude that the report was a confabulation. But that would not be the end of the issue. Five years later, *Look* magazine published a two-part article describing the possibility of the Hills' abduction by space aliens. As in Mattoon, others came forward with their own stories, and a nationwide factoid industry of alien abductions was spawned. And as with the gasser of Mattoon, police and private investigators have been unable to produce evidence to substantiate claims of alien visitation, prompting still more factoids—this time of government conspiracy and cover-up.

Today entire newspapers, magazines, and television programs, under the guise of presenting "news," are devoted to inventing and circulating believable rumors. Witness the trial of O. J. Simpson, where one rumor after another—that a bloody ski mask had been found in Simpson's home, that damaging evidence had been found in Simpson's golf bag, that Simpson had allegedly confessed to the crime—was repeated and elaborated on by the "news" media. There was little attempt to check these rumors, since the public's thirst for entertainment and the media's quest for ratings required that new and even more exciting "details" of the crime be presented every day—lest anyone lose interest.

Further advancing the spread of rumors and factoids is the practice of flaming on the Internet. *Flaming* is the Internet term for vicious attacks and unfounded rumors.[6] Some cyberspace factoids have included: a major fashion designer made racist statements on the "Oprah Winfrey Show"; the homepage of a major software producer contained a virus; and a major cookie maker gave free cookies to O. J. Simpson, thereby stimulating a nationwide boycott of the cookies. All of these rumors were false.[7]

In politics, the art of innuendo in the United States goes back to the birth of the nation in what were called "whispering campaigns." For example, rumors circulated that Thomas Jefferson was an atheist and had debauched a well-born Virginia belle, that Martin van Buren was the illegitimate son of Aaron Burr, that Andrew Jackson had lived with his wife before marriage, and that John Quincy Adams had acted as a pander for a Russian nobleman. The tradition continues into the modern era. In the 1970s, Richard Nixon's campaign staff hired "dirty tricksters" to spread rumors about leading Democratic candidates—rumors that many political analysts believe were at the heart of the withdrawal of front-running Edmund Muskie from the presidential race. Factoids continue to be transmitted even today by presidential and congressional "leaks," by mudslinging in election campaigns, and by journalists' reports based on information from "well-placed" sources.

The modern version of the whispering campaign could be observed during the mass media coverage of the Monica Lewinsky–Bill Clinton saga. At one point, the *Dallas Morning News*, on its Internet site, reported that a Secret Service agent was about to come forward as a witness to a sex act between Lewinsky and Clinton. The next day, headlines in the *New York Post* and *New York Daily News* read: CAUGHT IN THE ACT. Not to be outdone, the *Wall Street Journal*, on its Internet site, reported that a White House steward had told a grand jury that he had seen Lewinsky and Clinton together. The wire services then picked up this story. Of course, all these stories were false. Nonetheless, they fed the impeachment frenzy that was sweeping the press, if not the nation, at the time. The Clinton administration was the target of many innuendoes and factoids, including criminal accusations against the Clintons for the unauthorized receipt of confidential FBI files by a low-level official (the so-called Filegate), as well as allegations that Hillary Clinton was somehow involved in the suicide of Vince Foster, that the firing of several White House workers in the travel office (for possible improprieties) was motivated by the Clintons' desire to use the positions as rewards for supporters (the so-called Travelgate), and even that a haircut that then-President Clinton got aboard Air Force One had caused a major delay in air traffic at the Los Angeles airport. All these accusations were false; indeed, Special Prosecutor Ken Starr (not known for being biased in favor of Bill and Hillary), after years of investigation, cleared the Clintons in both the Filegate and Travelgate matters.

The use of factoids is also a common practice in campaigns against other nations. Adolf Hitler and his propaganda minister, Joseph Goebbels, mastered the art of what has been termed "the big lie." According to Nazi propaganda theory, one effective way to persuade the masses is to develop and repeat falsehoods—for example, "The German people are a master race; Europe is menaced by the Jewish conspiracy." Such big lies are difficult to prove false. For example, the fact that there is no evidence that a Jewish conspiracy exists is just further evidence regarding the cleverness of Jews. The big lie is then supported by many small but often irrelevant facts to make the big lie all that more believable—for example, some Jews own banks and Karl Marx, the founder of communism, was Jewish. The big-lie technique continues to be used by many governments today. As just one example, Iranian government officials circulated the story that the Iraqi invasion of Kuwait had been masterminded by the United States as a pretext for the U.S. invasion of the Persian Gulf region.

But do factoids really influence our judgments and beliefs? After all, some of them are often just plain unbelievable. Much research continues to show that the reaction of the citizens of Mattoon is not an isolated example; factoids can have a powerful effect on belief and human action. Let's look at some of that research.

Daniel Wegner and his colleagues have conducted a series of simple experiments looking at people's reactions to innuendo.[8] In their studies, participants were asked to rate the favorability of political candidates on the basis of a newspaper headline. For example, participants read either a directly incriminating head-

line (BOB TALBERT LINKED WITH MAFIA), a questioning incrimination (IS KAREN DOWNING ASSOCIATED WITH A FRAUDULENT CHARITY?),
a denial of unseemly behavior (ANDREW WINTERS NOT CONNECTED
TO BANK EMBEZZLEMENT), or a neutral headline (GEORGE ARM-
STRONG ARRIVES IN CITY).

The results showed, not surprisingly, that candidates linked
with a directly incriminating headline were perceived more negatively. Strikingly, however, merely questioning whether a candidate had performed an undesirable behavior or simply denying
that the candidate had performed an undesirable behavior also
resulted in negative perceptions of the candidate—just slightly
more positive than those evoked by a direct incrimination. It appears that simply questioning a candidate's connection with
unseemly activities can be enough to damage that candidate's
public image. What's more, the source of the innuendo made little difference: The candidates were still rated negatively even if
the source of the headline was a newspaper lacking in credibility
(the *National Enquirer* or the *Midnight Globe* as opposed to the
New York Times or the *Washington Post*). Negative political advertising and slur campaigns often do indeed pay off. As just one
example of the power of a negative accusation: During the trial
of William Kennedy Smith for rape, the popularity of President
John F. Kennedy (who was assassinated almost thirty years
before the trial of his nephew) declined, even though the majority of Americans agreed with the verdict of not guilty rendered in
the Smith trial.

Sometimes a false accusation can be more brazen and
direct. Some recent research we conducted with Derek Rucker
looked at what we called the projection tactic—accusing someone else of the misdeed you yourself are committing.[9] The
research was inspired by numerous historical examples. For
example, before invading a country, Adolf Hitler would often
accuse the leaders of that country of plotting aggression against
Germany. At the beginning of testimony before his committee,
Joseph McCarthy would accuse the witness of lying, as he,
Joseph McCarthy, was preparing to tell one lie after another
about the witness. We wondered if such projections would
change how events are perceived.

In our research, we asked people to view a competitive game
or to read about students cheating on a chemistry test or about

countries going to war. In some cases, one of the characters in the story would accuse others of a misdeed—for example, accusing an innocent person of lying or cheating on a test or blaming another country for a war. In four separate experiments, we obtained the same results: The person making the accusation was exonerated from blame, whereas the target of the projection was seen as the culprit of the misdeed. We obtained these results despite raising suspicions about the motives of the accuser, providing evidence that the accuser was guilty of the misdeed, and timing the accusation so that it occurred after the accuser's misdeeds came to light. In other words, when it comes to false accusations and blaming others for your own negative behavior, Adolf Hitler and Joseph McCarthy knew what they were doing!

If you think that projection is only effective in the laboratory of social psychologists, go ask Gary Dotson about his experiences. He spent six years in prison because of a young girl's false allegations. In the summer of 1977, Cathleen Crowell Webb, then sixteen years old, reported that she had been raped. Webb showed police her torn blouse and scars allegedly inflicted by the rapist; she also described the rapist to a police sketch artist. The police sketch just happened to match the likeness of Gary Dotson. Two years later, on the strength of this "eyewitness" evidence, Dotson was sentenced to not less than twenty-five years and not more than fifty years in the Illinois State penitentiary. Six years later, in March 1985, Webb retracted her story. She told authorities that she had made up the rape charge in order to cover up a sexual experience with her boyfriend.[10] Dotson asked that his conviction be overturned. The original judge would not reverse the decision. The governor of Illinois refused a pardon but did commute Dotson's sentence to the six years served. Both the judge and the governor continued to believe the original story—the false allegation was more believable than the recantation and the truth. It took Dotson four more years to clear his name through DNA tests showing that the semen on Webb's underwear could not have come from Dotson but could have come from her boyfriend. The effects of a teenager's projections lasted for twelve years, ruining twelve years of an innocent person's life.[11]

Other researchers have found that unsubstantiated evidence in a court of law can have an impact on juries, even when the judge explicitly tells the jury to ignore the factoid.[12] For example, in one experiment, Saul Kassin and his colleagues found that the credibility of an expert trial witness could be damaged merely by asking accusatory questions, such as, "Isn't it true that your work is poorly regarded by your colleagues?" The expert's credibility was damaged regardless of whether the accusation was denied or withdrawn by the lawyer after an objection was raised. Stanley Sue and his colleagues found that evidence prejudicial to a defendant would result in more convictions even when the evidence was ruled inadmissible. Numerous studies have found that negative pretrial publicity—such as reports of a confession, a failed lie detector test, the defendant's prior record, details of the case, and other information that was not admitted into trial testimony—can have a serious impact on jury decision making.

Factoids can influence not only political and judicial but also consumer decision making. Just a decade ago, a flier called the "Leaflet of Villejuif" had been circulating in France and other European nations.[13] The leaflet, typed on ordinary typewriters and then photocopied, urged parents to protect their children by boycotting popular brands of food and beverage such as Coca-Cola, Schweppes, Canada Dry, and others because they contained cancer-causing agents.

Surveys of the French population found that about half of all housewives had read or heard about the leaflet and that it was likely to have affected their behavior. In a study of 150 housewives who received the leaflet, 19% stated that they had stopped buying the listed brands and another 69% stated that they planned to do so. In a survey of primary school teachers and physicians who had heard of the leaflet, almost all of the teachers and nearly half of the physicians agreed with what the leaflet stated. Only a few teachers or physicians (less than 10%) attempted to check out the validity of the claims, although many schools stopped providing the offending brands at meals out of fear of doing harm to children.

What is so remarkable about the persuasiveness of the "Leaflet of Villejuif" is that the claims it made were completely false. For example, the additive identified by the leaflet as the most serious cancer-causing agent was E330. E330 is the European Common Market code for harmless citric acid, an ingredient found in many nutritional fruits such as oranges. Further, the leaflet also identified other ingredients as "harmless" and therefore good for you, even though some of these ingredients were actually known carcinogenic agents. In other words, the leaflet not only contained false and misleading information, it also contained harmful information. After a year or two of circulation, the original source of the leaflet was changed from "a hospital in Paris" to the "Hospital of Villejuif," a hospital internationally recognized for its advanced research on cancer. The hospital at Villejuif denied any association with the leaflet and repeatedly denounced its fraudulent claims. Despite these efforts, the leaflet continued to be passed from one person to the next and continued to be believed.

As Mark Twain once put it, "A lie can travel halfway around the world while the truth is putting on its shoes." Why are factoids so persuasive? We can suggest three reasons.

First, few attempts are made to verify the truth of a factoid. We often hear rumor and gossip directly from trusted friends whom we are not in a habit of questioning. We also turn to the "news"—whether on television or in other mass media—expecting, quite frankly, "the news" and are often not prepared to debunk each and every presented "fact." Factoids often just sneak by our persuasion defenses. We rarely think to ask, "Is this factoid really true? Who gains by repeated telling of this factoid?" Even when we seek to verify a factoid, it is often difficult, since many rumors deal with "secret information," "secret conspiracies," and "esoteric knowledge" that is hard to critically evaluate and scrutinize.

Second, we accept factoids because they often meet one or more psychological needs. For example, many factoids are entertaining and thus capture our attention—it is fun to look for clues that Paul McCartney is dead. More seriously, the very best factoids help us rationalize and justify our most fundamental worries and concerns. The "Leaflet of Villejuif" confirms the belief held by many that big corporations have conspired to harm us for profit. Accepting as true a damaging factoid about a well-known person can make us feel better about ourselves by showing us that even the great "Mr. So-and-So" has his faults, too. Believing that a black youth killed Mrs. Stuart or Susan Smith's children helps confirm many people's mistaken ideas about the nature and character of black Americans. Spreading a factoid may also enhance our self-images by showing others that we are in the "know" about secret information and by helping us address some of our most threatening fears. As a factoid is spread, it is often "modified and elaborated" to better serve our psychological needs.

Finally, and perhaps most importantly, factoids function as a form of pre-persuasion; they create social reality. Factoids serve as bits and pieces that are used to construct our picture of the world. As such, factoids direct our attention and suggest how we should interpret the world. For example, consider a citizen of Mattoon who wakes up one morning with an upset stomach or a pair of tired, aching legs (as undoubtably someone in the town will do). What will he or she think? *"It must be the gasser. That's why I feel this way."* That person may go on to interpret other random occurrences, such as a passing cat or a gust of wind, as supporting the notion of a visit from the gasser. *"You know, I did hear the porch creak and what sounded like a rapping at the window last night."* The rumor is thus given credence and then spread, going on to help others create their social worlds. Even when the factoid is shown to be false, it can still direct attention and thinking. For example, a political candidate falsely accused of embezzling must spend his or her time refuting and denying the charge instead of proposing substantive new programs in an attempt to win the election. And, as we saw in the research by Daniel Wegner and colleagues, such denials are usually doomed to fail, because they often serve to remind the casual reader of the original accusation.

Given that factoids can be so persuasive, it is understandable that a number of attempts have been made to limit their influence, with varying degrees of success. For example, during World War II, the U.S. government was particularly worried about how rumors and gossip could undermine the war effort. A well-placed rumor could raise unrealistic expectations of a quick victory or could dash all hopes of ever winning the war, thereby damaging morale. Further, spreading rumors about troop movements and the like could alert the enemy to Allied plans.

During the war, the U.S. government attempted to persuade citizens that repeating rumors was unpatriotic and could handicap the war effort—as the old saw went, "Loose lips sink ships." Citizens were instructed to treat rumors as Nazi propaganda.

Rumor-control clinics were also created to identify harmful rumors and to take measures to defuse them. For example, one government pamphlet recommended that harmful rumors be referred to the appropriate government agency (e.g., Army, Navy, FBI), which would then present a logical and factual refutation of the rumor. In order to stand a chance of succeeding, such refutations should not overstate the case, should embed the rumor in a negative context (or damn it, refute it, then damn it again and replace it), and should not repeat verbatim particularly memorable rumors.

Unfortunately, these tactics can be used to stop even truthful facts. For example, an effective use of rumor refutation can be seen in Bill Clinton's handling of accusations of marital infidelity made by Gennifer Flowers in the 1992 presidential campaign. On CBS's *60 Minutes*, Bill and Hillary Clinton denied the affair and said that their marriage had gone through some rough times, but now things were better than ever. The Flowers allegation probably cost Clinton a win in the New Hampshire primary, but it did not knock him out of the race. Clinton tried this tactic again when he went on nationwide television and, as he wagged his finger at the American public, stated in forceful terms, "I did not have sexual relations with that woman" in an attempt to deny his affair with Monica Lewinsky. And the tactic worked again—for a short time. Immediately after the statement, his trusted aides and cabinet members rallied to his defense, and many Americans (including his wife) sought to give him the benefit of the doubt. However, in the long run, the evidence finally accrued to show otherwise (as it did in the Flowers case as well), and the United States soon found itself in the midst of a costly and divisive impeachment trial.

Another attempt to regulate the influence of factoids, at least in the courts, is the development of evidence law. Since the rise of jury trials in twelfth-century England, some judges have been fearful that untrained, lay jurors would be misled by false testimony and would succumb to improper appeals to their emotions and sympathies.[14] As a means of lessening the impact of such information, courts have developed rules of procedure that specify who can present evidence, what evidence can be admitted, how evidence is to be introduced, and how a jury is to deliberate about the evidence. For example, evidence may be excluded from a court of law because it is hearsay, or secondhand, and therefore of questionable validity; because it is not relevant to the case and its value to the court is outweighed by the risks of prejudicial impact; because it is the opinion of an ordinary witness, not fact; or because it is from a privileged communication (such as that between attorney and client or husband and wife).

Evidence law is still evolving and generates much controversy even today. As a case in point, recall the controversies generated by whether the Fuhrman tapes—those recordings of LAPD officer Mark Fuhrman repeatedly using racial slurs—should have been admitted as evidence in the trial of O. J. Simpson and whether Judge Ito should have thrown out all the evidence collected at Simpson's Rockingham estate on the basis of an illegal search by police. On the one hand, some claim that evidence law can be frustrating to those seeking an efficient means of convicting criminals, especially those rules that require the police and prosecution to observe citizens' rights to privacy and undue search and seizure. Trial procedure and rules of evidence can present obstacles to the prosecution in arguing a case, thereby giving the impression that evidence law is designed to protect the criminal. (In some cases, these same evidence laws can also be used to exclude material that would make conviction of a defendant more likely.) On the other hand, evidence law can be an important safeguard for insuring the right of both the innocent and guilty to a fair trial, one that is devoid of innuendo and hearsay.

We would argue for even stronger evidence rules, noting that while some rules, such as changing the location of a trial if there is considerable prejudicial pretrial publicity, are usually helpful in insuring a fair trial, other procedures, such as ruling that a piece of prejudicial evidence is inadmissible and instructing a jury to ignore it, do not prevent a jury from being unfairly influenced by that evidence. In practice, the value of evidence laws for insuring a fair trial ultimately resides with the fair application of the laws and a judiciary willing to risk the possible anger of the public and politicians for the sake of protecting the constitutional right to a fair trial. Regardless of one's own views on the matter, the controversy over evidence law should further underscore the importance of factoids in the persuasion process.

If the control of factoids is difficult in a relatively well-controlled environment such as a court of law, it is all the more complicated in the mass media.[15] Attempts to diminish the effects of factoids in the mass media are relatively recent. The first court cases involving deceptive advertising in the United States occurred in the late 1950s and early 1960s. One of the most important cases was brought by the Federal Trade Commission (FTC) against Colgate-Palmolive, the makers of Rapid Shave. In one of their television commercials, an actor was shown squirting Rapid Shave onto sandpaper and then, moments later, shaving it clean with just one stroke. When the FTC attempted to repeat this demonstration, they found that sandpaper could not be shaved clean unless moisturized for an hour. Indeed, the makers of the original ad had used Plexiglas covered with sand, not sandpaper. The courts ruled that this ad was deceptive—it led consumers mistakenly to believe that Rapid Shave could shave even the toughest textures quickly—and Colgate-Palmolive was ordered to cease showing the commercial.

However, just stopping a deceptive advertisement may not be enough. We have seen that a belief in a factoid can linger for a considerable length of time. Such deceptive advertising can unfairly place business competitors at a disadvantage and can confuse and mislead consumers. During the 1970s, the FTC argued that manufacturers who make misleading claims must not only cease making the claims but correct and dispel any false beliefs created by the advertisement. For example, Profile Bread claimed to be a "diet" bread having fewer calories than other breads. (In reality, it had the same number of calories—but slices were cut thinner to reduce the number of calories per slice by seven.) Profile Bread was ordered to spend at least one-fourth of its advertising budget for a year to correct this misleading claim. Other firms, including other bakers, Ocean Spray (maker of a brand of cranberry juice), and various manufacturers of analgesics, were similarly ordered to spend a percentage of their advertising budgets to correct false claims. What did the manufacturers do? Some merely stopped advertising for a year—one-quarter of $0 is $0 spent on corrective advertising. Others spent the money to buy ads that not many people would read—for example, classified ads in the daily newspaper. In response, the FTC required subsequent deceptive advertisers to take specific steps to dispel false beliefs. In particular, Warner-Lambert, maker of Listerine, was required to dispel the myth that Listerine kills cold-producing germs by spending $10 million to promote the following statement: "Contrary to prior advertising, Listerine will not prevent colds or sore throats or lessen their severity." The FTC also issued guidelines on how to spend the money.

However, correcting mistaken beliefs may not be the most efficient method for dealing with factoids; perhaps a better approach is to nip them in the bud before they become factoids. During the 1970s, the FTC attempted to do this through its program on ad substantiation. This program required advertisers in selected industries to submit to the FTC evidence that would substantiate their advertising claims. The response of automakers was typical: They sent hundreds upon hundreds of technical documents that were nearly impossible to understand. Later, the FTC amended its procedures to require more focused and readable documents.

In the 1980s, however, much of the FTC's attempt to control factoids was abandoned when the United States elected a president who emphasized a free market as opposed to the use of "big-government" regulation. During the Reagan years, the staff of the FTC was cut by almost half. Other advertising regulatory bodies followed suit, with the major networks cutting many of their employees responsible for policing television advertising. This relaxing of government controls reopened the door to blatant abuses. The attorneys general of various states initiated their own lawsuits in an attempt to stem the deceptions. When Bill Clinton came to office in 1992, he gradually restored some of the regulatory powers of the FTC, especially in high-profile areas such as ads for violent movies, crimes of economic fraud, food labeling, and tobacco advertising. We should note, however, that many of the Clinton administration's attempts to curb tobacco advertising were overruled by the U.S. Supreme Court, which claimed that the Food and Drug Administration (which issued the guidelines) did not have the authority to regulate tobacco.

Nevertheless, when it comes to factoids, the stakes can be high. Look what happened politically during the Clinton administration. False allegations against the Clintons and false denials by Bill Clinton resulted in a year-long mass media frenzy and preoccupation with all things "Monica." The frenzy was compounded when several of Clinton's ardent accusers were themselves confronted with evidence of their own sexual indiscretions. We can certainly appreciate the feelings of many Americans who are tempted to say "a plague on all their houses."

When a rumor is answered with an innuendo that in turn prompts a lie that is then refuted with gossip leading to more rumors, a sane person just doesn't know what to believe. The end result is cynicism and deep distrust of all those involved. But here is the rub: The plague isn't on their houses, but on ours. Ultimately we all have a responsibility to challenge factoids— first, when confronted by a rumor, by asking just what the evidence is for the claim and then by consciously deciding not to create or spread false rumors and to counter them if we can.

Citizens worried about commercial and political factoids do have one recourse—themselves. Both *Consumer Reports* and *Advertising Age* publish lists of advertisements that have been found to make false or misleading claims. Consumers can also ask manufacturers to substantiate their claims. This is exactly what students in one of our courses did. They culled magazines and television to identify ninety-nine advertising claims and then wrote to the manufacturers of the products asking for any information that would substantiate their claims. The responses they received would startle even the most cynical critic of advertising. Just under 50% of the companies responded to the request. Of those responding, only five companies sent information that adequately substantiated their claims. The great majority sent more advertising. Indeed, for every page of materials directly related to the claim, the students received eighty-six pages of additional unrelated advertising and promotional materials.

Although the students did not find the answers to their ad-substantiation questions, their project is still of considerable value. First, it provides yet more evidence for a basic point of this chapter: Factoids are abundant in the age of propaganda. Second, the students' project suggests a method for dealing with potential factoids. Suppose consumers and voters began questioning and confronting the makers of factoids directly. It is just possible that many of our advertisers and politicians would be forced to begin replacing factoids with facts.

Communicator Credibility: Real and Manufactured

The Credible Communicator

Picture the following scene: Your doorbell rings; when you answer it, you find a middle-aged man in a rather loud, checkered sports jacket. His tie is loose, his collar is frayed, his pants need ironing, he needs a shave, and his eyes keep looking off to the side and over your head as he talks to you. He is carrying a small can in his hand with a slot in the top, and he is trying to convince you to contribute a few dollars to a charitable organization you have never heard of. Although his actual pitch sounds fairly reasonable, what is the possibility of his succeeding in prying you loose from your money?

Now let's turn back the clock a few minutes: You open your door in response to the bell, and standing there is a middle-aged man in a conservative business suit, well tailored and well pressed. He looks you squarely in the eye, introduces himself as a vice-president of the City National Bank, and asks if you would contribute a few dollars to the same charitable organization, using exactly the same words as the fellow in the loud, checkered jacket. Would you be more likely to contribute some money?

We were struck by the likely response to such a substitution several years ago when Allen Ginsberg appeared on one of the late-night talk shows. Ginsberg, one of the most popular poets of the "beat" generation, was at it again; his poem "Howl" had shocked and stimulated the literary establishment in the 1950s. On the talk show, having just finished boasting about his homosexuality, Ginsberg was talking about the generation gap.

The camera panned in. He was fat, bearded, and looked a trifle wild-eyed (was he stoned?); long hair grew in unruly patches from the sides of his otherwise bald head; he was wearing a tie-dyed T-shirt with a hole in it and a few strands of beads. Although he was talking earnestly—and, in the opinion of some, very sensibly—about the problems of the young, the studio audience was laughing. They seemed to be treating him like a clown. In all probability, the vast majority of the people at home, lying in bed watching the poet from between their feet, were not taking him seriously either—no matter how sensible his message, no matter how earnestly he delivered it. His appearance and his reputation were, in all probability, overdetermining the audience's reaction.

The scientist in us longed to substitute the conservative-looking banker in the neatly pressed business suit for the wild-eyed beat poet and have him move his lips while Ginsberg said the same words off-camera. Our guess is that, under these circumstances, Ginsberg's message would have been well received.

No need. Similar experiments have already been done. Indeed, speculations about the effects of character and prestige on persuasion are ancient. More than 300 years before the Christian era, Aristotle wrote:

> We believe good men more fully and more readily than others: this is true generally whatever the question is, and absolutely true where exact certainty is impossible and opinions are divided. It is not true, as some writers assume in their treatises on rhetoric, that the personal goodness revealed by the speaker contributes nothing to his power of persuasion; on the contrary, his character may almost be called the most effective means of persuasion he possesses.[1]

It required some 2,300 years for Aristotle's observation to be put to a scientific test. This was accomplished by Carl Hovland and Walter Weiss.[2] What these investigators did was very simple: They presented large numbers of people with a communication that argued a particular point of view—for example, that building atomic-powered submarines was a feasible undertaking (this experiment was performed in 1951, when harnessing atomic energy for such purposes was merely a dream).

Some of the people were informed that the argument was made by a person possessing a great deal of public credibility; for others, the same argument was attributed to a source with low credibility. Specifically, the argument that atomic-powered submarines could be built in the near future was attributed to J. Robert Oppenheimer, a highly respected and nationally known atomic physicist, or to *Pravda*, the official newspaper of the Communist party in the Soviet Union—a publication not famous in the United States for its objectivity and truthfulness.

Before reading the arguments, the participants were asked to fill out a questionnaire that revealed their opinions on the topic. They then read the communication. A large percentage of those people who believed the communication came from J. Robert Oppenheimer changed their opinions—they then believed more strongly in the feasibility of atomic submarines. Very few of those who read the identical communication attributed to *Pravda* shifted their opinions in the direction of the communication.

This same phenomenon has been repeatedly confirmed by several different investigators using a wide variety of topics and attributing the communications to a wide variety of communicators. Careful experiments have shown that a judge of the juvenile court is more likely than most other people to sway opinion about juvenile delinquency, that a famous poet and critic can sway opinion about the merits of a poem, and that a medical journal can sway opinion about whether or not antihistamines should be dispensed without a prescription.

What do the physicist, the judge, the poet, and the medical journal have that *Pravda* doesn't? Aristotle said we believe "good men," by which he meant people of high moral caliber. Hovland and Weiss used the term *credible*, which removes the moral connotations present in the Aristotelian definition. Oppenheimer, the juvenile court judge, the poet, and the medical journal are all credible—that is, they are not necessarily "good," but they appear to be both *expert* and *trustworthy*.

It makes sense to allow yourself to be influenced by communicators who are trustworthy and who know what they are talking about. It makes sense for people to be influenced by an editor of *Consumer Reports* when she is voicing an opinion about consumer safety, and it makes sense for people to be influenced by someone like Dr. C. Everett Koop, the former surgeon general, when he is talking about the use of condoms to prevent AIDS or about the addictive properties of nicotine. These are expert, trustworthy people.

But not all people are equally influenced by the same communicator. Indeed, the same communicator may be regarded by some people as possessing high credibility and by others as possessing low credibility. Moreover, certain peripheral attributes of the communicator may loom large for some people; such attributes can serve to make a given communicator either remarkably effective or remarkably ineffective.

The importance of peripheral attributes in persuasion was forcefully demonstrated in an experiment we performed in collaboration with Burton Golden.[3] In this study, sixth-graders heard a speech extolling the usefulness and importance of arithmetic. The speaker was introduced either as a prize-winning engineer from a prestigious university or as someone who washed dishes for a living. As one might expect, the engineer was far more effective at influencing the youngsters' opinions than the dishwasher. This finding is consistent with previous research; in and of itself, it is obvious and of some interest.

But, in addition, we varied the race of the communicator: In some of the trials the communicator was white, and in others, black. Several weeks prior to the experiment, the children had filled out a questionnaire designed to measure the degree of their prejudice against black people. The results were striking: Among those children who were most prejudiced against blacks, the black engineer was *less* influential than the white engineer, although both delivered the same speech. Moreover, among those children who were the least prejudiced against blacks, the black engineer was *more* influential than the white engineer.

It seems unreasonable that such a peripheral attribute as skin color would affect a person's credibility. It might be argued that, in a purely rational world, a prestigious engineer should be able to influence sixth-graders about the importance of arithmetic regardless of the color of his or her skin, but apparently this is not a purely rational world. Depending upon listeners' attitudes toward blacks, they were either *more* influenced or *less* influenced by a black communicator than by an otherwise identical white communicator. More recently, Paul White and Stephen Harkins have found that whites, in an attempt not to appear prejudiced, will often pay more attention to what a black communicator is saying.[4] This results in more persuasion if the message is strong and compelling, but less persuasion if the message is weak.

Clearly, such responses are maladaptive. If the quality of your life depends on the extent to which you allow a communication about arithmetic to influence your opinion, the expertise and trustworthiness of the communicator would seem the most reasonable factors to heed, and it would seem foolish to take into account factors irrelevant to the issue (such as skin color).

But, although such responses are maladaptive, it should not be very astonishing to anyone who has ever watched commercials on television. Indeed, advertisers bank on this maladaptive behavior and often count on irrelevant factors to increase the effectiveness of a spokesperson. For example, several years ago Bill Cosby starred in a series of commercials in which he playfully interacts with children. He tells the children how delicious a particular brand of pudding is, and together they chat, laugh, and enjoy their snacks. He also reminds the audience that the product not only "tastes good" but is "good for you," because it's made with milk. What made Cosby an expert on children and nutrition? In the 1980s, on "The Cosby Show," he had played Dr. Cliff Huxtable, a pediatrician as well as a warm, funny, and insightful father to five children.

Similarly, Karl Malden once starred in a series of commercials in which Americans traveling in a foreign country either lose all their money or have it stolen. The tourists are distraught, humiliated, traumatized, panicky. At the end of the commercial, Karl Malden appears and, in an authoritative voice, warns us not to carry money while traveling and recommends "American Express Travelers Cheques—don't leave home without them." What makes Karl Malden an expert on vacation financing? Nothing, but he is perceived as somewhat of an expert on *crime*. For many television seasons, Malden portrayed Lieutenant Mike Stone in "The Streets of San Francisco," a popular detective show.

More recently, the makers of Nicoderm—a stop-smoking patch—hired a young actress to promote their product. And who was she? The same actress who played "Dr. Olivet," a psychologist who often evaluated the mental stability of criminals on the hit TV show "Law & Order." Apparently, pretending to be a psychologist on TV for a couple of seasons is enough to allow this actress to voice her opinion about the best way to quit smoking.

And then there is our favorite in this genre. An actor from the hit daytime soap opera "General Hospital" comes on the TV screen and announces, "I'm not a real doctor, but I play one on TV"—and then goes on to recommend a brand of painkiller.

Though Cosby, an actor from "General Hospital," "Dr. Olivet," and Malden probably do not know a great deal more about nutrition, medicine, crime, nicotine patches, or even travelers checks than the average viewer, they almost certainly gain credibility and trust when they are identified with their particular roles.

The fact that we humans often use the credibility of a communicator to guide us in the acceptance or rejection of a message opens the door once again for mindless propaganda. Although it makes sense to believe the credible source when her or his expertise and trustworthiness are directly related to the issue at hand, it is often easier to *feign* credibility than to actually *achieve* it. For example, in the 1992 presidential election, Bill Clinton was adept at creating credibility with a variety of target audiences—such as by appearing on MTV and playing a saxophone on a late night talk show to attract young voters, eating at McDonald's to appeal to working-class folks, and playing up his "Bubba" image to break the Republican stronghold in the South. In the 1996 election, Clinton abandoned the Bubba schtick and used the trappings of the White House in an attempt to establish an image of leadership.[5]

One of the important tasks of media research is to keep tabs on the "reputation and credibility" of public figures, such as movie stars, sports figures, and other public "personalities." Advertisers want to know which celebrity figures are most believable, who among the stars is most liked by the public, who has been on the cover of leading magazines, and who has been overexposed. The answers to such questions determine the celebrity's value as a spokesperson for the advertiser's product. Credibility has become a commodity not only to be feigned but also to be bought and sold on the open market.

How can we recognize when a communicator is merely feigning credibility as opposed to actually possessing it? This is a difficult question. In order to know that someone is an expert in a given domain, we have to know enough about that topic to be able to recognize who is and isn't an expert. And if we know that much, then we are probably experts ourselves. Fortunately, students of rhetoric such as Douglas Walton have provided us with a set of questions that can be used to recognize when the use of an expert to guide our acceptance of a proposition is fallacious.[6] Walton suggests that we ask these questions: Is the expert clearly identified (or is it a vague attribution such as "leading experts say")? Is the person really an expert or someone who is merely quoted because of his or her prestige, popularity, or celebrity status? Does the judgment put forward fall within the field of competence of the expert? Is there consensus among the experts as to the judgment or opinion? Could the expert cite objective evidence to support her or his claim? And is the expert trustworthy and unbiased (or does he or she have a self-interest in the cause)?

When Aristotle wrote his description of the effects of "good character" on persuasion, a debate was raging in Greece. Many people, such as Socrates and Plato, saw those engaged in persuasion, such as professional speechmakers and the Sophists, as deceitful and untrustworthy persons. Rhetoric was a worthless art practiced by worthless people. In order to justify a place for persuasion in society, Aristotle argued that not only *should* a persuader be of good character for moral reasons but also that the trustworthy source *would* be more effective than the speaker lacking in character. Modern research on persuasion has supported Aristotle's belief in the effectiveness of the trustworthy communicator—with a few notable exceptions to be discussed later. Modern propaganda practices, with their ability to manufacture credibility and buy and sell it as a commodity, raise anew the ethical concerns prominent in Aristotle's times. As the psychotherapist Erich Fromm once noted, when everything and everybody is for sale—including persons, convictions, feelings, and a smile—then fewer people can be trusted because fewer people have a character and an identity that can be depended upon.[7] Without trust, communication becomes difficult, if not impossible.

13 |ıııııııııııııııııı

Breakfast of Champions, Junk Food for the Self

The celebrity endorsement has been a common feature of America's advertising landscape for decades. In the 1950s, future president Ronald Reagan described the revolutionary collars of Arrow shirts and the high-quality tobacco of Chesterfield cigarettes. In the 1960s, pro quarterback Joe Namath urged viewers to "take it off" with Noxema shaving cream. In the 1970s, Rodney Dangerfield, Bob Uecker, and a collection of madcap football players told us about the less-filling, great taste of Miller Lite beer. In the 1980s, Priscilla (the wife of Elvis) Presley told us to go ahead and buy that new car, because it really isn't our father's Oldsmobile. And today, basketball star Michael Jordan sells everything from breakfast cereal to cologne to phone service.

The use of such celebrities may seem quite irrational and bizarre. After all, when we think about it in a rational manner, who is an expert on the topic of razor blades or shaving cream? Well, perhaps a barber; maybe a dermatologist or a cosmetologist. Who is it that tells us what blades or lather we should use? Most often, it is a professional basketball or football player.

The use of athletes to sell products has a long history. Throughout the 1950s and 1960s, one of the most persistent peddlers of breakfast food was former Olympic decathlon champion Bob Richards, who was probably far more effective at selling Wheaties than some learned professor of nutrition, no matter *how* expert he or she might have been. In the 1970s, Richards was replaced by another gold-medal decathlon champion, Bruce Jenner. How effective are these sports stars? Well, when Jenner was finally replaced in the 1980s, the Wheaties people again decided not to use a nutritionist and hired Mary Lou Retton, an Olympic gold medalist in gymnastics. She was later replaced by a succession of sports heroes, including Pete Rose, Walter Payton, Chris Evert Lloyd, Michael Jordan, Joe Montana, Dan Marino, Cal Ripken, and the gold-medal winners from the 1996 Olympic games. By the time you read this, we would be surprised if Marion Jones, American premier track star of the 2000

Olympics, has not already graced the Wheaties cereal box. This would suggest that whoever handles advertising for Wheaties is convinced of the effectiveness of famous athletes. Indeed, the sports endorser is such an effective persuasion tactic it appears to be used worldwide. When the German chocolate maker Jacob Suchard wanted to advertise its Milka brand chocolates, whom did they hire? They asked Franziska von Almsick—a fourteen-year old swimmer and winner of four medals at the 1992 Olympics in Barcelona—to appear on TV milking their trademark purple cow.

Is this conviction justified? Will people be influenced by an ad just because a prominent celebrity is involved? Even if we admire the skills and talents such individuals display on the movie screen or the playing field, can we really trust them to be telling us the truth about the products they endorse? After all, we all know that the star peddling shaving cream, beer, or breakfast cereal is getting paid handsomely for her or his time. Indeed, the multimillion-dollar deals celebrities such as Madonna, Michael Jackson, and Bill Cosby cut with various sponsors have become part of the common knowledge touted in the news magazines. So we know better. Surely we cannot be influenced by such blatant hypocrisy. Or can we?

Our guess is that most people would be quick to say, "No; maybe *other people* might be persuaded to run out and buy something because a movie star or sports figure tells them to, but certainly I wouldn't trust even my favorite celebrity's advice on how to spend my hard-earned cash." But can people really predict their own behavior?

Not necessarily. Although most of us might not *trust* movie actors and sports stars, that does not necessarily mean we wouldn't buy the products they endorse. Another significant factor determining the effectiveness of spokespersons is how attractive or likable they are, regardless of their overall expertise or trustworthiness.

Several years ago, we and our colleague Judson Mills did a simple laboratory experiment demonstrating that a beautiful woman—simply because she was beautiful—could have a major impact on the opinions of an audience on a topic wholly irrelevant to her beauty and, furthermore, that her impact was greatest when she openly expressed a desire to influence the audience.[1] There is a sense in which people act as if they are attempting to please someone they find attractive, even though that person may never know about it. A later experiment not only replicated the finding that more likable communicators are more persuasive but went on to show that attractive sources are *expected* to support desirable positions.[2]

Perhaps the most amazing demonstration of the power of attractive and likable spokespersons to persuade is the use of fictitious spokespersons—cartoon characters such as Joe Camel, the Pillsbury Dough Boy, and Snap, Crackle, and Pop or imaginary personalities such as the Lonely Maytag Man, Aunt Jemima, and the suave yet unidentified spokesman for Infiniti automobiles. What could be of more suspect credibility? These "people" don't even exist except to sell you a product. Does it work? Consider Joe Camel, that sophisticated and smooth symbol for Camel cigarettes. Once Joe Camel began appearing on the nation's billboards, in magazines, and on a variety of promotional items such as T-shirts and ballcaps, Camel's market share among underage smokers increased from 0.5% to a whopping 32.8%, especially among young smokers—who were the target audience.[3]

Are we condemned to follow the desires of the beautiful and the famous? Richard Petty, John Cacioppo, and David Schumann have demonstrated that there is at least one circumstance in which we do not follow the dictates of the socially attractive— when we are motivated to *think* about the issue at hand.[4] That is, the attractiveness of the source has less of an impact when we operate in the central, as opposed to the peripheral, route to persuasion. In their experiment, subjects received one of four different ads for a fictitious new product, "Edge Disposable Razors." Two ads featured photographs of well-known and well-liked sports celebrities, and two ads featured middle-aged citizens from Bakersfield, California. Further, two ads contained six cogent and compelling arguments for Edge Razors (e.g., the handle is tapered and ribbed to prevent slippage) and two ads contained six specious and vague statements (e.g., it is built with the bathroom in mind).

The researchers varied subjects' motivation to think about Edge Razors by telling half of them that, at the end of the study, they would be allowed to select a gift from among several brands of disposable razors. The results showed that for subjects motivated to think about the communication by the prospect of choosing a gift razor, the quality of the message's arguments, not the attractiveness of the source, was the most important determinant in the subjects' ratings of Edge Razors. The other subjects were strongly influenced by the source of the message, more often rating Edge Razors as superior when the ad used sports personalities than when it used citizens of Bakersfield, California.

The Petty, Cacioppo, and Schumann findings notwithstanding, it is still somewhat disconcerting that under most circumstances attractive communicators can wield such influence. Again, we all know that the football player holding up his can of shaving cream is clearly trying to influence us—the shaving cream company is not paying him all that money not to sell shaving cream. Moreover, he seems to be operating in his own self-interest; when we take a good look at the situation, it's clear the only reason he's up there with the shaving cream is to make a buck.

The effectiveness of attractive sources in selling products and changing our beliefs indicates that we hold our beliefs for other reasons in addition to our desire to be correct and to size up the world accurately. We hold our beliefs and attitudes in order to define and make sense of our *selves*. By shaving with the right razor or eating the right cereal, we are saying, "I am just like that ballplayer; I am part of the attractive in-group." By purchasing the "right stuff," we enhance our own egos and rationalize away our inadequacies as we "become" just like our favorite celebrity. Perhaps we should remember what basketball star Charles Barkley frankly said on "Saturday Night Live": "These are my shoes. They're good shoes. They won't make you rich like me; they won't make you rebound like me; they definitely won't make you handsome like me. They'll only make you have shoes like me. That's it." Too bad Demetrick James Walker didn't watch this episode of "Saturday Night Live" before he decided to kill another boy for his Nike high-tops.

Advertisers know all too well that we believe what we believe and buy what we buy in the service of our self-image. They imbue their products with a "personality." Marlboro cigarettes are macho. Dr. Pepper soft drink is unconventional. A BMW automobile is yuppie. Calvin Klein is chic. To claim the desired persona, all we need to do is to purchase and display the right products.

And political pundits and consultants are increasingly learning that appeals to our self-image make good politics. Candidates for political office are given attractive personalities; their images are created by making speeches about the American flag, by posing in an Army tank, and by being photographed with schoolchildren in prayer. All we need to do to be patriotic, to be strong and tough, to be holy, is merely to cast a vote for the right candidate. It would be sad indeed if we lost our more than 200-year-old tradition of democracy because, like the unthinking subjects of Petty, Cacioppo, and Schumann, we were never motivated to scrutinize the candidate's image and evaluate the substance of her or his message.

14 ||||||||||||||||||||

How Do You Persuade if Everyone Knows You Are Untrustworthy, Unbelievable, and Disliked?

When you think about it, the professional propagandist has a difficult task. We commonly respond to persuasive messages by questioning the speaker's bias and noting how his or her self-interest is being served. This general skepticism can serve a useful purpose for the target of the appeal. By identifying a message as biased, the audience can prepare to defend its position and either to scrutinize carefully the contents of the message or to reject it out of hand, depending on the circumstances. But from the propagandist's perspective, this constitutes a formidable obstacle to securing compliance. Accordingly, the propagandist finds it important not to *appear* to be a propagandist. In order to be successful, the communicator must appear unbiased and trustworthy. In this chapter we look at two general strategies for making the untrustworthy, the unbelievable, and the disliked look trustworthy, believable, and liked.

The Chinese rhetorician Han Fei-tzu, who advised rulers in the third century B.C., told the following story to illustrate how a ruler can improve the perception of his credibility.[1] The Duke of

Wu wished to invade the country of Hu. The Duke pulled aside one of his most trusted counselors and asked him to argue in public that the Duke should attack Hu, which the counselor then did. The Duke immediately put the counselor to death as a dramatic way of reassuring the ruler of Hu that he had no intention of attacking. Assured that the Duke was a trustworthy leader—after all, he had just put one of his most trusted advisors to death—Hu disarmed. The Duke of Wu immediately launched a surprise attack and the country of Hu was captured.

One of the morals of Han Fei-tzu's story is that communicators can make themselves seem trustworthy by apparently acting against their own self-interest. If we are led to believe that communicators have nothing to gain and perhaps even something to lose by convincing us, we will trust them and they will be more effective. When the Duke of Wu put his counselor to death, he appeared to be arguing against his own self-interest—"No! Invading Hu, even though it may result in benefits to my country, is wrong. I believe this so strongly that I will put my favorite advisor to death for merely suggesting it." The problem—for the citizens of Hu—was that the Duke's position was an illusion; he had arranged it so that it would appear he was acting and arguing against his own self-interest. This leads us to the second moral of Han Fei-tzu's story: When it comes to propaganda, appearances can be deceiving.

The strategy of acting or arguing against your own self-interest can be used to increase the perception of your trustworthiness without actually putting your best friend to death. An illustration may be helpful. Suppose a habitual criminal, recently convicted as a smuggler and peddler of cocaine, was delivering a talk on the harshness of the American judicial system and the overzealousness of its prosecutors. Would he influence you? Probably not. Most people would probably regard him as biased and untrustworthy. The cocaine peddler occupies a position clearly outside the Aristotelian definition of a "good person." But suppose he was arguing that criminal justice was too *soft*—that criminals almost always beat the rap if they have a smart lawyer and that even if criminals *are* convicted, the sentences normally meted out are too lenient. Would he influence you?

The evidence from one of our own experiments suggests that he probably would. In a study conducted in collaboration with

Elaine Walster and Darcy Abrahams, we presented our subjects with a newspaper clipping of an interview with Joe "the Shoulder" Napolitano, who was identified in the manner described above.[2] In one experimental condition, Joe "the Shoulder" argued for stricter courts and more severe sentences. In another condition, he argued that courts should be more lenient and sentences less severe. We also ran a parallel set of conditions in which the same statements were attributed to a respected public official.

When Joe "the Shoulder" argued for more lenient courts, he was totally ineffective; indeed, he actually caused the subjects' opinions to change slightly in the opposite direction. But when he was arguing for stricter, more powerful courts, he was extremely effective—as effective as the respected public official delivering the same argument. This study demonstrates that Aristotle was not completely correct: A communicator can be an immoral person and still be effective, as long as it seems clear that the communicator is not acting in her or his self-interest by attempting to persuade us.

Why was Joe "the Shoulder" so effective in the experiment? Let's take a closer look. Most people would not be surprised to hear a known convict arguing in favor of a more lenient criminal justice system. Their knowledge of the criminal's background and self-interest would lead them to expect such a message. When they receive the opposite communication, however, these expectations are disconfirmed. To make sense of this contradiction, the members of the audience might conclude that the convict had reformed, or they could entertain the notion that the criminal is under some kind of pressure to make the anti-crime statements. In the absence of any evidence to substantiate these suppositions, however, another explanation becomes more reasonable: Maybe the truth of the issue is so compelling that, even though it apparently contradicts his background and self-interest, the spokesman sincerely believes in the position he espouses.

Evidence for this phenomenon comes from an experiment by Alice Eagly and her colleagues, who presented students with a description of a dispute between business interests and environmental groups over a company's polluting of a river.[3] The students then read a statement about the issue. In some conditions the spokesman was described as having a business background and was said to be speaking to a group of business people. In others, his background and audience were varied, thereby altering the subjects' expectations of his message. The results supported the reasoning above: When the message conflicted with their expectations, listeners perceived the communicator as being more sincere and they were more persuaded by his statement.

It is hard to imagine a more convincing spokesperson for an anti-smoking campaign than someone whose fortune was made off the habits of millions of American smokers. In fact, Patrick Reynolds, who inherited $2.5 million from the R. J. Reynolds Tobacco Company founded by his grandfather, has taken a strong public stand against smoking and has gone so far as to urge victims of smoking-related illnesses to file lawsuits against tobacco companies![4]

Similarly, during the height of the Cold War the most effective opponents of the nuclear arms race were several professionals who took stands that seemingly contradicted their backgrounds. These communicators—for example, J. Robert Oppenheimer, a respected nuclear physicist who, for many years, cautioned against the further development of nuclear technology; Carl Sagan, a trusted astronomer who warned the world about nuclear winter; and Admiral Elmo Zumwalt, a former naval commander who campaigned for a halt to certain military developments—were perceived as highly credible precisely because of the discontinuity between their messages and the apparent interests of their professions. First of all, they were experts. Second, since they had nothing to gain (and perhaps even collegial esteem to lose), it seemed that only the compelling need for disarmament led them to speak out. Not only do we tend to take more notice of unexpected events, but we also attribute more credibility to speakers who appear to resist the pressures of their colleagues and who take stands in opposition to their backgrounds.

Today one of the nation's most respected authorities on health issues is the former U.S. surgeon general, Dr. C. Everett Koop. That was not the case when Koop was first appointed to the position in the early 1980s by President Reagan. Koop is an evangelical Christian whose position on abortion and contraceptives caused many Americans, especially those with a more liberal bent, to worry that Koop would use his position to advance his own view of morality. As the full meaning of the AIDS epidemic began to be discovered, Dr. Koop made a dramatic recommendation: Obviously the best way to avoid the AIDS virus is sexual abstinence or monogamy; however, if you plan to be sexually active, you should use a condom. Koop's recommendation resulted in a firestorm from those on the Right and, especially, evangelical Christians. They believed that Koop's recommendation to use condoms promoted promiscuity.

The firestorm did not end there. In the last days of his appointment, Koop released a report stating that there was no evidence that an abortion causes emotional harm to the woman—although Koop himself still believed that abortion was morally wrong. The report dismayed many in the Reagan administration, who had hoped to use evidence of emotional harm as an argument against abortion.

In 1996 C. Everett Koop was once again the center of controversy. This time Koop supported the Clinton administration's efforts to limit the sale of tobacco to children. Koop took this position because nicotine is a highly addictive substance. Smoking among teenagers is at the highest level in nearly two decades. Each day 3,000 kids start smoking (more than a million a year); approximately a third will die from their newfound addiction. Most smokers take up the habit in their early teens.[5] Koop's support of efforts to prevent teenagers from taking up the smoking habit irritated the 1996 Republican presidential candidate Bob Dole, who believes that cigarettes are not addictive and claimed that Koop had been brainwashed by the liberal media. Nevertheless, C. Everett Koop has repeatedly demonstrated that he is a man of impeccable integrity who has earned his reputation as a trustworthy source.

The Chinese philosopher Mencius, who lived in the fourth century B.C., provides us with another technique for increasing the perception of trustworthiness.[6] Mencius had gained fame as a wise counselor. The king sent a polite note asking Mencius to come to court so that he might advise the king. Mencius replied that he was not well and was unable to come to court. The next day he walked conspicuously around town. The king was outraged and sent several men to find out why Mencius showed so little respect and to beseech him once more to come to court. Mencius would not receive the men and left to visit a friend. The king could stomach Mencius's impertinence no more and accused him of disloyalty. Mencius replied that far from being disloyal and disrespectful, he had shown the most loyalty and respect for the king in all the land. He could be useful to the king only if the king absolutely trusted his integrity and independence of mind. If the king suspected that he might do or say things merely to please, his counsel would be ignored.

Mencius's actions illustrate another way of increasing the perception of credibility: The apparent trustworthiness of a person can be *increased* and the apparent bias of the message *decreased* if the audience is absolutely certain the person is not trying to influence them. To illustrate, let us bring this discussion into the twentieth century. Suppose a stockbroker calls you up and gives you a hot tip on a particular stock. Will you buy? It's hard to be sure. On the one hand, the broker is probably an expert, and this might influence you to buy. On the other hand, the broker has something to gain by giving you a tip (a commission), and this could lower the effectiveness of the message. But suppose you accidently happened to *overhear* the broker telling a friend that a particular stock was about to rise. Because the broker was obviously not *trying* to influence you, you might be more readily influenced.

This is exactly what was discovered in an experiment by Elaine Walster and Leon Festinger.[7] In this study, a conversation was staged between two graduate students in which one of them expressed his opinion on an issue. The situation was arranged such that an undergraduate student was allowed to overhear this conversation. In one experimental condition, it was clear to the undergraduate that the graduate students were aware of his presence in the next room; therefore, the undergraduate knew anything being said could conceivably be directed at him with the intention of influencing his opinion. In the other condition, the situation was arranged so that the undergraduate believed the graduate students were unaware of his presence in the next room. In this latter condition, undergraduates' opinions changed significantly more in the direction of the opinion expressed by the graduate students.

There are many tactics for making it appear that you are not really trying to influence someone. A few years back, the brokerage firm of E. F. Hutton ran a series of commercials in which, when one person began to pass on some stock advice from E. F. Hutton, a sudden hush fell over the room and everyone strained toward the speaker to better "overhear" the tip. The implication is clear: Everyone is getting in on advice that was not intended for them, and the information is all the more valuable as a result. Another example of this phenomenon is the "hidden camera" advertisements on television: If we are convinced a person has been caught unaware, we do not attribute a persuasive intent to the message; believing the person is acting spontaneously, we are more persuaded by his or her testimony. Finally, politicians are notorious for claiming that, unlike their opponents, they are above "politics" and are merely taking the position that they do because they have the best interest of the public at heart. When communicators do not appear to be *trying* to influence us, their potential to do so is increased.

Throughout this book, we look at how clever propaganda tactics can be used to manipulate our beliefs and behavior. Indeed, in the next chapter we look at the wholesale manufacture of source credibility. The second moral of Han Fei-tzu's story—that appearances can be deceiving—is often all too true; but the acceptance of this moral can breed an unhealthy cynicism.

For this reason, it is good to pause and reflect on the behavior of a person such as Dr. C. Everett Koop. In an era in which political self-interest appears to dominate—where, for example, congressional leaders opposed to excessive military spending are in favor of shutting down military bases except, of course, for the ones in their districts—it is refreshing to run into a public servant of high integrity. When Koop, as surgeon general, was confronted with the AIDS crisis, he conducted a thorough investigation so that he could render an expert judgment. At great risk to his career and at the cost of alienating his friends and supporters, Dr. Koop spoke what he knew to be true. The cost to Dr. Koop's career for his honesty should not be downplayed. Although he made it clear that he would like to continue in public service and would enjoy a promotion to secretary of the Department of Health and Human Services, Koop was not reappointed by the Bush administration. His accomplishments should not be taken lightly either. There are untold numbers of Americans—perhaps the people who live next door to you, perhaps your own son or daughter—who will not die of AIDS but will go on to live long and productive lives as a result of Dr. Koop's actions. In this age of propaganda, Dr. Koop's behavior reminds us that there is still a place for Aristotle's communicator of good character.

15

The Manufacture of Credibility

Imagine the following hypothetical situation: Two men are running for the Senate. One of the candidates has far less money to spend on his campaign than the other. Accordingly, in order to get maximum free exposure, he consents to numerous interviews, gives frequent news conferences, agrees to performances before hostile audiences in an attempt to generate news media interest in the campaign, and appears often on panel-type programs on television. The interviewers on these occasions are opponents and seasoned reporters who frequently ask him difficult questions, even hostile ones. The candidate finds himself forever on the defensive. Sometimes the camera catches him at an unflattering angle or in the act of scratching his nose, yawning, or fidgeting. Watching at home, his mother is surprised at the bags under his eyes and at how tired and old he looks. Sometimes, when faced with a tough or unexpected question, he has difficulty finding the right response; he hems and haws and sounds inarticulate.

His opponent with the well-stocked campaign chest does not need to appear in such forums. Instead, he spends vast amounts of money videotaping spot commercials. Because he pays the camera crew and the director, his countenance is captured only from the most flattering angles. His personal makeup artist works hard to mask the bags under his eyes and to make him appear young and dynamic. His mother, watching him at home, never saw him looking so well. The interviewer asks him questions prepared and rehearsed in advance, so that his answers are reasonable, concise, and articulate. If the candidate does happen to stumble over a word or to draw a blank, the cameras are stopped and the scene is shot over and over again until it portrays him in the best light.

This situation is no nightmarish projection into the future; it closely approximates what occurred, on a much more important and dramatic scale, during the 1968 presidential election. In an extraordinary behind-the-scenes account of Richard Nixon's campaign, journalist Joe McGinness reported on the adeptness with which Nixon's advisors controlled the image of the candidate that was projected to the American people.

In reporting these events, McGinness claims that television is a powerful means of seducing voters to vote for *images* of candidates rather than the candidates themselves. Or, as one Nixon staffer put it: "This is the beginning of a whole new concept. . . . This is the way they'll be elected forevermore. The next guys up will have to be performers."[1]

This proved to be a prescient statement indeed, for in 1980 a seasoned movie and television personality was swept into office and reelected by a landslide in 1984. Moreover, he managed to retain his *personal* popularity, despite the fact that public opinion polls indicated most Americans felt he was not doing a good job. As this fortieth president of the United States put it, "Politics is just like show business, you have a hell of an opening, coast for a while and then have a hell of a close."[2]

When Nixon's staffer made his prediction, he was referring specifically to a television program that was arranged to look as though candidate Nixon was spontaneously answering questions phoned in by voters. In reality, he was giving carefully rehearsed answers to questions prepared by his staff. When a voter asked a question on the telephone, Nixon's staff simply reworded it in the form of a prepared question, attributed the question to the voter, and allowed Nixon to recite his prepared answer. And Nixon and his supporters continued to stage such events throughout his presidency. For example, on November 3, 1969, amidst growing protests against the Vietnam war, Nixon gave his famed "silent majority" speech, calling on the great silent majority of Americans to support him and dismiss anti-war demonstrators. After the speech, Nixon received 50,000 favorable telegrams and 30,000 letters of support from what seemed to be that silent majority. Three decades later the truth came out: According to Nixon aide Alexander Butterfield, those telegrams and letters were manufactured. Before the speech, Butterfield had contacted several operatives and arranged for them to send in the letters and telegrams.[3] Three decades later, the technique of staged events is still used by politicians. For example, in the 1996 and 2000 U.S. presidential elections, both parties staged "nominating" conventions that looked more like coronations than a debate over who was best qualified to lead this nation.

When McGinness's book appeared, many people were shocked and appalled at what they considered to be unethical and dishonest behavior. On the other hand, the overwhelming majority of voters either did not care or thought Nixon's deceptiveness was merely an indication that he was a clever, shrewd politician. Richard Nixon's popularity remained high throughout his first term in office, and in 1972 he was reelected in one of the most lopsided landslides in the nation's history, despite the fact that, at the time, it was known that a group of individuals financed by the Committee to Reelect the President had been caught breaking into the offices of the Democratic National Committee in a building called Watergate.

How extensive is the use of advertising to create seductive images of political candidates? According to Kathleen Hall Jamieson, U.S. presidential candidates have always tried to create images of themselves that would appeal to voters, at least since the 1828 victory of Andrew Jackson over John Quincy Adams.[4] However, it was not until 1952, when Dwight D. Eisenhower hired as key campaign advisors two ad agencies (BBDO and Young & Rubicam) and received volunteer help from a third (the famed advertiser Rosser Reeves of the Ted Bates agency), that professional ad agencies were used extensively in presidential campaigns. Today ad agencies, political pollsters, and media consultants are a common political fixture and can be found in the highest echelon of political advisors.

How effective are media advisors in electing a candidate? Nixon's victory in 1968 could be interpreted as indicating that such deceptive programming was effective in spite of its blatant manipulativeness. On the other hand, one astute observer, John Kenneth Galbraith, has commented that Nixon may have won in

". . . And I plan to go forward with the help of you, the voters, my family, my campaign staff, and, last but certainly not least, my advertising agency."

1968 in spite of these devices. Jamieson offers another perspective: Spending a large amount of money does not guarantee success in a campaign; success depends on how *well* you spend it. If you are fortunate enough to have a large wad of cash to spend, it will not insure your election unless, according to Jamieson, you use it to run a campaign that presents a clear, consistent image of your candidacy and an appealing vision for the nation. Obviously, if you don't have a big bankroll, you are going to have a difficult time presenting any image, much less a consistent one, and, needless to say, you will be at a disadvantage. For example, the typical winner of a seat in the U.S. Senate spends

$3.4 million (compared to $1.9 million for the loser) and the typical winner of a seat in the House of Representatives spends $410,000 (compared to $200,000 for the loser).[5]

And, of course, image consultants are not just limited to the political arena. For example, Amway, a manufacturer of home products sold directly to the consumer, tells its new soap detergent sales agents always to appear in public in their best clothes—coat and tie or dress—even if they are just going to the corner grocery. You never know whom you will meet, they are cautioned, and you should always maintain your image.[6]

The historian Daniel Boorstin has called attention to the use of pseudo-events to create celebrities and sensations.[7] A pseudo-event is a planned event for the immediate purpose of being reported by the news media—for example, a presidential photo-op with a veterans' group or staged hysteria for the Wonderbra. A celebrity is a person who is only known for being well known, such as Fabio or Dr. Joyce Brothers or Kato Kaelin. How do you become a celebrity and a sensation in your own time? Simply create your own pseudo-event that will get you into the news.

And don't worry if you are charged with a heinous crime such as murder. For the right amount of money, your image problems can be fixed. Before taking the O. J. Simpson case, trial lawyer Robert Shapiro had developed a detailed strategy for managing the public image of his clients.[8] Some of his advice: Develop a relationship with reporters, make sure your client looks good on TV, choose the setting for your interviews, and limit your comments about the trial to a few, select soundbites that promote your client's cause. It appears both sides in the Simpson trial were well schooled in the art of public relations.

Even the credibility of a fabric can be manufactured.[9] By the early 1980s, polyester had acquired the image of being "tacky," "in bad taste," and "unnatural," and it was the butt of frequent jokes. No problem for PR expert Mary Trudel, who was hired by manufacturers such as du Pont and Monsanto to turn the image around. A series of events were staged to put polyester on a positive footing—the 1987 winner of the Miss America pageant toured the country in a synthetic wardrobe; press releases were used to stimulate newspaper stories, such as "Beyond Leisure Suits: New Life for Polyester"; and a touch test was arranged for fashion designers that convinced Pierre Cardin, Calvin Klein, and others to start using more polyester in their clothes. Although most of us probably still feel negatively about polyester, it is appearing in our clothes (courtesy of clothes designers) and we probably don't have as negative a reaction to its variants, such as Lycra.

But, to return to the world of selling political candidates rather than criminals or synthetic fabrics, suppose you did have a sufficient wad of cash and you aspired to elected office, whom could you hire and what could they do for you? You'd want to hire a public relations expert such as Roger Ailes, who served as advisor to both the Reagan and Bush campaigns and is now chair and CEO of Fox News. Or maybe you could employ Robert Dilenschneider, former CEO of the PR firm of Hill and Knowlton who has given advice to such entities as Metropolitan Edison on how to handle public reactions to the Three Mile Island incident, the Chilean government on how to calm fears about a scare that their grapes were laced with cyanide, and Columbia University on how to deal with the student protests of the 1960s. And if you are really lucky, you can hire the Spin Doctors in Love—the husband and wife team of James Carville (he's a Democrat and has helped elect Governor Robert Casey, Senator Harris Wofford, and President Bill Clinton) and Mary Matalin (she's a Republican and has worked on the Ronald Reagan and George Bush presidential campaigns). What advice would you receive?

According to Ailes, a great speaker has one major characteristic. As he puts it:

> If you could master one element of personal communications that is more powerful than anything we've discussed, it is the quality of being *likable*. I call it the magic bullet, because if your audience likes you, they'll forgive just about everything else you do wrong. If they don't like you, you can hit every rule right on target and it doesn't matter.[10]

Some of Ailes's specific advice for making yourself likable: Say what the audience thinks (which you can find out through polling), make others feel comfortable, and control the atmosphere (the situation) for your best advantage.

Here is some of the general advice Dilenschneider gives in his best-selling book, *Power and Influence*, for increasing your credibility:[11] Set easy initial goals and then declare victory (this will create the perception that you are a strong leader); use setting to support image (for example, Reagan designed his presidential podium to look powerful but soft and understated; interviews should be done in settings that fit the message); choose the negatives that will be written about you (most journalists seek a balanced report; provide the reporter with negatives that you can then refute and thus look good); and understand how people see things, then appeal to what they prefer.

Matalin and Carville have some advice, too.[12] Why not float an idea (a tax cut, a health care proposal) without attribution (that is, circulate it as a rumor)? If everyone likes the idea, then claim it as your own. If it gets shot down, then deny your campaign ever said it. In this manner, you can always be sure to say exactly what everyone wants to hear. Another piece of advice: Make sure you appear consistent in the media. And the best way to do this? Just say a few things over and over again (that way, you don't contradict yourself). For example, in a focus group held during the 1992 election, the major complaint about Bill Clinton was that he appeared to be inconsistent and willing to say anything to get votes. Carville's recommendation, which Clinton followed, was to stick to a basic theme (a different kind of Democrat) and state it repeatedly. The result: Clinton appeared more consistent in the latter part of the campaign. And finally, don't lie to the press, but do feel free to manipulate the media. For example, in the 1986 gubernatorial race in Pennsylvania, Democratic candidate (and Carville's boss) Robert Casey made a statement that he would not make his opponent's— Republican William Scranton III—admission that he had smoked pot in the 1960s a campaign issue. However, as we have seen in recent U.S. presidential elections, drug use by a candidate is too juicy a campaign issue to pass up. So what is a Carville to do? Simple. Circulate a rumor that the campaign is preparing an ad on Scranton's use of drugs. The news media cover the rumor and talk about Scranton's drug use, and the Casey campaign denies everything. Carville and Casey are double winners—Scranton has to defend himself in the media, and Casey appears to have taken the high ground.[13]

The advice of Ailes, Dilenschneider, Matalin, and Carville is a far cry from Aristotle's prescription that a communicator be of good character. Credibility is manufactured, not earned. Credibility is created by carefully managing the situation so that the star of the event, the communicator, looks just the way he or she is supposed to look—likable, credible, strong, expert, or whatever image is needed at the time. Once the image is created in the form of a celebrity or a politician, then it can be bought and sold like a commodity to advance any cause that has the resources to purchase the "rights" to the image.

The manufacture of credibility can lead to a cult of personality. Instead of thinking about important issues for ourselves, we turn to credible-looking leaders for their solutions. This strategy would make some sense if the people we turn to do indeed possess the required expertise. Sadly, it is often the case that "credibility" has been subtly manufactured and sold for propaganda purposes. And the media often serve as handmaidens in this charade. Consider, for example, the post-debate "analyses" served up by many of the TV network pundits, who, instead of talking about the issues, seem to prefer to discuss such superficialities as which candidate "looked more presidential" or appeared to handle complex issues "more adroitly." Such reporting contributes to the cult of personality and promotes propaganda at the expense of careful and deliberate persuasion. The image becomes far more important than the substance.

16

Prizefighter Slays Eleven with One Look: The Influence of Mass Media Models

The checkout stand at the local supermarket is lined with newspapers claiming to have "the largest circulation of any paper in America" and to be "America's fastest-growing weekly." Recent issues have contained prophecies to take us well into the new millennium.[1] The psychics predict that a freak change in world weather will bring torrential rains to the Sahara Desert; Oprah Winfrey will dump her boyfriend and start dating Chris Darden, the O. J. Simpson prosecutor; a tunnel under the Hudson River will suddenly rupture and flood; genetic engineers will isolate the "compass gene" that directs spawning salmon to the place of their birth and will use the discovery to help dogs and cats find their way home. Of course, it is doubtful that many of these predictions will come to pass.*

However, there is a sociologist at the University of California at San Diego named David Phillips who can, with remarkable accuracy, foretell some striking future events.[2] Phillips's latest startling prediction: Within four days of the next nationally televised heavyweight championship prizefight, at least eleven innocent U.S. citizens who would not otherwise have died will be murdered in cold blood. The reason: People learn from the behavior of those they see and admire on television.

Here's how Phillips came to make his startling prediction. He first gathered an exhaustive list of past heavyweight championship prizefights and examined the fluctuation of daily homicide rates before and after each fight. After correcting for the influence of seasons, days of week, holidays, and other trends, he discovered that homicide rates rose significantly on the third and fourth days after the fights. Sadly, homicide rates did not decrease at any time after the fight to compensate for the immediate effects of the bout. Thus one can safely conclude that most (if not all) of these eleven murdered individuals would still be alive had there not been a publicized prizefight.

---

* Here are the predictions from the first edition of Age of Propaganda made by psychics for the early 1990s: Princess Di will divorce Charles to become a nun; a mysterious virus will turn Barbara Bush's hair bright red; a meteorite will plow into the White House Rose Garden; Mikhail Gorbachev will buy a beach home near the Reagans in Bel-Air, California; the AIDS virus will be shown to have been developed by religious fanatics as a plot to wipe out gays; deep-sea explorers will discover a sunken Spanish galleon full of gold and artifacts from an alien spaceship. Only "half" of one of these predictions has come to pass, and one didn't need to be a psychic to predict it: Princess Diana did get a divorce, but she did not sign up for a nunnery before her untimely death (which was not predicted by the psychics). The other predictions failed to materialize—at least, not yet! But we have our eye on Barbara Bush's hair.

What is even more haunting about Phillips's research is that the type of person killed just after a prizefight is likely to be similar to the fighter beaten in the bout. That is, if a young black male was beaten, then murders of young black (but not white) males increased. Similarly, if a young white male was beaten, more young white (but not black) males were murdered. Furthermore, the effects of prizefights on homicides increased with the amount of fight publicity: The more people who knew about the fight, the greater the number of homicides.

Phillips has found that mass media models can influence other behavior as well. In March 1986, four teenagers in New Jersey made a suicide pact and then carried out their plan. Within a week of this multiple suicide, two teenagers in the Midwest were found dead under similar circumstances. Media reports no doubt spotlighted the confusion and grief surrounding teenage suicide. But did the media's coverage of these tragedies actually inspire copycat suicides? According to Phillips, the answer is a qualified "yes."

How can he be sure? Phillips and his colleagues studied suicide rates among teenagers following network television news or feature stories about suicide. Their research tracked fluctuations in teenage suicides by comparing suicide rates before the stories with rates after the stories. Within a week of the broadcasts, the increase in teenage suicides was far greater than could be explained by chance alone. Furthermore, the more coverage major television networks devoted to suicide, the greater the subsequent increase in suicides among teenagers. These increases held even when the researchers took other possible causes into account. Thus the most likely explanation for the increase in teenage suicides following media publicity is that such publicity actually triggers subsequent copycat suicides in a process similar to the copycat poisoning scare of the 1980s triggered after seven people died from taking Tylenol laced with cyanide.

More recently, we have witnessed a string of school slayings in places such as Pearl, Mississippi; West Paducah, Kentucky; Jonesboro, Arkansas; Edinboro, Pennsylvania; Fayetteville, Tennessee; Springfield, Oregon; Conyers, Georgia; and Littleton, Colorado (in a school called Columbine). Each of these tragedies was covered in depth by the news media; often, the killings were broadcast live in real time to a watching, horrified nation.

Although these news reports most certainly conveyed the anguish of these slayings, they also conveyed one other fact of life: Murdering your classmates can get you national attention and is one way of dealing with life's problems.

The effects of mass media models on violence and other social behaviors have been known for almost four decades. In the early 1960s, the noted psychologist Albert Bandura began an extensive laboratory program looking at television models and aggression.[3] In a typical study, children would watch, on a television monitor, an adult beating a Bobo doll—a large, plastic doll with a weight at the base. When punched, the doll falls backwards and then springs upright. In the Bandura-produced television show, models would punch, kick, fling, hit with a mallet, and scream at a Bobo doll. The children would then have the opportunity to play with various attractive toys, including a Bobo doll. The results repeatedly showed that children were likely to do what they had previously seen; those exposed to the violent model were more likely to strike, hit, punch, kick, and fling the Bobo doll.

Much subsequent research supports Bandura's initial findings. Aggressive models have been shown to influence the aggression of both males and females, children and adults; to influence behavior in and out of the laboratory; and to teach aggression regardless of whether the model is a cartoon character or a real person and whether the aggression is an isolated act or part of a complex plot, such as a television crime story. Watching aggressive models has led people to kick a Bobo doll, electrically shock a classmate, verbally assault a stranger, and harm a small animal.[4] Strikingly, one of the first TV advertisements directed at children appeared on "The Mickey Mouse Club" and offered for sale the Burp gun, a cap-firing machine gun developed by Mattel to look like machine guns used in World War II. Before Christmas 1955, Mattel sold more than 1 million Burp guns; the company quickly followed with a line of toy .45 six-shooters like those wielded in Westerns so that children could pretend to kill their friends just like they saw on TV.[5]

Fortunately, modeling works in two directions; that is, the power of mass media models can also be used to teach pro-social behavior. For example, social models have been used to increase people's likelihood of helping a stranded motorist with a flat tire and to increase the amount of donations dropped into a Salvation Army kettle.[6] Similarly, models have been used to teach nonviolent responses and to lower levels of aggression in a violent situation.[7]

However, teaching is not the same as preaching; models persuade far more effectively than words. In a series of insightful studies, James Bryan and his colleagues exposed children to adult models who *preached* either greed or charity or *practiced* either greed or charity.[8] The results: Children were more influenced by what the model *did* than what the model *said*. This finding takes on increased importance in an era when the mayor of Washington, D.C., lectures children about the evils of drugs and subsequently is caught using cocaine, when piety-pandering politicians preach family values and sexual abstinence and then commit repeated acts of adultery while complaining about the adultery of others, or when televangelists engage in illicit sexual behavior or pocket money from the collection plate.

The power of models to persuade has not been lost on advertisers. Thirty-second spots are full of chubby people losing weight with the right diet aid; housewives impressing their husbands with clean houses brought about by an advertised cleanser; boyfriends and girlfriends being rewarded with love, affection, and prestige for just one smile polished by a special toothpaste; young couples achieving the good life with the use of a major credit card; Barbie dolls dressed in the latest fashions. These models do more than just sell products; they also reinforce values (e.g., thin is good) and teach lifestyles (e.g., housewives should be husband pleasers, the road to success for little girls is through fashion and physical attractiveness, the good life can be obtained with a quick fix such as a diet pill).

Politicians use models, too. One effective technique is to create a *bandwagon* effect—the impression that everyone is for the candidate. Politicians do this by staging large rallies attended by what appears to be a multitude of supporters in the hopes of convincing the as-yet-uncommitted voter. Success in the polls— an indication of popular support—is essential if the candidate hopes to secure campaign contributions.

Mass media models are effective for two primary reasons. First, they teach new behavior. For example, a young child learns the "specifics" of how to shoot and kill a "suspect" by watching television crime shows such as "NYPD Blue" or "Power Rangers." A newly married couple discovers that the good life can be purchased on credit by watching others on television use a credit card. A teenager gleans the mystique of committing suicide or killing classmates from a news report.

Of course, just because someone *knows how* does not necessarily mean that he or she will *do it*. Most of us know how to beam someone down to the surface of an alien planet from watching "Star Trek" or to protect Superman from kryptonite by using a lead shield, but it is unlikely we will ever engage in such behavior. What, then, causes us to behave like our media models? One important factor is that we believe the rewards received by a model for a given behavior will also come to us. That is why advertisers often use models "just like us" and place them in familiar situations such as at home, work, school, or the supermarket.

This brings us to the second reason why mass media models are persuasive: They serve as a cue to indicate that a certain behavior is *legitimate* and *appropriate*. After watching a prizefight, it appears to be OK to "punch someone's lights out"; hearing about a teenage suicide or a schoolhouse murder suggests that this may be a reasonable way to deal with life's problems or that those who have wronged us will now be forced to grieve for us or will now be dead; watching a housewife mop the floor convinces us that this is an appropriate lifestyle for women (but not necessarily for men). A steady diet of mass media models can shape and twist our understanding of what is right and wrong with the world.

Let's take a closer look at the Columbine High School incident. On April 20, 1999, Dylan Klebold and Eric Harris murdered fifteen of their classmates and seriously wounded another twenty-three. The death toll could have been much worse. Klebold and Harris had rigged a number of bombs that fortunately failed to detonate. The Columbine tragedy came on the heels of seven other similar school slayings—all of which had been well publicized in the mass media. Did the coverage of these previous school slayings lead Klebold and Harris to murder their classmates? It is not that simple to answer. The social reality of Columbine, like many schools, was one of winners (athletes, class officers, cheerleaders) and losers (nerds, Goths, shy loners) who, like Klebold and Harris, are often tormented, bullied, and ridiculed by others. Being a teen is hard enough. Being a teen who is tormented, bullied, and ridiculed by classmates cries out for a solution. In this context, TV violence, along with the ubiquity of violent video games, prescriptions for bomb making on the Internet, and news coverage of schoolmates killing schoolmates, teaches not only how to kill but that killing can be a legitimate and appropriate way to resolve a problem. What can be done? Quite obviously we can reduce our intake of violent mass media models. But this doesn't go far enough. We also need to attack the source of frustrations by offering our children more pro-social ways to deal with their problems by teaching empathy and conflict resolution and by making our schools a more compassionate place by actively reducing bullying and by instilling norms of cooperation. (Recently, one of us [E. A.] has written a book on the massacre at Columbine High that describes these prescriptions in more detail.[9])

What characteristics make a mass media model *most* persuasive? The accumulation of much research shows that a model is most effective when he or she is high in prestige, power, and status, is rewarded for performing the behavior to be learned, provides useful information on how to perform the behavior, and is personally attractive and competent in facing life's problems. In other words, the model is a credible and attractive source. Think for a moment about an advertisement that uses models to persuade. We bet that the people in these ads possess most, if not all, of these attributes.[10]

The immediate persuasiveness of mass media models is clearly known by professional persuaders, although the subtle, but nonetheless important, effects of such models are often ignored by everyone. For example, if it were known that in three or four days eleven people would die, perhaps trapped underground, perhaps at the hands of foreign terrorists, the nation would mobilize. The major networks would send camera crews and reporters. CNN would carry around-the-clock coverage. The story would dominate the front pages of newspapers. The person who predicted such an event would become an overnight celebrity, being asked to appear on the Leno and Letterman shows, invited to give his or her opinions on morning talk shows, and, perhaps, become a regular pundit asked to comment by the news media on every conceivable issue facing or not facing this nation.

But Phillips's prediction is *not* about eleven people whom the nation will come to know personally by media coverage of the event. The eleven people who will be murdered as a result of the next publicized prizefight will be, for the most part, nameless faces known only to their loved ones. They will die not in exotic places or lands but in their own neighborhoods. They will not die of supernatural causes, of a freak accident of nature, or at the hands of a ruthless dictator. Indeed, the cause of their deaths will not be known immediately, if at all. But they will certainly die, and they will die as a result of the simple fact that mass media models are persuasive.

The Message and
How It Is Delivered

Packages

The cereal aisle at the local supermarket is the battleground for many a weekly war of words. The battle usually goes something like this: Seven-year-old Rachel spots her favorite cereal, Lucky Charms, picks up a box from the shelf and quietly delivers it to the shopping cart. Her mom looks at the box in disgust. It is bright red. A leprechaun is sprinkling shining stars (must be sugar) over pink and purple marshmallow bits. On the back of the box she reads that a special pair of glasses is enclosed to be used in spotting hidden leprechauns.

Mom sternly announces, "Rachel, put that junk back on the shelf. It's loaded with sugar and nothing but empty calories."

Rachel replies, "But mom, it tastes good. The other stuff tastes yukky."

Being a smart woman, mom offers Rachel another choice and a little inducement, "Why not this one? It's 100% Natural. It's good for you. You'll be a big girl."

Rachel looks at the box. It is small, but heavy. The front features a bowl of light brown cereal set against a wood-grain background and a couple of stalks of unprocessed grains. On the back of the box is a lot of small print.

Rachel exclaims, "Yukko! I don't want to be a big girl."

How would you resolve the great breakfast cereal standoff? Would you side with the mother and opt for nutrition even though Rachel may not eat it? Or would you feel that Rachel, even at this young age, should be making her own decisions regardless of the consequences? Our recommendation may surprise you. The fight is for naught. Tell Rachel and her mom to buy the Lucky Charms because, quite truthfully, it is more nutritional than the "natural" cereal.

Every year Americans spend roughly $6.9 billion on breakfast cereals. *Consumer Reports*, a highly respected source of consumer information, conducted a test of some of these breakfast cereals.[1] Their researchers fed young rats, which have nutritional requirements remarkably similar to humans, an exclusive diet of water and one of thirty-two brands of breakfast cereals for a period of fourteen to eighteen weeks. They found that the rats grew and remained quite healthy on a diet of such cereals as Cheerios, Grape-Nuts, Life, Shredded Wheat, and Lucky Charms. On the other hand, fifteen ready-to-eat cereals such as Captain Crunch, Corn Flakes, Product 19, and Quaker's 100% Natural either prevented the rats from growing or were judged to be not sufficiently nourishing to support life.

A comparison between Lucky Charms and 100% Natural shows that Lucky Charms is lower in calories but slightly higher in sodium and sugar than 100% Natural, although the differences probably do not matter very much. However, 100% Natural, like many granola-style cereals, is higher in saturated fats, which raise blood cholesterol levels. Whereas Lucky Charms contains no saturated fat, a cup of 100% Natural is equivalent in fat content to about half a rack of greasy beef ribs. (Recently the maker of 100% Natural announced a low-fat version, which has slightly more than a quarter of the fat of the original version).[2]

What caused the disagreement between Rachel and her mom? It is clear that they used the cereal package (not the cereal) as what is technically called a *heuristic*—a simple cue or rule for solving a problem. In this case, the problem for mom was to select a nutritious cereal; for Rachel the problem was to get a cereal that is fun and tasty. The bright colors, the cartoon character, and the kids' game on the box of Lucky Charms suggest that this cereal is for kids—and we all know that kids' food is junk food. On the other hand, the earth tones and pictures of unprocessed grains on the 100% Natural box indicate that this cereal is "all natural" (even the brand name agrees). Nature is good and wholesome; this cereal must be nutritious. In both cases, the cereal packages were designed so that Rachel and her mom would infer certain attributes about the products—qualities that may or may not be present. Armed with these conclusions, the choice of which cereal to purchase can proceed without much additional thought; persuasion occurs in the peripheral route.

It appears that just about anything can be sold to the American public simply by placing the label "natural" on it—cereal, alternative medicines, juices, vitamins, soft drinks, ice cream, junk food such as potato chips and popcorn seasoned with fatty cheese, overpriced vegetables, and now even cigarettes. In an attempt to appeal to "health-conscious" smokers, manufacturers have developed new brands of cigarettes—American Spirit, Buz, Born Free, and Sherman's—that claim to be 100% additive-free and all natural.[3] The logic (if you want to call it that) is that the manufacturers of mass-marketed cigarettes use more than 700 chemical additives, some of which are toxic. An all-natural cigarette supposedly gives a purer, cleaner smoke. Reminiscent of the cigarette ads of the 1940s claiming that smoking built lung capacity, one brand of herbal cigarettes actually claims to be good for you—an effective remedy for asthma, various lung problems, and nervousness. And many smokers and would-be smokers are buying the pitch. Sales of "natural" cigarettes have grown by 60% to 90% over the last ten years to a $50-million market. The "natural" appeal worked so well that R. J. Reynolds adopted it for its Winston brand, touting the cigarette as additive-free. The ads claim: "I get enough bull at work. I don't need to smoke it." And the sales skyrocketed. Health professionals are astonished by the gullibility of the American public and are alarmed by the claims. The simple truth of the matter is that cigarettes of all types are loaded with toxins and carcinogens that can kill you. Smoking natural cigarettes is like asking a murderer to make sure the bullet is clean before using it to kill you. Indeed, the FTC ruled that Winston's "no-additive claim" was deceptive, implying

". . . Or do you think we should go with this one?"

that the cigarette was less harmful than others. As a result, R. J. Reynolds includes this disclaimer in its "no bull" ads: "No additives in our tobacco does not mean a safer cigarette."

Marketers have been using packages to guide consumer decision making for nearly a century. Since the 1890s, Quaker Oats has been boxing rolled oats in a container with a picture of a religious Quaker to suggest the purity and consistency of their breakfast cereal. In 1898 a man named C. W. Post reinforced the image of a healthy breakfast food by enclosing a copy of the pamphlet "The Road to Wellville" in each box of Grape-Nuts cereal. Sales took off. Packaging is such a successful heuristic device that generic and store brands often try to take advantage of it by making their packages—the color of their labels, the shape of the container, and so on—resemble the bestselling national brands.

Other heuristics are also used to encourage consumers to infer product quality and thus buy a particular brand. Three of the most important are price, store image, and brand name. Each heuristic comes with its own rules for inferring product quality. For example, the higher the price, the better the quality—which is probably true when it comes to such products as Yugos and

Rolls Royces but is not necessarily the case for wines, medicines, sport sneakers, prepackaged foods, and a host of other products. The same pair of jeans looks better in a high-class department store than in the local discount mart. Nationally recognized brand names are automatically deemed superior to store brands and generics. In addition, advertisers spend vast sums of money to link their brand name to a brand-specific proposition, such as "Michelob is classy" or "Bud is for the everyday working Joe," to guide our supermarket visit.

Persons can be packaged, too. The first information that we typically pick up about a person—gender, age, race, physical attractiveness, and social status—is usually associated with simple rules and stereotypes that guide thought and behavior. Gender and racial stereotypes tell us "just how men and women differ" and "what a particular member of an ethnic group is like." Much research has demonstrated that beautiful people are assumed to be more successful, more sensitive, warmer, and of better character than less physically appealing persons and that we often act in accord with those assumptions. Persons of high social stature, which is often inferred from their dress and mannerisms, are respected and held in high esteem. Is it any wonder that "get-ahead" self-help books often describe how to take advantage of these heuristics by urging their readers to "dress for success," that is, to wear the *right* clothes to create the *right* image or to use the *right* cosmetics to enhance their attractiveness?

Heuristics can also be used to judge whether a persuasive communication is worthy of acceptance and belief. In the previous section of this book, we looked in detail at one such heuristic—the source of the message. We saw that, in general, the more credible, attractive, or expert the source, the more effective is the communication; we also saw that we are more likely to use the source to guide our opinions if we are operating in the peripheral, as opposed to central, route of persuasion.

There are other persuasion heuristics. For example, the advertisers John Caples and David Ogilvy argue that advertisements are most effective when they contain long, compelling copy—in other words, a long message with many arguments. Obviously, such a message would be more effective than a short message containing weak arguments—*if the message is read*. But what about cases where the message is only skimmed or not read at all? According to research in social psychology, when people are not thinking very carefully about an issue, long messages, regardless of whether they contain weak or strong arguments, are most persuasive.[4] It appears that we operate on the principle that "message length *equals* message strength." If the message is long, it must be strong.

If you have watched an infomercial, those half-hour "shows" that feature knives, blenders, political candidates, cleansers, and sandwich makers for sale, you have seen another persuasion cue in action. These shows inevitably feature a "daring" demonstration of the product—a knife cutting up an old tennis shoe and then slicing a tomato perfectly, a blender making mayonnaise from scratch, or a magic powder removing a difficult stain. What is the audience's reaction? At first there is murmuring, as disbelief fills the air with tension. And then the audience, acting as one, bursts into loud, thunderous applause.

The thunderous clapping and cheering serves as a *social consensus* heuristic—a cue that says, "Everyone accepts the conclusion of this message, so you should, too!" This technique was employed in the nineteenth century by the sellers of patent medicines, who would plant shills in the audience to pretend to be cured of an affliction and to sing the praises of whatever product was for sale. Recognition of the power of the applause-makes-right heuristic leads politicians to schedule major talks in favorable settings, television producers to insert canned laughter and applause, advertisers to use testimonials and portray their products as being in great demand. Once again, the evidence shows, social consensus heuristics are most likely to have an impact when people are unmotivated to think about a message's meaning.[5]

Another common persuasion heuristic is based on the confidence of the speaker—the more self-assured and confident a communicator appears, the more likely that we will accept what is said. Research on trial testimony in courts of law, for example, has found that juries are more likely to believe testimony when it is given by an eyewitness or expert who exudes confidence. Similarly, nonverbal behavior that suggests confidence in the message, such as a low rate of speech errors, an authoritative tone of voice, and a steady body posture, are positively related to persuasion.[6] For example, many jurors from the O. J. Simpson trial noted in post-trial interviews that prosecutor Marcia Clark showed signs of stress and frustration; she would often sigh and make gestures with her hands as though she was throwing in the towel. All of this undermined her credibility with the jury. As one juror put it, "It made me think; Well, if your case is so strong, why are you so frustrated?"[7]

Still another frequently used persuasion tactic is to load a speech with the "correct" symbols and buzzwords as a means of informing the recipient that the message is acceptable and worthwhile. For example, car dealers and politicians often appear with the flag or invoke God, as if to say, "My position is patriotic and religious, so it is worthy of acceptance." Of course, history reveals that just about any scoundrel can wrap him- or herself in the flag—as often for personal profit as for the nation's best interest.

Often the symbols and buzzwords are tailored to a specific audience. For example, one craze popular on college campuses and in liberal groups is "PC"—political correctness. PC is a fast-changing set of symbols, phrases, and actions that, when properly used, lets everyone know that the message is right and the communicator is doing the right thing. To gain acceptance, one should not wear fur in public; one should always say "he or she"—never the generic "he"; one should eat free-range chicken, not formula-fed, assembly-line chicken; one should never eat veal; one should use cloth, not disposable, diapers; one should demand paper bags at the grocery store, never accepting plastic ones; one should claim to be boycotting certain brands or products; and above all, one should not be critical of PC.

Never mind that some of the rules are contradictory and ineffective. For example, if fur is unacceptable, why not forgo leather? Careful analysis shows that paper bags, unless they are recycled, produce more environmental waste than plastic, and that cloth diapers result in more pollution in their manufacturing and cleaning than do disposables and greatly disadvantage working and single parents. But that is the nature of heuristics—they aren't meant to be thought about, lest they appear as silly as applauding a sliced tomato.

Consider the case of McDonald's.[8] In the early 1970s, environmentalists launched a campaign criticizing McDonald's for its use of paperboard packaging. Ray Kroc, McDonald's founder, commissioned the Stanford Research Institute to conduct a study comparing the environmental impact of different forms of packaging. The study concluded that when all aspects of the issue were considered—from manufacturing to disposal—polystyrene is better for the environment than paper. When paper and cardboard are used to package food, they must be coated with a plastic film, making them nearly unrecyclable. The manufacture of polystyrene uses less energy and conserves more natural resources than does the production of paper, and polystyrene takes up less room in landfill and is recyclable. The infamous McDonald's clamshell was born.

In the 1980s, environmentalists raised another, quite legitimate, concern: the manufacturing of polystyrene releases chlorofluorocarbons, which contribute to the destruction of the ozone layer. In 1987, McDonald's directed its polystyrene suppliers to eliminate the release of chlorofluorocarbons from their manufacturing process. However, the clamshell had become a symbol of environmental irresponsibility and McDonald's, in response to pressure groups, ceased using it in the early 1990s, returning to unrecyclable, plastic-coated paper wrappers. Ironically, McDonald's image of being "concerned about the environment" has suffered because it was responsive to environmental concerns. One of McDonald's competitors, which had not responded to earlier pressures to adopt the clamshell, actually ran ads claiming that they had always used cardboard out of concern for the environment. In truth, many American households and businesses would find it difficult to compete with McDonald's record on the environment. McDonald's earmarks 25% of its capital budget ($100 million) for purchasing recycled building materials (thus helping to create this industry), allocates $60 million to purchase recycled paper products, and developed forty-two initiatives aimed at holding down the volume of garbage at its restaurants by more than 80%. The destruction of the environment is a complex problem, requiring more than just symbolic finger-pointing and heuristic thinking to resolve.

Of course, as we have stressed earlier, persuasion does not have to be peripheral and decisions do not have to be based on heuristics. Rachel's parents could carefully read the ingredients on the cereal box, subscribe to a consumer magazine, or consult nutrition textbooks. Similarly, we could base our judgment of what a politician is saying not on buzzwords, audience reactions, and source demeanor but on the actual content and implications of the message itself.

This raises an important question: What conditions are most likely to lead to heuristic rather than rational decision making? Research has identified at least five such conditions.[9] Heuristics are most likely to be used when we do not have *time to think* carefully about an issue, when we are so *overloaded with information* that it becomes impossible to process it fully, or when we believe that the issues at stake are *not very important*. Heuristics are also used when we have *little other knowledge or information* on which to base a decision and when a given heuristic *comes quickly to mind* as we are confronted with a problem.

A moment's thought will reveal that the persuasion landscape faced by Rachel and her parents contains many of the features that lead to heuristic decision making. If they are like most Americans, Rachel and her family are feeling increasingly pressed for time. As consumers, they face a message-dense environment complete with a choice of, for example, more than 300 different brands of cereal currently on the market. They probably have had little consumer education or training. They have been, however, the recipients of millions of advertisements, each repeating and repeating a brand image, so that this image will quickly come to mind in the aisles of the local supermarket. Given this state of affairs, it is a wonder that *all* decisions are not made heuristically.

 One of the dilemmas of modern life is that with increasing time pressures, increasing amounts of information, and an increasing number of choices, we must rely more and more on heuristic decision making. Although relying on heuristics is sometimes a useful way of dealing with the onslaught of the message-dense, decision-rich environment, basing our decisions primarily on heuristics can present some problems.[10]

First, the heuristic cues that we possess may be false. There is little reason to assume that brand images and ethnic stereotypes have a reliable basis in fact. Relying on such heuristics may result in the purchase of an unwanted product and the missed opportunity to hire a qualified employee or fall in love with that special person. Furthermore, a rule may be appropriate in certain situations but be misapplied in others. For example, spontaneous, legitimate audience applause can signal that this is an entertaining show worthy of our attention. Canned laughter does not.

Another serious problem is that heuristics can be easily faked and manipulated. Cereal boxes can be redesigned to look increasingly wholesome. Laughter and applause can be dubbed into a broadcast. Politicians can be coached to exude winning mannerisms. Physical attractiveness can be improved with makeup and surgery. Speeches and advertisements can be peppered with buzzwords and symbols. Anyone with a little cash can buy a new blazer and a sincere tie. The essence of propaganda is a well-designed package.

What can be done to lessen our dependence on faulty heuristics? One way to address these concerns would be to enact legislation to ensure that the cues that we do use—for example, phrases on product labels such as "low-calorie," "low-sodium," or "100% nutritious"—are accurate and are applied correctly. The Federal Trade Commission has established guidelines for the use of some labels, such as "low-fat" and "lower calories." (The term "natural" is not included in these guidelines because the FTC found it nearly impossible to define. In addition, just because something is supposedly natural doesn't mean it is good to eat; mistletoe berries are 100% natural and eating them will kill you.) This, along with other efforts to improve the quality of product information, is a step in the right direction. However, such efforts are unlikely to succeed in stamping out heuristic thinking. After all, no government, no matter how vigilant, can protect us from our own prejudices. In the long run, we must depend on our own knowledge of propaganda tactics and our own efforts to treat important issues as if they truly are important.

18

Self-Sell

World War II was a war not only of bombs and bullets but of words and propaganda as well. The Nazi's propaganda offensive was first outlined by Adolf Hitler in *Mein Kampf* and then executed by Joseph Goebbels and his Ministry of Propaganda. The United States relied on a loose collection of social psychologists and other social scientists to develop its campaign, to boost the nation's morale, and to diffuse the impact of Nazi propaganda.

One of the unlikely combatants in this propaganda war was the U.S. Department of Agriculture's Committee on Food Habits, headed in part by the famed anthropologist Margaret Mead. Its mission during the wartime emergency was to maintain the health of the American people despite shortages of certain types of high-protein foods. One specific project was to increase the consumption of meat products that, in the United States, had often been thrown away or used as pet food—meats such as beef hearts, kidneys, and intestines. To do so, the committee made use of a tactic that is now ubiquitous in attempts at persuasion.

Any parent who has ever tried to get a child to eat green vegetables can appreciate the difficulty of convincing a nation that beef hearts, kidneys, and intestines are nourishing and tasty, much less to get people to actually eat them. To accomplish the task, the Committee on Food Habits called on Kurt Lewin, the father of social psychology and himself a recent refugee from Nazi Germany.

How did Lewin do it? Well, he *didn't*—not directly. What Lewin *did* do was to get people to persuade themselves to eat these intestinal meats. To demonstrate the effectiveness of participatory, self-generated persuasion, Lewin conducted a simple experiment to convince housewives (who at the time made most of their family's food decisions) to eat intestines and other undesirable meats.[1]

Half of the housewives received an intriguing lecture on the merits of intestinal meats. The forty-five-minute lecture emphasized the importance of eating these meats for the war effort; it stressed the meats' health and economic advantages; mimeographed recipes were distributed. The lecture concluded with a testimonial from the speaker about her success in serving intestinal meats to her own family.

The other housewives spent their forty-five minutes persuading themselves in a group discussion. This discussion began with a short introduction by the leader on the problem of maintaining health during the war. The leader then enlisted the help of the housewives by asking them, "Do you think that housewives like yourselves could be persuaded to participate in the intestinal meat program?" The group discussion covered many of the same arguments as the lecture but produced much more dramatic effects. Of the housewives who had heard the lecture, only 3% served intestines. In stark contrast, 32% of the housewives who had engaged in self-persuasion served their families intestinal meats.

Subsequent persuasion research has shown that self-generated persuasion—whether induced by group discussion, by getting someone to role-play an opponent's position, or by asking a person to imagine adopting a course of action—is one of the most effective persuasion tactics ever identified.[2] Indeed, one recent set of studies found that just thinking about how to transmit a persuasive message to others will result in changes in attitude that persist for at least twenty weeks.[3]

And why shouldn't the tactic be extremely effective? The technique of self-generated persuasion combines many of the facets of successful persuasion discussed throughout this book. It gains its power from providing subtle social cues and directions that ask the target of influence, in effect, to "think up as many positive cognitive responses about the issue as you can and, if you do happen to come up with some counterarguments, to be ready to refute them." The resulting message will come from a source that you almost always consider credible, trustworthy, respected, and liked—yourself. The act of generating arguments is an act of commitment to the cause. After all, they're your ideas, aren't they?

World War II may be over, but the use of self-sell in propaganda is certainly not. Larry Gregory, Robert Cialdini, and Kathleen Carpenter conducted a series of experiments illustrating the effectiveness of a form of self-persuasion called "self-imagining" in selling consumer products.[4] In one of their studies, salespersons went door-to-door in Tempe, Arizona, selling subscriptions to cable television. Some of the potential customers were informed of the advantages of cable TV (e.g., it is cheaper and involves less hassle than going out to a movie; you can spend more time with your family). Others were asked to "take a moment and imagine how cable television will provide *you* with broader entertainment." They were then induced to imagine how they would use and enjoy each benefit of cable television. The results showed that 19.5% of those merely receiving information about cable television subscribed to the service, whereas a whopping 47.4% subscribed after they had been asked to imagine using the service.

The self-generated persuasion technique fits well with the American values of participation, self-reliance, and deciding for one's self. Ironically, while the technique trades on the value of self-reliance, in reality we can be manipulated into a course of action that is often of primary benefit to the manipulator.

A trip to a car dealership (like one we took) will illustrate the point. Much of the friendly salesman's banter is targeted at getting the potential customer to think about possessing that car and to come up with his or her own reasons for doing it right *now:*

> "Sir, can I get you to do me a favor? I know we just met. These babies are selling like hotcakes and my boss keeps bugging me to find out just why people like yourself love 'em so much. What should I tell him?"

As we inch closer to the car and an actual test drive, the salesman persistently asks personal questions (Where do you live? What do you do? What music do you like?) in an attempt to gather information that can later be used to help us imagine owning that car. When a seat is taken at the wheel, the salesman states, "The car looks good on you; and I don't tell that to everyone."

During the test drive, the personal information is used and the pitch continues. "Did you get a look at the backseat? Plenty of room to pick up those professor friends of *yours* at the airport." "Hmmmm, who left this classical station on the radio? Like you, I normally listen to rock. Let's switch it over to *your* station." "Really punch that pedal, professor. I want you to see how it'll handle those inclines on *your* commute from Forest Hills."

The test drive over, the salesman dramatically delivers his lines, "Professor, I'm going in to see the boss and try to get you the best deal on *your* car." The keys to the car are pressed into the flesh of the palm and the hand gently closed. We are left alone in the showroom, tightly holding a key to our beautiful car—left alone to think, to dream, to imagine owning that car.

This nice, friendly social interaction actually emerges as cunning and blatantly manipulative once we know the principles and power of self-influence. But what can be done about it? Here's what we did. It would be difficult for anyone not to imagine owning that car. You've just daydreamed about it for almost half an hour. But what also can be imagined is getting that car at a rock-bottom price and driving it home to show friends and neighbors and hearing them exclaim: "That car? At that price? What a deal!" Imagining this latter scenario led to a stalemate that eventually produced a lengthy negotiation (almost two hours) in which each party dug in his heels.

This tiresome negotiation was getting nowhere slowly. Why not try self-generated persuasion tactics ourselves? "Hey, Bill [the salesman]. I notice this dealership gives an award for the salesperson of the month. Just how do they decide who gets this award and can you get me a sales rep who really wants to win that thing?" Bill took the bait. He wheeled around in his chair, leaned back, and began a fifteen-minute free association about the award. A few minutes later, we were writing a check as a deposit on a very good deal.

Car dealers are not the only merchants who have discovered self-generated persuasion. Mass media advertisers have developed their own set of variants. One effective type of commercial is the "slice-of-life" ad that allows us to dream with characters, much like ourselves, as they successfully solve life's problems using, of course, the advertiser's brand. Some ads require us to complete the incomplete jingle, as in "Where's the . . . [beef]?" and "You can take Salem out of the country, but you . . . [can't take the country out of Salem]." Still other ads are in a foreign language, such as a recent campaign for IBM computers which requires the viewer to translate along with the subtitles. Marketing promotions and contests often ask us to "Tell us why you like Acme-brand widgets in fifty words or less?" Politicians send out questionnaires and surveys asking for our opinions in "helping to plan the next election campaign and prioritize our goals." A new variant of self-generated persuasion can be found in multilevel sales organizations such as Amway. In these organizations, customers are recruited to serve as sales agents with the task of finding more customers. By trying to sell the product, the customer-turned-salesperson becomes more convinced of the product's worth.

Perhaps you can further convince yourself of the effectiveness of self-generated persuasion by generating even more examples of self-generated persuasion!

·····················

Naked Attics and Neighborhood War Heroes: On Vividness in Communication

Way back in the 1950s, a local community was about to vote on whether or not to fluoridate the water supply as a means of combating tooth decay. An information campaign that seemed quite logical and reasonable was launched by the proponents of fluoridation. It consisted largely of statements by noted dentists describing the benefits of fluorides and discussing the evidence on the reduction of tooth decay in areas with fluoridated water, as well as statements by physicians and other health authorities to the effect that fluoridation has no harmful effects.

The opponents used an appeal that was much more vivid and emotional in flavor. By vivid appeal, we mean a message that is (1) emotionally interesting (it attracts our feelings), (2) concrete and imagery-provoking, and (3) immediate (it discusses matters that are personally close to us). For example, one antifluoridation leaflet consisted of a picture of a rather ugly rat, along with the inscription "Don't let them put rat poison in your drinking water." The referendum to fluoridate the water supply was soundly defeated.

Of course, this incident does not demonstrate conclusively that vivid appeals are superior, mainly because the incident was not a scientifically controlled study. We have no idea how the people would have voted on fluoridation if no publicity had been circulated, nor do we know whether the antifluoridation circular reached more people, whether it was easier to read than the proponents' literature, and so forth. But it does raise an interesting question: Are vivid appeals more persuasive than other less interesting and more pallid messages? Research is accruing that indicates the answer is "yes"—under certain conditions.

A stunning scientific demonstration of the power of vivid arguments to persuade comes from the area of energy conservation. If homeowners could be induced to make their homes more efficient (by adding insulation, weatherstripping, and the like), it could result in a savings of about 40% of the energy that is now wasted. This would not only be in the national interest, reducing dependence on Persian Gulf oil, but would also result in substantial financial savings for the individual homeowner.

In 1978, the government began requiring utility companies to offer the consumer a free home audit, wherein a trained auditor carefully examines one's home, recommends what needs to be done to make it more energy-efficient, and offers the consumer an interest-free loan to get the work done. What a deal! The problem is that, while a great many homeowners requested a home audit, only 15% of them actually followed the recommendation of the auditor—even though it was clearly in their best financial interests to do so.

Why? In order to answer this puzzling question, we and our students Marti Hope Gonzales and Mark Costanzo interviewed several homeowners and found that most of them had a hard time believing that something as small as a crack under a door or as "invisible" as the paucity of insulation in the attic could be very important.[1] Armed with this information, we conducted a workshop in which we trained several auditors to communicate in more graphic, more vivid terms. For example, instead of simply saying "You would save money if you weatherstripped your doors and put some additional insulation in the attic," the auditors were trained to say something like this:

Look at all the cracks around that door! It may not seem like much to you, but if you were to add up all the cracks around each of these doors, you'd have the equivalent of a hole the circumference of a basketball. Suppose someone poked a hole the size of a basketball in your living room wall. Think for a moment about all the heat that you'd be losing from a hole of that size—you'd want to patch that hole in your wall, wouldn't you? That's exactly what weatherstripping does. And your attic totally lacks insulation. We professionals call that a "naked" attic. It's as if your home is facing winter not just without an overcoat but without any clothing at all! You wouldn't let your young kids run around outside in the wintertime without clothes on, would you? It's the same with your attic.

Psychologically, cracks around the door may be seen as minor, but a hole the size of a basketball feels disastrous. Similarly, insulation is something people don't often think about—but the idea of being naked in winter grabs attention and increases the probability of action.

The results were striking. Auditors trained to use compelling images increased their effectiveness fourfold: Whereas previously only 15% of the consumers had the recommended work done, after the auditors began to use more vivid communications, this number increased to 61%.

Why do vivid appeals work? Vivid messages affect our cognitive responses in at least four possible ways. First, vivid information attracts *attention*. It helps the communication stand out in the message-dense environment. Second, vividness can make the information more *concrete* and *personal*. We saw earlier the persuasive power of self-generated arguments and images. Third, the effective vivid appeal *directs* and *focuses* thought on the issues and arguments that the communicator feels are most important. Finally, a vivid presentation can make the material more *memorable*. This is especially important if we do not reach an immediate conclusion but base our later judgments on information that comes readily to mind.

Our cognitive response analysis also suggests that vivid information may sometimes fail to convince—and do so in a quite dramatic fashion. Just because a message is vivid does *not* insure that it will induce positive thoughts and thus be effective. A case in point is the now-infamous Dukakis tank ad used during the 1988 presidential campaign. In this ad, the Dukakis campaign staff sought to make Michael Dukakis's commitment to a strong national defense vivid in the minds of voters by showing him in an army tank. The ad was attention-getting, and it did succeed in reducing the issue to one concrete, memorable symbol. The end result was not very persuasive, however. Instead of the reaction hoped for by the Dukakis campaign (i.e., he surely is tough on defense), many viewers responded with thoughts such as, *"Gee, he looks silly in that tank."* The vividness of the appeal just made it all the worse for Dukakis.[2]

Nevertheless, a vivid presentation can make a strong argument even more persuasive; it may also make a more dubious proposition ring true. Consider the following example. Suppose you are in the market for a new car and the single most important thing you are looking for is reliability and longevity. That is, you don't care about looks, style, or mileage—what you do care about is the frequency of repair. As a reasonable and sensible person, you consult *Consumer Reports* and learn that the car with the best repair record is clearly a Toyota. No other car even comes close. Naturally, you decide to buy a Toyota.

But suppose the night before you are to make the purchase, you attend a dinner party and announce your intention to one of your friends. He is incredulous. "You can't be serious," he says, "my cousin bought a Toyota last year and has had nothing but trouble ever since. First the fuel-injection system broke down; then the transmission fell out; then strange undiagnosable noises started to come from the engine; finally, oil started to drip from some unknown place. My poor cousin is literally afraid to drive the car for fear of what will happen next."

Let's suppose the ranking made by *Consumer Reports* was based on a sample of 1,000 Toyota owners. Your friend's cousin's unfortunate experience has increased the size of the sample to 1,001. It has added one negative case to your statistical bank. Logically, this should not affect your decision. But a large body of research by Richard Nisbett and Lee Ross (from whose work we drew this example) indicates that such occurrences, because of their vividness, assume far more importance than their logical, statistical status would imply.[3] Indeed, such occurrences are frequently decisive. Thus it would be very difficult for you to rush out and purchase a Toyota with the example of the plight of your friend's cousin firmly fixed in your mind. All other things being equal, most people are more deeply influenced by one clear, vivid, personal example than by an abundance of statistical data.

Vivid examples and case studies are also used by politicians to get us to buy their programs and policies. In *Eloquence in an Electronic Age*, communications researcher Kathleen Hall Jamieson addresses the question of why Ronald Reagan was considered, by foe and admirer alike, to be a great communicator.[4] The Reagan presidency produced no major addresses—no speeches as eloquent or as memorable as Lincoln's Gettysburg Address, Franklin D. Roosevelt's fireside chats, or Kennedy's *Ich bin ein Berliner* speech. In their stead were a series of catchphrases such as "Make my day" and "There you go again."

Jamieson argues that Reagan's communication style differed greatly from that of past presidents. Previous presidents had used the devices of classical rhetoric to advance their causes—well-constructed arguments, the contrasting of possible options, argument by metaphor. Reagan relied on dramatization and storytelling to make his points. His speeches persuaded by creating visual images, by personalizing the central themes of his administration, and by involving us in a dramatic narrative of American life.

For example, in his first inaugural address, Reagan sought to assure his audience that America's involvement in the Vietnam war was just and honorable. There are a number of ways to argue for this proposition. One could provide the listener with a list of reasons for the war: It helped stay the spread of communism; it was designed to prevent the overthrow of a democracy and the rise of yet another totalitarian regime; it was ostensibly supported by the people of South Vietnam; and so on. The war could also be contrasted with other options available at the time. Such was *not* Reagan's style.

Instead Reagan, from his location at the Capitol building, described the sights of Washington, D.C., as TV cameras panned the scene—the Washington Monument, the Jefferson Memorial, the Lincoln Memorial, and, finally, across the Potomac River, the hills of Arlington National Cemetery, where rows of simple white crosses and Stars of David mark the graves of those who gave their lives for their country. Reagan continued:

> Their lives ended in places called Belleau Wood, the Argonne, Omaha Beach, Salerno, and halfway around the world on Guadalcanal, Tarawa, Pork Chop Hill, the Chosin Reservoir, and in a hundred rice paddies and jungles of a place called Vietnam.

By including the Vietnam war dead in a succession of symbols and images exemplifying the best of American heroism, Reagan had transformed the war in Vietnam into a just and honorable mission with a single vivid image.

Perhaps Reagan's most memorable addresses were to Congress. In these speeches, Reagan would describe the personal acts of service performed by private citizens. The members of

Congress would applaud, the viewing public would be filled with pride at the accomplishments of their fellow citizens, and Reagan would gain national approval of his policies.

For example, to gain acceptance of the U.S. invasion of the island of Grenada, Reagan singled out Sergeant Stephen Trujillo. During the attack on Grenada, Trujillo had saved the lives of many of his fellow soldiers. As Congress applauded Trujillo's valor, Reagan quickly noted, "you [Trujillo] set a nation free," thereby justifying America's invasion.

To convince the nation that poverty was not a major social problem, Reagan frequently used rags-to-riches and neighbor-helping-neighbor stories. On one occasion, he singled out Jean Nguyen, a Vietnamese refugee who was now, after a successful academic career, graduating from West Point. On the same night, he also singled out Clara Hale, a black woman and founder of a home for the infants of drug-addicted mothers. Hale served as a concrete example that poverty and drug abuse were problems for private citizens, not the federal government, to solve and that Reagan's policies did not systematically disadvantage black Americans.

We can analyze Reagan's arguments concerning the lack of poverty in this country in much the same way as we looked at our friend's story about the problematic Toyota. Near the beginning of the Reagan years, one out of every nine American children lived in poverty. At the end of his term, that figure was one in four children. It would be a simple matter, depending on our propaganda purposes, to find vivid examples of either children living in poverty or children whose parents had gotten themselves out of such circumstances. Such human examples may make our arguments more persuasive, but they do little to address the issue of poverty in America. This would require a detailed look at how various government policies have affected indicators of poverty. The communist leader Joseph Stalin anticipated the current use of vividness in the tactics of propaganda when he remarked perceptively: "The death of a single Russian soldier is a tragedy. A million deaths is a statistic."[5]

We would be remiss in our duties if we failed to point out that vivid appeals are not used only by Republicans. A case in point is Democratic strategist James Carville's book *We're Right,*

They're Wrong.[6] This volume is chock-full of vivid appeals, such as a story of how Carville's grandmother, Octavia Duhon, worked with pride for the federal government; how Carville went to college on the G.I. Bill; and the rags-to-riches drama of Dr. Joseph Giordano, who went to medical school on government loans and who later removed an assassin's bullet to save Ronald Reagan's life. Carville uses these images and stories to make a point opposite to that made by Ronald Reagan: Government can do good things for good people.

Vivid appeals can be found in a wide range of domains. Turn on Saturday morning TV and you'll see a steady stream of ads directed at children—all showing graphic, vivid images of a toy supposedly in action. Keep the set on that night and you will see such vivid demonstrations as ball-bearings rolling down a car, a lonely Maytag repairman, and an Energizer bunny that appears to keep on going. Do any of these images prove their point?

Anyone who watched the O. J. Simpson trial should be familiar with the use of vivid images in the courtroom: As one lawyer tried to outdo the next in producing the most dramatic, vivid image possible—from 911 tapes of domestic abuse, to graphic descriptions of police misconduct and incompetence, to, perhaps most vivid of all (at least for television viewers), O. J. Simpson trying on the gloves.[7] Indeed, defense lawyer Gerry Spence believes that an effective attorney is one who tells the client's story in compelling, vivid terms. As he puts it:

> In my mind's eye I see my client coming home at night and I tell the story: I see Joe Radovick trudging home at night to face a heap of unpaid bills sitting on the kitchen table. Nothing but the cold bills greets him . . . a tired man, worn-out, exhausted, a man without a penny, without pride, without hope. An empty man. The bank had it all.[8]

Such vivid appeals can also work for the prosecution; here the prosecution needs to paint a vivid, sympathetic picture of the victim of the crime rather than the perpetrator. In a recent study with our student Lillie Ibayan, we asked subjects to evaluate the evidence in a murder case and then recommend a verdict and sentence.[9] For some of the subjects, we included vivid, emotional information about the victim—for example, pictures of the victim's family and testimony that the victim was at the top of her class and that her young sister was having trouble sleeping through the night as a result of the murder. The results showed that this victim-impact information resulted in harsher punishments meted out by death-qualified jurors (that is, those subjects who believed in the death penalty).

Throughout American history, vivid, personal appeals have moved the soul of the nation—such novels as Harriet Beecher Stowe's *Uncle Tom's Cabin*, Upton Sinclair's *The Jungle*, John Steinbeck's *The Grapes of Wrath*, and Kurt Vonnegut's *Slaughterhouse-Five* are just a few examples. But although novels have been effective, it is television's ability to present vivid, emotional images that is unsurpassed.

Some communications scholars believe that anti-war sentiment during the Vietnam war—America's first televised war—was due in part to the constant stream of war images cast onto the nation's television screens.[10] The U.S. military, having learned its lesson in Vietnam, went to great lengths to restrict the flow of vivid images of the Persian Gulf and Kosovo wars to Americans watching on their TV sets at home. Indeed, government officials saw to it that only images that supported U.S. involvement in the Persian Gulf, such as a U.S. guided missile surgically striking an Iraqi command headquarters or an Iraqi Scud missile being shot out of the sky, consistently made it to our television screens. Americans protested when CNN aired footage, supplied by Peter Arnett, of harm to Iraqi civilians caused by U.S. bombing raids. The Kosovo conflict received even less news coverage, much of it centered on the plight of refugees.

In recent years, Americans have been angered by watching blindfolded hostages on exhibit in Iran, impassioned by the sight of young servicemen's coffins on an airplane tarmac or the destruction and loss of life caused by terrorist bombings in Oklahoma and aboard Pan Am Flight 103, and moved to compassion by scenes of devastation after hurricane Andrew and the Santa Cruz and Kobe earthquakes. And each day, still more vivid and moving images are being televised to replace those of the day before. The power of television to dramatize warrants our concern and scrutiny, so that compelling and sometimes vivid arguments are not replaced by merely vivid, moving tales.

20 ■■■■■■■■■■■■■■■■■■■

Why Do They Keep Repeating the Same Ads?

In 1882, Harley T. Procter of Cincinnati, Ohio, began to market his new soap, which he called Ivory, with newspaper and magazine ads proclaiming that "it floats" and is "99 44/100% pure." In 1922, Gerald Lambert, son of the founder of Lambert and Lambert, hired the Chicago ad agency William and Cunnyngham to improve the sluggish sales of Listerine—at the time, a product used as an antiseptic in surgery and to fight throat infection. The resulting campaign: "Even your best friend won't tell you. Listerine is good for halitosis." Five decades later, in 1954, a delegation from the Philip Morris tobacco company asked the famed Chicago adman Leo Burnett to help solve a marketing problem—to develop an ad campaign that would sell filter cigarettes (regarded at the time to be feminine) to men. The next year, Burnett released his first ads for Marlboro cigarettes featuring a virile, macho cowboy riding the range with cigarettes in hand.[1]

What do these three advertisements have in common (in addition to having sold millions of products)? These ads have been seen, in one form or another, countless times by generations of countless Americans. Repetition of ads, slogans, and selling points is a common feature of the landscape of twentieth-century American advertising. Yet, in surveys about what people think about advertising, one of the most common and consistent complaints is that it is annoying to see the same old stuff over and over again. If repetitive advertising is so irritating, why do advertisers continue to do it?

From a business perspective, frequent repetition of an advertisement helps to meet multiple marketing objectives in a cost-efficient manner. Repeatedly exposing consumers to an ad is a good way to introduce a new product or to remind customers of the value of an older brand. Often, repeat exposure is an unintended consequence of attempting to present an ad to multiple target audiences (the members of which may overlap). With the high cost of creating and producing new advertising ideas and

*"This is the twenty-seventh time we've seen this commercial.
I guess it's time to buy the stuff."*

slogans, it makes sense to stick with proven winners. As a further inducement to repeat an ad, advertising agencies typically receive 15% of media costs as their fee. So the more times an ad is run, the larger the billing. However, the accomplishment of such marketing objectives and cost benefits would amount to very little if message repetition did not do one thing more and do it very well—persuade you to buy the product.

The Greek storyteller Aesop once advanced the notion that familiarity breeds contempt. Although Aesop's moral may apply to the social gatherings of foxes and lions, it certainly does *not* describe the persuasive effects of familiarity brought about by repeated exposure to advertising. The modern-day Aesop writing about advertising would probably conclude the opposite: *Familiarity breeds attraction, liking, and even "truth."*

How familiarity can result in sales can be seen in a typical trip to the grocery store in search of a laundry detergent. We go to the detergent section and see a staggering array of brand names. Because it doesn't much matter which one is purchased, we may simply reach for the most familiar one—and chances are it is familiar because we've heard and seen the name on television commercials over and over again. If this is the case, then sudden increases in television exposure should produce dramatic changes in familiarity and, perhaps, in sales.

Let's look at the data. Several years ago, the Northwest Mutual Life Insurance Company conducted a nationwide poll to find out how well the public recognized its name. It came out thirty-fourth among insurance companies. Two weeks and $1 million worth of television advertising later, the company repeated the poll. This time it came out third in name familiarity.

Of course, familiarity does not necessarily mean sales, but the two are frequently linked. Thus A&W root beer boosted its share of the market from 15% to 50% after six months of television advertising. By switching channels on a Saturday morning, a child can watch ads for McDonald's in up to a dozen colorful, fast-paced commercials each hour; perhaps this is one reason why the chain continues to sell billions of hamburgers.

Robert Zajonc of the University of Michigan has demonstrated in a laboratory setting that, all other things being equal, the more a person is exposed to an item, the more attractive it is.[2] In three separate studies, Zajonc presented nonsense words, Chinese ideographs, and photographs of students taken from a college yearbook. The items were repeated from zero to twenty-five times. The results showed that attraction to the item increased with the number of exposures. Much subsequent research has supported Zajonc's basic finding: More exposure results in increased liking.

But is voting for a presidential candidate the same kind of decision as choosing a laundry detergent or a breakfast cereal or evaluating nonsense words and Chinese ideographs? The answer may very well be "yes." After the 1972 congressional primaries, Joseph Grush and his colleagues examined the amount of money candidates spent on political advertising during the elections and found that a large majority of races were won by big spenders.[3] Subsequently, Grush found again that candidates who spent the most money in the 1976 Democratic presidential primaries typically received the most votes. In both studies, however, those

who tended to gain the most from media exposure were candidates who were relatively unknown to the voters prior to their
campaigns. But in presidential elections in which candidates are
highly familiar, massive media blitzes are less influential.[4] Nevertheless, even minimal impact may be large enough to swing
some close races.

The power of repetition in propaganda was well understood
by Joseph Goebbels, the head of the Nazi propaganda ministry.
His propaganda crusades were based on a simple observation:
*What the masses term truth is that information which is most
familiar.* As Goebbels put it:

> The rank and file are usually much more primitive than
> we imagine. Propaganda must therefore always be essentially
> simple and repetitious. In the long run only he will achieve basic
> results in influencing public opinion who is able to reduce prob-
> lems to the simplest terms and who has the courage to keep
> forever repeating them in this simplified form despite the objec-
> tions of intellectuals.[5]

According to Goebbels, the repetition of simple messages,
images, and slogans creates our knowledge of the world, defining what is truth and specifying how we should live our lives.

A set of recent experiments illustrates Goebbels's point—repetition of a piece of information increases its perceived validity.[6]
In these experiments, participants were exposed to statements
such as "Leonardo da Vinci had two wives at the same time"
and "Tibet, with 1.2 million square kilometers, occupies one-
eighth of China's total area." Some of these statements were
repeated on multiple occasions. The results: The participants in
these studies judged the repeated statements to be more "true"
than those not repeated.

Consider something as simple as the Marlboro man, an
image we have probably seen hundreds of times but one that we
probably have not thought much about. What does this cowboy
teach us? First, that smoking is for the rugged, self-confident
individual (as opposed to being a health hazard). Second, that
American men should be macho (as opposed to, say, caring and
sensitive). And finally, that you can be rugged and macho simply

by smoking Marlboros—it is that easy. A lifetime of exposures to black Americans as Uneeda Slicker boys and Aunt Jemima, to Hispanics as Juan Valdez and Frito Banditos, and to women as either endlessly arguing about the benefits of a brand of paper towels or sexily draped on the hood of an automobile can reinforce and maintain pervasive social stereotypes.

This problem does not seem to worry all advertisers. What they do worry about is annoying the viewers to the point where they refuse to listen to the advertising and to buy the product. Recall that many American consumers find repetitive advertising to be irritating. Such annoyance can diminish and even reverse the effects of repetition, but this reversal is often short-lived. For example, Rick Crandall, Albert Harrison, and Robert Zajonc showed subjects the same Chinese ideographs over and over again.[7] Immediately after the repetitive presentation, subjects did not rate these ideographs as any more attractive than less familiar ones, presumably because the frequent exposures were boring and tedious. However, after a week's delay, the repeatedly presented Chinese ideographs gained in attractiveness. Apparently the annoying effects of repetition wore off faster than the familiarity-induced attraction.

Even so, advertisers know that repeated exposure can lead to what is known as "wear-out"—when an ad loses its effectiveness because consumers find repeated exposures to be tedious and annoying. Wear-out effects are most likely to occur with ads that attract much attention, such as humorous ads and informational messages. Advertisers attempt to eliminate wear-out by using a technique known as "repetition-with-variation." In this technique, the same information or theme is repeated many times, but the presentation format is varied. For example, the Marlboro man is posed at different angles and is seen in different settings, or the halitosis-fighting power of Listerine is demonstrated in the home, at work, and on a date.

Does repetition-with-variation work? A study conducted by David Schumann illustrates the effectiveness of repetition-with-variation in overcoming wear-out effects and identifies an important condition in which variation does not succeed in producing attraction.[8] In this study, participants watched a simulated television show, complete with advertising for a fictitious pen called the "Omega 3." Half of the participants viewed the *same* ad for the Omega 3 pen presented either one, four, or eight times, whereas the other participants watched either one, four, or eight *different* ads for the Omega 3—in other words, repetition-with-variation. (These differing ads contained the same information about the Omega 3 but varied irrelevant features such as wording, print type, and setting.) Schumann also varied whether the ad was processed using the central or peripheral route by encouraging some participants to think about the Omega 3 advertising with a promise that, at the end of the study, they could select a gift from among several brands of ballpoint pens. Other participants were told that they would receive a free bottle of mouthwash as a gift and were thus not motivated to think about ballpoint pens and the Omega 3.

What did Schumann find? Let's look first at the effects ad repetition had for those participants who were not motivated to think much about the pens—a state we often find ourselves in when watching television and its advertisements. When the same ad was repeated, the participants' opinion of the Omega 3 pen became more favorable with four repetitions but less favorable after eight—in other words, a wear-out effect occurred. However, when a different ad was repeated, the participants' opinion of the Omega 3 became more favorable with every exposure. Repetition-with-variation had reduced the tedium and eliminated the wear-out effects.

For those participants who were motivated to think about pens, wear-out occurred when both the *same* and *different* ads were repeated. Specifically, opinions of the Omega 3 pen became more favorable with four repetitions but *less* favorable after eight. For thinking participants, even repetition-with-variation could not counter the annoying effects of repeat exposure. In this case, the extra exposures provided an opportunity to scrutinize and critique the advertisement's message.

The rub, of course, is that we see and hear many, many persuasive messages each day, and we see and hear them over and over again. It is difficult to think deeply about each and every one of these communications. After all, how often do we think, in depth, about the meaning of the Marlboro man or the significance of the fact that Ivory soap floats? Repetition is thus left to create its own truths.

21 ||||||||||||||||||||

If You Have Nothing to Say—Distract Them

When confronted with a persuasive communication, especially one that runs counter to important beliefs, we tend, whenever feasible, to invent counterarguments on the spot. This tendency serves us very well: It prevents our opinions from being unduly influenced. This resistance can serve to defeat the propagandist's purpose, especially when the arguments for the cause are weak and specious and therefore easily refuted.

But professional persuaders, aware of our tendency to counterargue, have discovered a way to overcome some of this resistance. Advertisers have an old motto: "If you don't have anything to say, sing it!" In other words, a mild distraction (provided by a song, an irrelevant picture, etc.) can disrupt counterarguing and increase the effectiveness of a persuasive message.

The song that was most on the lips of the typical American in the 1940s was not a great tune by Irving Berlin, Cole Porter, or Rodgers and Hammerstein. It was a ditty that was as meaningless as it was simple: "Rinso *white!* Rinso *white!* Happy little washday song!" Rinso, a laundry detergent, was no better or worse than its competitors—but the song, ah, the song. In the 1970s, Coca-Cola hit the charts with "I'd like to teach the world to sing." Pepsi, just before the turn of the century, spent millions to have Ray Charles serenade us with "You've got the right one, baby—Diet Pepsi—uh-huh, uh-huh."

What effect does a song have on persuasion? Does it make people feel happy, with this happiness somehow increasing the persuasiveness of the message? The answer is a sometimes "yes"—a lively song can make us happy and thus help us think happy thoughts about a product.[1] At other times the song may get stuck in our head, reminding us of the brand name (as in "Rinso *white!*"). At still other times a catchy song or a big production number can attract our attention to the ad so that we don't change the channel or go to the bathroom and we at least hear the advertiser's message. However, when advertisers say "If you don't have anything to say—sing it," they usually mean that a song or, for that matter, a steamy love scene or a picture of an elephant using the telephone or any other irrelevant element can serve as a distraction to disrupt our typical counterarguing of a weak or discrepant message.

An early experiment by Leon Festinger and Nathan Maccoby was the first to demonstrate the validity of the advertiser's motto.[2] In this experiment, two groups of students who belonged to a college fraternity were required to watch a film that presented arguments about the evils of college fraternities. The arguments were intended to be powerful and were widely discrepant from the beliefs of the audience. As you might imagine, the students were motivated to counterargue this message. In one version of the film, a young professor delivered the attack on fraternities. In the other version, the young professor was replaced by an entertaining beatnik artist working on an abstract expressionist painting. The students still heard the arguments against fraternities but watched an entertaining and distracting film as they listened.

Festinger and Maccoby reasoned that because this group was engaged in two tasks simultaneously—listening to the arguments against fraternities and watching an entertaining film—their minds would be so occupied that they would have a limited capacity to think up arguments to refute the message. The members of the control group, on the other hand, were not distracted by the entertaining film; therefore, they should be better able to devote some of their thoughts to resisting the communication by thinking up counterarguments. The results of the experiment confirmed this reasoning. The fraternity men who were distracted by watching the film underwent substantially more opinion change (against fraternities) than did the fraternity men who were not distracted.

How do advertisers try to disrupt our counterarguing of their messages? Sometimes they literally sing, as with the Rinso commercial and many like it. Another class of distraction techniques is the extensive use of creative license in the layout and presentation of an advertisement. For a print ad in a magazine or newspaper, examples of such *artsy* techniques would include pictures of attractive models or unique objects that command attention, reverse white-on-black print, strange layouts that confuse the reader, and typefaces that are difficult to read. For television, artsy could mean a commercial with many short scene changes (similar to an MTV video); the use of strange camera angles; the playing of fast, rhythmic music in the background; and the inclusion of offbeat characters and yelling, screaming spokespersons. All of these techniques can provide a mild distraction and thus prevent counterarguing. The trick for the advertiser is to provide just enough of a distraction to disrupt counterarguing but not so much that it eliminates the reception of the message.[3]

But not all advertisers agree with the "sing-it" dictum. In his advice to fellow advertisers, David Ogilvy calls this kind of creative license "art-directoritis" and urges his colleagues to avoid it.[4] Ogilvy claims, based on his own observations and years of advertising experience, that the techniques associated with art-directoritis often fail to achieve their desired effects. How does this square with what we know about distraction and persuasion?

Ogilvy achieved his fame as an advertiser in the 1950s with a series of influential print ads for Hathaway shirts, Rolls-Royce, and Schweppes tonic. Although for different products, the ads employed a similar style. Each ad contained an interesting picture featuring the product. A headline would tell readers why the product was of special value for them, and lengthy copy would explain the reason for this assertion. For example, one ad showed a picture of a Rolls-Royce with the headline: AT 60 MILES AN HOUR THE LOUDEST NOISE IN THIS NEW ROLLS-ROYCE COMES FROM THE ELECTRIC CLOCK. The copy listed thirteen unique benefits of owning a Rolls. Similarly, a more recent ad for Acura automobiles merely shows the car and states that for three consecutive years, the Acura has been number one in surveys of owner satisfaction. In this kind of situation, when one can state compelling, cogent arguments, Ogilvy is right. An artsy ad would distract the reader from the cogent arguments and might actually *decrease* persuasion. But that is only half of the equation. For weak arguments or when one fears counterarguments, well . . . the persuader can always sing it.

Our speculation has been confirmed by a neat little experiment by the social psychologists Richard Petty, Gary Wells, and Timothy Brock.[5] In this study, the investigators distracted students by asking them to monitor a television screen for X's while they listened to one of two messages arguing for an increase in their tuition. One message consisted of weak, easily counterargued arguments, whereas the other consisted of strong, hard-to-refute arguments. Distraction *increased* the effectiveness of the weak message (because it disrupted counterarguing) but *decreased* the impact of the strong communication (because it disrupted the ability to pay close attention to the cogent arguments being made).

Recently television advertisers have introduced a new, more subtle technique that can serve to distract and disrupt message processing—time compression. To save media costs, advertisers can, for example, "compress" a thirty-six-second television ad into a thirty-second time slot by running the ad at 120% of its normal speed. Psychologically, time-compressed ads are harder to argue against. Metaphorically speaking, the advertiser is persuading at 100 miles an hour while you maintain the speed limit and try to defend yourself at 65 miles an hour. You are bound to lose.

A series of studies by consumer psychologist Danny Moore and his colleagues confirm this relationship between time compression, distraction, and persuasion.[6] Specifically, they found that participants were less able to develop counterarguments to a time-compressed message and that time-compressing a message consisting of strong arguments reduced persuasion whereas it increased the persuasive impact of a message containing weak arguments.

In sum, advertisers (and other influence agents) use a variety of tactics to distract us from processing and counterarguing a message. This distraction, if it is mild, can lead to more persuasion when our natural inclination is to argue—for example, if the message is weak or disagreeable. The end result, of course, is just a little more mindless propaganda and a little less thoughtful persuasion.

---

22 ||||||||||||||||||||

If You Want to Gain an Inch, Ask for a Mile—Sometimes!

Suppose you are talking to an audience that strongly disagrees with your point of view—for example, an anti-abortionist speaking to a pro-choice lobby or an automaker trying to convince consumers that the car they believe to be quite worthless is, in reality, excellent. Will it be more effective to present the arguments in their most extreme form or to modulate the message by presenting it in such a way that it does not seem terribly different from the audience's position?

For example, suppose you believe people should exercise vigorously every day to stay healthy; any physical activity would be helpful, but at least an hour's worth would be preferable. Your audience consists of couch potatoes who seem to believe that switching TV channels with the remote is sufficient exercise for the average person. Would you change their opinion to a greater extent by arguing that people should begin a rigorous daily program of running, swimming, and calisthenics or by suggesting a briefer, less taxing regimen? In short, what is the most effective level of discrepancy between the opinion of the audience and the recommendation of the communicator?

This is a vital issue for any propagandist or educator. For example, the attorney Gerry Spence has been extremely successful in persuading juries to award multimillion-dollar settlements to his clients. When asked by other lawyers how he does it, Spence replies: "I simply ask for the money. I tell the jury what I want."[1] And what he asks for is a lot, at least by the standards of a typical settlement. Spence asked for and received from a jury $10 million in punitive damages for the children of Karen Silkwood and $26.5 million from *Penthouse* magazine for destroying the reputation of a former Miss Wyoming. How sound is Gerry Spence's strategy of asking for large awards?

Let's look at this situation from the audience's point of view. Most of us have a strong desire to be correct—to have "the right" opinions and to perform reasonable actions. When someone disagrees with us, it makes us feel uncomfortable because it suggests our opinions or actions may be wrong or based on misinformation. The greater the disagreement, the greater our discomfort.

How can we reduce this discomfort? One way is by simply changing our opinions or actions. The greater the disagreement, the greater our opinion change would have to be. This line of reasoning, then, would suggest that the communicator should adopt the Gerry Spence strategy and argue for the daily program of rigorous exercise; the greater the discrepancy, the greater the opinion change needed.

Several investigators have found that this "linear" relation does hold true. A good example of this relation was provided by an experiment by Philip Zimbardo.[2] Each woman who was recruited as a participant for the experiment was asked to bring a close friend with her to the laboratory. Each pair of friends was presented with a case study of juvenile delinquency, and then each of the participants was asked, separately and in private, to indicate her recommendations on the matter. Each woman was led to believe her close friend disagreed with her, either by a small margin or by an extremely large margin. Zimbardo found that the greater the apparent discrepancy, the more the women changed their opinions toward what they supposed were the opinions of their friends.

However, a careful look at the literature also turns up several experiments disconfirming this line of reasoning. For example, Carl Hovland, O. J. Harvey, and Muzafer Sherif argued that, if a particular communication differs considerably from a person's own position, it is, in effect, outside of one's "latitude of acceptance" and the individual therefore will not be much influenced by it.[3] They conducted an experiment and found a curvilinear relation between discrepancy and opinion change. By "curvilinear," we mean that a small discrepancy increased the degree of opinion change; but as the discrepancy continued to increase, opinion change began to slacken; and finally, as the discrepancy became large, the amount of opinion change became very small. When the discrepancy was very large, almost no opinion change was observed and in some cases could actually decline.

To see how it differs from the Zimbardo study, let's take a closer look at this mid-1950s experiment. The communication was based on a red-hot issue of the day, one the participants felt strongly about: whether their state of Oklahoma should remain "dry" or go "wet." The voters of the state were virtually equally divided on this issue, and the participants in the study were a representative sample: Some of the subjects felt strongly that the state should remain "dry" and continue to prohibit the distribution and sale of alcoholic beverages, others felt strongly it should go "wet," and the rest took a moderate position.

The members of each group were presented with communications supporting one of the three opinions, so that, in each group, there were some who found the communication close to their own position, some who found it moderately discrepant from their own position, and some who found it extremely discrepant from their own position. Specifically, some groups were presented with a "wet" message, which argued for the unlimited and unrestricted sale of liquor; some with a "dry" message, which argued for complete prohibition; and some with a moderately "wet" message, which argued for legalization of some drinking but with certain controls and restrictions.

Unlike the Zimbardo findings, Hovland, Harvey, and Sherif found that the greatest opinion changes occurred when there was a *moderate* discrepancy between the actual message and the opinions of individual members of the groups.

What an exciting state of affairs! In science, when there are a substantial number of research findings pointing in one direction and a similarly substantial number of research findings pointing in a different direction, it does not necessarily mean someone has to be wrong; rather, it suggests there is a significant factor that has not been accounted for—and this is indeed exciting, for it gives the scientist an opportunity to play detective.

We beg the reader's indulgence here, for we would like to dwell on this issue—not only for its substantive value but also because it provides an opportunity to showcase one of the more adventurous aspects of social psychology as a science. Basically, there are two ways of doing the detective work necessary to find the missing factor. We can begin by assembling all the experiments that show one result and all those that show the other result and (imaginary magnifying glass in hand) painstakingly scrutinize them, looking for the one factor common to the experiments in group A and lacking in group B; then we can try to determine, conceptually, why this factor should make a difference. Or, conversely, we can begin by speculating conceptually about what factor or factors might make a difference, then glance through the existing literature with this conceptual lantern in hand to see if the experiments in group A differ from the experiments in group B on this dimension.

Let's follow this second mode and speculate about what factor or factors might make such a difference. We can begin by accepting the notion discussed above: The greater the discrepancy, the greater the discomfort for the members of the audience. But this does not necessarily mean the members of an audience will change their opinion.

There are at least four ways in which the members of an audience can reduce their discomfort: (1) They can change their opinion; (2) they can induce the communicator to change his or her opinion; (3) they can seek support for their original opinion by finding other people who share their views, in spite of what the communicator says; or (4) they can derogate the communicator—convince themselves the communicator is stupid or immoral—and thereby invalidate that person's position.

In a great many situations, including those in these experiments, the message is delivered either as a written statement (as a newspaper or magazine article, for example) or by a communicator who is not approachable by the audience (as on television, on the lecture platform, on the witness stand, etc.). Also, the subject is often either alone or is part of an audience whose members have no opportunity to interact with one another. Under these circumstances, it is virtually impossible for the recipients of the communication either to have immediate impact on the communicator's opinion or to seek immediate social support. This leaves the recipients two major ways of reducing this discomfort—they can change their opinion or they can derogate the communicator.

Under what circumstances would an individual find it easy or difficult to derogate the communicator? It would be very difficult to derogate a liked and respected personal friend; it would also be difficult to derogate someone who is a highly trustworthy expert on the issue under discussion. But if the communicator's credibility were questionable, it would be difficult not to derogate him or her. Following this line of reasoning, we suggest that, if a communicator's credibility were high, the greater the discrepancy between the communicator's opinions and the audience's opinions, the greater the influence exerted on the opinions of the audience. However, if the communicator's credibility were not very high, he or she would be, by definition, subject to derogation.

This is not to say that the communicator with lesser credentials could not influence the opinions of the audience. Such a communicator would probably be able to influence people to change their opinions if his or her opinions were not too different from theirs. But the more discrepant such a communicator's position is from those of the audience, the more the audience might begin to question the communicator's wisdom, intelligence, and sanity. The more they question, the less likely they are to be influenced.

Let's return to our example involving physical exercise: Imagine a seventy-three-year-old man, with the body of a man half his age, who had just won the Boston Marathon. If he told us that a good way to stay in condition and live a long, healthy life was to exercise vigorously for at least two hours every day, we would believe him. Boy, would we believe him! He would get much more exercise out of us than if he suggested we should exercise for only ten minutes a day.

But suppose a person somewhat less credible, such as a high school track coach, were delivering the communication. If he suggested we exercise ten minutes a day, his suggestion would be within our own latitude of acceptance and he might influence our opinion and behavior. But if he advised us to embark on a program of two hours of vigorous exercise every day, we would be inclined to write him off as a quack, a health freak, a monomaniac—and we could comfortably continue being indolent. Thus we would agree with Hovland, Harvey, and Sherif: People will consider an extremely discrepant communication to be outside their latitude of acceptance—but only if the communicator is not highly credible.

Armed with these speculations, we, with two students—Judith Turner and J. Merrill Carlsmith—scrutinized the existing experiments on this issue, paying special attention to the ways in which the communicator was described.[4] Lo and behold, we discovered that each of the experiments showing a direct linear relation between discrepancy and opinion change happened to describe the source of the communication as more credible than did those whose results showed a curvilinear relation.

We next constructed an experiment in which we systematically investigated the size of the discrepancy and the credibility of the communicator. In this experiment, women college students were asked to read several stanzas from obscure modern poetry and to rank them in terms of how good they were. Each student was then given an essay to read purporting to be a criticism of modern poetry that specifically mentioned a stanza she had rated as poor. For some subjects, the essayist described this particular stanza in glowing terms—thus creating a large discrepancy between the opinion of the communicator and the opinion voiced by the subjects in this experimental condition. For some subjects, the essayist was only mildly favorable in the way he described the stanza—thus establishing a moderate discrepancy between the essayist and the subjects. In a third condition, the essayist was mildly scornful in his treatment of the stanza—thus placing the recipients of this communication in a situation of mild discrepancy. Finally, to half of the women in the experiment, the writer of the essay was identified as the poet T. S. Eliot, a highly credible poetry critic; to the other half of the subjects, the essay writer was identified as a college student.

The subjects were subsequently allowed to rank the stanzas once again. When T. S. Eliot was ostensibly the communicator, the essay had the most influence on the students when its evaluation of the stanza was most discrepant from theirs; when a fellow student of medium credibility was identified as the essayist, the essay produced a little opinion change when it was slightly discrepant from the opinion of the subjects, a great deal of change when it was moderately discrepant, and only a little opinion change when it was extremely discrepant.

The conflicting results are accounted for: When a communicator has high credibility, the greater the discrepancy between the view he or she advocates and the view of the audience, the more the audience will be persuaded; on the other hand, when a communicator's credibility is doubtful or slim, he or she will produce maximum opinion change at moderate discrepancies.

So, is Gerry Spence correct when he advises other lawyers to ask for large awards for their clients? The answer is "yes"—when the lawyer has established a credible relationship with the jurors, laid a strong foundation for arguments, and presented a highly vivid and convincing case; in other words, when the juror has no other way to reduce the discomfort of rendering an extreme award other than to give the award. We should note that as a master trial attorney, Mr. Spence goes out of his way to treat the jurors with respect and dignity, to tell the story of his clients in a compelling manner, and to spell out the damages suffered by the plaintiff at the hands of the defendant in no uncertain terms. On the other hand, if any factor that makes the extreme request appear ludicrous (the appearance of greed, poor arguments, dislikable lawyer, unsympathetic plaintiff, etc.), the request will fall flat and may even backfire. For example, consider the judge who is later asked by the defendant to overturn the jury's decision. This judge probably doesn't know much about Mr. Spence and may even harbor suspicions about a lawyer who can extract such sizable awards from jurors. With a busy calendar, the judge quickly skims a rather pallid trial transcript and thus doesn't feel the pain suffered by the plaintiff. In the judge's experience, large awards for everyday people seem out of place. In the judge's eye there are ample reasons why Mr. Spence's extreme request appears incredulous. In such cases, the scientific evidence indicates that the appeals judge is not likely to go along with a request for a large damage award. Indeed, many of Gerry Spence's awards have been reduced and overturned by judges on appeal, including those awarded in the Karen Silkwood and Miss Wyoming cases.

In this chapter, we have taken a slightly different approach to the topic of persuasion from that found in the rest of the book—here we looked at it not from the propagandist's or the target's point of view but from the perspective of a scientist. In other words, we sought to answer the question of what works, when, and how. This does not mean that the principles we discussed are not without their propaganda purposes—the politician, the advertiser, the lawyer, the sales clerk will all modulate their positions so as best to fit with those of the audience. We took this perspective, however, to provide a peek behind the scenes at how the principles of persuasion discussed throughout this book have been identified. The social psychologist's knowledge of persuasion has not developed from idle, armchair speculation. Each little fact about persuasion is often the result of extensive study and research, often performed by many researchers over many years. Such research is a vital antidote to the propaganda of our times.

23 ||||||||||||||||||||

Protagoras' Ideal: One-Sided Puffery versus Two-Sided Debate

The Greek historian Herodotus tells the following tale about the origins of the Persian war. In 480 B.C., Xerxes, the Persian leader, had decided to go to war against the Greek city-states in retaliation for their humiliating defeat of the Persians ten years earlier at Marathon. Artabus, Xerxes' uncle, argued against the war on the grounds that the Greek army and navy could easily defeat Persia. He began his speech with these words.

> O king, it is impossible, if not more than one opinion is uttered, to make choice of the best; a man is forced to follow whatever advice may have been given him; but if opposite speeches are delivered, then choice can be exercised. In like manner pure gold is not recognized by itself; but when we test it along with baser ore, we perceive which is the better.[1]

Artabus' words, at first, fell flat. Xerxes was filled with rage and publicly condemned Artabus for his disloyalty to Persia. However, after a period of "cooling off," Xerxes came around to Artabus' position and canceled the attack.

But then a strange event occurred. In the dead of night, Xerxes was visited repeatedly in a dream by a ghostly figure urging war. Haunted by the vision, Xerxes reversed himself once more. The Persians went to war against the Greeks and, after some initial victories, were soundly defeated. The Persian Empire went into decline, and the Greek city-states experienced their Golden Age. The moral of the story was not lost on Herodotus' Greek compatriots: Basing a course of action on irrational considerations results in disaster; full discussion and debate offer the possibility of choosing wisely in public affairs.

When it comes to persuasion, the early Greeks possessed a vision of the ideal. The Sophist Protagoras believed that there are two sides to every issue. His fellow citizens agreed; they thought that persuasion happened best when all parties concerned knew both sides of the issue at hand. By juxtaposing one argument against an opposing one, the issue is made clear; the advantages and disadvantages of the available courses of action are revealed.

Aristotle made Protagoras' belief in the advantages of a two-sided message a component of his theory of effective communication.* The confrontation of opposites is a fundamental process of reasoning. As Aristotle put it:

> [a two-sided message as] a form of speech is satisfying, because the significance of contrasted ideas is easily felt, especially when they are thus put side by side, and also because it has the effect of a logical argument; it is by putting two opposing conclusions side by side that you prove one of them false.[2]

The influence of the Greek love for two-sided debate is still felt today—somewhat. Rhetoric textbooks extol the communication that explores carefully the pros and cons of an issue. The American legal system is based on the ideal that each party to a litigation should present its best case, with a jury of peers deciding which side of the issue will prevail. Contrast this with the old Soviet system, in which there was one truth embodied in the party and the state served as judge, jury, prosecutor, and defense.

In our own century, the journalist Walter Lippmann argued that opposing viewpoints are essential to democracy;[3] we learn most from those who tell us what we don't know or don't find agreeable. Reminiscent of the early Greeks, Lippmann believed that it was only through listening to various positions on an issue that truth could be found.

But Protagoras' ideal is a long way from the type of persuasion one finds in the mass media today. The typical ad is one-sided and consists of little information, much puffery, and many exaggerated claims. "This pain reliever is gentler, faster, best." "Brand X will take fat off fast." "You can't beat the taste of Brand Y." "Only presidential candidate Z will strengthen defense, increase domestic spending, and balance the budget (Congress

---

* Of course, consistent with Protagoras' belief that there are two sides to every issue, some Greeks argued that one-sided persuasion was best. Plato in his dialogues Gorgias and Protagoras chided the Sophists as "word tricksters and hucksters" who obscured the path to the one truth, or what has since become known as the Platonic ideal.

willing)." For the most part, debate and comparison are missing from today's persuasion landscape.

Consider the simplest form of "debate," one that hardly approaches the Greek ideal: the comparative advertisement, that is, an ad that explicitly compares two or more brands of a product on at least one attribute. Studies have found that only 7% to 25% of all advertising in the major media is comparative in its claims.[4] It wasn't always possible for advertisers to present comparative ads. In the early 1960s, major ad agencies and television networks strongly discouraged comparative ads and the mentioning of a competitor's brand name on the grounds that it was unsporting. In 1964, NBC dropped its ban on such advertising, but the other two networks did not follow, thereby requiring an advertiser wishing to use a comparative campaign to create two separate ads—one for NBC and one for ABC and CBS. In the early 1970s, the Federal Trade Commission (FTC) threatened lawsuits over restraint of trade to force ABC, CBS, and the major advertisers to reverse their policy. The result, according to advertising historian Stephen Fox,[5] was an increase in comparative advertising and the development of a new philosophy of advertising termed *brand positioning*.[6]

According to the philosophy of brand positioning, market share can be gained by linking a product to one specific selling point or consumer benefit. One of the best ways to position a brand in the consumer's mind is to compare it with a competitor, especially if that competitor is well known. Some highly successful examples: 7-Up doubled its sales by calling itself the uncola in contrast to Coke; Tylenol became the number-one aspirin substitute by pointing out that "aspirin can irritate the stomach lining, trigger asthmatic or allergic reactions, and cause small amounts of gastrointestinal bleeding"; Scope improved its market share by claiming that Listerine produces *medicine breath;* Avis gained valuable ground on Hertz by arguing that because they were number two, they would try harder.

In all of these positioning ads, a comparison is made that makes the advertised brand appear superior. Of course, other contrasts can be made that would make it look inferior. For example, number-one Hertz may not need to overexert itself since it is already delivering what the consumer wants. Although brand positioning is comparative, it frequently makes comparisons on

only a few advantageous dimensions and thus falls short of the Greek ideal of a full discussion of the pros and cons of an issue.

Given the complexity of many public issues, one would hope that the speeches of politicians and government officials would resemble more the ideals of Protagoras than the practices of modern consumer advertisers. Alas, the structure of modern mass media does not always facilitate the ideal. It is difficult to contrast opposing viewpoints in a thirty-second advertisement or a network news soundbite. In the televised era, U.S. presidential campaigns look more like an advertising campaign positioning brands than an ideal debate. For example, in 1964, Lyndon Johnson positioned his opponent, Barry Goldwater, as a trigger-happy threat to unleash nuclear arms. (Goldwater failed to reciprocate in kind and lost by a landslide.) Richard Nixon and Ronald Reagan were both successful in portraying their Democrat rivals as liberal extremists. In 1988, George Bush carried this theme further by branding his opponent, Michael Dukakis, as the "ACLU liberal"; Dukakis portrayed Bush as the

"rich boy who became a wimp." Although this positioning strategy failed for Dukakis, it worked four years later for Bill Clinton,
who painted George Bush as a "rich boy born with a silver foot
in his mouth." In the 2000 election, George W. Bush attempted
to link Al Gore with Bill Clinton, hoping that some of the negative aspects of Clinton would rub off on Gore. To counter, Gore
selected as his running mate Joseph Lieberman, one of Clinton's
harshest moral critics, and then depicted George W. Bush as a
pawn of the rich. Sadly, these tactics diminish the amount of
time spent discussing some of the larger issues facing the country, such as education, health insurance, child welfare, nuclear
arms proliferation, and foreign policy.

Is it ever possible for a two-sided argument to be more persuasive than a one-sided message? Or, to put it more bluntly,
what factors make a one-sided argument so effective that they
seem to be the tactic of choice for most modern propagandists.
To sharpen our understanding of the uses and abuses of one- and
two-sided communications, let's examine the conditions under
which each is most persuasive.

Suppose you are about to make a speech attempting to persuade your audience that more spending on education is necessary or that the budget surplus should be used to fuel tax cuts.
Would you persuade more people if you simply stated your view
and ignored the arguments against your position, or would you
be more persuasive if you discussed the opposing arguments and
attempted to refute them?

Before trying to answer this question, let's look closely at the
factors involved. If a communicator mentions the opposition's
arguments, it might indicate that he or she is an objective, fair-
minded person; this could enhance the speaker's trustworthiness
and thus increase his or her effectiveness. On the other hand, if
a communicator so much as mentions the arguments on the
other side of the issue, it might suggest to the audience that
the issue is a controversial one; this could confuse members of
the audience, make them vacillate, induce them to search for
counterarguments, and ultimately reduce the persuasiveness of
the communication.

With these possibilities in mind, it should not come as a surprise that there is no simple relation between one-sided arguments and the effectiveness of the communication. It depends to

some extent on how well informed the audience is and on the audience's initial opinions on the issue.

Research generally finds that the more informed the members of the audience are, the less likely they are to be persuaded by a one-sided argument and the more likely they are to be persuaded by an argument that brings out the important opposing arguments and then attempts to refute them.[7] This makes sense: A well-informed person is more likely to know some of the counterarguments; when the communicator avoids mentioning these, the knowledgeable members of the audience are likely to conclude that the communicator is either unfair or is unable to refute such arguments. On the other hand, an uninformed person is less apt to know of the existence of opposing arguments. If the counterargument is ignored, the less informed members of the audience are persuaded; if the counterargument is presented, they might get confused.

The message-dense nature of the mass media often makes it difficult to respond intelligently to what we receive. It takes considerable mental effort to process effectively the stream of one short message after another. Advertisers have observed that consumers frequently find comparative advertising confusing; they mistake one brand for another, leading to a situation in which the advertiser is publicizing the competition. For this reason, comparative advertising is rarely used by the leading brand (why give a new upstart free publicity?); it is used mostly by a challenger that might gain from being confused with the leader. For example, in the domain of fast-food burgers, Burger King and Wendy's often compare themselves with the market leader, McDonald's, which never mentions its competitors. Pepsi often mentions Coke; the reverse is almost never true. In the domain of political campaigns, attack advertising is most often used by the challenger, not the incumbent, and by a candidate who is behind or slipping in the polls.[8] In the confusing, message-dense environment of the mass media, one-sided messages make sense for all but a few propagandists.

Another factor influencing the effectiveness of one- versus two-sided persuasion is the partisanship of the audience. As we might expect, if a member of the audience is already predisposed to believe the communicator's argument, a one-sided presentation has a greater impact on his or her opinion than a two-sided presentation. If, however, a member of the audience is leaning in the opposite direction, then a two-sided refutational argument is more persuasive. We should underscore that the research does not favor the effectiveness of a simple two-sided argument: It favors the effectiveness of presenting both sides and pointing out the weaknesses in your opponent's position.

Most politicians seem to be well aware of the partisanship phenomenon; they tend to present vastly different kinds of speeches, depending upon who constitutes the audience. When talking to the party faithful, they almost invariably deliver a hell-raising set of arguments favoring their own party platform and candidacy. If they do mention the opposition, it is in a derisive, mocking tone. On the other hand, when appearing on network television or when speaking to any audience of mixed loyalties, they tend to take a more diplomatic position, giving the opposing view a less emotional airing.

The evidence about the conditions under which a two-sided communication is more effective is a cause for concern for those who appreciate the ideal of Protagoras. The message-dense environment of the mass media is not conducive to thoughtful, intelligent processing of message content. The ease with which we can switch television channels allows us easily to find the most agreeable and entertaining message. Competing in this environment, communicators may come to rely more and more on the one-sided, partisan communication, reducing further the audience's understanding of the issues of the day.

All is not lost for those who favor the Greek ideal of persuasion—after all, there are two sides to every issue. During the 1988 presidential campaign, the League of Women Voters refused to sponsor the presidential debates, as they traditionally had done. The reason: The political pundits had designed the rules of the debate so that true discussion could not occur; the candidates were thus free to deliver their one-sided stump speeches and were never placed in danger of being embarrassed by a careful comparison of their positions on the issues.

The 1992 presidential campaign was different—somewhat.[9] Many citizens seemed legitimately upset about the way the 1988 campaign was conducted, and the news media appeared embarrassed at its lack of coverage of the issues. The result was some attempt to stimulate debate and fair discussion in the campaign. For example, many newspapers and CNN carried analyses of deceptive ads and statements by the candidates. Ross Perot, an independent candidate who garnered 19% of the popular vote, attempted to move beyond short soundbites and outlined his proposals in 30-minute infomercials. All the candidates fielded questions from average citizens on talk shows such as "The Phil Donahue Show" and "Larry King Live." One of the highlights of the 1992 campaign came in Richmond, Virginia, when, during the presidential debates, audience members reminded candidates to quit the mudslinging and irrelevant character attacks and get to the issues.

The success, albeit limited, of the FTC in the 1970s in increasing the number of comparative advertisements on television suggests that the League of Women Voters and the citizens of Richmond, Virginia, may be on the right track. John Chancellor, the NBC news commentator, would take it one step further. Given that American taxpayers, through funding laws, now pay for a major chunk of the campaign, taxpayers are entitled to determine the campaign rules and norms. Chancellor argued that the government should no longer provide money for thirty-second spots and soundbites. In their place would be taxpayer-supported debates, press conferences, and forums that would lead to in-depth discussions.

As U.S. presidential elections subsequent to 1992 and many state and local races have shown, if we want issue-oriented elections, citizens must demand them. By paying attention to the form and style of the persuasive message, we can achieve the type of persuasion a democracy requires. Perhaps one attribute of a communicator's credibility should be the degree to which he or she considers and communicates fairly and intelligently on both (or even multiple) sides of an important issue. The next time a presidential candidate tries to terminate debate and discussion by responding to an opponent's challenge with the words "There you go again," as Ronald Reagan did to Jimmy Carter in the 1980 presidential debates, perhaps the best response, regardless of our own position, would be to jeer and laugh as the early Greeks might have done. After all, whose intelligence is being insulted when debate is limited to a one-sided communication?

Emotional Appeals:
Touch the Heart,
Persuade the Mind

The Fear Appeal

In 1741, in the small New England town of Enfield, Connecticut, Jonathan Edwards delivered a sermon entitled "Sinners in the Hands of an Angry God." In this sermon, he preached:

> Thus it is that natural men are held in the hand of God, over the pit of hell; they have deserved the fiery pit, and are already sentenced to it . . . the devil is waiting for them, hell is gaping for them, the flames gather and flash about them, and would fain lay hold on them, and swallow them up. . . . In short, they have no refuge, nothing to take hold of; all that preserves them every moment is the mere arbitrary will, and uncovenanted, unobliged forbearance of an incensed God.[1]

Eyewitness accounts indicate that the sermon left the congregation "breathing of distress and weeping." The records show that thousands gave over their lives to Christ as part of the Great Awakening of eighteenth-century America.

Two centuries later, Adolf Hitler offered these words to his fellow countrymen and -women:

> The Jew regards work as a means of exploiting other peoples. The Jew is the ferment of the decomposition of peoples. This

means that the Jew destroys and has to destroy. The Jew is harmful to us. . . . What then are the specifically Jewish aims? To spread their invisible State as supreme tyranny over all other States in the whole world.

Communism is the forerunner of death, of national destruction, and extinction. . . . The red mob is threatening Berlin. . . . Today we may be convinced that there are more than 600,000 to 700,000 Communists in Berlin. How do people imagine a German future, as long as this increase is not checked? We must fight to the very end those tendencies which have eaten into the soul of the German nation.[2]

Millions of Germans gladly embraced Hitler's National Socialist party.

Although the goals of Edwards and Hitler were quite different, their method was the same—instilling fear. Both Edwards and Hitler threatened their audiences with dire consequences if a certain course of action was not followed.

Fire-and-brimstone preachers and Nazis are not the only ones who arouse fear in order to motivate and persuade. Life insurance agents play on our anxieties to induce purchase of their policies. Parents try to scare their children in hopes of having them come home early from a date. Physicians use fear to insure that patients adopt and maintain a prescribed medical regimen. The nightly news carries reports of one sensational crime after another, thus increasing our fear of the streets. The political party that is out of office treats us to tales of the economic and moral collapse of the nation in hopes of gaining power. And special-interest groups announce one food fear after another—coffee may cause pancreatic cancer, the use of aluminum pots can produce Alzheimer's disease, corn flakes contain hazardous amounts of the pesticide EDB—despite the fact that Americans' life expectancy continues to increase.[3]

Sometimes these fear appeals are based on legitimate concerns—smoking does cause cancer; "unsafe sex" increases one's chance of contracting AIDS; failure to brush and floss can led to painful tooth decay. But often fear appeals are based on dark, irrational fears—fears stemming from racial prejudice or the notion that there is a Communist under every bed. At times a regime instills fear by terrorizing its own citizens, as in Hitler's Germany, Stalin's Soviet Union, Mao's Cultural Revolution, the

Cambodia of the Khmer Rouge, the Argentina of the junta, Saddam Hussein's Iraq, and at countless other times and places. Fear appeals are powerful because they channel our thoughts away from careful consideration of the issue at hand and toward plans for ridding ourselves of the fear. When illegitimate fears are used, the message promotes deception—not to mention the cruelty of the fear itself. It behooves us to look closely at just when and how fear appeals are effective.

Not all fear appeals are successful in achieving their objectives. For the past few years, public service announcements have alerted viewers to the dangers of drug abuse and have frightened Americans about the possibility of contracting AIDS. Opponents of the nuclear arms race paint a graphic picture of nuclear winter. Yet drug abuse remains *high*, the practice of safe sex *low*, and the possibility of world annihilation through the use of nuclear weapons ever present. Just what are the factors that make a fear-arousing appeal more or less effective?

Let's begin with a seemingly simple question: Suppose you wish to arouse fear in the hearts of your audience as a way of inducing opinion change. Would it be more effective to arouse just a little fear, or should you try to scare the hell out of them?

For example, if your goal is to convince people to drive more carefully, would it be more effective to show them gory technicolor films of the broken and bloody bodies of highway accident victims, or would it be more effective if you soft-pedaled your communication—showing crumpled fenders, discussing increased insurance rates due to careless driving, and pointing out the possibility that people who drive carelessly may have their driver's licenses suspended?

Common sense argues on both sides of this street. On the one hand, one might suppose that a good scare will motivate people to action; on the other hand, it can be argued that too much fear can be debilitating—that is, it might interfere with a person's ability to pay attention to the message, to comprehend it, and to act upon it. We have all believed, at one time or another, that it only happens to the other guy, it can't happen to me. Thus people continue to drive at very high speeds and to insist on driving after they've had a few drinks, even though they know better. Perhaps this is because the possible negative consequences of these actions are so great that we try not to think about them. Thus, if a communication arouses extreme fear, we tend *not* to pay close attention to it.

What does the scientific evidence tell us? Experimental data overwhelmingly suggest that all other things being equal, the more frightened a person is by a communication, the more likely he or she is to take positive preventive action. And there are certain conditions that will enhance the impact of a frightening appeal.

Fear can be a powerful motivating psychological force, channeling all our thoughts and energies toward removing the threat so that we don't think about much else. Consider the series of experiments conducted by Dariusz Dolinski and Richard Nawrat.[4] In their research, they aroused fear by blowing a police whistle as a pedestrian jaywalked or placing a piece of paper that resembled a ticket used to administer fines on the windshield of cars. In the modern urban world, police whistles and tickets are sure to startle and create some fear in our hearts. However, this fear was quickly relieved—no arrest was made among the jaywalkers and that piece of paper that looked like a ticket turned out to be an ad for a hair-growth medicine. Next, Dolinski and Nawrat asked the jaywalkers and motorists to comply with a request (in some studies, to complete a questionnaire and in other studies, to aid a charity). The results: When fear was aroused and then relieved, the jaywalkers and motorists were significantly more likely to comply with the request than those who jaywalked without a whistle or did not receive the "ticket." Dolinski and Nawrat conclude that the arousal of fear and its subsequent relief distract attention from evaluating the request, resulting in more compliance. The principle of fear-then-relief is well known by terrorists and rogue interrogators. For example, one common method of extracting a confession from "witches" during the Inquisition was to torture, terrorize, and inflict harsh pain on the accused and then show kindness. Dazed and confused, the falsely accused would sign a confession that then served as their death warrant.

Now let's turn to looking at the use of fear in a persuasive message. The most prolific researchers in this area have been Howard Leventhal and his colleagues.[5] In one experiment, they tried to induce people to stop smoking and to obtain chest X-rays. (At the time, medical authorities considered routine chest X-rays important in the fight against tuberculosis.) Some subjects were exposed to a low-fear treatment: They were simply presented with a recommendation to stop smoking and get their chests X-rayed. Others were subjected to moderate fear: They were shown a film depicting a young man whose chest X-rays revealed he had lung cancer. The people subjected to the high-fear condition saw the same film the "moderate-fear" people saw—and, in addition, they were treated to a vivid, gory color film of a lung cancer operation. The results showed that those people who were most frightened were also most eager to stop smoking and most likely to sign up for chest X-rays.

Is this true for all people? It is not. There is good reason why common sense can lead us to believe that a great deal of fear leads to inaction: It does—under certain conditions.

What Leventhal and his colleagues discovered is that the people who had a reasonably good opinion of themselves (high self-esteem) were the ones most likely to be moved by high degrees of fear arousal. People with low opinions of themselves were the least likely to take immediate action when confronted with a communication arousing a great deal of fear—but (and here is the interesting part) after a delay, they behaved very much like the subjects with high self-esteem. People who have a low opinion of themselves may have difficulty coping with threats to themselves. A high-fear communication overwhelms them and makes them feel like crawling into bed and pulling the covers up over their heads. Low or moderate fear is something they can more easily deal with at the moment they experience it. But, given time—that is, if it is not essential they act immediately— they will be more likely to act if the message truly scared the hell out of them.

Subsequent research by Leventhal and his colleagues lends support to this analysis. In one study, subjects were shown films of serious automobile accidents. Some subjects watched the films on a large screen from up close; others watched them from far away on a much smaller screen. Among those subjects with high or moderate self-esteem, those who saw the films on the large screen were much more likely to take subsequent protective action than were those who saw the films on the small screen. Subjects with low self-esteem were more likely to take action when they saw the films on a small screen; those who saw the films on a large screen reported a great deal of fatigue and stated that they had great difficulty even thinking of themselves as victims of automobile accidents.

It should be relatively easy to make people with high self-esteem behave like people with low self-esteem. We can overwhelm them by making them feel there is nothing they can do to prevent or ameliorate a threatening situation. Much research has shown that if recipients of a fear appeal perceive that there is no way to cope effectively with the threat, they are not likely to respond to the appeal but will just bury their heads in the sand— even those who have high self-esteem.[6] Franklin D. Roosevelt knew the debilitating effect of extreme fear and sought to counteract it when he announced, in his first inaugural address, "The only thing we have to fear is fear itself."

Conversely, suppose you wanted to reduce the automobile accident rate or to help people give up smoking, and you were faced with people with low self-esteem. How would you proceed? If you were to construct a message containing clear, specific, and optimistic instructions, it might increase the feeling among the members of your audience that they could confront their fears and cope with the danger.

These speculations have been confirmed; experiments by Howard Leventhal and his colleagues show that fear-arousing messages containing specific instructions about how, when, and where to take action are much more effective than recommendations that omit such instructions. For example, a campaign conducted on a college campus urging students to get tetanus shots included specific instructions about where and when they were available. The campaign materials included a map showing the location of the student health services and a suggestion that each student set aside a convenient time to stop by.

The results showed high-fear appeals to be more effective than low-fear appeals in producing favorable *attitudes* toward tetanus shots among the students, and they also increased the students' stated intentions to get the shots. The highly specific instructions about how to get the shots did not affect these opinions and intentions, but the instructions did have a big effect on the *actual behavior:* Of those subjects who were instructed about how to proceed, 28% actually got the tetanus shots; but of those who received no specific instructions, only 3% got them. In a control group exposed only to the instructions, with no fear-arousing message, no one got the shots. Thus specific instructions alone were not enough to produce action—fear was a necessary component for action in such situations.

Very similar results were obtained in Leventhal's cigarette experiment. Leventhal found that a high-fear communication produced a much greater *intention* to stop smoking. Unless it was accompanied by recommendations for specific behavior, however, it produced little results. Similarly, specific instructions (buy a magazine instead of a pack of cigarettes, drink plenty of water when you have the urge to smoke, etc.) without a fear-arousing communication were relatively ineffective. The combination of fear arousal and specific instructions produced the best results; the students in this condition were smoking less four months after they were subjected to the experimental procedure.

In sum, a fear appeal is most effective when (1) it *scares* the hell out of people, (2) it offers a *specific recommendation* for overcoming the fear-arousing threat, (3) the recommended action is perceived as effective for reducing the threat, and (4) the message recipient believes that he or she *can* perform the recommended action. Notice how the fear appeal works. The recipient's attention is first focused on the painful fear. In such a frightened state it is difficult to think about anything other than getting rid of the fear. Next, the propagandist offers a way to get rid of that fear—a simple, doable response that just happens to be what the propagandist wanted you to do all along.

This is exactly what Jonathan Edwards and Adolf Hitler offered their listeners. Both men described rising menaces—sin or Jews and communists—that, if allowed free rein, would devastate the soul or the national spirit. Each man offered a specific remedy for the crisis—commitment to Christ or joining the Nazi party. These courses of action were easy enough to perform—one needed only to answer the altar call or to vote for a Nazi candidate.

In contrast, fear appeals to increase nuclear disarmament or to decrease drug abuse rarely incorporate all four components of a successful fear appeal. We have all been alerted to the dread of nuclear weapons and the personal and social destruction of drug abuse. However, there have been few specific recommendations for removing these threats that have been generally perceived as *effective* and *doable*.

Two counterexamples of effective anti-nuclear arms appeals will make our point. First, during the 1950s and early 1960s, many people purchased and installed "nuclear fallout shelters" in their homes. The reason: Fear of nuclear war was high and the installation of a home fallout shelter, at the time, appeared to be an effective, doable response.

Second, during the 1964 presidential campaign, Lyndon Johnson, in a series of television ads, was able to sway voters by portraying his opponent, Barry Goldwater, as a supporter of the use of nuclear weapons. One controversial ad featured a young girl counting to ten as she pulled petals from a daisy. A moment later, the television screen filled with the mushroom cloud of a nuclear bomb. Johnson's appeal was successful because it linked the fear of nuclear war to Goldwater and then proposed a vote for Johnson as a specific, doable way to avoid this threat. In contrast, there doesn't appear to be such a simple response to today's threat of nuclear winter or a terrorist's use of nuclear arms, so we have a tendency to avoid our fears by ignoring the issue.

Consider also the campaign to reduce the incidence of drug abuse by telling kids to "just say no." Although many teenagers are probably frightened by the drug scene, most will not perceive "just saying no" as an effective and doable response. Imagine yourself as a teenager whose friends are getting high by snorting cocaine and are pressuring you to try one little snort. Just saying "no" is likely to result in even more pressure—"Come on, just one try. What are you? A loser?" Such pressure is not easy to resist.

Solving the drug problem, given its scope and complexity, will require more than just a cleverly worded advertisement. However, we can design our appeals so that they are more effective. For example, recently a teacher asked her elementary school class to come up with specific ways to say "no" when their friends pressure them to use drugs. The students produced a book of "ways to say no"—for example, walking away, calling the dealer the loser, offering the friend an alternative to doing drugs. Such an approach has the advantage of "self-selling" the class not to use drugs and also provides a list of specific ways that children might perceive as effective for dealing with peer pressure; such a list can then be illustrated on television or role-played in the schools. But in the final analysis, for our fear appeals to work, we need to offer our children a more effective and doable solution to life's problems than the advice to "just say no"—we need to offer them something to say "yes" to.

The use of fear appeals—for pro-social or for more unseemly crusades—raises a broader question: Should fear appeals be used at all? Given the power of fear to motivate and direct our thoughts, there is much potential for abuse. Illegitimate fears can always be invented for any given propaganda purpose. As persuaders, it is our responsibility, if we decide to use a fear appeal, to insure that the fear we instill is, at least, legitimate and that it serves to alert the target to potential dangers as opposed to obscuring the issue with emotion. If we don't, then we run the risk of establishing our credibility as little more than that of Chicken Little. As targets of such appeals, we owe it to ourselves to first ask "How legitimate is this fear?" before taking the propagandist's bait. If we don't, we could spend our lives running around in a vain attempt to keep the sky from falling.

The Granfalloon Technique

"My God," she said, "are you a Hoosier?"

I admitted I was.

"I'm a Hoosier, too," she crowed. "Nobody has to be ashamed of being a Hoosier."

"I'm not," I said. "I never knew anybody who was."

—Kurt Vonnegut, *Cat's Cradle*

One of the most interesting and often most unbelievable set of findings in social psychology is induced by what has come to be known as the *minimum group paradigm*, which forms the basis of an emotionally powerful persuasive technique. In this procedure, first identified by the British social psychologist Henri Tajfel, complete strangers are formed into groups using the most trivial, inconsequential criteria imaginable.[1] For example, in one study, subjects watched a coin toss that randomly assigned them to Group X or Group W. In another study, subjects were first asked to express their opinions about painters they had never heard of and were then randomly assigned either to a group that appreciates Klee or to one that enjoys Kandinsky, ostensibly due to their picture preferences. To use a term coined by the American novelist Kurt Vonnegut, Tajfel and his colleagues are creating *granfalloons*—proud and meaningless associations of human beings.[2]

What makes Tajfel's research so curious are the results that are often obtained. Despite the fact that the subjects were total strangers prior to the study, that they had never interacted with one another before and never would again, and that their actions were completely anonymous, they acted as if those who shared their meaningless label were their good friends or close kin. Subjects indicated that they liked those who shared their label. They rated others who shared their label as more likely to have a pleasant personality and to have produced better output than out-group members. Most strikingly, subjects allocated more money and rewards to those group members who shared their label and did so in a competitive manner—for example, subjects were more likely to prefer giving fellow group members $2 and members of the "other" group $1 rather than giving fellow group members $3 and the members of other group $4.

What makes the granfalloon tick? Researchers have uncovered two basic psychological processes, one cognitive and one motivational. First, the knowledge that "I am in this group" is used to divide up and make sense of the world, much in the same way that words and labels can be used to pre-persuade (see Chapter 6). Differences *between* groups are exaggerated, whereas similarities among members of the granfalloon are emphasized in the secure knowledge that "this is what our type does." One serious consequence is that out-group members are dehumanized; they are represented in our mind by a simple, often derogatory label—gook, jap, redneck southerner, kike, nigger—as opposed to unique individuals—Nguyen, Susumu, Anthony, Elliot, Doug. It is a lot easier to abuse an abstraction. Second, social groups are a source of self-esteem and pride, a form of reverse Groucho Marxism—"I'd be more than happy to join a club that would have me as a member."* To obtain the self-esteem the group has to offer, members come to defend the group and adopt its symbols, rituals, and beliefs.

Herein lies the secret to the persuasiveness of the granfalloon. If the professional persuader, the advertiser, the politician, the televangelist can get us to accept his or her granfalloons, then we have a ready-made way to make sense of our lives—the propagandist's way—and as our self-esteem becomes increasingly linked to these groups, we have a strong motivation to defend the group and to go to great lengths proudly to adopt its customs. What the propagandist is really saying is: "You are on my side (never mind that I created the teams); now act like it and do what we say." Let's look at some specific examples of how granfalloons can be used to persuade.[3]

A study by Robert Cialdini and his colleagues illustrates the attraction power of a granfalloon.[4] Every autumn Saturday, many of America's universities and colleges battle it out on the gridiron—half win and the other half lose. Cialdini and his colleagues

---

* Based on one of Groucho Marx's legendary statements. On learning that he was admitted to an exclusive club, he remarked, "I would not want to belong to a club that would have me as a member."

counted the number of college sweatshirts worn on the Monday following a football game at seven universities that take football seriously—Arizona State, Louisiana State, Notre Dame, Michigan, Ohio State, Pittsburgh, and Southern California. The results: More students wore their university insignias after a victory, and especially after a big win. Nothing succeeds like a winning granfalloon. Is it any wonder that advertisers pay dearly to link their products with winners, such as Michael Jordan for sneakers or Cindy Crawford for makeup, and to create merchandise-selling granfalloons based on a designer label, movies such as *Star Wars* or *Pokémon*, or the latest Saturday-morning cartoon?

We are also attracted to the people in our granfalloon as well, even if those people are disreputable and unscrupulous. For example, suppose you found out that you shared a birthday with Grigori Rasputin, the "Mad Monk of Russia." What would you think of him? As you know, Rasputin was a scoundrel who used his position as a religious figure to exploit others mercilessly for his own gain. If you shared his birth date, would you think more positively of Rasputin? A pair of experiments by John Finch and Robert Cialdini suggests that you would.[5] In this research, college students were led to believe that they shared the same birthday as Rasputin. After reading a description that painted Rasputin in unsavory terms, the students were asked to rate the monk. Those who thought they shared his birthday rated Rasputin as better, more effective, more pleasant, and stronger than those who did not share his birthday. In other words, we like those who end up in our granfalloon, even when membership is based on something as trivial as a birthday. We are also more likely to cooperate with those in our granfalloon. In another study, college students played a highly competitive game with someone they thought shared or did not share their birthday.[6] The results showed that the students tended to cooperate with and not compete against their birthdaymates (relative to those who did not share a birthday). Do these results seem surprising to you? If so, we hasten to point out that many people believe that they share personality traits, fates, and destiny with those who share their zodiac sign—a collection of twelve granfalloons based on birthdays.

Sometimes granfalloons come ready-made. In recent decades, marketers have put forth extraordinary effort to classify

America into groups and lifestyles, with the goal of designing communications and products to fit each group.[7] For example, one scheme advanced by the Claritas Corporation divides America into forty types of neighborhoods based on values, lifestyles, income, and so on. You could be a member of the "Young Influentials," "Blue-Collar Nursery," or "Blue-Blood Estates." Each group is associated with a certain self-image and lifestyle. Advertising and products are then targeted to profitable markets. In other words, products are given a "personality" that fits the image of the target market; this advertising then goes on to create further the image of each granfalloon by specifying what needs to be done to maintain a certain image.

When ready-made groups don't exist, the skilled propagandist can create them by inventing new distinctions or by emphasizing old, forgotten ones, just as Tajfel and his colleagues have done in their laboratories.

A trip with a friend of ours to purchase a microwave oven illustrates the invention of a granfalloon in a sales situation. He loves to cook. In contrast, his wife, who accompanied him on this shopping trip, is of the mind that a woman's place (especially this one's) is not necessarily in the kitchen, but in the office. As is common, the salesman began by directing his pitch about the advantages of microwave cooking to the female. The salesman was abruptly informed by the wife, "He does the cooking; you should tell him about it." The salesman, without breaking stride, turned to our friend, positioning his body so that a two-person group was formed with the wife excluded, and said: "That's great. I think it's wonderful that more men are cooking. There's nothing I like better than to get in the kitchen and do some cooking myself." The inherent persuasive message: "We share the same attitudes; we are of the same type; trust me!"

Or consider this more unseemly example of the phony use of a granfalloon. In an interview discussing his technique, a fraudulent telemarketer—a person who would routinely call people on the phone, lie to them that they had won a prize, and then seduce them into giving up their hard-earned cash—put it this way: "Any good con artist is going to use whatever [a victim] tells them about themselves against them. If you tell me you are a veteran of World War II, well, great, sir, I am a veteran of Desert Storm. We've got something in common. You always look for an angle with the victim to legitimize what you are doing and to make yourself more believable."[8] In other words, the con criminal tells the target of the scam, "We are in one big happy granfalloon; you can trust me and do what I say."

Shared emotion and feeling can also create a granfalloon. A sense of oneness with others can be produced by sharing a fun time, a sad situation, or a harrowing experience. Kathleen Hall Jamieson identifies this as one skill that made Ronald Reagan so persuasive a president—the ability to express the emotions we are currently feeling or would like to feel.[9] Reagan's speeches often described the emotional experiences of others—what it felt like to carry the Olympic torch; the feelings of a family as they watched their only son go off to war; the experience of a daughter who honored her promise to her father, a World War II veteran, to visit the beach at Normandy. By expressing our common feelings, Reagan provided the nation with a sense of unity and, not inconsequentially, made an attack on the Teflon president seem tantamount to attacking ourselves.

Office politics provides yet another arena for the granfalloon technique. One common ploy used by organizational politicians is to create personal fiefdoms, complete with their own agenda and goals and, of course, enemies. For example, an office gamesplayer may rally the troops by declaring it is us against them— the marketing department versus production, the psychiatrists versus the psychologists, the city versus the college. Once the identities are fixed, the agenda is set.

Often workplace distinctions can be so trivial that they are not easily understood by an outside observer or a new group member. The cunning office politician may be so bold as to create temporary, fluctuating group identities. For example, today's Machiavellian may set one group against another by going to one person and saying "we women must stick together," to another and saying "we newcomers have to watch out for the old guard," and to a third and saying "those of us with an eye to the bottom line better pull together on this one"—all in an attempt to secure allegiance to a proposal.

Another office persuasion tactic is subtly to change a person's granfalloon—a technique known as *co-option*. This tactic is often used to squelch opposition. For example, consider a social activist who has been highly critical of a corporation's policies or a feminist who argues that his or her university's hiring practices are discriminatory. The corporation or university then gives the critic a new position, often highly visible but without real power within the organization—for example, a place on the board of directors or appointment as head of a women's affairs center. The position usually comes with a nice office, secretaries, letterhead, stationery, and maybe even a parking place. Gradually, the critic becomes increasingly isolated from old "activist" friends and increasingly dependent on the corporation or university for material resources and a sense of identity. The opposition is defused as ties with the old granfalloon are dissolved.

Tragically, granfalloons are not limited to business offices but can appear at national and international political levels, where the stakes are much higher. Adolf Hitler was able to create a strong German identity by manufacturing a "Jewish" and a "Communist" threat and by emphasizing a common "Aryan" heritage. During the Cold War, American and Soviet propagandists portrayed each other as imperialistic warmongers with little regard for human rights and dignities. Today there continues to be strife in the Balkans among Serbs, Croats, and Muslims. Once such identities form, the right and moral course of action becomes abundantly clear.

The modern masters of the granfalloon are televangelists—Christian fundamentalist ministers such as Oral Roberts, Pat Robertson, Jimmy Swaggart, Jim Bakker, and Tammy Faye Messner (formerly Bakker) who use television to promote not only the gospel but also, with rapid-fire frequency, their sales message.[10] For example, one study looking at the content of Christian programs found that a typical show makes requests for donations averaging $189.52 per hour, with the average Bible selling for a pricey $191.91. (Jerry Falwell wins the title of "God's biggest solicitor," offering Bibles, books, tapes, and other religious trinkets for sale at a rate of $1,671 per hour.) The results are quite profitable. In 1980, the top four religious programs took in over a quarter of a billion dollars, with the Jimmy Swaggart Ministry alone collecting more than $60 million in 1982. They succeed by defining the image of a "Christian" and then using the electronic media to create a "family of believers" based on this image.

Roughly 10 million Americans (or 4% of the U.S. population) regularly watch Christian programming. Although this is a large number of viewers (it is estimated that Jesus preached to no more than 30,000 souls in his entire lifetime), it is not exactly a moral majority, but more like, in marketing terms, a small but potentially profitable market segment. Who, then, are the members of the electronic church? Surveys and interviews reveal two broad categories of viewers: persons who are already converted to Christianity and those who are lonely and isolated or have recently suffered a loss, such as a personal disability or the death of a loved one. The success of Christian programming lies in directly matching the needs of both types of viewers.

The electronic church creates a "Christian identity" for its viewers. The identity, most clearly expressed by the minister-leader, comes complete with political attitudes (typically conservative ones, such as opposing abortion and supporting a strong defense), religious beliefs (a literal interpretation of the Bible, the principle of "seed-faith," or the giving of money to later receive more in return), shared feelings (the joy of a spontaneous, televised healing; the tears of Tammy Faye Messner), goals (the creation of a Christian nation, ridding the nation's schools of evolutionary teaching, returning prayer to the classroom), enemies (secular humanists; liberal politicians; at least until recently, the Supreme Court; homosexuals; intellectuals), and rituals and symbols (the 700 Club, PTL bumper stickers and buttons, "speaking in tongues").[11]

For those who already believe, Christian broadcasting becomes a means for further expressing their identity. For those who are lonely or have suffered a loss, it is a way to replace, repair, or rationalize a self-conception that may be damaged by, say, loss of job status or of a close family member. A satisfying self-identity as one of "God's chosen people" can be obtained by watching, subscribing, donating, and adopting the behaviors suggested by religious programs. This image can then be used by the televangelist to sell and market products and ideas.

Given the booming buzz of modern reality, it is perfectly human to try to reduce the vast amounts of information we receive to a more manageable level by categorizing and labeling it. It is also perfectly human to want to belong to groups and to be proud of membership in these groups. Such feelings can have positive consequences: "We Are the World" and Jerry Lewis telethons have raised millions of dollars for worthy causes by tapping into our self-images as global, caring citizens. Many church, mosque, and synagogue members find great meaning and religious identification in feeding the hungry, caring for the less fortunate, and taking the beam out of their own eye first.

At other times, however, granfalloons can be manipulated to get us to purchase unwanted products, to vote for less than qualified candidates, and to hate innocent people. What can be done to lessen the chances of falling prey to the granfalloon tactic?

Here are five simple rules of thumb that might help. First, be wary of those who attempt to create minimum groups and to define you as a member of a certain category. There are many ways to define and label a person. Ask yourself, "Why is this particular label being suggested?" Second, follow the old civil rights motto, "Keep your eye on the prize." Try linking your self-esteem to achieving an objective—be it a quality purchase at a reasonable price or a social good—rather than maintaining a self-image. Third, don't put all of your self-esteem eggs in one basket, one granfalloon—it might lead to fanaticism. Fourth, look for common ground—goals that might be acceptable to both the in- and the out-group—as a means of reducing the importance of group boundaries. And finally, try to think of an out-group member as an individual, someone who may share more in common with you than you might have previously thought.

26

Guilt Sells

In an annual Girl Scout cookie sales drive, thirteen-year-old Elizabeth Brinton sold 11,200 boxes of cookies. When asked how she did it, Brinton replied, "You have to look people in the eye and make them feel guilty."

Guilt sells—a fact of persuasive life that seems to be intuitively grasped by parents, teachers, clergy, charities, and life insurance agents. But guilt, the feeling that we are responsible for some wrongdoing, can be used to sell more than cookies and life insurance. Guilt can also lead you to admit to a crime you did not commit, as social psychologists Saul Kassin and Katherine Kiechel recently discovered.[1]

In a fascinating experiment, Kassin and Kiechel invited college students into their lab for what appeared to be a study measuring reaction time. Each student was to type a series of letters read aloud by another student (who was really working with the experimenters). Before the study began, the experimenter warned: "Do not touch the ALT key near the space bar because the program will crash and the data will be lost." After about a minute of data entry, lo and behold, the computer supposedly ceased to operate and froze. A highly distressed experimenter accused the typist of pressing the forbidden ALT key. All the typists initially denied the charge. The experimenter then tinkered with the keyboard, confirmed the data were lost, and asked, "Did you hit the ALT key?" The typist was then asked to sign a handwritten confession stating, "I hit the ALT key and caused the program to crash. Data were lost," which they were told would result in a phone call from the principal investigator.

How many typists confessed to a crime they never committed? Kassin and Kiechel found that a whopping 69% of the subjects signed the confession. What is more, 28% of the subjects later told another student (supposedly unrelated to the experiment) that they had hit a wrong button and ruined the study. In other words, these subjects actually believed they had committed the offense, with some of them actually making up details about how they came to hit the ALT key.

Kassin and Kiechel found two factors that increased the likelihood that the typist would make a false confession. First, if the typists were asked to enter data at a quick pace, then they were more likely to confess. Second, and perhaps most interesting, rates of confession were dramatically increased if the typist was confronted with false incriminating evidence—that is, they were told that the other student who read the letters aloud saw them hit the ALT key. Police commonly employ this tactic when they question suspects, leading them to believe that they have evidence of guilt that they often do not possess.

Of course, this is just a social-psychological experiment. Such things couldn't happen in real life, where the stakes are much higher and people have more to lose than just some course credit. Don't bet your life or liberty on it, or you might discover what Brad Page learned the hard way: Feelings of guilt, even if falsely induced, can lead one to comply with a police request to confess to a crime.

On the morning of November 4, 1984, Brad and his fiancée, Bibi Lee, had decided to go jogging with their friend Robin in Redwood Park in Oakland. Brad and Robin, both strong runners, lost sight of Bibi after a few miles and stopped to wait for her to catch up. After waiting for several minutes, they became concerned, doubled back, and began to search for her.

The park is a large one, with several trails that wind through the woods. Brad and Robin surmised that Bibi might mistakenly have wandered off the main trail. When they couldn't find her, they decided to head back to the parking lot and wait near the car, thinking that she would eventually head there. After a long wait, Brad decided that it would be more efficient if he searched for her by car, so he asked Robin to wait in the lot in case Bibi came looking for them, while he drove around the perimeter of the park.

After about fifteen minutes, he returned, reporting that he was still unable to find her. They waited for her for another half-hour or so. Then Brad suggested that they drive back home. He felt that Bibi could easily have hopped a bus back home; besides, he later admitted, he was a little annoyed at Bibi because he suspected that she might have disappeared on purpose in order to punish him for a minor squabble they had had earlier that day.

Five weeks later, Bibi's body was found in a shallow grave in a wooded area of Redwood Park. Who killed Bibi Lee? It might have been a serial killer who had been active in the area. Indeed, an eyewitness reported seeing a burly, bearded man (fitting the description of the serial killer) dragging a young woman fitting Bibi's description into a van; at the time the witness wasn't certain whether it was a playful or an aggressive act, so she didn't bother to report the incident until after she read about Bibi's disappearance.

But as time progressed, and there were no hot suspects, the police asked Brad Page to come in for additional questioning. Their reasoning was that he might have found Bibi during the fifteen minutes that he left Robin waiting in the parking lot—

and, in a fit of anger, might have killed her. After inducing Brad to waive his right to an attorney ("We're all friends, here, aren't we?"), the police interrogators had him go over his story several times. During the interrogation, they kept asking him how he could possibly have left his girlfriend alone in the park and driven back home.* Brad felt terribly guilty about it, saying several times, "It was the biggest mistake of my life!" Each time they asked the question, his guilt seemed to grow.

Finally, the interrogators told Brad that, late on the night that Bibi had disappeared, he had been seen near the site of the shallow grave and that his fingerprints had been found on a rock that had been used as the murder weapon. As with the false incriminating evidence used in the Kassin and Kiechel experiment, neither of these statements was true. Brad said that he had no recollection of having left his apartment that night and had no idea how his fingerprints could have gotten on the murder weapon (he didn't even know what the weapon was). But he had no reason to distrust the interrogators, so, understandably, he became terribly confused and asked them if it is possible for a person to commit a horrible crime like this and "blank it out." The interrogators informed him that such things were common occurrences and that it might help him recall the circumstances and ultimately might help him relieve his *guilty* conscience if he closed his eyes and tried to imagine how he *might* have killed Bibi *if he had killed her.*** Brad proceeded to do as he was told, inventing (as did some of the subjects in the Kassin and Kiechel experiment) what he later described as an imaginative scenario. Two hours after his alleged confession, when he was told that the police considered it to be a confession, he seemed genuinely astonished and immediately recanted.

The police continued to consider this to be a confession, even though a great many important details did not coincide with the

---

* One of the authors (EA) testified at Brad Page's trial as an expert witness on noncoercive persuasion and, accordingly, was given access to the audiotapes of the interrogation.

** It should be noted that this is the one aspect of the interrogation that is disputed; the interrogators deny that they stated these instructions in a hypothetical manner, whereas Brad Page insists that they did. Unfortunately (and unaccountably), the police had turned off the tape recorder during this part of the interrogation, so it is impossible to obtain objective evidence on this disagreement.

actual physical evidence. Brad Page was indicted for first-degree murder. The jury was unable to decide whether or not the confession was real, and a mistrial was declared. In a second trial, the jury was similarly confused; they deliberated for six days before finally deciding that while he was not guilty of murder, he *was* guilty of manslaughter! Brad Page was sent to prison. In spite of numerous attempts by lawyers and the media to reopen the case, he served his full term.

We are in no position to state with absolute certainty that Brad Page did not kill Bibi Lee. But we are convinced that his confession was not a valid one. Moreover, we have a pretty good idea of why he complied with the police request to imagine how he might have killed Bibi. Guilt, whether real or imagined, leads to compliance. During the interrogation, Brad Page was made to feel guilty about how he had driven off and left Bibi alone. "You mean to say you actually drove off and left her alone?" It is likely that the feelings of guilt helped to make him susceptible to the influence of his interrogators. The Brad Page case is not exceptional.[2] Police interrogation manuals recommend playing on the suspect's guilt and suggesting incriminating evidence has been found (even when it hasn't been). Surveys show that confession evidence plays a role in the majority of trials and, in the minds of jurors, is one of the most powerful and damning forms of evidence against a defendant. Unfortunately, some confessions are false, as studies of innocent persons who were falsely imprisoned often reveal.[3]

But just how does guilt work as a propaganda device? The effects of guilt on compliance have been isolated in a clever set of experiments performed by Merrill Carlsmith and Alan Gross.[4] In their studies, subjects were induced to deliver a series of painful electric shocks to another individual as part of an experiment on teaching. (In actuality, no shocks were received, but the subjects were led to believe that the shocks were real.) Such an experience would undoubtedly lead the participants to feel guilty about their behavior. Other, "not-guilty" subjects were merely instructed to ring a buzzer to indicate a wrong answer. All subjects were then asked by the shock "victim" to make phone calls on behalf of a "Save the Redwood Forest" committee. The results showed that subjects who were induced to feel guilt were three times as likely to comply with the request than were the "not-guilty" subjects. Guilt sells!

Why is guilt so effective in motivating human behavior? Carl-smith and Gross reasoned that there are at least three possible explanations for why guilt sells: (1) *sympathy,* or feeling sorry for the victim; (2) *restitution,* or feeling the need to compensate for the wrongdoing; and (3) *generalized guilt,* or the desire to repair a self-image tarnished by a transgression.

A second study by Carlsmith and Gross teased apart these three explanations by varying who was transgressing against whom. To induce sympathy for the victim, some subjects first watched someone else supposedly shocking a third person and then were asked by the shock "victim" to help save the redwoods. To induce a need for restitution, other subjects were first led to believe they were shocking a person and later were asked by this "victim" to help save the redwoods. To induce generalized guilt, a third group of subjects was also led to believe that they were shocking a person, but this time the request to save the red-woods came from another individual who was unrelated to the administering of shocks. The results showed little compliance by those subjects who felt only sympathy for the victim. However, those subjects who either felt a need for restitution or who were experiencing generalized guilt were significantly more likely to volunteer to make more phone calls in an attempt to save the redwood forests.

What happens when the victim of a transgression offers the guilty party forgiveness? As strange as it might seem, the trans-gressor is more likely to comply with a request when all is absolved. Forgiveness of guilt and compliance were recently investigated in an experiment conducted by Brad Kelln and John Ellard.[5] In their research, college students were led to believe that they had mishandled some scientific equipment and thereby ruined the experimenter's study. As in the Carlsmith and Gross study, the students were more likely to comply with a request to aid the experimenter in other research when they felt guilty about mishandling the equipment compared to those students who did not damage the machine. But here is the interesting twist. One group of students was forgiven their supposed mis-deed. They were told by the experimenter: "Don't worry about it. That's OK."

What would you do in such a situation? Often the act of for-giveness is seen as "wiping the slate clean"—the transgressor is absolved of guilt and the person offering forgiveness is perceived as a friend. However, that is not what Kelln and Ellard found. In fact, they found that just the opposite occurred. The offer of forgiveness served as a double whammy; first they felt guilty about damaging the equipment and then they were offered no means of making it up to the researcher. The only way to make restitution and to show that they were "good" people was to comply with the experimenter's request to do more work. And that they did, offering to do almost twice the work as the other students in the research. But all of these guilty feelings had a cost. When the students were forgiven their transgressions, they came to dislike the experimenter—the person who had absolved them of their crime. Apparently, people do not like people to whom they feel beholden.

We should note that another common response to feelings of guilt produced by transgressing against another is to derogate the victim. For example, in an experiment by Keith Davis and Ned Jones, students were asked to watch another student being interviewed and then to tell the student that they found him or her to be a shallow, untrustworthy, and dull person.[6] The major finding of the study was that students who volunteered for this assignment succeeded in convincing themselves that they didn't like the victim of their cruelty. In other words, after we attack another person we look for ways to justify, or "make right," our actions. One way to do that is to blame the person we attacked for our own behavior: He or she is stupid or careless or evil or whatever and therefore deserved our maltreatment; thus our misbehavior is rationalized. The victim becomes the scapegoat for our guilt. Skillful propagandists will make this rationalization coincide with their goals.

The power of guilt to convince and to persuade stems, as with most emotional appeals, from its power to direct our thoughts and to channel our energies. When we feel guilty we typically pay little attention to the cogency of an argument, to the merits of a suggested course of action. Instead, our thoughts and actions are directed to removing the feeling of guilt—to somehow making things right or doing the right thing. We fall into the rationalization trap.

Guilt can have its pro-social uses. Imagine a society in which no one felt remorse for any transgression that he or she

performed. Many social commentators have noted that the success of Martin Luther King, Jr.'s, campaign to desegregate the
South was due, in part, to the guilt feelings induced in many
white southerners when his nonviolent actions were met with
billy clubs, fire hoses, and attack dogs.

Nevertheless, many effects of guilt are, of course, not positive;
many guilty feelings are undeserved. Guilt can be induced by
reminding the target of past sins that have long since been
atoned for, by making small transgressions loom large, or by
making it appear that the target is responsible for a crime that
he or she did not commit. Once we are filled with guilt, our
thoughts and behavior are directed toward ridding ourselves of
this feeling. The end result is, at best, the manipulation of our
behavior and, perhaps at worst, long-term damage to our self-
esteem or even the loss of our freedom.

27

What Is the Influence of One Flower Given?

A. C. Bhaktivedanta spent much of his life in India as a manager
of a successful pharmaceutical company. In the early 1960s,
after leaving his wife and family and accepting the name of
Swami Prabhupada, he came to America and founded the International Society for Krishna Consciousness, a movement
devoted to improving the world's spiritual health by chants and
love for Lord Krishna. Starting from a storefront mission on
Manhattan's Lower East Side, the swami, in less than a decade,
was able to gather the resources to establish a worldwide network of more than a hundred Hare Krishna temples and communes, including forty located in the United States.[1]

Swami Prabhupada's primary source of income during this
period of rapid expansion came from public donations and sales
of religious merchandise, including his two most popular items,

Back to Godhead magazine and a designer edition of the *Bhagavad Gita*. What makes the Hare Krishnas' success so remarkable was the sales force the swami recruited to sell the society's merchandise. The swami selected young people—often teenagers, many of them with psychological problems—dressed them in saffron robes, holy beads, and B. F. Goodrich sandals, shaved the heads of the males, fed them a diet consisting primarily of vegetables (most notably dahl and chickpeas), and then sent them into the marketplace singing, dancing, and chanting the Hare Krishna. Would you buy a copy of the *Bhagavad Gita* (or anything else, for that matter) from a chanting, orange-clad, stubble-headed sales agent? Not likely. The Hare Krishna sales force breaks just about every persuasion rule (save one) found in this book—they were low in source credibility, low in interpersonal attraction and liking, and high in vested self-interest.

How did the swami get thousands of people to part with their hard-earned cash to finance his spiritual kingdom? Robert Cialdini, one of the world's leading authorities on influence tactics, wondered how he did it, too.[2] At first, Cialdini notes, the Hare Krishnas were quite unsuccessful in their solicitations. Indeed, many towns enacted laws and ordinances prohibiting Krishna begging and even banned them from certain parts of town, especially airports. Occasionally violence would erupt between Krishnas and townspeople. All of this turned around, according to Cialdini, when the Krishnas discovered one of society's most effective persuasion devices, one capable both of overcoming the Krishnas' negative image and of placing an overpriced copy of the *Bhagavad Gita* into the hands of many a weary traveler. Their technique made use of what is called the *norm of reciprocity*.

A norm is a specific guide to conduct—for example, tip 15% of the dinner bill; don't cut in front of people standing in line at the movies; don't urinate in public; don't read other people's mail.[3] If we break a norm, we most likely receive some form of social sanction and disapproval—a glaring look, gossip and ridicule, shunning and ostracism, and sometimes even physical punishment, jail, banishment, or death. (Note the reaction of some people to the Krishnas because they broke society's dress and social-interaction norms.) As a consequence of these sanctions, even a young child begins to learn not to break the norms. Indeed, when put in a position of transgressing a norm, we often feel highly anxious—a feeling that we would like to avoid. We may end up obeying the norm almost automatically without much thought as to why.

Often norms can be associated with a specific role (cooking is women's work; businessmen are competitive) or a specific culture (eat with a fork as opposed to chopsticks; don't overproduce in this workshop). Other norms are widely shared and appear in many cultures and societies (incest is taboo; honor your commitments). The norm of reciprocity is one such norm. It states: "If I do something for you, then you are obligated to return the favor and do something for me." Perhaps one reason why this norm is found in so many cultures is its value to a society. The norm of reciprocity regulates exchange in a culture; it insures that the person who makes the first exchange will not be cheated.

A study by Dennis Regan illustrates the persuasive power of the norm of reciprocity, a tactic so powerful that it can even overcome the effects of being disliked.[4] In his experiment, two male students reported for a study that supposedly was investigating "aesthetic judgments." One of the men was really an accomplice who, at the beginning of the study, attempted to make himself unlikable (by being rude and inconsiderate to another person) or likable (by being kind and considerate to another). After both "subjects" rated art slides for about five minutes, the accomplice slipped out of the room for a couple of minutes and returned either empty-handed or carrying two Cokes and said, "I asked him [the experimenter] if I could get myself a Coke, and he said it was OK, so I bought one for you, too." At the end of the study, the accomplice asked the real subject if he would like to buy some raffle tickets. The results showed that when the accomplice gave the other student a Coke and thus invoked the norm of reciprocity, he sold nearly twice as many raffle tickets, compared to when no Coke was given and regardless of how socially attractive he was perceived to be!

How did the Krishnas use the norm of reciprocity to solicit money? Quite simply, they gave the influence target a gift of a flower. As Cialdini, who spent hours at the airport observing the Krishnas in action, tells it, the sect member would spy a "victim," who would suddenly find a flower pressed into his or her hand or pinned to a jacket. If the target attempted to give it back, the Krishna would refuse by saying, "It is our gift to you." Only then was the request made for a donation. The gift of a flower established a feeling of obligation and indebtedness. How could this favor be repaid? Quite obviously by providing the Society with a donation or with the purchase of an attractive edition of the *Bhagavad Gita.*

Hare Krishnas are not the only ones to employ the norm of reciprocity for persuasive purposes. This may have started on a mass scale with the well-known "Fuller Brush man," a fixture of the 1930s who went from door to door selling brushes. He always began by giving the home owner a small, inexpensive brush as a way to establish the reciprocity norm. A phenomenon of the 1950s, Tupperware parties, began with a gift from the company (typically a small Tupperware item) and a gift from the party host (refreshments), thereby obligating the party goer to both company and host (who receives a gift from the company if you and your friends buy enough). A recent television ad for an antacid began with an authoritative-looking man stating, "We believe in our product so much, that, after watching this ad, if you would like to try our product just call us toll-free and we will send you a pack." Marketers know that a free sample—a taste of sausage or orange juice at the supermarket or a trial packet of cold medicine or shampoo in the mail—can greatly increase product sales. Sales presentations for such things as vacuum cleaners, automobiles, encyclopedias, and beachfront property in Florida often begin with a free prize, such as a road atlas, a transistor radio, or a trial magazine subscription. Charities and political parties frequently mail free gifts of buttons and bumper stickers with catchy slogans when they ask for a contribution. Many university professors will receive a free copy of this book in the hopes that they will assign it to their classes. Former President Lyndon B. Johnson, widely known for his powers of influence in Congress, kept a drawerful of small trinkets—key chains, coffee mugs, and pens with an official seal. He would hand these keepsakes out to friends and acquaintances alike, thereby establishing a social relationship of indebtedness.

There are a number of variations on the use of the norm of reciprocity to increase compliance. One ingenious version has been dubbed the *door-in-the-face* technique. Here's how it works. Imagine that you work for a local blood bank and you want to increase blood donations. Using the door-in-the-face technique, you would begin by asking for a very extreme favor—say, donate blood once every two months for at least three years. Such a request would surely be rejected (hence the name "door-in-the-face") but might lead to more acceptances of a compromise—say, donating one unit of blood—than would otherwise be the case. This is exactly what Robert Cialdini and Karen Ascani found.[5] In one study, they asked passersby on an Arizona State University walkway to either (1) donate a unit of blood sometime tomorrow or (2) donate a unit of blood once every two months for a period of three years and, when this request was rejected by the passerby, he or she was asked merely to donate a unit of blood sometime tomorrow. The results showed that more people agreed to give blood and actually gave more blood when they received the extreme request first.

Another use of the norm of reciprocity can be found in the *that's-not-all* technique commonly used on late-night TV ads to peddle small kitchen appliances. This technique was investigated in a set of clever experiments conducted by Jerry Burger.[6] Here's how this technique works. In one experiment, Burger set up a bake sale to sell cupcakes. No prices were listed. When a passerby stopped and asked about the cupcakes, he or she was told that the price was 75¢. But before the customer could respond, the seller held up a hand saying: "Wait, that's not all—you also get these cookies along with the cupcakes," as the customer was shown two medium-sized cookies. Other passersby were merely told at the start that for 75¢ they could get the cupcakes and two cookies. Burger found that nearly double the amount of cupcakes and cookies were sold when the seller announced the cookies as an extra "that's-not-all" item as opposed to telling the customer about the cookies from the start.

The door-in-the-face and that's-not-all techniques make use of two basic psychological processes. First, both the large initial request and the small initial offer set up a contrast effect, similar to the one that occurs with decoys (see Chapter 10)—giving a pint of blood doesn't seem nearly so bad when compared to donating at regular intervals for the next three years, and "a cupcake—plus some cookies" sounds better than just "a cupcake." Second, the immediate concession by the requester invokes the norm of reciprocity. The requester is implicitly saying, "I just reduced my request from three years of blood donations to just once; now it is your turn to reciprocate my concession." Similarly, in the that's-not-all technique, the request implies, "I just added an extra two cookies to the deal; now it is your turn to make a concession and make the purchase." And many an influence target does just that!

Car dealers have learned the value of the door-in-the-face technique. Dealers often pad the asking price for an automobile by adding an extra price sticker that raises the cost of a car by as much as a few thousand dollars. Early in the negotiations, the dealer will graciously concede this extra charge. Now it is *your turn* to reciprocate and to pay *more* for that car then you might have intended to. Similarly, infomericals often make use of the that's-not-all technique. A common ploy on these half-hour-long commercials is to first describe a product—a blender, fruit dehydrator, or similar product—and to offer it for sale. But before you can decide whether you want it or not, another item—a set of six steak knives, a fruit roll-up attachment, or an apple corer—is announced as a part of the deal and as a concession to you, the consumer. And again, it is your turn to reciprocate and buy!

In general, the norm of reciprocity is successful as a persuasion device because it directs our thoughts and carries its own motivation to act on those thoughts. We are directed to think *"How can I repay my obligation?"* as opposed to *"Is this a good deal?"* Our primary motivation is to avoid the uneasy feeling that comes from transgressing the norm. Other norms can similarly motivate our thinking. Next, we will look at just one of these norms to see how the rule "honor your commitments" can be exploited.

28

The Committed Heart

A visit from the encyclopedia salesman can illustrate many persuasion tactics. The "free" road atlas given for listening to the sales representative invokes the norm of reciprocity. The features of the volumes are described in glowing, influential words. The salesman encourages you to generate dozens of good reasons (at least you think so) for owning an encyclopedia set. The fact that your children and other loved ones don't already have access to a world of knowledge makes you feel a little guilty.

But perhaps one of the most powerful inducements to buy occurs "after" the sales presentation. The salesman continues: "Well, if there are no more questions about the books, that will conclude the presentation. Oh yes, one more thing. My boss would really like it if I could get your opinion about our encyclopedias. Would you mind completing a form with me?"

You respond, "OK."

"It's a series of questions about what *you* would like in an encyclopedia. It would really help if you would respond *as if you were buying a set today.*"

The salesman goes on to ask a series of questions. "Which color binding do you like—white, maroon, or black? With or without gold leaf? With or without double-strength binding?" and so on. You answer each question mindlessly as the salesman checks off your responses on a preprinted official form.

At the end of the inquiry he asks, "Would you mind initialing this sheet as a way of authorizing your answers?" Again, you do so in a half-mindless state.

From that point on, that formal-looking paper is treated as *your* order for a set of encyclopedias. The salesman suggests, "Let's see how much it would cost to buy *your* set of encyclopedias today; hmmmmm, with a 5% discount, that would be _____," as he hands you a slip of paper with a handwritten number on it. As you read it, the salesman asks, "Shall I order *your* set today?" You stammer, half-confused, "Well, 'em, I'd . . . well."

We don't know whether you will buy that set of encyclopedias today or not. Many of us will undoubtedly see through his ploy. But we bet this procedure of "taking your order" will increase encyclopedia sales significantly and will do so because of the feelings it engenders. In general, it is important to all of us to be "persons of our word," that is, to be self-consistent and to honor our commitments. Granted, we did not say we would buy an encyclopedia, but the salesman seems to think so—perhaps we *did* indicate we would like one. When we go back on our word, we often feel uneasy, even when it is a seemingly flimsy commitment like the one given to the encyclopedia salesman. To maintain a positive view of ourselves, we act on our commitments. The rationalization trap has captured another unsuspecting victim.

Preying on our sense of commitment as a way to induce persuasion is often accomplished in small doses. Suppose you would like to enlist someone's aid in a massive undertaking, but you know the job you have in mind for the person is so difficult, and will require so much time and effort, that the person surely will decline. What should you do? One possibility is to get the person involved in a much smaller aspect of the job, one so easy that he or she wouldn't dream of refusing to do it. This action serves to commit the individual to "the cause." Once people are thus committed, the likelihood of their complying with the larger request increases.

This phenomenon was demonstrated by Jonathan Freedman and Scott Fraser.[1] They attempted to induce several homeowners to put up a huge, unattractive sign in their front yards reading "Drive Carefully." Because of the ugliness and obtrusiveness of the sign, most residents refused to put it up; only 17% complied. A different group of residents, however, were first "softened up" by an experimenter who "put his foot in the door" by getting them to sign a petition favoring safe driving. Because signing a petition is an easy thing to do, virtually all who were asked agreed to sign. A few weeks later, a different experimenter went to each resident with the ugly "Drive Carefully" sign. More than 55% of these residents allowed the sign to be put up on their property.

Thus, when individuals commit themselves in a small way, the likelihood they will commit themselves further in that direction is increased. This process of using small favors to encourage people to accede to larger requests had been dubbed the *foot-in-the-door* technique (a technique opposite in form to the door-in-the-face tactic described in Chapter 27). It is effective because having done the smaller favor creates pressure to agree to do the larger favor; in effect, we comply with the large request to be consistent with our earlier commitment.

Similar results using this technique have been found in studies of charitable donations and voting. For example, people induced to wear a lapel pin publicizing an American Cancer Society fund-raising drive were approximately twice as likely to give a donation the next day as were those who were simply approached for a contribution.[2] Other investigators have found that the chances of getting people to vote on election day could be increased just by asking them if they planned to go to the polls.[3] In this study, the researchers contacted potential voters and asked them to predict whether they would vote in an election to be held on the upcoming Tuesday. All of those contacted, perhaps out of a desire to appear civic-minded, said "yes," they would be voting. The respondents then acted on this commitment, with 86.7% of them voting in the election compared to 61.5% of those not asked to make self-predictions.

Car dealers also know how to use commitment to sell automobiles. Indeed, when social psychologist Robert Cialdini temporarily joined the sales force of an automobile dealer, he discovered a common and successful ploy called *lowballing* or *throwing the customer a lowball*.[4]

The technique works this way. Suppose you enter an automobile showroom intent on buying a new car. You've already priced the car you want at several dealers—you know you can purchase it for about $11,300. Lo and behold, the salesman tells you he can sell you one for $10,542. Excited by the bargain, you agree to the deal and write out a check for the downpayment. While the salesman takes your check to the sales manager to consummate the deal, you rub your hands in glee as you imagine yourself driving home in your shiny new car. But alas, ten minutes later, the salesman returns with a forlorn look on his face—it seems he made a calculation error and the sales manager caught it. The price of the car is actually $11,684. You can get it cheaper elsewhere; moreover, the decision to buy is not irrevocable. And yet, far more people in this situation will go ahead with the deal than if the original asking price had been $11,684—even though the reason for purchasing the car from this dealer (the bargain price) no longer exists.

What is going on in this situation? There are at least three important things to notice. First, while the customer's decision to buy is certainly reversible, a commitment was emphasized by the act of signing a check for the downpayment and handing it over to the salesman. Second, this commitment triggered the anticipation of a pleasant or interesting experience: driving out with a new car. To have the anticipated event thwarted (by not going ahead with the deal) would produce disappointment. Third, although the final price is substantially higher than the customer thought it would be, it is only slightly higher than the price somewhere else. Under these circumstances, the customer in effect says, "Oh, what the hell. I'm already here, I've already filled out the forms—why wait?

Commitment can be self-perpetuating, resulting in an escalating commitment to an often failing course of action. Once a small commitment is made, it sets the stage for ever increasing commitments. The original behavior needs to be justified, so attitudes are changed; this change in attitudes influences future decisions and behavior. The result is a seemingly irrational commitment to a poor business plan, a purchase that makes no sense, a war that has no realistic objectives, or an arms race gone out of control.

The process of escalating commitment appears to have played an important role in the deepening U.S. involvement in the war in Vietnam. As Robert McNamara, secretary of defense under presidents Kennedy and Johnson and a major protagonist in the buildup of America's forces in Vietnam, put it in his recent book: "The beginnings of all things are small, and the story of my involvement in Vietnam is no different."[5] According to McNamara, America's involvement began innocently enough with the sending of 16,000 military advisors in 1961 to help the Vietnamese defend themselves against communism. In 1963, South Vietnam's leader, Ngo Dinh Diem, was assassinated (due in part to a confusing directive issued by the Kennedy administration), resulting in political chaos in the country. To buy time for a new regime, the United States in 1964 began a small covert action program consisting of propaganda distribution, intelligence gathering, and general sabotage against North Vietnam. When this didn't work, the United States developed plans for bombing the Ho Chi Minh Trail and then more plans for an "integrated political-military attack." In response to a covert action, North Vietnam attacked the U.S. destroyer *Maddox*. The United States retaliated in August 1964 with sixty-four sorties against patrol boats and an oil complex.

The war was now on. The administration privately made the commitment to take additional military action by January 1, 1965, although there was no agreement on what this action would be. On January 28, 1965, President Johnson initiated the bombing of North Vietnam. With the air strikes came a request for troops to protect the bases. As McNamara put it:

> Once you put the first soldier ashore, you never know how many others are going to follow him. But the need appeared

pressing and the commitment small, and besides, how could the president decline a commander's petition for ground troops to protect the lives of airmen?[6]

The number of troops increased from 23,000 to 175,000 in 1965, with an additional 100,000 more in 1966. And when the bombing failed to repel the Viet Cong, more ground troops were sent to Vietnam. And then even more were sent as the Viet Cong retaliated. By the war's end, 543,400 U.S. troops had been sent to Vietnam. More bombs were dropped on North Vietnam in three years than in all of Europe in World War II. In all, 58,191 U.S. citizens were killed in action.

With each commitment and then failure, U.S. objectives would change and grow increasingly ill defined and vague as those involved in the escalation decision sought to rationalize and justify their previous actions. At first, the U.S. purpose was to train the Vietnamese to defend themselves. When it became obvious that there was little hope of accomplishing this objective, the goal became to retaliate against attacks from North Vietnam. As the commitment grew, the goal changed first to crushing North Vietnam's will to fight, and then to just bolstering the morale of our South Vietnamese allies, and then finally to a vague wish to "win at any cost."

As a 1971 analysis by the newsmagazine *Time* stated:

> Yet the bureaucracy, the *Pentagon Papers* indicate, always demanded new options; each option was to apply more force. Each tightening of the screw created a position that must be defended; once committed, the military pressure must be maintained.[7]

In a thought-provoking analysis, Ralph White suggested that previous commitments blinded our leaders to information incompatible with the decisions they had already made.[8] As White put it, "There was a tendency, when actions were out of line with ideas, for decision-makers to align their ideas with their actions." To take just one of many examples, the decision by the Joint Chiefs of Staff to continue to escalate the bombing of North Vietnam was made at the price of ignoring crucial evidence from the CIA and other sources which made it clear that bombing would not break the will of the North Vietnamese people but, quite the contrary, would only strengthen their resolve. White surmises the reason the Joint Chiefs prevailed in their efforts to escalate the bombing was that their advice was consonant with decisions already made and with certain key assumptions that later proved to be erroneous. In other words, the Joint Chiefs' escalation of the war was in part an attempt to reduce their own dissonance about their previous war efforts, a process reminiscent of what happened after Mrs. Keech's end-of-the world prophecy failed and after the city of Santa Cruz was informed about an impending destructive earthquake (see Chapter 4).

As with other self-motives and emotions, commitment and consistency can have their purpose and value. No one wants to live in a society of inconsistent, two-faced liars! However, commitments can form a propaganda trap—we commit ourselves, sometimes inadvertently, sometimes inappropriately, and then live out our commitments in all honesty.[9] The clever propagandist will know how to secure our commitment and set a rationalization trap.

In such cases, it may be useful to ask, "How did I get myself into this situation?" Fortunately, when we are dealing with major purchases many states require that consumers be given a period of time to "change their minds" about that purchase—a time to rethink mistaken commitments. Unfortunately, when it comes to acts of war and international policy such decisions may be irrevocable. In the Vietnam war, we finally closed it down and got out. Sadly, this was several years (and thousands of casualties) *after* Robert McNamara, by his own admission, realized that the war was unwinnable. In such cases, it may also help us if we remember that the most *honorable* action is *always* that of *ceasing* to honor *dishonorable* commitments.

29 ▪▪▪▪▪▪▪▪▪▪▪▪▪▪▪▪▪▪

To Practice What You Preach

Occasionally, we humans do things that bring us immediate pleasure but put us in grave danger as well. To take a poignant example, let's look at the spread of AIDS. During the past two decades, AIDS has become an epidemic of monumental proportions. At the start of the new millennium, more than 16 million persons worldwide had died from AIDS; currently more than 35 million persons are living with AIDS, with millions more infected but not currently showing symptoms. A particularly vulnerable group is sexually active young adults; in recent years, AIDS has become the leading cause of death among individuals between the ages of eighteen and thirty in the United States.

Although medical researchers have made some progress in slowing down the ravages of the disease, neither a cure nor a vaccine currently exists. Accordingly, the major weapon we have for reducing the spread of AIDS is persuasion—to find an effective way of convincing people to change their risky behavior. Toward this end, the U.S. government has spent hundreds of millions of dollars on AIDS information and prevention campaigns in the mass media. Although these campaigns have been reasonably effective at conveying information about how AIDS is spread (for example, by having sex with a partner who carries the AIDS virus), by and large they have failed to prevent young people from engaging in risky sexual behavior. For example, interviews with sexually active college students show that, although they are aware of AIDS as a serious problem, most are reluctant to stop having casual sexual intercourse and only a surprisingly small percentage seem willing to use condoms regularly. The reason? They consider condoms to be inconvenient, unromantic, and reminiscent of death and disease—and they do not want to be thinking about dying of a horrible disease while getting ready to make love.

Needless to say, this is a serious problem. If attempts to change behavior by rational arguments have been ineffective, is there anything that can be done to safeguard sexually active teenagers and young adults against the ravages of AIDS? A few years ago, at a congressional hearing on AIDS, the dominant conclusion among public health officials was: Since teenagers and young adults do not seem to be taking AIDS seriously enough, educators need to get their attention by devising communications that would (to quote one witness) "scare the hell out of them."

Unfortunately, the solution is not that simple. As we saw in Chapter 24, the problem with fear appeals is that, while fear-laden messages can be effective under some circumstances, they do not always trigger reasonable problem-solving behavior. Indeed, when we are trying to solve a thorny problem like getting young, sexually active people to change their sexual behavior, we may be dealing with precisely the kind of situation in which inducing a high degree of fear is likely to have the opposite effect. That is, when something pleasurable like sex is involved, if you try to frighten people into doing something they don't want to do or perceive to be difficult or annoying to do (like using condoms), they tend to deny it and to convince themselves that such a frightening thing as AIDS is extremely unlikely to happen to them.

And this seems to be what has been happening. Interviews with sexually active college students have demonstrated that they will go through all kinds of mindless denials, extremely convoluted justifications, and other cognitive gymnastics in order to continue to have unprotected sex without thinking about the possible negative consequences. For example, some have succeeded in convincing themselves (erroneously) that they are able to spot someone with AIDS just by looking at them or that, "Surely none of my friends could possibly have AIDS." In short, these young people seem to be saying, "AIDS is a serious and deadly problem, all right, but not for me!"

The tendency for young people to engage in denial is by no means a recent phenomenon. Indeed, this strategy was documented by Thucydides some 2,500 years ago when he wrote with obvious chagrin about the fact that young Athenian soldiers, on preparing to depart for a dangerous war in Sicily, simply refused to believe there was any possibility of dying; instead of getting their minds in order and preparing themselves for the strong possibility of death, these young men occupied themselves with talk of their excitement about seeing faraway places. Denial is a powerful mechanism—and it can be self-destructive because it allows people to block out or distort rational argument and thus keep them from taking useful preventive action.

Given this state of affairs, how might one induce sexually active young adults to make a more realistic assessment of their vulnerability to AIDS and, therefore, resolve to use condoms during sexual encounters? One promising strategy is to find a way to obviate denial. Instead of trying to sell people on the virtues of safe sex through direct rational argument, we might try to make an end run around the denial mechanism by appealing to our human need to consider ourselves to be people of high integrity.

Here's how it works. Suppose Dave is a sexually active college student and, like most students, (1) does not use condoms regularly, (2) has managed to blind himself to the personal dangers inherent in having unprotected sex, but yet (3) realizes the dangers of unprotected sex and the transmission of AIDS. Suppose, on going home for the holidays, Dave finds that Charley, his sixteen-year-old kid brother, has just discovered sex and is in the process of boasting about his many and varied sexual encounters. What might Dave say to him? Chances are, as a caring, responsible older sibling, Dave will dampen his younger brother's enthusiasm a bit by warning him about the dangers of AIDS and other sexually transmitted diseases—and urge him to, at least, take proper precautions.

Suppose that we are friends of the family who were invited to dinner and who happen to overhear this exchange between Dave and Charley. What if we were to pull Dave aside and say something like this: "That was very good advice you gave Charley—we are very proud of you for being so responsible; by the way, how frequently do *you* use condoms?"

Psychologically, we are setting up a situation in which an individual is being forced to confront his own hypocrisy; that is, we are making Dave mindful of the fact that he is not practicing what he just got through preaching. The astute reader will see this situation as the beginning of a rationalization trap. We human beings want to see ourselves as people of integrity. People of integrity practice what they preach. In the hypothetical situation, Dave's self-concept as a person of integrity is threatened by his own behavior—behavior that suggests he might lack integrity and that he might be behaving hypocritically. How might Dave rationalize his behavior and reestablish his self-concept as a person of high integrity? There is only one sure-fire way: by beginning, forthwith, to put into practice what he has just finished preaching to his brother Charley. In short, to start using condoms immediately.

In a series of experiments, we, along with Jeff Stone, Carrie Fried, and other former students of ours, constructed a procedure very much like the example mentioned above.[1] Specifically, we induced college students to deliver a convincing speech, talking about the dangers of AIDS and urging the audience to use condoms every time they had sex. We videotaped the speech after informing the speakers that we would be showing the tape to high school students as part of a sex-education class. Next, we asked the speakers to dredge up and tell us about all the situations in their day-to-day lives when they found it difficult or impossible to use condoms themselves—thus making them mindful of the fact that they were preaching one thing but doing something quite different.

Nobody wants to be a hypocrite. When confronted with their own hypocrisy, how might college students reestablish their belief in their own integrity? Exactly like Dave did in the hypothetical example: by resolving to change their behavior to bring it into line with their own preaching. In our experiments, we compared the behavior of these college students with a similar group who simply composed and videotaped their arguments in favor of condom use—but were not made mindful of their own hypocrisy. The results of these experiments are clear and powerful. College students who were made to feel like hypocrites purchased far more condoms after leaving the experiment; even more impressive is the fact that, some three months later, when interviewed on the telephone about their sexual behavior, 92% reported that they were now using condoms regularly. This percentage is almost twice as high as that of the students whom we did not confront with their own hypocrisy.

The implications of this experiment are striking. For the past two decades, we have been begging, cajoling, scaring, and imploring our loved ones to take steps to avoid the AIDS virus by practicing safer sex. And all the while, the deadly virus has continued to spread and we have watched, helplessly, as one friend after another has succumbed to it. We now have one persuasive technique that works: Simply get people to preach safer sex—and then remind them that they themselves are not practicing what they are preaching.

Can we apply this strategy to other domains—to issues regarding which almost all people agree that certain behaviors are important but simply do not engage in those behaviors? Let's look at the issue of protecting the environment. In this domain, many of us are potential hypocrites. That is, most Americans profess to being environmentalists and are in favor of protecting our natural resources, such as the air we breathe and the water we drink. But when it comes to actually doing it—recycling, conserving water and energy, car pooling—most of us fall far short of the behaviors we would endorse. U.S. citizens comprise 6% of the world's population but consume about 33% of the world's resources. Many of us seem to feel we are doing our share if we simply put a "Save the Whales" bumper sticker on our car. How might we use the hypocrisy tactic to make people more aware of the fact that they are not practicing the environmental behavior that they are implicitly preaching?

We and our students set out to tackle this problem. In one study, we asked people to make a speech urging others to recycle bottles, cans, and newspapers—and then we asked them to think about some of the times that they themselves had failed to recycle.[2] Just as in the condom experiments, this made them mindful of their own hypocrisy. Subsequently, when we asked them to volunteer to help with recycling activities, these people were far more willing to help than were people who made the speech but were not confronted with their own hypocrisy. Again, when made to feel like a hypocrite, these people found the one sure way to restore their feelings of integrity: to begin to practice what they were preaching.

We also used the hypocrisy tactic to help ameliorate another pressing environmental problem—the conservation of drinking water.[3] A few years ago, there was an acute water shortage in central California. The administration of our university had been trying hard to use rational arguments to persuade students to take shorter showers in order to conserve water. They posted signs in the dormitories and in the locker room of the field house; they gave students pep talks about how dangerous the water shortage was and what they could do to use less water. It should be pointed out that, when it comes to matters of the environment, the students at our university are an unusually conscious and conscientious group. They care about saving the whales and preserving the redwoods; they care about the habitat of the spotted owl; they are deeply opposed to indiscriminate dumping of toxic waste material. But, alas, these urgings had very little impact on the shower-taking behavior of most of our undergraduates. Apparently, taking long, luxurious showers proved to be too attractive an activity for the overwhelming majority of our students to give it up easily. Our guess is that each probably felt that an occasional long shower "by just me" would not hurt the conservation effort very much. But, of course, if almost all the students felt and acted that way, it would indeed hurt a great deal.

Given the failure of direct communication to make a dent in the shower-taking behavior of the students, we decided to attempt to make our students aware of their hypocrisy as a way of getting them to take shorter showers. In our experiment, a research assistant stationed herself in the women's locker room of the university field house and intercepted, at random, several students who had just finished working out and were on their way to take a shower. The research assistant asked each student if she would be willing to sign (in big block letters) a poster encouraging others to conserve water. The poster read: "Conserve Water! Take shorter showers! If I can do it, so can you!" Next, they were asked to respond to a "water-conservation survey" consisting of items designed to make them mindful of the fact that their showering behavior was often wasteful. In short, we made the students aware of the fact that, when it comes to water conservation, they were not practicing what they preached.

We then compared their shower-taking behavior with that of a group of students who merely signed the poster but who were not made mindful of their hypocrisy by taking the water-conservation survey. We were able to measure the length of their showers directly: A second research assistant was unobtrusively waiting (with hidden waterproof stopwatch) to time their showers. Our intervention was phenomenally successful. As in the condom experiments, hypocrisy had a major impact on the students' behavior. That is, those students who were induced to advocate short showers and also were made mindful of their own past behavior took very short showers, lasting just a bit over three and a half minutes—a fraction of the time of a typical student shower.

What is going on in these experiments? We should note that the results are not due simply to hypocrisy; that is, it is not simply people's hypocrisy that induces them to use condoms or to take shorter showers. Hypocrisy is all over the place and does not usually result in major changes in behavior. To illustrate, the political comedian Al Franken recently told what has become an old, out-of-date joke: "Quick; what do Newt Gingrich, Bob Dole,

Phil Gramm, and George Will have in common? They've all been married one less time than Rush Limbaugh."[4] (Limbaugh has been married three times.) It's an old joke because, as Franken was telling it, Newt Gingrich was cheating on his second wife, whom he then divorced in order to marry his third wife. What gives the joke its bite is the fact that these pundits and political leaders have been making speeches and writing columns extolling the value of strong families for a very long time. If one considers that making a marriage work is part of family values, their behavior might be considered hypocritical. Will this hypocrisy, in and of itself, affect their behavior? Probably not. Regardless of political stripe, politicians and ordinary people like you and us engage in hypocritical activities from time to time, with little impact on our overall behavior.

This tendency for us humans to engage in all sorts of mental contortions to deny our hypocrisy can be seen in some recent research conducted by Daniel Batson and his colleagues.[5] In this series of experiments, college students were confronted with a moral dilemma. They were required to assign themselves and another person to one of two treatments in an experiment: a positive condition where the student could win prizes or a dull and boring condition with no prizes. Fairness requires that each person (the student and the other person) have an equal chance of getting into the positive condition. However, who wants to sit around in a dingy old lab for an hour working on a boring assignment, especially when you can be having fun winning prizes? What would you do in such a situation—play fair or take the good time for yourself? Batson and his colleagues found that the students attempted to do both! First, most of the students assigned the other person to the boring task; in a typical study, only 15% took the boring task for themselves—far below the expected 50% if the fairness norm had been used. However, the vast majority of those who took the fun task sought to *appear* moral and fair by doing such things as flipping a coin to determine the assignment (but rigging the outcome) or pretending that they were merely accepting someone else's unfair decision as fair. In other words, they engaged in moral hypocrisy: pretending to be fair when in fact they were not. Batson and his colleagues did find one way of preventing moral hypocrisy. The students were most likely to play fair when they were (1) reminded of the moral standard to be fair *and* (2) made self-aware of their own moral standards.

And that's our point: In our experiments, what makes the hypocrisy phenomenon work—what makes it lead to a powerful change in ingrained behavior—is that the people are made fully aware of their hypocrisy and are handed a perfectly sensible way to allow them to polish their tarnished integrity (such as using condoms or taking shorter showers). If we are not made starkly aware of our hypocrisy, we all share a tendency to push the hypocritical behavior out of sight and do nothing about it. Without an obvious, available, pro-social pathway toward restoring our integrity, we might settle for symbolic action such as wearing a politically correct T-shirt or placing a high-minded bumper sticker on our car.

Thus far, we have been talking about using hypocrisy to promote goals and behavior that most people would consider worthwhile or even noble. That is, most of us would probably agree that it is a good idea to invoke a powerful mechanism such as hypocrisy if the goal is to induce people to behave in a responsible manner toward their environment—and especially if the goal is to save their own lives and the lives of their sexual partners. But there is a darker side to hypocrisy-induction. Like most of the persuasion strategies discussed in this book, hypocrisy-induction is a double-edged sword. What if the goal of invoking hypocrisy were simply to gain a financial profit?

Here is a case in point. A short time ago, some of our students reported to us that they were thinking of joining a commercial health spa. When they went in for the orientation, they were asked to fill out a "lifestyle" questionnaire that included questions such as these: Do you think your health is important? Do you think it is important to exercise regularly? How much exercise do you get now? Would you like to get more?

Naturally, they answered "yes" to all of the "yes/no" questions. After all, they were thinking of joining a health spa—it would be ludicrous to say that they didn't think their health was important! Later their answers were used to make them look like hypocrites if they balked at the hard-sell sales pitch or showed any hesitation at paying the rather large monthly fee. "What do you mean that sounds like a lot of money? It is your health that is at stake. You still consider your health important, don't you?"

One might argue that the goal (physical fitness) is good for the person and therefore the use of this strategy by the proprietors of the health spa is just as important as is water conservation, recycling, or AIDS prevention. We might find that argument more convincing if the proprietors were not turning a handsome profit. We hasten to add that it appears that the proprietors of the health spa had been using this technique for several years; they initiated it before the scientific experiments on hypocrisy were conducted. People who are out to make a buck often stumble on diabolical ways of doing it, without the aid of social psychologists.

However, when it comes to hypocrisy and persuasion, there is a silver lining to this particular cloud. The students who visited the health spa spotted the hypocrisy-induction tactic and were able to debunk it for what it was—an attempt to play on their emotions, make them feel hypocritical, and part them from their money. The reason? They had recently heard a lecture on the hypocrisy-induction strategy and were delighted at their newfound ability to identify and resist propaganda. And that is the way it often is with knowledge of persuasion.

30

The Psychology of Scarcity and the Mystique of Phantoms

Potatoes have not always enjoyed the popularity that they do today. In the late eighteenth century, the French believed that potatoes caused leprosy; the Germans grew spuds only for cattle and for prisoners; the Russian peasant considered them to be poisonous. All that changed when Catherine the Great, ruler of Russia, cleverly ordered fences built around potato fields. Large notices were posted warning the populace not to steal potatoes.[1] The potato became a staple of the Russian diet, and the rest is potato history.

Catherine the Great's campaign to introduce the potato into the Russian diet made use of a common, but nonetheless effective, principle of persuasion—*scarcity sells*. The attractiveness of an object can be increased by making it appear scarce and unavailable, by erecting barriers that make the object difficult to obtain. To paraphrase an old saw, "Scarcity makes the heart grow fonder."

Advertisers and sales agents are well aware that scarcity sells. Their ads announce: "not available in any store," "get 'em while supplies last," "limited edition," "available for a limited time only." Sometimes they deliberately limit supplies. For example, the Franklin Mint, a direct marketer of such "collector items" as commemorative dinner plates, keepsake figurines, and souvenir coins, regularly claims: "Only a limited number of items were produced. No more will be made. The molds will be destroyed." Another gold coin merchant restricts sales to "only five coins per order." Car dealers often make such remarks as, "We only received two models like this one, and we sold the other one yesterday." The local salesclerk will gladly tell you, "That's all we have in stock; we can't keep 'em on the shelf—sorry."

Beginning with the Barbie doll in 1959, almost every year there has been a toy (or two) that becames the hot, scarce item— one year, Cabbage Patch dolls; the next, Ninja Turtles; then Power Rangers, Furby babies, and the Tickle Me Elmo doll. What will it be next year? The story of the Elmo doll is instructive. The doll had features that many found appealing—it giggled and vibrated when stroked. However, the Tickle Me Elmo dolls had one feature that especially made the cash registers ring— they were frequently out-of-stock. Parents would line up for hours in the hope of getting dolls for their children. Battles would break out in toy departments over who would get that last doll. Stores would conduct lotteries to see who would win an opportunity to buy a doll. Some owners auctioned off their dolls at upwards of $500. Sales for the dolls skyrocketed.

What is the lure of scarcity? What happens when an object is made unavailable and thus becomes a *phantom* choice? Consider what the typical Russian peasant must have thought and felt upon seeing a newly restricted potato field: *"Hey, why are they roping off these potatoes? They must be valuable. I wonder if they will post a guard? Sure they will; they'll see to it that only the rich get to eat potatoes. Not if I can help it. I'm sick of beet soup day in and day out. I want potatoes."*

As indicated by our hypothetical peasant, phantoms can capture the imagination. The unavailable becomes exotic. When we discover that a commodity is scarce or may be unavailable, one of our first inferences is that it must also be desirable. Why else would it be so rare? We tend to use a simple rule, or heuristic: If it is rare, if it is unavailable, then it must be valuable. This is what lies behind research findings showing that female college students believed that a scarce pair of nylon hosiery should cost more than a readily available pair, that children rated cookies in scarce supply as more desirable than similar cookies in abundant supply, and that, in response to news of an upcoming shortage of imported beef, orders by supermarkets and other food stores increased to between two and six times the normally ordered quantities.[2] Given the ease with which information about scarcity and availability can be manipulated, the propaganda potential of this technique is nearly unlimited and is available to all.

Scarcity and unavailability can do more than just make an object appear more desirable. When a phantom alternative is present, it can also result in a change in the perception, evaluation, and ultimate choice of the available options. We, along with Peter Farquhar and Doug Calvin, have conducted a series of experiments in which college students were asked to choose among brands of products.[3] In some sets of the choices, a very attractive alternative was included, but the students were told that the item was unavailable and that they could not select it. In other words, a phantom alternative was presented.

What do the results show? First, the presence of an attractive phantom made the other brands look less attractive—a contrast effect similar in nature to, but opposite in direction from, that found with decoys (see Chapter 10). Second, the phantom changed the relative importance given to the criteria for making a decision. Specifically, the attribute on which the phantom was superior was rated as most important for making the decision. For example, if the phantom was a new computer with lots of memory or a new car that gets great gas mileage, then the attributes of computer memory and gas mileage became the focus of decision making. This change in decision criteria also resulted in a change in choice; the students were much more likely to indicate that they would purchase an available brand that rated high on the attribute on which the phantom was best.

Thus the presence of a phantom may subtly affect our perceptions. For example, hearing about the possibilities of a defense shield in the sky, commonly referred to as the Strategic Defense Initiative, or Star Wars, may cause us to view our present defense capabilities as inadequate. It can also cause us to shift the focus of our attention toward strategic high-tech weapons systems and away from conventional military hardware, even though conventional hardware has been proven to be more useful in fighting a limited war in places such as the Balkans or the Middle East.

Phantoms, like scarce but available alternatives, can also arouse our emotions—emotions that can be played upon by the skilled propagandist.[4] As with most consumer goods, owning an object that is scarce for or unavailable to everyone else is a means of defining one's self: "I am unique and special because I own something that no one else (or at least not many) has been able to obtain." Just hearing about a phantom may induce worry and concern: "If they bring out a better product, I'll be stuck with this thing. Maybe I should wait." This experience is so common in the computer industry that computer experts have a special term for preannounced but unavailable products—vaporware. Not obtaining a hoped-for phantom can be a frustrating experience leading to aggression (one explanation for why riots and revolutions occur) or sour grapes (devaluing the once hoped-for phantom as a way to reconcile oneself with not getting it). Being the only child on the block without that new toy can often arouse feelings of inadequacy and incompetence. Finally, taking away an object or choice can result in what has been termed psychological reactance—the individual, upset at having his or her freedom denied, attempts at all costs to restore a sense of autonomy and control.

Given the power of scarce and unavailable items to alter our perceptions and to arouse our emotions, it is not surprising that propagandists often use a phantom as a persuasion device. We call this the *phantom trap*—marshaling most, if not all, of one's resources in an attempt to obtain that which cannot be reached.

One important aspect of the phantom trap is *phantom fixation:* a tendency to focus attention on the scarce or unavailable item. By concentrating on the scarce or unavailable, we may forget and overlook the possible. A program of research by Walter Mischel illustrates the point.[5] Mischel was investigating the ability of children to delay gratification. In his studies, children were given a choice: They could get a small candy bar right away or they could wait and receive a much more attractive prize later (a big candy bar). Which children were most likely to wait for the currently unavailable prize? Mischel found that children who could distract themselves from focusing their attention on *either* prize—for example, by thinking of other things—would wait the longest and therefore fared better. Children who became fixated on receiving the prizes experienced considerable conflict that was hard to resist and thus were more likely to take the immediate but lesser prize.

The Mischel experiments demonstrate how phantoms can direct thought. The presence of an attractive but currently unavailable object can focus our attention and resources on obtaining the desired prize. Settling for less than the phantom becomes a conflict that can only be resolved by "strength of willpower," a test that many of us often fail.

Such a fixation can have positive consequences; it may be helpful in mobilizing energies to obtain an elusive goal of perhaps great personal or societal benefit. It can also be exploited for propaganda purposes. For example, early promoters of the New World such as Ralph Hamor recruited settlers with promises of fountains of youth, gold, riches beyond belief, and (as one pamphlet put it) "lands so marvelous as to seem incredible."[6] Many signed on, having become increasingly dissatisfied with their own lives as a result of the propaganda, and went in search of the phantom, *El Dorado*. Today, the promoters of Pokémon make use of phantom fixation—"I just can't get some of those trading cards"—to literally make a few billion dollars. In many cases, phantom fixation can be a waste of time and energy, especially when the phantom is really a "red herring" of sorts—a truly unavailable option. In such cases, an individual or organization may expend great amounts of resources to obtain a desired new employee or access to new markets, only to find that the effort was wasted and the phantom never existed.

An experiment we conducted with Ken Freeman and Peter Farquhar demonstrates another side of the phantom trap—how emotions aroused by a phantom can serve to persuade.[7] In our study, students first earned money by completing a manual-labor task of turning screws and refilling a box of spools. The money was used to purchase common office supplies such as erasers and paper clips. However, when some of the students went to purchase the paper clips, they encountered a surprise phantom—after selecting the most attractive option, they were told that they had not earned enough money to purchase it. Although the students probably didn't care much about the paper clips, the news that they couldn't get what they wanted (even something as trivial as a paper clip) was in many ways personally threatening—just as many people feel threatened when told that they are too late for a sale or that they don't qualify for financing of that new car.

Because the students felt vulnerable, their emotions could be easily aroused and their choices were susceptible to manipulation. For example, half of the subjects encountering the surprise phantom were told, "Given that you are short of money for the paper clips you want, I'll give you the next most similar clip. *It's your only choice.*" Such a communication was designed to arouse reactance (a desire to restore lost freedom), and it did: All but a few subjects pointedly refused to select the brand the experimenter recommended, instead opting for another, quite different alternative. In a different condition, subjects, after finding out that they could not have their first choice, were manipulated much more subtly; they were told, "You might want to consider the next most similar clip." This communication was designed so as *not* to arouse reactance but to inform subjects how to be consistent with their original choice. Consequently, almost all subjects chose the paper clips subtly recommended by the experimenter. The astute reader will recognize this subtle strategy as being almost identical to the "lowballing" tactic (commit the customer, then switch 'em) used by many unscrupulous sales agents and described in Chapter 28.

What is particularly interesting in both conditions is that, whether subjects resisted direct pressure or succumbed to subtle pressure, their decisions were based not on the merits of the products but on the emotions aroused by a phantom.

Another version of the phantom trap has been termed the "consumer Catch-22 carousel" by C. R. Snyder.[8] As we mentioned

"This car is not for everyone, sir.
Would you care to take our aptitude test?"

earlier, obtaining a scarce and rare product adds to one's self-image as a unique and special person. Manufacturers know this and design and market their products accordingly. If the marketer does a good job of creating a perception of the product as unique, then you desire and acquire it. But the catch is, *so does everyone else*; suddenly you are no longer an original. Instead of acquiring a product that makes you unique, you have obtained one that makes you just like everyone else. This further heightens the need for uniqueness, and off we go in an endless pursuit of the next faddish phantom. As Erich Fromm points out, once we begin using material goods to define ourselves, we are doomed to be on an endless treadmill of dissatisfaction.[9]

The phantom trap also points up some of the possible pitfalls in using censorship to regulate human behavior. Attempts to make something "unavailable" through censorship may increase the perceived value of the forbidden item. For example,

The Satanic Verses was an interesting novel by Salman Rushdie, but it certainly was not blockbuster material. Its sales might have been limited to several thousand copies except for one thing: The Ayatollah Khomeini declared it was sacrilegious and urged Muslims to assassinate the author. The book immediately rocketed to the top of the best-seller list. A similar event took place recently in China: Zhou Weihui wrote a sexy but typical romance novel entitled *Shanghai Baby*. The Chinese Communist party banned the novel—not for its contents, but because Weihui apparently showed "too much skin" at a book signing. However, unlike previous attempts at censorship by the Chinese leadership, this time the ban was made public. Demand for *Shanghai Baby* soared. Pirated copies are sold everywhere. Weihui sold the rights to her book to publishers in South Korea, Taiwan, Italy, and Japan (where a guidebook to the bars and dives of *Shanghai Baby* is available for the tourist); and, of course, a film version is being discussed.

Further, by limiting commodities such as X-rated movies and "nudie" magazines to adults only, we provide children a ready-made method of proving their adulthood and defining themselves as "grown-up"—in a sense, we unwittingly encourage them to go out and get the fruit forbidden to all but adults. The point is nicely illustrated in an experiment conducted by David Zellinger and his colleagues.[10] In this study, college students received a description of a book much like the descriptions that appear on dust jackets. Half of the students were told that the book had a "21-year-old age restriction." When such a message was given, the book was rated as more desirable—the students indicated they would like to read it to a far greater extent than did the students in the control condition.

How can the phantom trap be avoided? We have three suggestions.[11] First, consider that phantoms may exist where you might not expect them—either through devious design or simply through unintentional unavailability. In such cases, it is wise to develop contingency plans in advance. For example, if the car you want proves to be unavailable, you could walk off the car lot rather than sliding to the "most similar" alternative. Second, when dealing with phantoms it may be a good idea to imagine other scenarios—for example, attempting to obtain other phantoms or accepting a readily available option. This will lessen the likelihood that you will become fixated on the unavailable. It can also make clear the relative costs and benefits of pursuing a phantom or perhaps suggest new, viable alternatives. Finally, use the emotions that often accompany phantoms as a cue that something is awry. Try to react not to the emotions but to the circumstances of the situation. Again, this may mean that the best strategy is simply to walk away and gain the time and composure needed to look more carefully before you leap. Whether one is talking about a defense system costing billions, a multi-million-dollar introduction of a new computer product, or merely a few hundred extra dollars for the family car, avoiding the potential pitfalls of phantom traps may be no small potatoes.

When Information Fails:
The Challenge of Propaganda
to Society

Education or Propaganda?

Legend has it that the Greek philosopher Protagoras was the first person in history to have his books burned in public. Protagoras, who lived in the fifth century B.C., was a Sophist—an individual who made his livelihood by *teaching* others the ways of *persuasion*. His incinerated volume, lost now to antiquity, was similar in many respects to the one you are currently reading; it, too, described various persuasion devices that could be used on any occasion. It appears that, almost from the beginnings of Western civilization, people have found the idea that one individual can influence another, using persuasion, to be distasteful if not downright despicable. Propaganda is often viewed as the work of an evil manipulator.

On the other hand, Protagoras' other profession, that of educator, is sometimes held in high esteem. We eagerly send our children to schools and universities hoping that they will learn a useful trade, develop an appreciation for the finer things of life, become productive citizens. But what really is the difference between propaganda and education?

Some would argue that breakfast cereal and aspirin commercials are obvious attempts to sell something at a high price by intentionally misleading the audience. They can be considered propaganda. "Selling" a presidential candidate, however, is more complicated. The devices used by political pundits and campaign staff to display a candidate in a favorable manner could conceivably be considered education—an attempt to educate the public on the policies and virtues of the candidate by presenting those views as clearly, efficiently, and articulately as possible.

The American Heritage Dictionary of the English Language defines *propaganda* as "the systematic propagation of a given doctrine" and *education* as "the act of imparting knowledge or skill." Again, we could all agree that breakfast cereal and aspirin ads are propaganda designed to promote the sale of certain brands. But what about American television programs, which still tend to depict women and minorities in stereotyped roles? Or, more subtly, what about the vast majority of school textbooks? American history textbooks typically distort the past by ignoring or downplaying less than meritorious events in U.S. history, portraying leaders as bigger than life and almost superhuman, and making it appear that the theory of American government is the way it is actually practiced. Until recently, the contributions of African-Americans and other minorities have been virtually ignored.[1] Is this merely imparting knowledge?

The problem of distinguishing between education and propaganda can be subtler still. Let us look at arithmetic as taught in the public schools. What could be more educational? By that we mean, what could be more pure, objective, factual, untainted by doctrine? The issue, though, isn't as clear-cut as it may appear. Remember the examples used in your elementary school arithmetic text? Most of the examples dealt with buying, selling, renting, working for wages, and computing interest. These examples do more than simply reflect the capitalistic system in which the education is occurring: They systematically endorse the system, legitimize it, and, by implication, suggest that it is natural and normal.[2]

As a way of illustrating multiplication and percentages, the textbook might have Mr. Jones borrowing $20,000 at 14% interest from a bank in order to purchase a new car. Would this example be used in a society that felt it was sinful to charge interest, as early Christian societies believed? Would this example be used in a society that believed people shouldn't seek possessions they can't afford? What would be the reaction to a textbook that replaced those problems with ones of this nature: (1) A family of four needs $100 per week for food, but after paying the rent has only $25 left for food. Assuming $100 worth of food represents full nourishment, what is the percentage of under-nourishment for this family? (2) The U.S. government spends $1.5 trillion annually, with $510 billion spent on the elderly (Medicaid and Social Security), $328 billion on defense, and $22 billion on education. How much money would need to be spent on education to bring it to the same funding level as defense? To the same funding level as the elderly?[3] We are not suggesting that it is wrong or evil to use these kinds of illustrations in arithmetic books, nor do we seek to declare a winner in this political struggle; we are merely pointing out that something as innocuous as an arithmetic textbook can serve as a tool for propaganda. If so, it might be useful to recognize it as such.

The debate over what is education and what is propaganda was brought to the fore once again with the advent of Channel One. In the early 1990s, Whittle Communications began Channel One as a "news service" for American schools.* Schools were offered this deal: Each class that adopted Channel One would receive a television set, a VCR, and twelve minutes per day of Channel One programming consisting of news snippets (short news stories of 50 to 175 words on topics such as the Queen of England visiting the United States, Winnie Mandela being found guilty of kidnapping, and U.S. Marines offering relief to cyclone victims in Bangladesh). In return, Channel One would show two minutes of advertising (embedded in ten minutes of "news"), which was offered to advertisers such as McDonald's, M&M/Mars, and Pepsi at $200,000 per thirty-second spot. Reebok, the makers of tennis shoes, sponsored one twelve-minute segment on physical education. Strapped for cash, nearly 12,000 schools and their 8 million students adopted Channel One in order to obtain the TV and VCR.

The decision was not without controversy. Advocates argued that today's children are brought up on TV and that Channel One is thus an effective means of awakening an interest in public affairs and training citizens. On the other hand, critics noted that Channel One is blatant commercial propaganda foisted upon a captive audience; some pointed out that American

---

*In 1994, Channel One was purchased by K-III Communications, which owns Seventeen and the Weekly Reader and is owned in turn by Kohlberg Kravis Roberts & Co., which is famous for its $25-billion leveraged buyout of RJR Nabisco.

democracy probably doesn't need more news snippets but could use more in-depth analysis of current affairs of the type that occurs in an energized classroom discussion.

What has Channel One accomplished? The research to date supports the fears of the critics. For example, in one study conducted by education researcher Nancy Nelson Knupfer and high school principal Peter Hayes, students who watched Channel One for a year showed no improvement in general knowledge of current events (relative to those students who did not watch Channel One); in addition, on quizzes given less than a day after watching the program, most students could not explain what the stories were about or why the news item was important. However, the students did demonstrate nearly perfect recall for the ads presented on the show.[4]

In practice, whether a person regards a particular course of instruction as educational or propagandistic depends, to a large extent, on his or her values. Reflect, for a moment, on the typical film about drug abuse that children are often required to watch in high school. Such films typically mention that many hard-core narcotics addicts began by sampling marijuana. Most school officials would probably regard the presentation of this piece of factual knowledge as a case of "imparting knowledge," and most marijuana users would probably regard it as "the systematic propagation of a given doctrine"—because it implies that smoking marijuana leads to the use of hard-core addictive drugs without mentioning that the vast majority of people who have sampled marijuana (such as former president Bill Clinton) do not become hard-core drug users.

By the same token, consider the topic of sex education in the schools as viewed by a member of the Christian Coalition on the one hand and by the editor of *Playboy* magazine on the other hand. For one individual it is propaganda; for the other, education. Similarly, advertisers are often known to argue that, far from serving a propaganda purpose, their advertising seeks to inform the consumer about brands of products and the benefits that may be obtained from them. In a similar vein, consider the debate on the teaching of evolution and creationism in biology class. Scientists see creationism as religion and therefore having no place in a science class. Fundamentalists see evolutionary theory as a kind of religious dogma and want to censor alternative religions or at least have equal time.

This is not to say that all communications are drastically slanted and one-sided. Rather, when we are dealing with an emotionally charged issue about which people's opinions differ greatly, it is probably impossible to construct a communication that people on both sides of the issue would agree was fair and impartial. Not surprisingly, researchers have found that pro-Israeli and pro-Arab partisans rated identical samples of major network television coverage of the Beirut massacre as being biased against their side.[5] Your opinion about the recount of votes in Florida in the 2000 U.S. presidential election most likely depended on which candidate you supported. If you backed Al Gore, you probably saw the recount as a great exercise in democracy in which all the votes of all the people mattered and should be counted. There is no need to rush democracy. In contrast, if you supported George W. Bush, then the recount of votes in selected Florida counties using questionable counting techniques was tantamount to stealing the election. Two recounts are enough for a democracy.

Research also shows that many Americans agree that the evening news is biased; they disagree, however, as to the nature of this bias.[6] Those who view the evening news as biased are evenly split, claiming that it is too liberal or too conservative, too Republican or too Democratic, too supportive of the status quo or too change-oriented. The point is that the bias of a communication is often in "the eye of the beholder." (Opinion polls generally show that members of the elite national media press tend to be more liberal on cultural issues and more conservative on economic issues than the average American.[7]) What is labeled as propaganda and what is labeled as education depend on one's own propaganda purposes. Protagoras' book was considered heretical in his day. Today, a similar volume might be called a "textbook." Undoubtedly some readers of this book may choose to question our educational purpose, preferring instead to see this volume as propaganda for the use of rational and fair persuasion strategies.

In many ways, it is dangerous to apply the labels "education" and "propaganda" to a communication merely on the basis of whether it agrees or disagrees with one's values. Consider the case of war propaganda, with its goal of convincing a nation to commit acts of aggression against an evil enemy. If the appeal is successful, the act of war becomes consistent with our values and the most blatant propaganda is labeled "news" and "information needed to pull the nation together." In such cases, we may let our guard down just at the moment when we need it the most. Consider the opposite case, in which we learn about a disagreeable fact—for example, that the policies of the president we elected are in many ways responsible for increased racism and poverty. To reduce our dissonance, we label the disconcerting information "propaganda" and deny the validity of the claim. Thus discredited, the fact no longer needs to be considered in our decision making. In such cases, we miss the opportunity to educate ourselves about important issues of the day and to discover perhaps more successful courses of action.

More than five decades ago, Max Wertheimer—a psychologist and a refugee from Nazi Germany—advanced a distinction between propaganda and education that we believe is well worth considering.[8] According to Wertheimer, propaganda tries to keep people from thinking and from acting as humans with rights; it manipulates prejudice and emotion to impose the propagandist's will on others. Education, in contrast, should provide the skills for people to stand on their own two feet and to make their own decisions; it should encourage critical thinking. In Wertheimer's framework, programs such as Channel One are propaganda; they immerse the student in a world of consumerism and not-so-hard-hitting "news" and fail to provide an opportunity to develop skills needed for participation in a democracy.

What is the educational response? It is unrealistic to expect children to have the sophistication to avoid propaganda—whether it appears on television, in advertising, or in their textbooks. Therefore, it is important that an education offers the tools for understanding propaganda. Consider these possible responses to Channel One (or to any other form of propaganda). Instead of grading papers while the students watched the show, suppose the teacher pointed out how the ads were made, what techniques the advertisers used, or how Channel One was financed. Suppose the teacher took the Channel One video and challenged the students to create a "better" newscast—a newscast that looked at the issues with more depth than did Channel One and from multiple points of view. We suspect that such experiences would alert students to how propaganda is made, increase their interest and knowledge of current events, and place them in a better position to make their own decisions about what to buy and what to believe.

At the heart of Wertheimer's view of education is critical debate and group discussion that explores an issue from multiple perspectives. How can this be accomplished? In the 1950s, N. R. F. Maier, an organizational psychologist, developed guidelines for structuring group discussion and decision making.[9] His research, along with research that we have recently completed with our colleague Marlene Turner, demonstrates that just exposing discussion groups to these guidelines can increase critical thinking and improve the quality of decision making.[10] Some of Maier's recommendations for generating critical discussion include:

1. Do not accept the first answer you hear as *the* answer. Explore alternatives. Ask, "What else should be considered?" "What else might we do?"

2. Keep any discussion problem-centered and avoid looking for excuses or seeking to blame others for a problem. Avoid saying things like, "That's a really stupid idea."

3. Keep track of all suggestions for solving a problem or making sense of an issue so that each may be explored fully.

4. After gathering a number of suggestions for addressing an issue, then probing and evaluative questions can be asked. These might include: "How would that work out?" "Do I understand the issue or do I need to search out more information?" "Am I mistaken in my assumptions about the issue?" "What are the advantages or disadvantages of each proposal?" "Is there a way to combine suggestions to generate an even better solution?"

5. Protect individuals from personal attacks and criticism, especially if they present minority or divergent viewpoints (after all, they may be right).

6. Make your objective one of understanding differences of opinion in the group and attempting to resolve them.

As our discussion indicates, the issue of whether a given piece of information is education or propaganda is complex and goes well beyond whether we simply like or dislike the content of the information. It behooves us, then, to look closely at how the tactics that we have presented throughout this volume are used in propaganda campaigns—a task we take up in this set of chapters. In taking up this charge, we do so with an eye toward asking, "What forms of education and persuasion will best serve our society and ourselves?"

32 | What Is News?

Imelda Marcos's shoes. There are very few people who were adults in the waning days of the Ferdinand Marcos regime who won't know what we are talking about when we use this simple phrase. Most of us will immediately see, in our mind's eye, a closet containing thousands of pairs of shoes, of various colors, styles, and uses. This image, which first appeared on ABC News's "Nightline," has served as the symbol of the corruption that characterized Marcos's long reign as president of the Philippines. As a symbol, the picture of Imelda Marcos's shoes is vivid and effective, but also simplistic. And very, very useful. It is characteristic of the type of news we are most likely to get—a vivid image as opposed to a thoughtful discussion.

On any given day, the world is full of happenings such as wars, riots, consumer frauds, spelling bees, family violence, scientific achievements, political speeches, and human sorrows and happiness. Obviously, the news media cannot (and does not) cover all these events. It has been estimated that, for the typical daily newspaper, more than 75% of the potential news items of the day are rejected and never see print. For national media such as network television news, the percentage of rejected news is much higher. For example, on any given day, there are many armed conflicts occurring throughout the world. The viewer of the nightly news or the reader of the daily paper typically learns of approximately two or three of these conflicts and, after years of watching and reading, could probably name fewer than a dozen current wars.

Selectivity of news is the beginning of propaganda. As Walter Lippmann once put it:

> Without some form of censorship, propaganda in the strict sense
> of the word is impossible. In order to conduct a propaganda

"By limiting the weather report to seven minutes, we'll have nine or ten seconds for the President's soundbite."

there must be some barrier between the public and the event. Access to the real environment must be limited, before anyone can create a pseudo-environment that he thinks wise or desirable. For while people who have direct access can misconceive what they see, no one else can decide how they shall misconceive it, unless he can decide where they shall look, and at what.[1]

Any revolutionary or would-be leader worth his or her salt knows that a primary objective is to secure the public's source of news. Very early in its existence, the Nazi party established its own publishing company, the Eher Verlag, which in its heyday controlled more than 150 publishing houses, employed an estimated 35,000 persons, and had profits exceeding 100 million marks a year. During his reign as *Führer,* Hitler was successful in holding the press captive by systematically rewarding agreeable journalists (with choice interviews, promotions, and party favors) and punishing those who disagreed with Nazi policy (by limiting their access to news, subjecting them to government investigations, and suspending their operating licenses).[2]

Five years before coming to power in the 1917 October revolution, the Soviets established the newspaper *Pravda.* For more than seven decades, until the fall of Communism, *Pravda,* which ironically means "truth," served the Soviet Communist party by censoring and filtering the news presented to Russian and Eastern Europeans.[3]

Managed news is not the exclusive province of totalitarian regimes. Closer to home, President Franklin D. Roosevelt, much like other U.S. presidents, attempted to influence the news, albeit more subtly than his European counterparts, by flooding the news media with pro-administration information. For example, during a typical three-month period in 1936, the Roosevelt administration employed 146 full-time and 124 part-time publicity agents who issued 7 million copies of about 4,800 public news releases. The Works Progress Administration alone spent more than $1 million in one year on printing—all in an effort to encourage the news media to convince the American people of the necessity of New Deal policies.[4]

In present-day Western democracies, what factors determine which news items are selected for television and radio newscasts and for publication in magazines and newspapers? In totalitarian regimes, news is routinely censored by ruling elites. Such blatant control is rare in Western democracies and when it does occur, it often results in immediate public outcries—witness, for example, reactions to the censorship of rap groups or the popularity of "network censor" jokes. The jokes tap into a wellspring of animosity to such censorship in spite of the fact that studies of network practices find that, by the time a script reaches the network censor, only minor changes, if any, are needed to make the show "airworthy."

However, there are certain circumstances in which direct censorship is not only accepted but appears to be encouraged by American citizens. Such was the case during the Persian Gulf war when the Pentagon established rules designed to regulate information flow concerning the war effort.[5] Journalists were permitted to cover the war scene only if they were in organized pools escorted by a military leader, a situation that kept them far from the real action. Any journalist operating independently was subject to arrest by military police. If reporters did happen to stumble onto newsworthy items, officials were assigned to guide them quickly away from the action. With few opportunities to gain firsthand information, reporters became dependent on official statements and government-issued videotapes. Few Americans complained. One "Saturday Night Live" skit poked fun at the coverage of the war by depicting reporters as comically self-absorbed, with little understanding of national security. John Sununu, at the time the White House chief of staff, ordered a videotape copy of the show for viewing at the White House as further evidence that the public supported the military's press policy.

Clearly, however, the selection of *everyday* news in Western democracies involves more than traditional censorship. Considering the mass of information that comes over the news wires, how do journalists select what to print in the papers and to show on TV? To answer that question, let's look at how the primary news gatherer—the reporter—goes about her or his job.[6]

News reporters typically work beats—that is, they are assigned a group of institutions to cover such as the local criminal justice system or the White House or Hollywood or sports teams. This immediately injects one source of bias into news coverage—something that happens off or between beats has a lower chance of being covered unless it is a major disaster or other spectacular event. For example, almost 60% of the stories appearing in the *New York Times* and the *Washington Post* are from routine channels and beats.[7] For the citizen, this means an endless stream of stories about events happening on a given beat, say, for example, a Hollywood starlet's feelings about home furnishings and nudity or daily reports on the well-being of our favorite athlete's injured toe. Off-beat stories rarely are covered and aren't even considered news. For example, we have come to expect that CNN's "Headline News" will run a little banner at the bottom of the screen listing sports scores and stock prices. It would appear quite strange if the network suddenly filled that space with the names of those who won spelling bees or National Merit Scholarships or listed statistics describing the health and well-being of workers.

Most reporters are on a deadline; they must prepare a given number of stories by a certain time regardless of what is happening. In order to meet their deadlines, reporters place a premium on sources that can be easily contacted (for example, politicians or bureaucrats) and trusted (ones the reporter has talked with before and who gave a "successful" interview). This also creates bias in at least two ways. First, the reporter develops a routine for covering a story; for example, the reporter covering the crime beats learns to look for stories in such places as police crime reports and trial calendars and develops relationships with police and district attorneys that keep the stories coming; others who might shed light on the causes of crime—for example, welfare agencies, churches, academics, or the homeless—are for the most part ignored. Second, the reporter's routine results in the same types of people appearing on the news repeatedly. For example, a survey of guests appearing on ABC News's "Nightline" finds that the vast majority of those asked to give their opinions on the show are white and male and employed primarily in government, university think-tanks, and corporations.[8] Women, minorities, labor leaders, and those representing the public interest are rarely asked to appear. Such a guest list results in a biased discussion of issues with some points of view clearly excluded.

Increasingly, reporters work for a corporation.[9] For the last decade or so, media ownership in the United States has become concentrated in the hands of a few organizations. Today, twenty-three corporations control most of television, magazines, books, and movies. Some facts about media ownership: 60% of local daily newspapers belong to one of fourteen corporate chains, three corporations dominate the magazine industry, six record companies control 80% of the market for recorded music, and nine film studios produce 70% of network TV's prime-time schedule. This concentration of ownership results in direct pressure on the reporter; certain stories are encouraged or not encouraged depending on their implications for the parent corporation. More subtly, however, corporate ownership biases programming and coverage. For example, although almost all Americans are workers and consumers, there is little sustained coverage of corporate policies and how they affect the welfare of employees; any attempt to inform consumers about the safety and quality of products is typically relegated to the back pages of newspapers and back channels of cable TV. In contrast, reporting on the ups and downs of the stock market, along with other business news, is a regular feature of both newspapers and television "news" programs.

A particularly interesting case in point is beautifully depicted in the 1999 film *The Insider,* based on the true story of Jeffrey Wigand. Wigand, a researcher for the Brown & Williamson tobacco company, decided to go public with evidence indicating that the cigarette industry was not only aware of the addictiveness of its product but actually tried to increase that addictiveness in order to boost sales. This evidence was particularly damaging because the CEOs of the major tobacco companies had previously sworn in testimony before Congress that they did not believe that cigarettes were addictive. Risking his job and arrest for contempt of court, Wigand bravely went on camera with TV journalist Mike Wallace for an interview on the TV news show "60 Minutes." But, at the last minute (on the advice of their attorneys), the top brass of CBS decided to shelve the interview in order to avoid the messiness of a lawsuit at the hands of the cigarette companies, leaving Wigand hung out to dry.

As difficult as these pressures may seem, the journalist faces one more pressure that may mean her or his livelihood—the ability of the news story to hold the audience's attention. All television programming, including the evening news, must strive for profits—and that translates into securing ratings and viewers that will attract advertising dollars. And what induces people to watch the news? A study of why people watch the news concludes that most viewers want to be amused and diverted; being informed is only a secondary motive for watching. As the director of the British Broadcasting Corporation has noted, television news is just another form of entertainment.[10] To guarantee high ratings and revenues, mass media content tends to be agreeable and to require little effort on the part of consumers, while still being arousing, emotionally engaging, and above all entertaining.

Accordingly, when those in charge of news programming make decisions about which events to cover and which fraction of the miles of daily videotape to present to the public, they make their decisions, at least in part, on the basis of the entertainment value of their material. Around-the-clock coverage of the O. J. Simpson trial or the JonBenet Ramsey murder or the latest rumor in the Monica Lewinsky saga is far more entertaining than, say, the events in Bosnia, the concentration of mass media ownership, or a U.S. presidential election (unless, of course, it is in dispute). Film footage of a flooded metropolis has much more entertainment value than footage devoted to a dam built to prevent such a flooding: It is simply not very exciting to see a dam holding back a flood. And yet construction of the dam may be more important news.

Just as such action events as football games are more entertaining on television than such quiet events as chess matches, it is more likely that riots, bombings, hijackings, earthquakes, massacres, and other violent acts will get more airtime than stories about people helping one another or people working to prevent violence. Indeed, news agencies station reporters at "action centers," such as courts, athletic facilities, and police stations as opposed to schools, churches, and research laboratories, where more important events may be occurring. Thus, local news devotes eight times more coverage to sports than to community problems such as school financing or housing,[11] and national TV news telecasts tend to focus on the violent behavior of individuals—terrorists, protesters, strikers, or police—because violent action makes for more exciting viewing than does a portrayal of people behaving in a peaceful, orderly manner.

What makes a great news story? In general, reporters and editors tend to look for stories that (1) are new and timely, (2) involve conflict or scandal, (3) concern strange and unusual happenings, (4) happen to familiar or famous people, (5) are capable of being made dramatic and personal, (6) are simple to convey in a short space or time, (7) contain visual elements (especially pictures for television), and (8) fit a theme that is currently prominent in the news or society.

Armed with this understanding of how the news media operate, we can comprehend how it came to pass that the image of Imelda Marcos's shoes was beamed into homes around the globe. By providing a frequent forum for her cause, the producers of "Nightline" had long befriended Corazon Aquino, the "housewife" who ended the twenty-one-year rule of Ferdinand Marcos. And the producers of "Nightline" were glad to do it. The Aquino/Marcos feud had all the elements of a great drama—a simple housewife who was carrying on the legacy of her assassinated husband, Benigno Aquino, pitted against a corrupt and arrogant ruler out of touch with his country and very poor at handling the American media. On the night the Marcos government fell, a "Nightline" crew was filming the crowds gathered outside the former palace of Ferdinand and Imelda Marcos when an aide to Corazon Aquino spotted them and invited the film crew inside for an exclusive tour of the private quarters. As they made their way through the palace, the "Nightline" crew filmed riches and opulence unknown to most people. However, it wasn't until they reached the bedroom that they found the visual image they were looking for. As "Nightline" host Ted Koppel and producer Kyle Gibson put it:

> And there, in the closet we saw these shoes. Thousands and thousands of shoes. Racks and racks. There was every style—pump, sling-back, flat heel, spiked heel. For every style, there were at least eight pairs of shoes in a row, each pair a different color.[12]

The estimated 3,000 pairs of shoes were the perfect media image—an ABC News exclusive. The shoes were a strange happening about a famous person; visually compelling, the shoes fit the current theme of "Nightline" that the Marcos rule was corrupt. Although the shoes are the perfect image to capture the corruption, we can ask: What did they really teach us about corruption in the Philippines? Do we understand anything of what happened in this country other than the fact that the first lady had a lot of shoes?

The news media's desire to satisfy our itch for entertainment and the resulting bias in coverage was dramatically illustrated by the way the media handled the 1970 Austin, Texas, "nonriot" in which one of us (E. A.) participated. Tensions had been running high between University of Texas students and local police following a confrontation at an impromptu student demonstration against the invasion of Cambodia by U.S. troops. But this was a mere preface compared to what seemed to be coming. A few days later, during a peaceful demonstration, four Kent State University students were slain by members of the Ohio National Guard. To protest this event, the Texas students planned a gigantic march into downtown Austin. The city council, fearing trouble, refused to issue a parade permit. In frustration and anger, the students decided to march anyway. Rumors spread that hundreds of armed rednecks and hooligans were descending on Austin with the intention of assaulting the students. Other rumors abounded to the effect that state troopers and Texas Rangers had been called in and were determined to take strong and violent action against anyone disobeying the law.

The situation seemed certain to be a prelude to extreme violence. Sniffing an exciting story, news teams affiliated with the major television networks were alerted and rushed to Austin. As it turned out, however, the explosive situation was defused at the eleventh hour: A federal judge issued a temporary restraining order to prevent the city from enforcing the anti-parade ordinance, in response to a request from university officials and several members of the police force. This event—especially because of the role played by the police—resulted not only in the total absence of violence but also in a genuine explosion of goodwill and solidarity among diverse elements of the community. Twenty thousand students did march, but they marched in a spirit of harmony. Some of them offered cold drinks to the police officers; students and police exchanged friendly greetings. This was an important event, coming as it did in an atmosphere of apparently universal distrust between students and police.

Interestingly enough, the national television networks completely ignored this encouraging turn of events. Given that teams of nationally prominent reporters from a variety of news organizations had descended on the city during the week, the lack of coverage seemed puzzling indeed. An unsettling explanation was provided by community psychologists Phillip Mann and Ira Iscoe: "Since there was no violence, news media teams left town and there was no national publicity, a commentary whose implications are by now sadly self-evident."[13]

It is interesting to note that years later in the same city, a great deal of coverage was given to an event of higher drama but far less importance. Some fifty members of the Ku Klux Klan staged a march and were greeted by about 1,000 hecklers. Some rocks and bottles were thrown, and a few people received minor cuts and bruises. The skirmish was featured in network television news reports and major stories in newspapers from coast to coast. Clearly, a minor Klan-and-town conflict was deemed more entertaining than a peaceful expression of goodwill.

The moral of both of the Austin, Texas, stories is simple: If you want access to the mass media, be entertaining.

Such coverage does not present a balanced or complete picture of what is happening in the world, not because the people who run the news media are evil and necessarily trying to manipulate us but simply because they are trying to entertain us. And, in trying to entertain us, they oversimplify and thus unwittingly influence our opinions about the world we live in. For example, as we noted before, people who watch a lot of TV tend to see the world as a far more violent place than those who watch very little TV.

The value of entertainment and the lesson of news as drama has not been lost on those who want to make the news, such as terrorists. Consider the Beirut hostage crisis of 1985, in which some forty innocent American passengers on a TWA jet were held captive by Shiite terrorists. TV cameras offered viewers back home around-the-clock coverage of all aspects of the crisis, important and trivial alike. There were press conferences held by the terrorists, press conferences held by the hostages, intimate shots of anguished families, demands, counterdemands, pistol-wavings, outrageous statements, luncheon menus. The TV cameras did everything but follow the hostages into the restrooms. The drama was spellbinding.

Advertisers and direct marketers constantly rediscover the observation that "news is entertainment." With the advent of interactive cable, computer bulletin boards, and the World Wide Web, some marketers, sincerely proud of their products, thought that these new technologies would afford them the opportunity to go beyond the usual thirty-second spot and provide some real information to the consumer. They dutifully prepared large databases containing information on product attributes, new usage ideas, what to do about typical problems, and so on—only to find that no one looked at the information. Marketers quickly came to realize that if they were to use this new technology effectively, then their presentations had to be entertaining; therefore they have replaced the information displays with product-oriented video games, contests, and bake clubs.

And the power of the itch for entertainment was not lost on Paragon Cable of New York. Instead of cutting off services to those who fall behind on their cable TV bill, Paragon fills each of its seventy-seven channels with C-SPAN programming. As you know, C-SPAN broadcasts mostly unedited speeches from the floor of the U.S. Senate and House of Representatives, along with other public affairs programs. Officials at the cable company report that, in the aftermath of this strategy, collection of overdue balances improved dramatically.[14] Apparently, news that isn't entertaining is more painful to watch than no news at all.

The result of this itch for entertainment is soundbite and photo-op news—a montage of brief visual images that play to the crowds. Each event and every idea must be part of a dramatic story amply illustrated with visual displays. Stories that are easily dramatized and visualized, such as a child trapped in an abandoned well, are readily covered. More complex issues, such as the details of the latest national health plan, the economy, or regulatory policy, receive little attention unless they can be made concrete and visual.

Would-be leaders, whether they be peaceful demonstrators, terrorists, advertisers, or candidates for president, must compete for attention in this entertainment environment. They do so by staging canned nominating conventions; using catchphrases guaranteed to make the evening news, such as "Make my day," "Just don't do it," "Read my lips," or "I will fight for you"; and engaging in endless photo sessions involving, for example, the Vietnam war memorial, a child with AIDS, a visit to a flag factory, or Arafat and an Israeli leader shaking hands in front of the White House.[15]

Television coverage of a political campaign comes to look more like an episode of a popular soap opera than a discussion of democracy and leadership. Just as we hear about the sex life of our favorite soap opera characters, who's ahead of whom in the competition for love and money, the latest rumors and gossip about the characters, and what sort of family troubles and squabbles they are having, so, too, we are likely to find out about the political candidates' sexual escapades, who leads whom in the most recent opinion poll, the latest rumors and gossip about the candidates, and the intricacies of intraparty squabbles. In a TV soap opera, image counts more than substance—the same as in a political campaign. A detailed analysis of our favorite character's business and home finances would be boring. So, too, would be a detailed analysis of the federal budget. However, there is a big difference: The characters on a TV soap opera use "play money." The government uses real taxpayers' real money.

And while we were all peeping into Imelda Marcos's closet and gawking at her shoes, what did we miss? First, the news media failed to present a detailed discussion of corruption in the Philippines: How widespread was it? How did it start? How was it maintained? What role, if any, did the United States play in this corruption? Such a discussion would be of enormous value in developing a U.S. policy toward the Philippines. Instead, the political events of the Philippines were reduced to a plot reminiscent of spaghetti westerns or an episode of the "A Team"—bad people take over the town; an honest citizen, with the help of her neighbors, cleans up the town and restores justice. Second, in all the interviews and photo-ops, we never heard Imelda Marcos's explanation for why those shoes were in her closet. According to Gerry Spence, the attorney who defended Imelda Marcos in her criminal trial for fraud and racketeering, Mrs. Marcos confided to him that she owned so many shoes because there are many shoe factories in the Philippines.[16] As the first lady, she received hundreds of shoes each year from companies that wanted to claim that Imelda Marcos wore their shoes. Most of the shoes were useless because they did not fit, but she stored them in the closet anyway. Of course, this could be little more than a self-serving explanation. (One wonders why she didn't give them to charity.) Regardless of where the truth lies, it is far more complex than a closet full of shoes. Anyone accused of wrongdoing is entitled to present her side of the story; as citizens in a democracy, we are entitled to hear both sides so that we can reach an informed opinion. In the criminal trial, we might add, Imelda Marcos was acquitted of all charges.

One wonders whether anyone would watch if television advertisers and politicians replaced all the slick thirty-second spots with ads that contained only useful information. One wonders what would happen to the ratings if journalists substituted in-depth coverage of important but possibly dull issues for the current barrage of entertaining but often distorting visual images now seen on the news. Advertisers, politicians, and journalists have come to rely on entertaining images and soundbites to convey their messages—a practice that distorts and simplifies reality by editing out all but the most entertaining information. In the long run, our seemingly insatiable desire for entertainment may succeed where Hitler and *Pravda* ultimately failed.

On the Ineffectiveness
of Information Campaigns

Suppose you inherited controlling interest in a television network. Here is a golden opportunity to influence people's opinions on important issues. Let's say you are an enthusiastic proponent of national health insurance, and you would like to persuade others to agree with you. Having read about the persuasion tactics described in this book, you know how to do it, and you are in control of a very powerful medium of communication. How do you set about doing it?

That's simple: You choose a time slot following a highly intellectual program (in order to be certain that well-informed people are watching) and, accordingly, you present a two-sided argument (because two-sided arguments work best on well-informed people). You arrange your arguments in such a manner that the argument in favor of national health insurance is stronger and appears first (in order to be fresh in the viewer's mind). You describe the plight of the poor, how they get sick more frequently and die earlier for lack of affordable medical care. You frame the need for national health care in terms of a personal loss for the viewer—the current piecemeal system is costly and driving up taxes. You use vivid personal examples of people you know. You discuss these events in a manner that inspires great fear; at the same time, you offer a specific plan of action, because this combination produces the most opinion change and the most action in the most people. You present some of the arguments against your position and offer strong refutation of these arguments. You arrange for the speaker to be expert, trustworthy, and extremely likable. You make your argument as strongly as you can, in order to maximize the discrepancy between the argument presented and the initial attitude of the audience. And then you sit back, relax, and wait for those opinions to start changing.

It's not that simple, however. Imagine a typical viewer: Let's say she is a forty-five-year-old, middle-class real estate broker who believes the government interferes too much in private life.

*"Does anyone really want to hear about a
fire in a shoe factory out in the boondocks?"*

She feels any form of social legislation undermines the spirit of
individuality, which, she believes is the essence of democracy.
She tunes in your program while looking for an evening's entertainment. She begins to hear your arguments in favor of free
health care. As she listens, she becomes slightly less confident in
her original convictions. She is not quite as certain as she had
been that the government shouldn't intervene in matters of
health. What does she do?

If she is anything like the subjects in an experiment conducted by Lance Canon, she would reach for the remote control,
switch channels, and begin to watch "Wheel of Fortune."[1] Canon
found that, as one's confidence is weakened, a person becomes
less prone to listen to arguments against his or her beliefs. Thus
the very people you most want to convince and whose opinions
might be the most susceptible to being changed are the ones
least likely to continue to expose themselves to a communication
designed for that purpose.

Information campaigns frequently fail to change attitudes, a fact of persuasive life that was observed by Herbert Hyman and Paul Sheatsley as far back as 1947.[2] In explaining the frequent failure of information campaigns, Hyman and Sheatsley noted that people tend to acquire information mostly about things that they find of interest and tend to avoid information that does not agree with their beliefs. Should someone find that they have been unavoidably exposed to uninteresting and disagreeable information, a common response is to distort and reinterpret that information, thus ignoring its implications for updating beliefs and attitudes.

Despite these apparent psychological barriers, attempts to influence attitudes and change behavior by providing reasonable information—whether it be a mass mailing on the AIDS epidemic from the U.S. surgeon general, crisis information in the front of the phone book, a Ross Perot political infomercial, or our hypothetical health insurance documentary—are as common as ever. To the extent that such campaigns fail to consider our tendency to expose ourselves selectively to information and systematically to distort discrepant communications, they are likely to fail.

Must you resign yourself to broadcasting your message to an audience composed of viewers who already support national health insurance? That may be the case—if you insist on airing a serious documentary devoted to the issue. After considering your alternatives, however, you might decide to take another approach.

You call a meeting of your network executives. The programming director is instructed to commission several scripts dramatizing the plight of families facing financial ruin because of high medical costs associated with serious illness. You order the news department to do some feature segments on the success of national health insurance in other countries. Finally, you provide the late-night talk show host with a couple of jokes he might tell about his inept but affluent doctor.

Although none of these communications would match the documentary in terms of the information provided, their cumulative impact could be more significant. Embedded in dramas or news segments, they would not necessarily come labeled as arguments supporting national health insurance; they seem innocuous, but their message is clear. Not appearing to be explicit attempts at persuasion, they should arouse little resistance, inhibiting the formation of counterarguments by distracting the audience. Most importantly, people will probably watch them without switching channels.

The use of entertaining programs to disseminate a point of view has been successful in achieving high audience ratings and in changing people's attitudes and behaviors.[3] For example, the Harvard Alcohol Project convinced TV producers to include "designated drivers" in the scripts of thirty-five prime-time television series during the 1989–1990 season as a means of promoting this alternative to drinking and driving. Subsequent research revealed an increase in the use of designated drivers as a result of the shows.

However, must we abandon the mass media as a means of communicating critical information and accept programs delivering only trivial entertainment? Cy Schneider thinks so, especially when it comes to our children. Schneider has created more than 1,000 kids' commercials for more than 400 products, including such notables as the Barbie doll, Chatty Cathy, and Agent Zero M. He has also been involved in the production of children's shows sponsored by the toymaker Mattel, such as "Matty's Funday Funnies" and "Beany and Cecil." He offers this apology for the state of children's television:

> The fact is that better shows, programs with more substance, have been tried over and over again by the commercial networks and stations. For the most part they have not attracted a large audience and consequently are not economically practical. There is only so much of this kind of programming that television is willing to support.[4]

Although it may be difficult to use the mass media to convey information, it is not impossible. Information campaigns *can* succeed if they follow these simple rules: (1) Make the program entertaining (a principle we observed in the previous chapter), (2) do not directly attack a viewer's attitudes and beliefs, and (3) use the tactics described in this book to make the program persuasive.[5] For example, during World War II, a radio program hosted by singer Kate Smith was highly successful in strengthening American commitment to the war effort and selling $39 million worth of bonds to finance the war.[6] In 1965, CBS sought to promote safe driving by airing "The National Drivers' Test," an involving show on which drivers were given a quiz about how to handle road situations; the show was viewed by 30 million Americans, 1.5 million of whom wrote to CBS for more information.[7] Both of these programs followed these rules.

Public television has attempted one of the most ambitious efforts to use the mass media to inform and teach with such shows as "Sesame Street" (to encourage academic achievement) and "Mister Rogers' Neighborhood" (to promote positive social relations). The logic behind these shows is clear: By the time a typical American child graduates from high school, he or she will have spent more time in front of a television set (17,000 hours) than in a classroom (11,000 hours).

The efforts appear promising.[8] "Sesame Street" has been on the air since 1969 and is watched on a weekly basis by about half of all preschoolers in America. It features a lovable set of characters—Bert and Ernie, Elmo, Big Bird, and Oscar the Grouch— and a sequence of fast-moving, attention-getting segments that teach such skills as counting, letter and number recognition, and vocabulary. Early evaluations of the program found that preschoolers who watched "Sesame Street" showed significant gains on education tests measuring knowledge of letters and numbers and on tests of matching, sorting, and classifying skills. However, there is a fly in the ointment: In natural settings, not all children watch "Sesame Street," particularly those from disadvantaged homes (the originally intended audience). However, this problem can be overcome if viewing is encouraged in the home or through highly successful early intervention programs such as Head Start.

Positive results have also been obtained for shows such as "Mister Rogers' Neighborhood." On this program, Fred Rogers creates an accepting atmosphere where children can discover such things as how plants grow or how tortilla chips are made, learn that each person (including you) is special, and take a trolley to the "land of make-believe" where imaginations explore the social world. Research finds that children who watch such shows on a regular basis are more likely to be altruistic and cooperative with their peers and to engage in other forms of prosocial behavior. Contrary to the opinion of Cy Schneider, it does appear that TV can offer higher-quality shows that inform and teach; we can educate as we entertain.

Although "teaching as we entertain" is a laudable goal (especially for our children), it is often easier said than done. This is particularly the case when dealing with "adult" issues that are complex, are rapidly developing, and require the communication of sophisticated and detailed information. In such cases, it may be difficult or impossible to provide the needed information in a highly dramatic, highly personalized, and very entertaining manner.

Robert Entman argues that, although the opportunity to gain more information about political affairs has increased dramatically in the last twenty years, Americans' interest in and knowledge of such affairs have not increased and may well have declined during this period.[9] The public, the press, and political leaders appear to be caught in a spiral. The communication of complex information requires an interested and informed public. Without an educated audience, journalists and leaders must simplify their message and package it as "entertainment," thus reducing further the sophistication of the public at large. The result may be, as Entman puts it in the title of his book, a democracy without citizens. Many of us lament the unrealistic cartoon world that our children view every day on television and demand more educational fare. We would argue that, as adults, we should have the same laments and demands for ourselves.

34

Subliminal Sorcery: Who Is Seducing Whom?

Imagine that it is the 1950s and you are off to see *Picnic*, one of the more popular films of the day. However, the movie theater, located in Fort Lee, New Jersey, is unlike any you have been in before. Unbeknownst to you, the projectors have been equipped with a special device capable of flashing short phrases onto the movie screen at such a rapid speed that you are unaware that any messages have been presented. During the film, you lean over to your companion and whisper, "Gee, I'd love a tub of buttered popcorn and a Coke right now." To which he replies, "You're always hungry and thirsty at movies, shhhhhh." But after a few moments he says, "You know, some Coke and popcorn might not be a bad idea."

A short time later you find out that you and your friend weren't the only ones desiring popcorn and Coke in the theater that day. Far from it. According to reports in newspapers and magazines, James Vicary, an advertising expert, had secretly flashed at 1/3,000 of a second the words EAT POPCORN and DRINK COKE onto the movie screen. He claimed that this had increased Coke sales by 18.1% and popcorn sales by 57.7%. Upon reading their newspapers, most people were outraged and frightened. It is a scary world indeed if advertisers can use such a devilish technique to bypass our conscious intellect and beam subliminal commands directly to our subconscious. By *subliminal* we mean a message so faint or fast that it is presented below the threshold of awareness.

In a 1957 article for the *Saturday Review* entitled "Smudging the Subconscious," Norman Cousins captured such feelings as he pondered the true meaning of such a device. As he put it, "If the device is successful for putting over popcorn, why not politicians or anything else?"[1] He wondered about the character of those who would dream up such a machine to "break into the deepest and most private parts of the human mind and leave all sorts of scratchmarks." Cousins concluded that the best course of action would be "to take this invention and everything connected to it and attach it to the center of the next nuclear explosive scheduled for testing."

Cousins was not alone in his concern about the use of subliminal techniques. In a series of four best-selling books, Wilson Bryan Key brought to national attention the possibility of widespread use of subliminal tactics.[2] Key argues that such techniques are not limited to television and movies. Cleverly hidden messages aimed at inducing sexual arousal are often embedded in the pictures and photographs of print advertisements. His concern about the use of subliminal persuasion is clear: "Every person reading this book has been victimized and manipulated by the use of subliminal stimuli directed into his unconscious mind by the mass merchandisers of media. The techniques are in widespread use by media, advertising and public relations agencies, industrial and commercial corporations, and by the Federal government itself."[3]

Governments have responded to the outcries of the critics. Subliminal advertising has been banned in Australia and Britain. In the United States, the Federal Communications Commission has ruled that the use of subliminal messages could result in the loss of a broadcast license. The National Association of Broadcasters has prohibited the use of subliminal advertising by its members. A Nevada judge has ruled that subliminal messages are not covered by the First Amendment protection of freedom of speech. In many ways, the furor over subliminal influence captures what many of us fear most about persuasion in general: Persuasion is a mysterious force that cannot be resisted.

Nevertheless, widespread media coverage and governmental rulings have not put an end to subliminal influence practices. In fact, such practices have spread to self-help products. Today a consumer needs only to visit the local bookstore or a vendor on the World Wide Web to find a vast array of subliminal audio- and videotapes designed to accomplish such worthwhile goals as increasing self-esteem, improving memory, reducing weight, controlling anger and temper, enhancing sexual responsiveness, and overcoming the trauma of sexual abuse. In their search for better self and health, American consumers have spent more than $50 million annually on subliminal tapes designed for therapeutic purposes.[4] The tapes work, according to one manufacturer, because subliminal messages bypass the conscious mind and imprint directly on the subconscious mind, where they create the basis for the kind of life the consumer wants.

Accusations concerning the sinister use of subliminal persuasion continue as well. Some have claimed that rock groups such as Led Zeppelin have implanted backward messages urging their listeners to worship Satan. In the summer of 1990, the rock band Judas Priest was placed on trial for allegedly recording, in one of their songs, the subliminal implant "do it." This message supposedly caused the suicide deaths of two avid young listeners of the group's music, Ray Belknap and James Vance.

In the 2000 U.S. presidential election, claims about the misuse of subliminal influence surfaced once again. This time the word RATS appeared for one-thirtieth of a second in an ad sponsored by the Republican National Committee. The supraliminal content of the ad attacked Al Gore's prescription coverage plan by claiming that it would be managed by bureaucrats. Supposedly, the subliminal RATS reinforced this message by likening Gore and the Democrats to rodents.

Given all the media coverage, the governmental involvement, and the dollars spent, surprisingly little public attention has been paid to a most basic question: Does subliminal influence really work?

During the last few years, we have been collecting published works on subliminal processes, gathering more than 150 articles from the mass media and more than 200 academic papers on the topic (a stack nearly 2 feet tall).[5] What does this collection of articles reveal?

First, there is some evidence for subliminal perception—minimal processing of information outside of awareness. One of the best examples of this is the cocktail party phenomenon. Suppose you are at a party and you are paying attention to what your friend is saying and ignoring all the other background noise. Someone in the background says your name. Your ears perk up and you start to pay attention to whoever said your name, even though a few minutes earlier you may not have known that the person was in the room. Such an effect indicates that you are doing some processing outside of awareness. Research tends to show that unconscious processes are limited to relatively minor cognitive feats.[6]

Second, in none of these papers is there clear evidence in support of the proposition that subliminal messages influence behavior. In other words, no study has conclusively demonstrated motivational and behavioral effects similar to those claimed by the advocates of subliminal seduction. Many of the studies fail to find an influence effect brought about by subliminal stimulation. Those few studies that do demonstrate an effect often either cannot be reproduced[7] or are fatally flawed on methodological grounds. For example, the studies failed to do such things as include a control group, use a double-blind procedure to rule out expectancy effects, and ensure that the stimuli were presented in a truly subliminal manner. On the other hand, these studies often engaged in such questionable practices as selectively presenting positive over negative findings, using unreliable measures, and describing internally inconsistent results as if they were consistent. Other reviewers of this literature have reached the same conclusion. As the cognitive psychologist Timothy Moore puts it, "There is no empirical documentation for stronger subliminal effects, such as inducing particular behaviors or changing motivation. Moreover, such a notion is contradicted by a substantial amount of research and is incompatible with experimentally based conceptions of information processing, learning, and motivation."[8] As Jack Haberstroh tells students and practitioners of advertising: "Does it work? No, it doesn't. The scientific research indicating subliminal advertising doesn't work is simply overwhelming."[9]

Let's look at some of this evidence. After reports of Vicary's EAT POPCORN/DRINK COKE study were circulated, there were a number of attempts to confirm his findings. For example, in one study conducted by the Canadian Broadcasting Corporation in 1958, the message PHONE NOW was subliminally flashed 352 times during a popular Sunday-night television show called "Close-Up."[10] Telephone use did not go up during the period. When asked to guess the message, viewers sent in close to 500 letters, not one of which contained the correct answer. But almost half the respondents claimed to be hungry or thirsty during the show. Apparently, they guessed (incorrectly) that the message was aimed at getting them to eat or drink. This not only shows that people *want* to believe the phenomenon works; it also demonstrates the power of expectations created by Vicary's theater study.

Evidence is now accruing that there is a good reason why the results Vicary claimed to have found in his EAT POPCORN/DRINK COKE study have not been obtained by other researchers: The study was probably never done and can best be described as a publicity hoax. Let us explain. Vicary's claims immediately drew the attention of advertisers, government officials, and researchers who demanded details of the study. To meet these demands, Vicary set up demonstrations of his machine. Sometimes there were technical difficulties in getting the machine to work. When the machine did work, the audience felt no compulsion to comply with subliminal commands. In 1958, the Advertising Research

Foundation pressed Vicary to release his data and a detailed description of his procedures. Vicary never did, and to this day the best description of his work appears in magazines such as the *Senior Scholastic*—intended primarily to be used in schools by junior high students. As negative evidence accumulated, James Vicary finally lamented in 1962 that he had handled the subliminal affair poorly. As he stated, "Worse than the timing, though, was the fact that we hadn't done any research, except what was needed for filing for a patent. I had only a minor interest in the company and a small amount of data—too small to be meaningful. And what we had shouldn't have been used promotionally."[11] This is not exactly an affirmation of a study that supposedly ran six weeks and involved thousands of subjects, as Vicary originally claimed.

Stuart Rogers provides additional evidence that the Vicary "experiment" was a hoax.[12] A psychology student at Hofstra University in New York at the time, Rogers thought that a report on Vicary's claim would make an interesting term paper. So he drove the short distance to Fort Lee, New Jersey, to talk with those who conducted the study. He found that the small-town theater was very small—too small to have hosted a test of nearly 50,000 movie-goers in six weeks. When he asked the theater manager about the study, the manager declared that no such test had ever been conducted at his theater. Stuart Rogers is now a marketing professor with a special interest in public relations. He views the Vicary EAT POPCORN/DRINK COKE affair as a publicity scam intended to increase customers for Vicary's marketing consulting business.

And what of Key's evidence for the effectiveness of subliminal seduction? Most of the studies he reports lack a control or comparison group. Finding that 62% of all subjects feel sexual, romantic, or satisfied when they see a gin ad with the word *sex* supposedly embedded in the ice cubes tells us nothing about the effectiveness of the "sex" implant. What would happen if the word *sex* was removed from the cubes? Perhaps 62% of the subjects would still feel sexy, romantic, or satisfied. Perhaps more, perhaps less would feel this way. Without such a comparison, we just do not know. There have, however, been controlled experiments that have shown subjects the same print ad—with and without a subliminally embedded message. These experiments—which have promoted all sorts of products from beer to cameras to Hershey bars—have failed to find evidence for Key's conjectures concerning subliminal seduction.[13]

Don't worry about those backward messages in rock music either. Although there is some evidence that some rock groups have put backward phrases on their records (mostly as a joke and to ride the subliminal craze to sell more records), research conclusively demonstrates that such messages have no effect on human behavior. For example, in a series of clever experiments, John Vokey and Don Read have played backward messages to college students.[14] They found that subjects were unable to (1) indicate whether a backward message was a statement or a question, (2) state whether two backward sentences had the same meaning, and (3) correctly classify a meaningful or a nonsense statement when played backwards. In another study, Vokey and Read found that subjects could not sort statements such as "Jesus loves me, this I know" when played backwards into one of five content categories: nursery rhymes, Christian, satanic, pornography, and advertising.

To illustrate further the *in*effectiveness of subliminal messages and to demonstrate the power of expectations, we, along with Jay Eskenazi and Anthony Greenwald, conducted a study of mass-market audiotapes with subliminal messages designed to improve either self-esteem or memory abilities.[15] Both types of tapes contained the same supraliminal content—various pieces of classical music. However, they differed in their subliminal content. According to the manufacturer, the self-esteem tapes contained such subliminal messages as "I have high self-worth and high self-esteem." The memory tape contained such subliminal messages as "My ability to remember and recall is increasing daily."

Using public posters and ads placed in local newspapers, we recruited volunteers who were interested in the value and potential of subliminal self-help therapies (and who would probably be similar to those people most likely to buy such tapes). On the first day of the study, we asked our volunteers to complete various self-esteem and memory measures. Next, they received their subliminal tape, but with an interesting twist. Half the tapes were mislabeled, so that some of the subjects received a memory tape but thought it was intended to improve self-esteem, whereas other subjects received a self-esteem tape but thought it was intended to improve memory. (Of course, half the subjects received correctly labeled tapes.)

The volunteers took their tapes home and listened to them every day for five weeks (the period suggested by the manufacturer for maximum effectiveness). After five weeks, they returned to the laboratory and completed, once again, self-esteem and memory tests; they were also asked to indicate whether they believed the tapes were effective. The results: The subliminal tapes had *no* effect (improvement or decrement) on either self-esteem or memory. But our volunteers had a different impression. Subjects who thought they had listened to a self-esteem tape (regardless of whether they actually had or not) were more likely to be convinced that their self-esteem had improved, and those who thought they had listened to a memory tape (regardless of whether they had or not) were more likely to believe that their memory had improved. In sum, the subliminal tapes did nothing to improve self-esteem or memory abilities, but, to our subjects, they appeared to have had an effect. As we put it in the title of the article, "What you expect is what you believe (but not necessarily what you get)."

Our results are not a fluke. We have repeated our original study on two separate occasions, using different tapes, and have yet to find an effect of subliminal messages on behavior as claimed by the manufacturer.[16] In addition, we are aware of six additional independent tests of subliminal self-help tapes.[17] In none of these nine studies were the manufacturer's claims for the efficacy of subliminal therapy substantiated—prompting both the National Academy of Sciences and the British Psychological Association to conclude that subliminal self-help tapes have no therapeutic value.[18]

The history of the subliminal controversy teaches us much about persuasion—but not of the subliminal kind. Despite the claims in books and newspapers and on the backs of subliminal self-help tapes, subliminal influence tactics have not been demonstrated to be effective. Of course, as with anything scientific, it may be that someday, somehow, someone will develop a subliminal technique that may work, just as some day a chemist may find a way to transmute lead into gold. Indeed, some researchers continue to present new claims for the power of the subliminal.[19] In the meantime, there are many other types of effective persuasion tactics (such as the ones described throughout this book) that warrant more attention than subliminal persuasion.

If subliminal messages are so ineffective, why is the belief in their power so widespread? One poll taken at the height of the subliminal hoax found that almost 81% of the respondents who had heard of subliminal advertising believed it to be a current practice and more than 68% believed it to be successful in selling products.[20] Most strikingly, surveys also reveal that many people learn about subliminal influence through the mass media and through courses in high school and college—a further indication of the need for better science education in American schools.

A partial reason for the appeal of the concept of subliminal influence lies in the coverage that the mass media have given subliminal persuasion. Many of the news stories about subliminal persuasion fail to mention negative evidence. When disconfirming evidence is presented, it is usually near the end of the article, giving the reader the impression that, at worst, the claims for subliminal effectiveness are somewhat controversial.

A second reason lies in our expectations, hopes, and fears. The issue of subliminal influence first emerged as a national concern soon after the Korean War—a time when other apparently mysterious mind-altering practices such as "brainwashing" and hypnotic suggestion captured the nation's imagination in films such as *The Manchurian Candidate*. Interest in subliminal seduction rose again in the post-Watergate years, when many Americans felt that their leaders were involved in devious conspiracies and massive cover-ups of the type dramatized in the movie *Network*. W. B. Key rejuvenated the issue of subliminal influence by portraying it as yet another example that big business and big government were conspiring to get us. In the late 1980s, the issue of subliminal messages was rejuvenated once more. This time it was linked into New Age beliefs that claim there is a powerful hidden force in the human personality that can be controlled for the good by magic, crystals, and subliminal commands. Our theories of what should be may have caused us to be too uncritical of claims for the power of subliminal influence.

Finally, a belief in subliminal persuasion serves a need for many individuals. In our age of propaganda, citizens are provided with very little education concerning the nature of persuasion. The result is that many feel confused and bewildered by basic social processes. Subliminal persuasion is presented as an irrational force outside the control of the message recipient. As such, it takes on a supernatural "devil made me do it" quality capable of justifying and explaining why Americans are often persuaded to engage in seemingly irrational behavior. Why did I buy this worthless product at such a high price? Subliminal sorcery.

But belief in subliminal persuasion is not without its cost. Perhaps the saddest aspect of the subliminal affair is that it distracts our attention from more substantive issues. By looking for subliminal influences, we may ignore more powerful, blatant influence tactics employed by advertisers and sales agents. Consider the tragic suicides of Ray Belknap and James Vance brought to light in the trial of Judas Priest.* They lived troubled lives—lives of drug and alcohol abuse, run-ins with the law, learning disabilities, family violence, and chronic unemployment. What issues did the trial and the subsequent mass media coverage emphasize? There was no spotlight on the need for drug treatment centers, no evaluation of the pros and cons of America's juvenile justice system, no investigation of the schools, no inquiry into how to prevent family violence, no discussion of the effects of unemployment on a family. Instead, we were mesmerized by an attempt to count the number of subliminal demons that can dance on the end of a record needle.[21]

In this trial, Judge Jerry Carr Whitehead ruled in favor of Judas Priest, stating: "The scientific research presented does not establish that subliminal stimuli, even if perceived, may precipitate conduct of this magnitude. There exist other factors which explain the conduct of the deceased independent of the subliminal stimuli."[22] Perhaps now is the time to lay the myth of subliminal sorcery to rest and direct our attention to other, more scientifically documented, causes of human behavior.

---

*One of us [A.R.P.] testified in this trial. His testimony consisted of much of the evidence presented in this chapter.

35 ıııııııııııııııııııı

Persuasion Direct

Every month the average American receives more than twenty-one pieces of direct mail—a total of more than twenty pounds of junk mail each year. Indeed, 39% of all U.S. mail consists of unsolicited sales pitches—a whopping 72 billion pieces of mail per year. These appeals are designed to sell everything from books to clothes to furniture to kitchen cutlery. They collect money for every conceivable political cause and needy charity. More than two million persons are employed in consumer mail-order selling.

Let's look at two pieces of such mail that we received to see how they work. One item came from Greenpeace, the liberal political organization that describes its purpose as environmental protection. The other came from Publishers Clearing House, which conducts a sweepstakes with the goal of selling magazine subscriptions and other products.

Before investigating this mail further, we should note that direct marketers—people who sell directly to the consumer via the mail or telephone or Internet—take great pride in identifying effective selling strategies. Typically, direct marketers receive most of their replies within a matter of weeks after posting the appeal. As such, they are very sensitive to what works and what does not. Often, simple split-mail experiments are conducted in which two versions of an appeal are sent out to see which yields a higher response rate. If you want to learn about persuasion tactics, watch what direct marketers do.[1]

One of the first things to notice about a direct-mail appeal is the envelope. It has the task of breaking through the message-dense environment to attract your attention and get you to open the piece and read on. The first line of persuasive attack is the name and address. To cut costs and increase response, the pieces are mailed primarily to those who would be most interested in the message. One source of Greenpeace's mailing list is the lists of contributors to other, similar causes. Publishers Clearing House has a larger target audience and is most interested in mailing to those who are likely to respond to direct-mail appeals in general (i.e., people who have purchased other direct-response items, have credit cards, own their own homes, and so on). It is unlikely that Rush Limbaugh will receive an appeal from Greenpeace or that a homeless person will receive an entry blank for the Publishers Clearing House sweepstakes.

The Greenpeace envelope is large (9 by 12 inches), brown, and official-looking. The return address features the distinctive Greenpeace whale. In bold print across the middle of the package is the message: "Enclosed: Community Toxic Report. Please return to Greenpeace within 10 days."

The Greenpeace envelope makes use of a number of fundamental persuasion tactics to encourage you to open it. First, the large envelope stands out among the smaller 4-by-9-inch envelopes that typically appear in the mailbox. Second, the brown envelope resembles government and other official mail. The half-mindful recipient may open it up, thinking it is something important. The technique of packaging the appeal as something official is quite common; many times the elderly will receive sales appeals in envelopes that look like government checks or inquiries. (A variant of this technique is to make the appeal look personal by using a "real" postage stamp and inscribing a "handwritten" note in blue ink on the envelope.) Third, the symbol of a whale serves as a heuristic for the environmentally conscious. Finally, the message concerning community toxins piques interest with a mixture of fear and urgency—an emotion that is further reinforced by the ten-day deadline for returning the questionnaire.

The envelope from Publishers Clearing House takes a less subtle approach. The 4½-by-11-inch envelope (still larger than most) is covered, front and back, with more than fifteen short messages and symbols. The messages are designed to create excitement and interest: "Twelve million dollars up for grabs in our new millionaire-a-month giveaways!" "Introducing E-X-P-R-E-S-S entry. Details inside." "Your 12 entry tickets are enclosed." Seemingly pasted on the envelope is a yellow note with blue lines. This fifty-six-word message (rather long for an envelope) congratulates the recipient on being eligible for a "SuperPrize"—implying either that you are special or that you've already won something. The return address features the distinctive Publishers Clearing House logo to alert the recipient that this is the "sweepstakes you've been hearing about on TV." Also displayed is the symbol of the Special Olympics to serve as a heuristic for the socially conscious. Needless to say, we've guessed what's inside this envelope: a chance of a lifetime to win millions. Let's open it immediately.

Once inside the envelope, the most striking feature is the amount of material. Greenpeace sent 1½ ounces of paper, a total of eight pages of information plus one reply envelope. Publishers Clearing House sent thirteen pages (plus a reply envelope and cents-off coupons), weighing in at 2½ ounces. Recall that message length equals message strength.

The first item of note in the Greenpeace package is a "gift" of twelve colorful stickers featuring the Greenpeace logo and cute but threatened animals such as kangaroos, dolphins, and penguins. The stickers are yours to use free of charge. As a persuasion tactic, they kill two not-so-rare birds with one stone. First, the stickers invoke the norm of reciprocity: "We've given you these nice stickers. Now it is your turn to return the favor." Second, by using the stickers, you adopt a "social identity" and join the Greenpeace granfalloon and thus become more agreeable to the cause.

The next item of note from Greenpeace is a four-page appeal addressed "Dear Friend" (another granfalloon technique). The letter begins with a request to complete the enclosed survey. It is doubtful that a survey with such a nonrandom sample could serve a legitimate "information-gathering" purpose. However, by completing the survey and thinking about toxic waste issues, the target begins the process of self-generated persuasion.

The survey is structured to produce cognitive responses sympathetic to Greenpeace's cause. Who would disagree with the thrust of these questions (and by default would not support the Greenpeace initiative)?

> Each year, more than 300 million tons of hazardous waste are produced in the U.S. alone. Do you believe your state, local, and federal authorities are doing all they can to protect you and your community from these wastes? [Are you opposed] to locating Toxic Waste Incinerators or Storage Facilities in or near your community?

Such questions elicit knee-jerk responses; note that such appeals never include difficult questions that might cause recipients to think twice about their answers. For example, they wouldn't dream of asking: "How much more would you be willing to pay for groceries that didn't use pesticides?" or "Would you be willing to sell your family car and use mass transit to decrease the need for offshore drilling?"

The bulk of the letter, however, uses a classic fear appeal. Recall from Chapter 24 that fear appeals are most effective when they raise high levels of fear and suggest a doable, effective response for coping with the feeling of fear. The Greenpeace appeal does just that. It states the problem in no uncertain terms: "Millions of our fellow citizens now agree that toxic waste is the most serious threat to public health today." Graphic examples of toxic pollution are included in the letter. What's the solution to this menace?

> Many people believe that the problem of toxic wastes is just too big to do anything about. Well, we at Greenpeace don't. *Greenpeace is one organization that is taking direct action* against the polluters of our water, our air, and our land—fighting to cut off toxics at their source. And with your help, we're going to do a whole lot more.

The letter goes on to list vivid examples of Greenpeace success stories and future action plans. It asks you, not necessarily to become a "front-line" activist confronting major polluters directly, but to send in your Community Toxic Survey along with a contribution. Note that the mention of front-line activists serves as a decoy to make the "act of a contribution" seem less difficult and more doable. To further underscore the threat of toxic waste and what you can do about it, Greenpeace offers, in a separate insert, a guide to home toxins. It's free with your contribution of $15 or more to Greenpeace.

One potential pitfall with fund-raising is that requests for money can often appear to be simply self-serving. Greenpeace minimizes this possible response by noting that its activists are putting their health and safety on the line for your environment.

The last item on the survey is a request for money. The target is asked to check the dollar amount—$15, $25, $35, $50, $100— of the contribution. Note how puny $15 or $25 appears next to a suggested contribution of $100—an example of contrast effects similar to those produced by decoys. A stamped, self-addressed reply envelope is included; the fact that these good, selfless people have already spent the money for a stamp puts additional pressure on the recipient not to "waste it" by pitching the appeal in the trash.

Publishers Clearing House uses some of the same persuasion tactics as Greenpeace, along with some additional ones. The goal of the communication is to induce you to subscribe to one or more magazines. Their reply card consists of space for ordering magazine subscriptions plus "12 lucky prize numbers" that could win you a million dollars. To order a subscription, you must find a stamp (from a 10½-by-22-inch sheet) corresponding to the magazine you want and paste it on your sweepstakes entry blank. Although you may enter the sweepstakes without ordering magazines (or else it would be illegal), ordering a subscription is encouraged with such phrases as "Express entry! Place at least one [magazine] coupon at left for automatic entry in all give-aways" and "If you haven't ordered lately, this may be the last bulletin we can send to you."

In the packet, Publishers Clearing House offers a free "gift" of coupons redeemable for more than $10 on Procter & Gamble products. As with the Greenpeace stickers, the gift of coupons invokes the norm of reciprocity. Further, by using the coupons one can adopt a self-image of "helpful and concerned" because Procter & Gamble will donate 10¢ to the Special Olympics for each coupon redeemed.

One insert states: "Don't throw away the number that can win you one million dollars." Recall that earlier we noted that it is more painful to lose money than it is pleasurable to gain the same amount. By framing the proposition as avoiding the loss of a million dollars, Publishers Clearing House provides extra moti-vation for returning an entry.

Other inserts describe possible sweepstakes prizes and past winners and, in a use of the self-sell technique, ask you to imag-ine "what it would be like to win a million dollars." Many of the inserts are personalized with the name of the recipient to attract attention and aid in self-persuasion. Other inserts describe mag-azines that can only be obtained through Publishers Clearing House or free gifts that cannot be obtained by purchasing the magazines at the newsstand (see the discussion of phantoms in Chapter 30). One flier even notes that you can win an American flag by returning your order (see the discussion of heuristics and symbols in Chapter 17).

One interesting feature of the Publishers Clearing House packet is what can be called the "sticker-hunt game." Customers are eligible for special prizes and bonuses if they find the right stickers and paste them in the right spots. The version we received offered double prize money for finding ten special stamps. How does this sticker-hunt game increase the likelihood that you will send in an order? One way to figure this out is to keep track of your cognitive responses as you hunt down the stickers and compare them to what your thoughts might have been if the sticker-hunt game were not there.

We once played the sticker-hunt game. The first few stamps were easy to find. After that, it was much tougher and we began to think: *"Where's that double-prize sticker? Hmmmm. It's not over here by the* Business Week *sticker or over there by the* Consumer Reports *stamp. Oh, here it is, taped to the entry form. Clever. Now, where's the bonus-prize sticker?"* After twenty minutes of such thoughts, we were able to locate all ten stickers. Notice, however, what we weren't thinking during this time: *"Gee, do I really need a subscription to yet another magazine?"* In other words, the sticker-hunt game was distracting us from counterarguing the true persuasive message. If you don't have anything to say, sing it! (A similar analysis can be made of the sweepstakes itself. By concentrating attention on the long shot of winning big prizes, thoughts are directed away from counterarguing the sales appeal.)

The sticker-hunt game offers another persuasive advantage—it invokes the need to rationalize one's efforts. The ease with which the first few stickers are found sucks you into the game and elicits a commitment to finding all ten. After twenty minutes of effort, you are not likely to say, *"Gee, that was stupid; I'll throw it all in the trash."* On the contrary, to justify your efforts, you are more likely to mail the entry immediately and to increase your chances of winning by purchasing some magazines.

Our description of direct-marketing techniques presents a rather cynical picture of this form of persuasion. Whenever techniques are carefully scrutinized, one can be left with a feeling of betrayal and manipulation. This might occur even if you are dissecting a work of art, such as Dali's *Last Supper* or Shakespeare's *The Tempest,* each of which has its own point of view. Our goal is not to cast aspersion on the products being peddled or condemn direct marketers for using these techniques. Indeed, the astute reader can doubtless pick out, from our own essays, numerous examples of the use of granfalloons, decoys, vivid images, and so on to illustrate the points of this book and, we hope, command your attention.

We are not opposed to the use of attention-getting devices per se. We *are* opposed to their use in a deceptive manner that obfuscates rather than clarifies the issues at hand. For example, a sticker-hunt game obscures legitimate reasons for purchasing a magazine, and biased wording of questions can cloud important environmental issues by falsely arousing emotions. Indeed, as we are writing this chapter, Publishers Clearing House, in response to a lawsuit brought by state attorneys general, has agreed to stop using some influence tactics and to make it clear that your chances of winning a sweepstakes are not improved by a purchase. Persuasion does not always need to result in deception and a confusion of the issues at hand.

In this context, we should mention that direct marketing is often the object of consumer complaints. The two most common objections to direct marketing are the existence of flimflam (fly-by-night operations that offer goods and services but either do not deliver or deliver a product far inferior to the one advertised) and the obtrusiveness of the appeal (the mailbox is cluttered with junk mail). Reputable direct marketers are concerned about these issues—after all, it cuts into their sales. For that reason, they have set up an association with a members' code of ethics and a procedure for having your name removed from members' mailing lists.*

Despite these complaints, the use of direct-marketing techniques is on the increase. More catalogs, mailers, 800 numbers, and dot com merchants appear every day. Television channels such as QVC and the Home Shopping Network now offer merchandise for purchase directly from your home. Direct marketing does offer the consumer a number of advantages: a wide variety of goods that cannot be profitably stocked at the local store, the ability to provide a high degree of customer service, and a quick and convenient means of shopping for today's time-pressed consumer. It also has the ability to offer the consumer a "superior"

---

*To have your name removed from mailing lists, write Direct Marketing Association, 6 East 43 Street, New York, NY 10017. In the United States, fraudulent telemarketers can be reported to your state attorney general or to the Federal Trade Commission at 1-800-FTC-HELP.

form of persuasion—one based not on irrelevant brand images and misleading "packages" but on useful information.

Consider a typical ad for a pair of sport shorts appearing in a Lands' End catalog. The ad shows a picture of the shorts, along with available colors and sizes plus an extensive list of features describing every detail of the shorts from fabric quality to waist design to the construction of the pockets. Admittedly, this information is not unbiased. No ad is. We all seek to put our best foot forward. However, the ad provides more information about the product than can typically be gained from a televised "image" ad featuring beautiful men and women actively wearing a pair of shorts. (Sadly, we probably know more about the quality of Lands' End sport shorts than we do about most political candidates.) A consumer equipped with catalogs from other merchants (and there are more than 12 million catalogs produced each year) could conveniently engage in comparison shopping and thus make selections with some degree of rationality.

Recall that we said earlier that direct marketers are very concerned with ensuring high rates of customer response. This affords customers the opportunity to influence a marketer's selection of persuasion tactics. If the merchant uses tactics that you do not find acceptable—for example, an inappropriate use of a fear appeal, devious use of distraction—you can throw the mail in the trash or recycle bin. Or, better yet, call the free 800 number and explain why you will not be buying the goods. Reputable merchants will learn from such complaints, and we should see more and more persuasive messages containing arguments that stand up to thoughtful scrutiny.

36

How to Become a Cult Leader

On November 18, 1978, not many people knew much about the small South American country of Guyana. Even fewer outside of the San Francisco Bay Area knew that a group of followers of the Reverend Jim Jones had set up a "model" community of believers in the jungles of Guyana. However, on that day 914 members of Jones's People's Temple committed mass suicide. A tub of fruit punch laced with cyanide and sedatives was brought out. Jones ordered his people to drink, informing them that they would soon be attacked by the CIA and that it would be better to die a revolutionary's death. Adult members induced their children to drink first and then drank the mixture themselves.

This, of course, was not the first time that mass murder and destruction transpired at the hands of a cult leader. Two examples from history illustrate the point. In 1534, Jan van Leyden lead a militant group of Anabaptists in the takeover of Münster, a German city in the throes of economic turmoil. The group believed that the end of the world was near and that they had been called to create the Kingdom of God on earth. Unlike other Anabaptist groups that espoused nonviolence, van Leyden's cult of New Jerusalem sought to establish their communist kingdom by force of arms. The result was a reign of terror in Münster for more than a year. It ended when authorities captured the city, resulting in mass destruction and death for many of the inhabitants.[1] At the beginning of the twentieth century in the Russian district of Kargopol, members of the 200-year-old sect called the Brothers and Sisters of the Red Death became convinced that the world was to end on November 13, 1900. The cult got its name because it banned marriage; members could have sexual intercourse provided they immediately submitted to the possibility of death by suffocation with a large red cushion. The group also believed that God would be pleased if they burned themselves to death before the end of the world. More than 100 members died as a sacrifice to God before czarist troops could arrive to prevent further slaughter.[2]

Nor was Jonestown the scene of the last cultic mass murder. In the spring of 1993 federal agents sought to investigate rumors of child abuse and weapons violations at the Branch Davidian compound in Waco, Texas. The members believed that their leader, David Koresh, was the last in a line of prophets who would open the seals of the Book of Revelation to usher in the Apocalypse and the Kingdom of God. In the siege, shoot-out, and conflagration that followed, eighty Branch Davidians (including twenty-one children) and four government agents lost their lives. In October 1994, fifty-three members of the apocalyptic Order of the Solar Temple died in a series of explosions and fires in

Canada and Switzerland. Their leader, Luc Jouret, a Belgian homeopathic doctor, taught a New Age mishmash of astrology, ecology, and health regimes; he believed that life on this planet was an illusion and would continue on other planets. In December 1995, sixteen more Solar Temple members were found dead in France. On March 19, 1995, five members of the Aum Supreme Truth cult placed bags leaking the poisonous gas sarin on the world's busiest subway system, resulting in the death of twelve people and injury of more than 5,500. The attack on the Tokyo subway was so cunning and cold-blooded that CNN even stopped its blanket coverage of the O. J. Simpson trial to report the Tokyo event live. Aum's leader, Shoko Asahara, taught a high-tech version of Tibetan Buddhism and worship of the Hindu god Shiva the Destroyer; the cult believed that nuclear war was imminent. On March 26, 1997, thirty-nine men and women of the group known as Heaven's Gate, dressed in purple shrouds and tennis shoes, killed themselves, thinking that they would board a UFO following the comet Hale-Bopp. This spaceship was supposedly to take them to the Kingdom of Heaven. On March 17, 2000, more than 500 men, women, and children perished in a church fire in Uganda apparently as part of a murder-suicide orchestrated by the leaders of the Movement for the Restoration of the Ten Commandments of God. The toll climbed to around 1,000 deaths as the bodies of other victims were found buried in graves in various locations controlled by the cult.

The behavior of cult members is as mysterious as it is frightening. Members of Sun Myung Moon's Unification Church periodically engage in a mass marriage, being randomly assigned by Moon and his associates to mates whom they have never previously met. Members of David Berg's Children of God (COG, or sometimes called Family of Love) willingly give all they own to the church. The backyard of one COG commune was filled with automobiles, buses, jeeps, and motorcycles that members had donated to Berg. Female members of COG practice "flirty fishing," or going to discos and bars with the sole aim of picking up men for sex and then trying to convert them to the cult. Berg called them "God's whores." The followers of Swami Rajneesh turned over all of their worldly possessions to their leader and smiled benignly as he accumulated eighteen Rolls Royces for his personal use. One member of the Church of Armageddon jumped from a tree to his death believing that, because he had purified himself, he could fly. Other members of the cult sit hand in hand in a circle and connect themselves to electrical devices to see how much electricity their bodies can stand because "all substances are from God." Members of the Aum Supreme Truth paid $7,000 per month to wear a PSI, or Perfect Salvation Initiation. What is a PSI? A cap covered with wires and electrodes that send 6-volt shocks (3 volts for children) to synchronize the brain waves of the wearer with those of the Master Shoko Asahara. Some of the members of Heaven's Gate castrated themselves in a desire to reach the Kingdom of God.

Many claim that cult members are "brainwashed." This rather frightening term was originally used to describe the persuasion tactics used on American prisoners in Communist Chinese prison camps during the Korean War. These camps were totalitarian environments in which the captors came to control the thoughts of the POWs by controlling all sources of information and by systematically rewarding and punishing appropriate and inappropriate thought. Since then, the term *brainwashing* has been used rather loosely and has taken on a meaning surrounded by menace and mystery. It has come to refer to exotic (and often undescribed) persuasion tactics that are assumed to be irresistible. Victims of brainwashing are depicted on television dramas and in the movies as if they are zombies led around by a mesmerizing leader.

This representation is extremely misleading; it suggests that only fools or those weak of will could fall into the clutches of a cult leader. Actually, anyone can be the target of a cult.[3] Cult recruiters often look for those who may be experiencing a vulnerable time in their lives—those who have just lost a close relationship, are at a point in their lives where they are not sure what they want to do next, or are feeling lonely or left out. However, research shows that the majority of those who join cults come from middle-class backgrounds, are fairly well educated, and are not seriously disturbed prior to joining. Today's cults have begun recruiting the elderly (particularly widowed women), professionals with small businesses such as dentists and lawyers, and college students.

Just what is a cult? First, a cult is not a label to be applied to any group that we happen not to like or that does things we

"I joined a cult over the weekend. They're letting
me keep my job, but I give them all my money."

think are bizarre. Using the term in this manner raises issues of
freedom of religion and expression and runs into some of the
traps we discussed in Chapter 31. Nor does the term apply only to
those groups promoting a certain form of religion. Today, cults
can be centered on a range of issues, including the occult, race,
politics, therapy, and self-help, as well as religion and spirituality.

The term *cult* is used to describe a pattern of social relations
within a group. At the core of these relations is dependency.[4] In a
cult, members are dependent on the group and its leader for
most if not all resources, including money, food and clothing,
information, decision making, and, perhaps most importantly,
self-esteem and social identity. This dependency results in a specific pattern of relations. First, cults tend to be highly leader-
oriented, since the leader is the source of all sustenance. Second,
because the leader is so important, he or she cannot be criticized
or second-guessed. Cults are marked by little or no checks and
balances on the leader's power (that is, no court of appeal and no

recourse to law for justice). The leader is typically exempt from the rules of the cult. Communication is highly centralized, with little information available from outside the group. The agenda, objectives, and work tasks are set by the elite. Finally, given the importance of the group to the individual, all influence and persuasion is directed toward maintaining the group. Rewards and punishments are used to maintain the leader's power. Dissent is immediately quashed. Persuasion is based on simple images and plays on emotions and prejudices.

Although cults may seem strange and mysterious, their persuasion tactics are nothing more or less than the same basic propaganda tactics that we have seen throughout this book. Cults simply use these techniques in a much more systematic and còmplete manner than we are normally accustomed to. Simply because the end result is dramatic and bizarre does not require that the means to get there be mystifying. Indeed, in case any of you would like to be a cult leader, we can list seven mundane but nonetheless "proven-effective" tactics for creating and maintaining a cult.[5]

1. *Create your own social reality.* The first step in creating a cult is to construct your own social reality by eliminating all sources of information other than that provided by the cult. Cult headquarters should be isolated from the rest of the world—a farm in Oregon, a secluded house on the outskirts of town, a jungle in Guyana, a complex in Waco, Texas, a community at the foot of Mount Fuji. If cult members must remain in the larger community (perhaps because income from their high-paying job is needed), then they should be isolated psychologically by keeping them busy chanting, reading cult literature, or working continuously for the cult. Members' mail should be censored. Family should be prevented from visiting members. Strict boundaries between "believers" and the "unredeemed" must be maintained. Such censorship can be physical, that is, forcibly excluding outsiders and physically restraining wayward members. However, it is much more practical to teach members self-censorship by labeling everything that is not "of the cult" as "of the devil."

The second step in constructing a social reality is to provide a cult's-eye view of the world. This picture of the world is then used by members to interpret all events and happenings. For example, Jim Jones taught that there is a constant threat of nuclear war and that the world is full of racism. To be prepared to live in this evil world, one must be ready to die. "Suicide" practice drills were conducted to prepare members for the inevitable attack on the Temple by this evil world. The Unification Church, which owns the *Washington Times* and *United Press International*, teaches the Divine Principle, a doctrine claiming that humanity must be restored to God's grace through payment of indemnity (penance) and the advent of a new messiah (the Reverend Moon). The believer is thus prepared to atone for sins through service to the church and to accept the leader's word as truth. David Berg, known as Moses to his followers, creates social reality for his Children of God through a series of "Mo Letters." These letters purport to be revelations from God and describe the cult's theology as well as providing guidance on how to interpret world events. For example, his letters advise cult members that they are special and thus above the law, that the world is rotten and thus it is acceptable to lie and steal for the church, and that sex with Berg is a good idea. Both Shoko Asahara and David Koresh taught that we live in the last days and that Armageddon would soon occur. The only way to survive was to prepare to defend oneself by stockpiling weapons. The Movement for the Restoration of the Ten Commandments of God also taught that the world would end (first on January 1, 2000, and then, when this prophecy failed, the date was postponed to January 1, 2001) and that the only way to salvation was through prayer, fasting, and sexual abstinence.

To get a real feel for the full power of a cult, imagine adopting their beliefs for just a moment. Try seeing the world as if you were a cult member. In a bizarre way, the world makes sense, perhaps for the first time in a cult member's life.

One useful technique for constructing social reality is to create your own language and jargon. For example, Divine Light Mission members call their services "satsang" and "darshan." The Unification Church refers to lying to the unredeemed as "heavenly deception." Scientology teaches that the "thetan" (soul) is impeded in its many lives by "engrams" (aberrations) that result from wrongdoing. Koresh believed that the Branch Davidians were in the "fifth seal" or the last events of human history. Asahara taught his followers that because they had entered a higher astral plane, returning to the world would cause great pain and suffering. Heaven's Gate referred to the body as a physical vehicle or container. Suicide meant failing to move to the next level (as opposed to killing one's self). In these terms, their suicide was nothing more than replacing one's present car with a new one in order to take a trip to a new land. A good vocabulary is useful for putting the "right" spin on things. By teaching a battery of clichés such as "bourgeois mentality," "Krishna consciousness," "of the world," and "in the Lord," any event is quickly defined as good or evil and critical thinking is abruptly terminated.

When it comes to teaching your social reality, here is one additional point to keep in mind: Repeat your message over and over and over again. Repetition makes the heart grow fonder, and fiction, if heard frequently enough, can come to sound like fact.

2. *Create a granfalloon.* The granfalloon technique requires the creation of an in-group of followers and an out-group of the unredeemed. The technique allows you to control members by constantly reminding them: "If you want to be a chosen one, then you must act like a chosen one. If you are not chosen, then you are wicked and unredeemed. To be saved, you must act like you are supposed to act." Seasoned group members serve as role models and guides on how to behave for new group members. Intense peer pressure is applied to secure conformity. The result is a uniformity of opinion and behavior in the cult, which then serves to further reinforce cult practices—if everyone is doing it, it must be right.

A man named Love Israel, head of the Church of Armageddon, teaches his followers that he is the "king" and "Christ's go-between connecting the members with heaven." He tells his followers, "Don't use your little mind inside. Use your big mind, the collective family's mind. We're your mind." Love Israel understands the granfalloon technique.

A new recruit is often brought into a granfalloon with a practice called "love-bombing"—the newcomer is showered with attention, approval, and support by cult members. Cult recruiters are taught to mirror the interests and attitudes of the potential new member, thus making it feel as if there is rapport and understanding between the recruit and the cult. In order to keep this support and approval, the recruit must conform to the group.

The essential ingredient in establishing an in-group of believers is the creation of a social identity—an image of who "we" are. Joining a cult represents a break from the "other" world and the acceptance of this new identity. Many cults require a "baptism" or other initiation to indicate acceptance of the new identity. A new name can be given; all the members of the Philadelphia-based group MOVE took as their last name "Africa"; the members of the Church of Armageddon use the last name "Israel." Hare Krishnas adopt distinctive orange robes and eat a special vegetarian diet. Early followers of Sun Myung Moon often did not possess their own clothes, but shared among themselves; when their clothes got dirty, they turned them in to be washed and took another set from the commune's supply. Thus a simple indicator of one's personal identity—what one wears—belongs to the group. The Divine Light Mission "satsang," or religious sermon, is designed to encourage new members to start answering the question: "What is a premie [the term for a member]?" Church of God followers adopt new biblical names. To further increase the cohesion of the group, all new recruits must learn three Bible verses in the morning before any of them can eat breakfast. The Branch Davidians believed they were select martyrs who would be called to rule in the coming Kingdom of God. Aum Supreme Truth members wore distinctive robes and ritual costumes, ate a unique diet of Aum food (unprocessed rice, seaweed, bean curd, and vegetable stew), and practiced purification rites such as vomiting 10 pints of water and flushing the nostrils with string and warm water.

The outward trappings of the believer—the new name, distinctive garb, a special diet—all confirm that the member is indeed a chosen one. To retain this valued membership, all one needs to do is continue to grow in this newfound life and, of course, continue to obey.

The reverse side of the granfalloon tactic is the creation of an out-group to hate. The Children of God teach members to hate their parents. One Mo letter states that parents are evil; they are not your true family; we are your family now. Chinese prison wardens taught American POWs that the capitalist system is corrupt. The Unification Church teaches that only believers will be resurrected at the final coming. The Church of Armageddon instructs that the "world" is bad. Playing on long-held Japanese prejudices, Aum Supreme Truth taught that Jews were the tools of Satan and that preparations were being made for a final war between Japan and the United States (which was run by Jews). Of course, any perceived enemy of Aum—the Japanese emperor,

Madonna, and Bill Clinton—were labeled "Jews." Heaven's Gate members believed that the outside society consisted of angels in the making that had flunked out, just as Lucifer had failed God. The creation of an evil out-group serves the dual purpose of making members feel good about belonging to their own group ("I'm glad I'm not like them") and increasing their fears about leaving and not supporting their own group ("I don't want to be like them; I can't let them take over the world.")

If granfalloon techniques are correctly applied, then you should be successful in creating fear of the "outside" world and the belief that the cult is the only solution to a happy life. Life is thus impossible outside the cult—the only solution to life's problems.

3. *Create commitment through a rationalization trap.* Cults can insure members' obedience by establishing a spiral of escalating commitment; the cult member, at first, agrees to simple requests that becoming increasingly more demanding. Jim Jones used such a technique, eliciting great trust from his followers one step at a time. Some light can be shed on what led to the final mass murder if we look at it as part of a chain of events.

Let's start at the beginning. Jim Jones was a dynamic speaker and preacher. It is easy to understand how a charismatic leader like Jones might extract money from the members of the church. Once they had committed themselves to donating a small amount of money in response to his message of peace and universal brotherhood, he was able to request and receive a great deal more. Next he induced people to increase their tithes to support the church. Jones would often ask his members to perform loyalty tests, such as signing a blank confession of "sins" and admitting to feelings of homosexuality or the commission of aberrant sexual acts. Jones would tell members, "If you were really committed, you would be willing to do anything for the church."

Next, Jones induced members to sell their homes and turn over the proceeds to the church. Soon, at his request, several of his followers pulled up stakes, leaving family and friends, to start life anew in Guyana. There they not only worked hard (thus increasing their commitment) but were also cut off from potential dissenting opinion; they were surrounded by true believers. The chain of events continued. Jones took sexual liberties with several married women among his followers, who acquiesced, if reluctantly; Jones claimed to be the father of their children.

Finally, as a prelude to the climactic event, Jones induced his followers to perform a series of mock ritual suicides as a test of loyalty and obedience. Thus, in a step-by-step fashion, the commitment to Jim Jones increased. Each step *in and of itself* was not a huge and ludicrous leap from the one preceding it.

After making an initial commitment, one does not feel comfortable reneging on the deal. To justify the sensibility of the initial commitment, the member is often willing to do more and then still more—to meet increasingly demanding commitments. In this way, the resolution of dissonance and maintenance of one's self-image as honoring commitments form a powerful rationalization trap.

Cults employ other emotional traps as well. They often shower new recruits with attention and gifts (for example, a free meal, fellowship, or, in the case of Children of God, free sex with a cult member); consistent with the norm of reciprocity, it is now time for the newcomer to do something for the group—or at least not be rude and leave in the middle of the leader's presentation. The guilt of a sinner can be reduced by a gift of everything one owns to the cult. Embarrassment over forced sex with a leader can be relieved by thinking that one needed such self-sacrificing "discipline." Cruelty to outsiders such as parents can be justified by seeing the need for even more cruelty. A feeling of stupidity for giving all to the cult can be overcome by rationalizing it as devotion to a noble cause. Confessions are used to reveal members' past undesirable behavior and feelings; with such information, the cult leader can make the member feel like a hypocrite for not accepting the "redemption" offered by the cult.

Note also that the member, after having done all these things, is faced with a dilemma: "How can I explain all that I have done to those outside the group?" This requires the creation of a sensible, coherent justification that is not easily forthcoming. The rationalization trap is sprung.

4. *Establish the leader's credibility and attractiveness.* Most cults have leader myths—stories and legends passed from member to member concerning the life and times of the cult leader. Unification Church biographers compare Moon's birth in Pyung-buk, North Korea, with Jesus' birth in Bethlehem—both were at night, both were in small unknown villages, and both marked the dawn of a cosmic transition. When Moon was sixteen years old, Jesus appeared and told him, "You will be the completer of man's salva-

tion by being the second coming of Christ." According to Divine Light legend, Maharaj Ji, as a young child, was already a great spiritual leader and teacher and was thus appointed to head a holy family in India. In answer to the question, "Just who is the Guru Maharaj Ji?" premies will often answer, "The Guru Maharaj Ji is God." After an initial period of indoctrination, wardens in Communist Chinese prison camps strove to maintain an image as wise and caring teachers whose job it was to instruct the wayward prisoner in the ways of the truth. Children of God leader David Berg, blessed in his mother's womb so he would be like Moses, Jeremiah, Ezekiel, Daniel, and his namesake, David, is the fulfillment of many biblical prophesies. David Berg's powers, described in his pamphlet "The True Story of Moses and the Children of God," are so great that "you can even rebuke the devil in the name of David and he will flee. No power in the world can stand against the power of David." The Branch Davidians considered Koresh to be a second Christ or a new messiah who would fulfill the prophecy of the Book of Revelation. According to Aum Supreme Truth legend, Shoko Asahara had amazing powers—he could live under water without oxygen for up to an hour and could levitate and fly. Asahara was shown in pictures with the Dalai Lama, who supposedly proclaimed that "he has the mind of a Buddha" and gave him his mission of saving Japan. Further reinforcing his divine nature, a sip of Asahara's blood was sold for $7,000 and his dirty bathwater went for $800 per quart.

What is the purpose of such myths? Cults require members to engage in extreme behavior—giving up children and family, having sex with leaders and strangers, practicing to murder oneself. Recall that earlier (Chapter 22) we noted that extreme requests arouse dissonance; we are more likely to comply with extreme requests if common means for reducing our dissonance are not available (e.g., derogating the requester) and we can rationalize our extreme actions—we must do it for God and to save all humankind. It is hard to disobey a person believed to be "the son of God" or, at least, blessed by a divine purpose. Anybody in his or her right mind should seek to identify with and be like such a holy person.

5. *Send members out to proselytize the unredeemed and to fund-raise for the cult.* Witnessing to the unconverted has the obvious advantage of bringing in new members. Perhaps just as important, proselytizing can ensure that members are constantly

engaged in self-sell, or self-generated persuasion. The act of witnessing requires the member to state anew to many different people the positive advantages of being in a cult. In arguing to convince others, members convince themselves. In testimonials given to other cult members, many cults encourage members to embellish how bad they were (on drugs, sexually permissive, living an empty life) before joining the cult. The worse you were, the more approval you receive from the group. By constantly recounting these stories, cult members come to believe in the power of the cult to effect change and how hopeless they would be without it.

Evangelical activity also strengthens resolve. Each instance of witnessing or attempt to sell the cult to outsiders is likely to elicit negative responses or an attack on the cult. In defending their beliefs, cult members learn to refute a wide range of attacks, thus inoculating themselves against attack and thereby maintaining belief in the cult (see Chapter 38).

6. *Distract members from thinking "undesirable" thoughts.* Most cult doctrines are hard to take seriously, much less accept. The cult member, especially a new recruit, is likely to question and counterargue such basic points as the value of giving all one owns, especially a new sports car, to the cult and the merits of working sixteen-hour shifts and turning over all proceeds to the cult leadership. The old advertising saw "If you don't have anything to say, sing it" probably never applied more. How, then, does a cult leader distract a member from carefully scrutinizing and questioning the cult's doctrine?

The Children of God use a combination of techniques. First, they never leave new recruits alone to think for themselves. Bible verses are played continually on a loudspeaker, and a trainer follows the new recruit around preaching Bible verses and Mo letters—even as the new recruit goes to the bathroom. The new recruit is deprived of food, water, and sleep. It is difficult to think when you are hungry and thirsty and fatigued. Famed deprogrammer Ted Patrick went through this indoctrination; having been deprived of sleep for forty-four hours, he describes his feelings:

> At first you are frantic for silence—just five minutes of peace and privacy. Then your senses begin to get numb—you grow accustomed to the constant noise. You also, as you get tired, stop

really registering what they tell you. You don't hear individual
words anymore, just a stream of babbling and shrieking. I guess
that's when the programming starts becoming effective—when
the conscious mind stops functioning out of weariness and all
that propaganda begins to seep into your unconscious.[6]

There are other ways to disrupt counterarguing in a cult.
Chanting and singing prevent thinking about anything else but the
chant and the song. Meditations such as those performed by the
Divine Light Mission, in which the premie spends hours trying to
visualize light, hear music, taste nectar, and speak the primordial
vibration of existence, prevent the meditator from focusing on
other, more worldly, concerns. Aum used a variety of techniques
for controlling thought, including drugs, PSIs, sleep deprivation,
and meditation. Nonstop activities such as proselytizing, working,
and cooking and cleaning for other members further limit the
opportunity for careful thought and personal reflection.

Once the recruit has accepted the cult, the task becomes one
of preventing further close scrutiny and thought about the merits of membership. This can be done by teaching that any "disagreeable thought" is evil and from the devil. For example, if a
member doubts a leader's command or starts to wonder about
the merits of a particular theological point, he or she is coun-
seled that this is "out of the Lord" or "from Satan" and should be
rebuked. Hare Krishnas are required to take frequent cold showers to eliminate thoughts about sex. Members thus become their
own mind police. Should this fail, more overt tactics may be necessary. For example, Jim Jones required a female cult member in
Jonestown to have sex in public with someone she despised as
punishment for wrong thoughts. Because their parents disobeyed Jones, daughters were forced to masturbate in public or
have sex in public with a disliked cult member. Aum Supreme
Truth placed those who disobeyed or tried to escape into painful
hot baths (of 117°F) or into tiny cells containing only a toilet and
a television blaring Asahara's voice all day and night. Observers
get the message, too: Control your own thoughts, or at least the
expression of those thoughts.

7. *Fixate members' vision on a phantom.* The successful cult
leader is always dangling a notion of the promised land and a
vision of a better world before the faithful. Unification Church

members follow and attend to the teachings of the "Lord of the Second Advent" so that they can be resurrected to the perfection state during the third and final testament stage. Jim Jones offered Jonestown to poor residents of San Francisco as a place that would, of course, require hard work but would also afford members the opportunity to "live comfortably—you'll have your own home, get a good school, college, swim, fish." Similarly, the nineteenth-century Oneida commune was working to build "heaven on earth." Amway asks new members to decide on their "Dream"—a new Cadillac, a summer cottage, a new ranch, or whatever they would like to get by selling Amway products. Divine Light Mission faithful are striving to see a light during their meditation and thus become a premie. It can be accomplished by service and devotion to Guru Maharaj Ji. Hare Krishnas believe that their chanting and dancing will stave off the inevitable decline and downfall of humanity. Aum and the Branch Davidians offered survival in the upcoming destruction of the world. In L. Ron Hubbard's Church of Scientology, members are working for a state of "clear." To become a "clear," members pay a high tuition to attend Scientology classes; devoted members may spend $10,000 to $15,000 in a matter of months.

By fixating a member's gaze on a future phantom, you provide a powerful incentive to maintain service to the group. Believers will be afraid to stop working, fearful that they or the world may lose the desired prize if they take even just one break. The average Moonie puts in an estimated sixty-seven hours a week working for the cause. It is also likely that most new recruits will be in a state of despair. Phantoms can establish hope—a powerful motivator of human behavior—by providing a sense of purpose and mission.

Our purpose in presenting these seven tactics is, quite obviously, not to have readers of this book go out and start their own cults. Because "brainwashing" can be viewed as "hocus-pocus," some people are apt to deny the very real power of cult tactics. Others are likely to attribute all sorts of magical powers to cults, standing in awe and fear of their abilities to control minds. By discussing the persuasion tactics utilized by cults, we are attempting to remove some of the mystery and ultimately reduce the danger of cults.[7]

But there is another reason for understanding the persuasion tactics of cults. Cults use the same persuasion tactics often used by other propagandists; cults just use them in a more thorough and total manner. It may be useful to reread this discussion and, instead of thinking of cults, consider your everyday social groups, such as family, church, country, or place of work, and ask, "What forms of propaganda are present in my life? How am I dependent on the groups I live in? Are the groups that I live in cultic and, if so, what should I do about them?"

37

Propaganda in the Third Reich: A Case for Uncertainty

The year was 1924 and a young aspiring artist named Adolf Hitler sat thinking in his jail cell. Like many of his generation, he had found it painful to accept Germany's defeat in the World War, a war in which he had served in vain as a combat soldier. He shared his country's humiliation over the punishments dictated by the Treaty of Versailles. Adolf Hitler considered just how it all came about.

Hitler believed that one of the key factors in Germany's defeat was the skillful use of propaganda by British and American governments. As Hitler put it:

> But it was not until the War that it became evident what immense results could be obtained by a correct application of propaganda. Here again, unfortunately, all our studying had to be done on the enemy side, for the activity on our side was modest, to say the least. . . . For what we failed to do, the enemy did, with amazing skill and really brilliant calculation. I, myself, learned enormously from this enemy war propaganda.[1]

What did Hitler learn from Allied war propaganda? Both the British and Americans established steering committees and organizations to develop and disseminate propaganda. For example, in the United States the Committee on Public Information (CPI), dubbed the Creel Committee after its chair, newspaper editor

George Creel, assisted in training "Four-Minute Men," volunteers who would speak at local gatherings on behalf of the war effort. The CPI encouraged the film industry to make pro-war films and saw to it that "facts" about the war were disseminated widely to the press.

The most striking aspect of British and American propaganda, however, was the "atrocity story"—reports of alleged cruelty performed by the enemy on innocent civilians or captured soldiers. The purpose of such tales was to stiffen the resolve to fight (we can't let this cruel monster win) and to convince citizens of the morality of the war (set the rationalization trap). For example, rumors circulated that the Germans boiled the corpses of enemy soldiers to make soap and that they mistreated the citizens of occupied Belgium. Much was made of the execution of an English nurse serving in Brussels for helping Allied soldiers return to the war and the German sinking of the luxury liner *Lusitania*, which, incidentally, happened to be carrying arms and war supplies. Although some of these atrocity stories contained a grain of truth, some were greatly exaggerated and others were pure fiction.[2]

Hitler realized that if Germany was ever to regain its dignity and win the next war, it would have to go the Allies one better in the war called persuasion.[3] He outlined his plan of attack in two chapters of the book he wrote in jail, *Mein Kampf* ("My Struggle"). For Hitler, propaganda was a means to an end—in this case, the promotion of the German state and the establishment and maintenance of the rule of the Nazi party. As such, there were no ethics that governed persuasion; there was only the rule of success or failure. As Hitler put it when talking about propaganda, "the most cruel weapons were humane if they brought about a quicker victory."[4]

Hitler was contemptuous of the ability of the masses to understand events. If he were alive today, he might remark that the people can operate only in the peripheral route to persuasion and that they use simple heuristics to guide their thinking. Effective propaganda relies on heuristics and appeals to the emotions. Hitler wrote in *Mein Kampf*:

> Its [propaganda's] effect for the most part must be aimed at the emotions and only to a very limited degree at the so-called intellect. We must avoid excessive intellectual demands on our

public. The receptivity of the great masses is very limited, their intelligence is small, but their power of forgetting is enormous. In consequence of these facts, all effective propaganda must be limited to a very few points and must harp on these slogans until the last member of the public understands what you want him to understand by your slogan.[5]

Having learned from the Allied efforts in World War I the value of an organization capable of coordinating and delivering effective propaganda, Hitler established an apparatus of his own. This organization was privy to all the dealings of the Reich and had the responsibility of selling the government's actions to the masses. To head up this organization, Hitler selected as his Minister of Popular Enlightenment and Propaganda Joseph Goebbels, the son of a lower-middle-class Catholic family from a small town in the Rhineland. Goebbels served as minister of propaganda from the time the Nazis came to power in 1933 until he committed suicide (after first poisoning his six children) near the end of the war. To get a flavor of what Nazi propaganda was really like, let's look at a few of the persuasion tactics used.

One of the first, and most important, tasks of the Ministry of Popular Enlightenment and Propaganda was to gain control of the mass media and to attract the attention of the masses. In the United States, Hitler and Goebbels hired public relations firms in an attempt to secure favorable press coverage of the regime. In Germany, the Nazis controlled journalists and filmmakers through a mixture of punishments and rewards, as we noted in Chapter 32. The Nazi regime made certain that it was the primary source of news and easily accessible to certain journalists. This treatment was extended to include foreign correspondents, thus putting U.S. reporters in a quandary: Report news unfavorable to Nazi Germany (such as the treatment of Jews) and be expelled or sanitize the news and be able to continue reporting.

The Nazis gained the attention of the masses by making their propaganda entertaining.[6] For example, Nazi posters used eye-catching graphics such as bold print and slashing, violent lines as well as attention-getting headlines. Radio news programs were often packaged as entertainment, featuring famous singers and celebrities. The 1936 Olympics, which were held in Berlin, were used as a vehicle to promote the image of a strong "Aryan" nation and to build the self-esteem of the German people. During the

Olympic Games, foreign correspondents were treated like royalty and given tours of the "successes" of the regime; as a result, many U.S. journalists filed stories stating that previous reports of attacks on Jews were either unfounded or greatly exaggerated. With such complete control of the press, radio, theater, cinema, music, and the arts, the essential themes of the Nazi party were repeated and repeated. It was nearly impossible in Germany during the 1930s to read a book or newspaper, listen to a radio broadcast, or see a film without coming into contact with the Nazi picture of the world.

Goebbels masterfully spread the Nazi agenda to the German nation by labeling events with easily learned slogans or terms that captured Germans' attention and directed their thinking. For example, he insisted that the word *Führer* ("leader") be used only to refer to Hitler. To belittle democracy, the Nazis referred to the Weimar Parliament as *Quasselbude,* or "chatterbox." To link the Russians and British as enemies of Germany, he labeled an aborted British raid as the "Maisky Offensive," after the Russian envoy to London, thereby creating the impression that the raid was conducted to appease the Soviets. To provide hope in 1942, Goebbels coined the phrase *schleichende Krise* ("creeping crisis") to suggest economic, social, and political unrest in England. Although in hindsight these phrases may seem contrived, they did create a "picture in the head" of world reality: "The Russians and the British are in cahoots to get us; fortunately, there is unrest in England and we have our leader."

Euphemisms were employed to lessen the sting of state-supported pillaging, torture, murder, and genocide. For example, the Gestapo didn't arrest citizens but took them into "protective custody"; they did not steal property, but "secured" it. The invasion of Poland was a "police action," and the subsequent murder of its citizens was termed "extraordinary pacification action." The buildings in the death camps were given cheery names, such as the Happy Nightingale, the Rose Garden, and the Baths and Inhalation Institutes. And Jews were never gassed or murdered in Nazi Germany; they were merely led to the final solution or given special treatment.

Goebbels also established "pictures in the head" through the use of innuendo and rumor. A common tactic was to attack the press (especially the foreign press) as liars and atrocity-mongers, thus leading German citizens to believe that any report unfavorable to the regime was biased. In the years of the Nazi party's rise to power, Goebbels would denigrate the character of members of the "opposition" by circulating rumors of scandals involving them. Toward the end of the war, as Germany suffered defeats on the battlefield, rumors were circulated that German scientists were nearing the completion of two new weapons—a U-boat capable of traveling underwater at high speeds and an anti-aircraft gun whose missiles were magnetically drawn to aircraft in the sky. The purpose of such rumors was to instill the belief that Germany could still win the war and should continue the struggle, despite a rash of defeats.

Nazi propaganda used heuristics extensively to secure agreement with its message. For example, rallies and propaganda films always showed masses of cheering, applauding, saluting Nazi supporters. We know this as the social consensus heuristic—if everyone else agrees, so should I.

Nazi slogans expressed an air of confidence: "Join Our Struggle," "Fight with Us," "Adolf Hitler Is Victory." Whenever Hitler spoke, he spoke with confidence and certainty of the Nazi purpose and the ability of the German people to accomplish this purpose. As we saw earlier, a speaker's confidence serves to increase the likelihood that a message will be accepted.

Hitler and Goebbels used historical symbols and monuments extensively to package the regime. As Hitler was coming to power, he announced his "Twenty-five Theses," reminiscent of the Ninety-five Theses that the German religious reformer Martin Luther had tacked to a church door in Wittenberg. Nazi artwork and posters often employed the style of Albrecht Dürer to suggest the historical roots of the regime. A popular genre of Nazi film was the historical biography. In such films, the life of a national historic hero such as Friedrich Schiller or Otto von Bismarck was depicted with an emphasis on parallels (often irrelevant) to the life and times of Adolf Hitler.

Architecture was also used to package the Third Reich. Under the direction of Albert Speer, the Nazis planned an extensive effort to erect public buildings of a special nature. Due to the war effort, few were built. Those that were served Nazi purposes. For example, priority was given to erecting sports arenas, gigantic assembly halls, cinemas, and theaters—all of which could be used for political purposes. The Nazi style, which might best be termed "Nordic Hellenism," was classical in design, but on a gigantic scale. Public buildings were designed to look like enlarged Greek temples, with towering steps and row upon row of columns. The design reinforced the image of the Nazis as heirs to the great cultures of the past. An individual who entered such an edifice would feel his or her own stature dwarfed by the power of the state as represented by the building. In contrast, the original Greek temples were always built to human proportions, leaving the visitor with the feeling that, as Protagoras said, "Humans are the measure of all things."

Another concern of Nazi propaganda was the creation of a band of supporters loyal to the Nazi party. As he was gaining power, Hitler dressed his supporters in brown shirts. Wearing the Nazi brown shirt in public became an act of commitment to the cause. The response of other Germans, at first, was one of ridicule. For many supporters, such a response likely produced even more commitment to the cause. As a means of rationalizing this commitment, the young brown-shirted Nazi would likely think, *This ridicule is just a small price to pay for the noble Nazi cause,* rather than admit that brown shirts and Nazi fanaticism were rather silly. He would undoubtedly turn to fellow brown-shirters for social support, and Hitler would add another loyal member to his band of cohesive followers.

Without a doubt the most demonic and effective Nazi propaganda ploy combined the fear appeal with the granfalloon tactic. After World War I, Germany's economy was in ruins, partly as a result of the demands of the Treaty of Versailles. The result was devastating for German citizens. A high rate of inflation coupled with high rates of unemployment disrupted families and left many in poverty. Many men felt humiliated because they could not support their families. Adding to these fears were racial prejudices that had existed for centuries in Europe. Aryans believed that they were a race of superhumans (directly descending from Adam, Japheth, or Atlantis, depending on the specific myth). It was their destiny to unite the Germanic people, to purify the Aryan identity, and to subdue the lesser races (most prominently, Jews, Negroes, and Gypsies).[7] Such racial prejudice continues to exist, as witnessed by neo-Nazi, Klan, and militia members who maintain the superiority of the white "race."[8]

Hitler and Goebbels were able to take advantage of the nation's fears and prejudices by proposing a granfalloon solution. A single theme was echoed in most, if not all, Nazi propaganda: The Jews were to blame for all the nation's problems. Couched as a documentary about the role of Jews in history, the 1940 film *The Eternal Jew*, for example, portrayed the Jew as a money-grabbing villain who not only is a drain on society but also carries diseases and lacks proper values. Scenes from the film showed "kosherstyle" ritual animal slaughter embellished to create the illusion of sadistic practices in the Jewish religion. In a similar vein, the film *The Jew Süss* vividly tells the story of a Jewish man raping a German maiden. The image of the Jew as despicable, inferior, and menacing was repeated over and over again in speeches, posters, films, newspapers, and even academic treatises.

What was the solution to this Jewish menace? The German people were once a proud nation; under the leadership of Adolf Hitler Germany can put an end to the Jewish threat and once again return to its past grandeur. To get this message across, Nazi propaganda first demonstrated that the party supported traditional German values. Nazi posters often featured scenes of traditional family life—a woman breastfeeding her child, children happily staring off into a distant future with the Nazi banner waving in the background, a father proudly standing next to his family.

Next, Nazi propaganda showed that a united Germany could achieve its goals. This theme was powerfully expressed in the 1934 film by Leni Riefenstahl entitled *The Triumph of Will*. The film opens with scenes of handsome young men in preparation to become soldiers. Hitler oversees their training. By the film's end, these young men have been turned into a powerful Nazi war machine. The message: By working together, we can be strong again.

Finally, Nazi propaganda located the source of this newfound achievement in one man—Adolf Hitler. As one campaign poster put it: "Hitler, our last hope." Goebbels's goal was to portray Hitler as a kind father whose nation had called him to serve in its time of greatest need. Propaganda thus needed to present two sides of Hitler. On the one hand, posters showed Hitler smiling and shaking the hands of children; newsreels showed him awkwardly accepting the praises of his nation. As Goebbels once wrote in a magazine article, "The simplest people approach him with confidence because they feel he is their friend and protector."[9] The other side of Hitler was that of *Führer*. To capture this side of the image, posters portrayed

Hitler in military garb standing erect and confident in purpose; newsreels presented endless scenes of Hitler reviewing the nation's troops.

The success of the Nazi propaganda machine, however, was based on more than just the use of some clever persuasion tactics. It was also due to a nearly wholesale acceptance of the idea that persuasion was to start at the top of society and be directed downward toward the masses. It was the responsibility of the ruling elite to make the decisions and then inform the masses of the wisdom of those decisions through propaganda; the responsibility of the masses was to follow. And what better role for the masses, since, by and large, they are ignorant and cannot think. We have seen this model of the role of persuasion in society before. Aristotle argued that persuasion was needed to instruct those who could not reason fully. Propaganda is a means to communicate the "truth" to the ignorant.

Although such a model of persuasion may more or less describe any society at a given time, it is not an inevitable outcome. The Greek Sophist Protagoras saw a different role for persuasion—through argument, the advantages and disadvantages of any course of action can be made clearer. The early founders of the U.S. government recognized that no party could be privy to the total truth; a society consists of competing interests. The U.S. Constitution, with its system of checks and balances, was one attempt to prevent any given group from gaining absolute control and to provide a forum for resolving differences of opinion.

The most dangerous aspect of Nazi propaganda, however, was its assumption that there is an absolute truth and that the ruling elite alone are privileged to know this truth. In his film series *The Ascent of Man*, the eminent scholar and humanist Jacob Bronowski catalogs the dangers of believing in this myth of absolute truth.[10] In one of the films, Bronowski looks at the culture and thought of Germany just before World War II and finds that there were two radically different philosophies, two fundamentally different ways of looking at the world—one represented by some of the scientists of the time and the other by the Nazi party.

These scientists were coming to the realization that human knowledge could never be absolute. There is no "God's-eye view." Based on their scientific findings, physicists such as Albert Einstein, Werner Heisenberg, and Max Born were proposing such ideas as the theory of relativity and the uncertainty principle, which led to the recognition that there is no absolute fixed point of reference and that human knowledge is limited. In the social sciences, the exploration of other cultures and other peoples was fast leading to the conclusion that habits and beliefs differ widely and that it was becoming increasingly difficult to say which is "best."

In the infancy of social psychology, Kurt Lewin was developing his theory of the psychological field. His theory emphasized how an individual's psychological needs and tasks influence his or her perception of the world. According to Lewin, different individuals with differing needs and tasks would come to perceive the same event differently. Ironically, the inspiration for Lewin's theory came from his experiences as a soldier in World War I, where he noticed that, as he approached the battlefield, his perception of the environment changed: No longer did he see beautiful gullies and interesting rock formations, but rather places to hide and things that could kill. Just before World War II, Lewin, who was Jewish, was forced to flee Nazi Germany. He came to America, where he trained many of the first generation of American social psychologists. The irony is that Kurt Lewin and Adolf Hitler fought on the same side in World War I. Both men experienced the same event; each reached a different conclusion.

The alternative position was one of dogma. The Nazi party embodied the truth; there was no need to tolerate other points of view. Hitler expressed this alternative philosophy succinctly:

> The function of propaganda is, for example, not to weigh and ponder the rights of different people, but exclusively to emphasize the one right which it has set out to argue for. Its task is not to make an objective study of the truth, in so far as it favors the enemy, and then set it before the masses with academic fairness; its task is to serve our own right, always and unflinchingly. . . . As soon as our own propaganda admits so much as a glimmer of right on the other side, the foundation of doubt in our own right has been laid.[11]

What are the fruits of the myth of absolute dogma? Six million of the 9.5 million Jews living in Europe were murdered. The Allied forces lost more than 11 million soldiers in battle, including 7.5 million Russian, 2.2 million Chinese, and a quarter of a million U.S. soldiers. The Axis powers lost more than 5 million soldiers in battle, including 3.5 million German and 1.2 million Japanese soldiers. Civilian casualties are harder to estimate. Direct civilian casualties as a result of the war include 2.5 million Russian, 860,000 Japanese, 300,000 German, and 60,595 British citizens. Another estimated 10 million Russians died as a result of indirect causes, such as famine and disease. In all, more than 36.5 million persons lost their lives. And for what reason?

At the end of his film, Bronowski offers an antidote to this "itch for absolute knowledge and power." There is a shallow pond just outside the concentration camp and crematorium at Auschwitz. The ashes of some 2 million people were flushed into this pond—an act caused by arrogance, by ignorance, by dogma. In one of the most dramatic moments on film, Jacob Bronowski walked out into this pond, bent down, and scooped up a handful of the ashes of some of these 2 million people. He made a simple request taken from Oliver Cromwell: "I beseech you, in the bowels of Christ, think it possible you may be mistaken."

If there is one thing to be learned from our study of persuasion, it is that we can be mistaken and misled. We have seen how information about our world can be selectively edited by news and entertainment organizations or managed by experienced political consultants. The picture of the world that emerges, mistaken as it may be, serves to guide our thinking and our actions. We have also seen that it is possible for a propagandist to play on our emotions and to take advantage of our decision-making processes by invoking simple heuristics. All of this leads to a single conclusion: *As human beings, we can be wrong.* Let us keep this fact in mind whenever we make decisions—especially those that cause damage to others.

One cannot study Nazi propaganda without passion and emotion. Both of the authors of this book lost friends and relatives during World War II, either in combat or in the Holocaust. We are sure that most readers of this book have suffered similar losses or have felt pain and anguish when watching footage of Nazi death camps or perhaps after a visit to our nation's Holocaust museum in Washington, D.C. Joseph Goebbels once boasted, "Nothing is easier than leading the people on a leash. I just hold up a dazzling campaign poster and they jump through it."[12] We owe it to the memory of his victims and to ourselves to learn as much as we can about the ways of propaganda and about the ways to promote democratic discussion so that we may prove Herr Goebbels false.

Counteracting the
Tactics of Propaganda

Is Forewarned Forearmed?
Or How to Really Resist
Propaganda

Throughout this volume we have attempted to explore the question: How credible and effective are obvious attempts to package and sell products and ideas (toothpaste, aspirin, presidential candidates) through clever influence tactics? On a personal level, many people claim that such blatant attempts at persuasion are so pitifully obvious that they are not much affected by them. Indeed, researchers have identified what is called the "third-person effect" in communication—a tendency to believe that the mass media will have a greater effect on others than on oneself; in other words, it is as if we say, "I will not be influenced, but others may very well be persuaded."[1]

Yet the prima facie evidence suggests such persuasion attempts are extremely effective. Success stories abound. The sales of Benson & Hedges 100s cigarettes increased sevenfold during a four-year period of heavy advertising. The Mattel Toy Company increased company size twenty-four-fold after it began to advertise extensively on television. Grape-Nuts, a venerable but nearly forgotten cereal, experienced a sudden 30% increase in sales when a well-known natural foods enthusiast began plugging this rather bland cereal. It appears that tremendous numbers of consumers set aside their skepticism even though they know the message is an obvious attempt to sell a product.

Moreover, as parents, most of us have seen our children being seduced by toy commercials and product packages that artfully depict the most drab toys in an irresistible way. Similarly, children watching cartoons on any Saturday morning are deluged by fast-paced ads for sugar-coated cereal, carryout food, and candy bars, and they in turn deluge their parents with requests for the products.

Much research confirms what every parent knows.[2] More than 90% of preschool-age children ask for toys or food they see advertised on television, according to a survey of their mothers. In fact, almost two-thirds of the mothers reported hearing their children sing commercial jingles they learned from television, most by the age of three. Another survey found that children who were frequent viewers of children's programs were more likely to want, request, and consume advertised snacks, cereals, and fast foods. In general, children under the age of eight demonstrate very good recognition of advertised brand names and poor recall of the specifics of the advertised claims, and they are highly persuaded by advertising. Perhaps one of the saddest demonstrations of the influence of advertising comes from an experiment which found that four- and five-year-old children, after watching an ad for a toy, were twice as likely to say that they would rather play with a "not so nice boy" *with* the toy than a "nice boy" *without* the toy.

That children are highly susceptible to persuasive appeals has not gone unrecognized by U.S. government agencies and officials. In 1934, in the case of *FTC v. R. F. Keppel & Brothers, Inc.*, the U.S. Supreme Court ruled that children were a special class of consumers "unable to protect themselves." How the government goes about protecting children depends on the political and economic circumstances of the era. For example, during the 1970s, pressure groups such as Action for Children's Television (ACT) lobbied the Federal Trade Commission (FTC) and the Federal Communications Commission (FCC) for greater regulation of television advertising directed at children. As a result of their support, the FTC negotiated an agreement with the National

Association of Broadcasters (NAB) to establish guidelines for children's advertising. Members of the NAB, which included the three major networks and approximately two-thirds of the local stations, agreed to reduce the amount of advertising to nine and a half minutes per hour for children's weekend programs and twelve minutes for weekday shows, require a clear separation between programming and advertising, and regulate advertising content to be consistent with values most parents endorse. In addition, the FTC and NAB also adjudicated consumer complaints about specific ads, often removing ads that violated the NAB standards.

However, in the early 1980s, as a result of President Reagan's deregulation policies, the FTC and FCC abandoned their roles as watchdogs of children's airwaves. The NAB also ceased to enforce its broadcast code of ethics, including those portions dealing with children and television. Regulation of children's advertising and programming was left to each individual television network and station—a case of the foxes becoming the guardians of the henhouse.

In 1996, President Clinton took a first step toward reversing this trend by announcing new federal rules regulating cigarette advertising directed at children. Some of these rules included banning tobacco ads on outdoor billboards within 1,000 feet of a school, prohibiting the sale or gift of items with tobacco brand logos, barring the use of any imagery supporting tobacco sales in magazines having a substantial number of readers under eighteen years of age, and banning the use of tobacco brand names in the sponsorship of sports events.[3] Clinton's goal, as he described it, was to put "Joe Camel and the Marlboro Man out of our children's reach forever." As we noted earlier, many of these attempts to protect children from tobacco advertising were later struck down by the U.S. Supreme Court.

Although regulation is important, even without it, some children do eventually catch on. We have seen our own children, after several disappointments, develop a healthy skepticism (even, alas, a certain degree of cynicism) about the truthfulness of commercials. One survey found that only 12% of sixth-graders believed television commercials told the truth all or most of the time; by the tenth grade, only 4% felt they were truthful most of the time. In general, research shows that many children under the age of eight find it difficult to detect a false utterance. However,

"*Kids, here I am, all hooked up to this lie detector, ready to tell you all about Zapples, the exciting new breakfast cereal. . . .*"

after this age, children show a growing distrust of advertisers and come to realize that the intention of advertising is not to inform but to persuade.

Needless to say, this kind of skepticism is common among adults as well. A public opinion poll showed that the overwhelming majority of adult respondents believe television commercials contain untruthful arguments. Moreover, the results indicate that the more educated the person, the more skeptical, and that people who are skeptical believe their skepticism makes them immune to persuasion.

This might lead us to conclude that the mere fact of knowing a communicator is biased protects us from being influenced by the message. But as indicated earlier, this is not always the case. Simply because we *think* we are immune to persuasion does not necessarily mean we *are* immune. For example, although attempts to teach children about advertising and its purposes have led to more skepticism about advertising, this skepticism seldom translates into *less* desire for advertised brands. Similarly, many adults tend to buy a specific brand for no other reason than the fact that it is heavily advertised. It behooves us, then, to look at just how being forewarned of persuasive intent influences persuasion.[4]

Research commonly shows that, under certain, but not all, conditions, to be forewarned is to be forearmed. In other words, members of an audience can be made less receptive to a message if explicitly forewarned that an attempt is going to be made to persuade them. This phenomenon was demonstrated in an experiment by Jonathan Freedman and David Sears.[5] Teenagers were told they would be hearing a talk entitled "Why Teenagers Should Not Be Allowed to Drive." Ten minutes later, the speaker presented them with a prepared communication. In a control condition, the same talk was given without the ten-minute forewarning. The subjects in the control condition were more thoroughly convinced by the communication than were those who had been forewarned.

Why were the forewarned teenagers less persuaded? We would argue that phrases such as "And now, a message from our sponsor" have the potential to render the message that follows less persuasive than it would have been if the communicator had simply glided into it without prologue. The forewarning seems to say "Watch out, I'm going to try to persuade you," and people tend to respond by marshaling defenses against the message. They tend to marshal their defenses in two ways—by playing attitudinal politics and by preparing a possible rebuttal to the anticipated communication.

By "attitudinal politics" we mean holding and expressing an opinion not because it is believed but in order to secure some strategic purpose. For example, many people dislike having their perceived freedom threatened by a communication and thus seek to appear independent but consistent. When these motives are invoked, the goal is to appear unpersuaded—regardless of the merits of the communication. One may claim: "I knew he was out to persuade me. But I make up my own mind. See—my opinion is unchanged." On the other hand, there are times when one seeks to appear informed, reasonable, and open to discussion. In such cases, a forewarning may result in *more* persuasion, or at least becoming more moderate in one's opinion.[6]

As a result of attitudinal politics, the effects of forewarning may be short-lived. As the audience for our beliefs or the strategic purpose for why we hold an opinion changes, so does the opinion. For example, one study found that the effects of forewarning wore off in about a week, resulting in little *immediate* persuasion but considerable *delayed* impact of a message.[7] Because of its often short-lived effects, forewarning does not always provide full protection from the tactics of persuasion. We may think skeptically about the advertisement as we view it comfortably in our homes. However, once at the supermarket, our skepticism may go out the window when the only information for making a decision is that which is recalled from the ad.

The second line of defense that may be engaged by forewarning—rebuttal—affords more protection but, alas, is not always used. By "rebuttal" we mean preparing oneself to scrutinize and counterargue an upcoming message. Much research indicates that a forewarning increases message scrutiny. However, it is often difficult to think about a message and fully prepare oneself for an influence attempt. For example, researchers have found that delivering a forewarning of persuasive intent immediately before delivering the message as opposed to five minutes before usually results in less resistance to persuasion, precisely because the target has little time to think of counterarguments. On the other hand, a forewarning has little effect when an individual is distracted from fully thinking about the message or has little time or opportunity to prepare a defense.

High-pressure sales agents appear to understand that forewarning can lead to a tougher sale. For example, Amway distributors are taught to set up meetings to recruit new Amway distributors by using a simple curiosity teaser that says nothing about the purpose of the meeting—and without allowing much time between this initial contact and the sales visit. Former Amway distributor Stephen Butterfield states he would call up possible customers and merely tell them: "Jack, listen! Money!" When Jack asked a question, Butterfield would respond: "My house! Eight o'clock! Bring your wife!"[8] Note that such an approach limits the ability of the potential customer to marshal defenses against the upcoming sales pitch.

Under certain conditions, even a clear forewarning will not *always* lead to an attempt to refute the message. One of these conditions is when the recipient believes the message or topic is unimportant. For example, Richard Petty and John Cacioppo warned college students that they would be receiving a persuasive message designed to change their beliefs about academic regulations.[9] They then heard a message arguing for the institution of an onerous senior comprehensive exam. Some of the students were told that the change would take place almost immediately (i.e., the onerous exam would impact them directly). Others were told that the exam would be instituted in the distant future or at another university. Forewarning reduced persuasion and increased counterarguing—but only among those students who thought they personally might be taking the exam. The other students, who did not believe the exam would affect them, found the argument quite convincing. Forewarning alone was not enough to induce these students to make the effort to scrutinize and counterargue the message.

Such results present a problem to those who believe that they are immune to persuasion just because they "know all about the advertiser's tricks." We often watch the mass media while we are in a mindless state. The communications are typically just not that involving or interesting. But, ironically, that often makes them all the more persuasive. In such cases, despite knowing that the advertiser is "out to get us," we still do not make much of an attempt to refute the message and, as a consequence, are often persuaded.

What, then, are the best ways to reduce susceptibility to the tactics of persuasion—recognized and otherwise? We can suggest three strategies.

One strategy, attempted by the FTC and FCC along with various consumer and industry groups, is to *regulate* and *legislate* persuasion practices so that they are fair and honest—for example, to forbid tactics that take advantage of special populations, such as children, or that deviously play on our emotions, such as lowballing. The idea is that, just as in a court of law some evidence is inadmissible and some legal maneuvers are not permitted, so, too, certain mass media persuasion tactics are unfair and not in society's best interest to allow.

Regulation of persuasion has potential pitfalls. One such problem is that rules regulating persuasion may violate First Amendment protections of free speech. Violations are especially likely to occur when content (e.g., prohibiting the teaching of evolution or the news coverage of a controversial event, such as a neo-Nazi rally in the United States or the effects of U.S. bombing raids on a civilian population) is regulated, as opposed to process (e.g., outlawing lowballing or particularly deceptive advertising). Another problem is that the idea of regulating mass persuasion is a relatively new one in American history. As such, the codes governing persuasion are limited in nature and can be easily overturned, thus affording the consumer and citizen minimal protection. Nevertheless, we would argue that it is beneficial for citizens of a society such as ours, which depends heavily on persuasion, to engage in discussions of what forms of persuasion are moral and what, if any, types of persuasion should be declared illegal—a task we begin in the next chapter.

A second defense against the tactics of propaganda is to play devil's advocate—to adopt for yourself, at least for the moment, the role of champion of the opposite cause—the position opposing that of the propagandist. The research on forewarning and persuasion suggests that simply knowing that you are about to be persuaded, in and of itself, is of little use in preventing persuasion. What matters is what you do with that forewarning—how it leads you to prepare for the message and to evaluate its content. Just because you know there will be an earthquake tomorrow doesn't mean you will be safe unless that forewarning leads you to take appropriate safeguards. It is the same with persuasion. To resist propaganda, you need to prepare for it. In the next chapter, we will look at some ways of playing devil's advocate as a means of reducing our susceptibility to propaganda.

A third strategy is to develop methods for resisting persuasion on a given issue or topic. Let's look at two techniques identified by researchers for accomplishing this goal.

Suppose you are faced with a situation in which negative information can be revealed that will hurt your cause. What can be done to limit the impact of this attack? One tactic for significantly reducing the impact of potentially damaging information is *stealing thunder*, or revealing the negative information about oneself or about the issue at hand before it is revealed by an opponent or others. An experiment by Kip Williams, Martin Bourgeois, and Robert Croyle illustrates the power of this technique.[10] In this study, subjects witnessed a reenacted criminal trial in which the defendant was accused of beating another man after a verbal altercation. Some of the subjects were informed by the prosecutor that the defendant had been previously convicted of the same crime twice; for other subjects, it was the defense attorney who brought up the evidence regarding the prior convictions and downplayed its significance. Williams and his colleagues found that stealing thunder (or admitting the evidence against you) significantly reduced the likelihood that the defendant would be viewed as guilty of the crime relative to having the prosecutor reveal the negative information.

Trial lawyers have long understood the importance of stealing thunder. As the distinguished defense attorney Gerry Spence puts it:

> I always concede at the outset whatever is true even if it is detrimental to my argument. Be up-front with the facts that confront you. *A concession coming from your mouth is not nearly as hurtful as an exposure coming from your opponent's.* We can be forgiven for a wrongdoing we have committed. We cannot be forgiven for a wrongdoing we have committed and tried to cover up.[11]

In his analysis of the O. J. Simpson trial, Vincent Bugliosi, a former Los Angeles County prosecutor who won 105 out of 106 felony jury trials, including the Charles Manson case, points out that Marcia Clark, Chris Darden, and the other prosecutors committed a number of strategic errors, including the failure to steal the defense's thunder. As he states, "when you know the defense is going to present evidence damaging or unfavorable to your side, you present that evidence yourself."[12] Bugliosi goes on to explain two reasons why stealing thunder works. First, stealing thunder enhances one's credibility; it shows that you are fair and willing to look at all the evidence regardless of its unfavorability to your cause. Second, it indicates to the jury that the negative evidence isn't all that bad (you're willing to admit it), and thus it takes the "sting" out of the potentially damaging information.

Stealing thunder can be used to limit the impact of damaging information in other domains. An interesting example comes from the U.S. presidential election of 1884.[13] Early in the campaign, rumors circulated that the Democratic candidate, Grover Cleveland, had fathered an illegitimate son by Mrs. Maria Halprin, the director of the cloak and lace department of a Buffalo, New York, store. Rather than deny or try to ignore the rumors (which were somewhat true), Cleveland stole the press's thunder by admitting and disclosing all the facts, presenting them in a manner that painted himself in a sympathetic manner: Halprin had had a number of affairs, making it difficult to know who was the real father; Cleveland accepted the responsibility for the child, including paying child support, because he was the only bachelor among Halprin's lovers; when Halprin began drinking heavily, Cleveland found a prominent family to adopt and raise the child. In contrast, James Blaine, the Republican candidate, denied rumors (which were also true) that his wife had given birth to their first child just three months after their wedding. Blaine told an unbelievable story—that they had had two weddings, six months apart, and had kept the first one secret because of the death of his father. (Interestingly, an informer gave Cleveland this information in advance of press coverage; rather than use it, Cleveland tore it up and then set it afire). Cleveland defeated Blaine handily.

A second technique for increasing resistance to persuasion on a given topic is *inoculation*. We have already seen that a two-sided (refutational) presentation is more effective for convincing certain audiences than a one-sided presentation (see Chapter 23). Expanding on this phenomenon, William McGuire and his colleagues have suggested that, if people receive prior exposure to a brief communication that they are able to refute, they then tend to become "immunized" against a subsequent full-blown presentation of the same argument, in much the same way that a small amount of an attenuated virus immunizes people against a full-blown attack by that virus.

In an experiment by McGuire and Dimitri Papageorgis, a group of people stated their opinions; these opinions were then subjected to a mild attack—and the attack was refuted.[14] These people were subsequently subjected to a powerful argument against their initial opinions. Members of this group showed a much smaller tendency to change their opinions than did the members of a control group whose opinions had not been previously subjected to mild attack. In effect, they had been inoculated against opinion change and made relatively immune. Thus not only is it sometimes more effective to use a two-sided refutational presentation, but, if it is used skillfully, such a presentation tends to increase the audience's resistance to subsequent counterpropaganda. Similarly, to protect ourselves from persuasion, we can begin to question our own beliefs, thereby discovering the strengths and weaknesses of the position we hold.[15]

In an exciting field experiment, Alfred McAlister and his colleagues inoculated seventh-grade students against existing peer pressures to smoke cigarettes.[16] For example, the students were shown advertisements implying that truly liberated women are smokers—"You've come a long way, baby!" They were then inoculated by being taught that a woman couldn't possibly be liberated if she was hooked on tobacco. Similarly, since teenagers tend to smoke because it seems cool or "tough" (like the Marlboro man), McAlister felt that peer pressure might take the form of being called "chicken" if one didn't smoke. Accordingly, the seventh-graders were asked to role-play a situation in which they practiced countering that argument by saying something like "I'd be a real chicken if I smoked just to impress you." This inoculation against peer pressure proved to be very effective. By the time the students were in the ninth grade, they were only half as likely to smoke as those in a control group from a similar junior high school.

In the war of persuasion, cigarette advertisers have also discovered the value of inoculation. Since institution of the ban on advertising cigarettes on TV, the percentage of Americans who have quit smoking or are trying to quit has dramatically increased (with the exception of young women, whose rate of smoking has increased). If tobacco companies are to maintain their sales, they must prevent the additional conversion of smokers to nonsmokers (and, of course, find new markets, such as children). To this end, the R. J. Reynolds Tobacco Company ran a series of two-sided magazine ads appealing for tolerance between smokers and nonsmokers. Half of the ad, titled "For those who don't," contained a series of arguments in favor of allowing smoking in public places. The other half of the ad, titled "For those who do," consisted of a gentle presentation of the anti-smoking position. The ad thus contained the information needed by smokers, who would probably be most interested in the topic, on how to counterargue and resist an anti-smoking campaign.

Research has found that inoculation is most effective in producing resistance when the belief under attack is a cultural truism—a belief accepted as unquestionably true by most members of a society, such as "The United States is the best country in the world to live in" or "If people are willing to work hard, they can succeed." Cultural truisms are rarely called into question; when they are not, it is relatively easy for us to lose sight of why we hold these beliefs. Thus, if subjected to a severe attack, such beliefs may crumble.[17]

To be motivated to bolster our beliefs, we must be made aware of their vulnerability, and the best way to do this is to attack those beliefs mildly. Prior exposure, in the form of a watered-down attack on our beliefs, produces resistance to later persuasion because (1) we become motivated to defend our beliefs and (2) we gain some practice in doing so. We are then better equipped to resist a more serious attack.

This is an important point frequently ignored or misunderstood by policy makers. For example, in the aftermath of the Korean War, when several American prisoners of war were supposedly "brainwashed" by the Chinese Communists, a Senate committee recommended that, in order to build resistance among the people to brainwashing and other forms of Communist propaganda, courses on "patriotism and Americanism" should be instituted in our public school system. But the research discussed above demonstrates that the best way to help soldiers resist anti-American propaganda would be to challenge their belief in the American way of life, and the best way to build resistance to pro-Communist propaganda would be to teach courses on Communism, presenting both sides of the argument.

If such an idea had been proposed in the 1950s, when the Cold War was in full swing and Senator Joseph McCarthy was conducting his witch hunt, it would probably have been considered to be part of the Communist conspiracy. The danger of susceptibility to Communist propaganda is a thing of the past, but the general principle still holds: We cannot resist propaganda by burying our heads in the sand. The person who is easiest to persuade is the person whose beliefs are based on slogans that have never been seriously challenged and examined.

39 ||||||||||||||||||||

What We Can Do to Stop Propaganda in Its Tracks

Throughout this book, we have delineated a great many persuasion and propaganda tactics and we have frequently discussed what we can do to counteract unwanted forms of propaganda. What we would like to do in this chapter is to pull together these recommendations with a simple goal in mind: How can we prevent propaganda from impacting us in our homes, workplaces, schools, courtrooms, and nation?

The answer to this question is complex. And why shouldn't it be? The propaganda we face is complex, taking a myriad of forms that often change in response to new environments, new opportunities, and our attempts to stop it.

In preventing propaganda, there appear to be two basic approaches we can take. First, we can take *defensive* action. In other words, learn how to detect propaganda, how to play the devil's advocate, what questions to ask about a communication, how to debunk and deflate a bogus appeal, and how to respond to unscrupulous propaganda attacks. Much of this book has been written with this goal in mind.

However, in a message-dense environment populated with propagandists of every ilk playing on our prejudices and emotions, even the best-trained warrior could not successfully defend against every attack. There is just too much flimflam—and too little time and too few resources to debunk it all. We also need to take *offensive* action—steps that will identify common propaganda forms and the seeds of propaganda and stop them at the source. Preventing propaganda from entering our homes requires both personal and institutional responses—that we take personal steps to end it and that we change some of the ways our society does things. In the remainder of this chapter, we offer some suggestions on things we can do to prevent, or at least slow, the spread of propaganda.[1] We begin by looking at some ways to defend ourselves personally and then move on to some societal actions we can take.

❑ Know the ways of persuasion and realize that you personally may be the victim of propaganda. In a series of important experiments, Brad Sagarin and his colleagues taught college students about the ways of persuasion.[2] Specifically, the students received materials that explained how to distinguish a legitimate use of source credibility from an illegitimate one—materials similar to our discussion of communicator credibility in Chapters 12–16. Next, Sagarin and his colleagues gave the students, in an unrelated context, a series of ads that used authority figures in appropriate and inappropriate ways. What did they find? The training alone did little to help the students resist a dishonest ad (although, interestingly, it did increase the influence of ads using legitimate communicators). However, the training did result in

more resistance to propaganda when it was coupled with a
"gotcha" procedure. In this case, before receiving the training on
source credibility, the students were initially shown that they,
too, could be taken in by dishonest communicators. The students were first asked to give their opinion of an ad that used a
fake stockbroker to recommend a product, and then asked to
take a look at their opinions to see whether they had noticed that
the stockbroker was a fraud. If they hadn't, they were told that
they had been fooled. Their illusion of invulnerability to propaganda weakened, the students eagerly applied the lessons they
had learned concerning source credibility and resisted phony
appeals. Extrapolating from this experiment, reading this book
is a good first step to bolstering your resistance to propaganda.
However, in order for you to gain maximum protection from
propaganda, you need to take one more step—don't fall prey to
the third-person effect whereby you think that everyone else can
be a victim of propaganda, but not you. Try to consider yourself
vulnerable and prepare yourself accordingly.

☐ Monitor your emotions. If you notice you are having an
emotional response to a communication, ask "Why?" Look for
things that might induce emotions, such as a false commitment,
a "free" gift that makes you feel obligated, a scarce item that
induces feelings of inferiority, a we–they distinction that elicits
the granfalloon, or speeches that make you feel fearful or guilty.
If you feel that your emotions are being played on, get out of the
situation and then analyze what is going on. If you can't physically remove yourself from the situation, redefine the situation
mentally until you can escape.

☐ Explore the motivation and credibility of the source of the
communication. Ask such things as: "Why is this person telling
me this information?" "What does the source have to gain?"
"Does the communicator really have the expertise and credibility
to be believed, or is it just a manufactured image?" "Can the expert explain the issue in terms that can be understood, or is it
just mumbo-jumbo designed to confuse and dazzle?"

☐ Think rationally about any proposal or issue. Ask such
things as: "What is the issue?" "What labels and terms are used
to describe it?" "Are these labels used fairly?" "What course or
courses of action are being discussed?" "What are the arguments
in support of the advocate's position?" "What are the arguments
opposing the position?" "How cogent are these arguments?"

☐ Attempt to understand the full range of options before making a decision. Ask such questions as: "Why are these choices being presented to me in this manner?" "Are there other options and other ways of presenting those options?" "What would happen if I chose something other than the recommended option?"

☐ "Don't watch your leaders' lips, watch their hands."[3] This metaphorical piece of advice comes from Theodor Plievier, an East German writer who has had vast experience with the ways of propaganda. In other words, don't base your evaluation on what someone *says* ("I am for the environment" "I am for education" "I am against crime") but on what the person actually *does* (how has the person protected the environment, supported education, or prevented crime?).

☐ Stop to consider the possibility that any information you receive may be a factoid. Let's take "idle" rumors and innuendo as an example. Human nature being what it is, most people take some pleasure out of hearing and repeating rumors. Why? As we noted before, rumors usually involve nasty, racy, or exciting negative stories about prominent people (national leaders, movie stars, or even well-known figures in our village, campus, or community). There is something about a nasty rumor about a prominent person that "takes them down a peg." The Germans have a word for it: *Schadenfreude*—the secret, guilty pleasure we derive from the misfortune or embarrassment of others. But such rumors are often untrue and are certainly not harmless—they can be painful and destructive of the character and reputation of the target. Accordingly, when you hear a rumor or innuendo, you might want to ask the source: "What is the evidence for this?" "Where did you hear it?" "Would you be willing to try to convince an impartial jury of the truth of this story?" In other words, insist that the repeater of the rumor put up or shut up. Each of us has a certain responsibility to challenge rumors rather than blindly accepting and repeating them.

☐ If everyone is "doing it" or you hear the same piece of "news" repeatedly, ask "why?" We recently completed a replication of the famous experiment by Solomon Asch in which subjects are asked to judge the relative lengths of lines.[4] In some of the trials, confederates of the experimenter intentionally agree on an obviously incorrect answer. Now it is the subject's turn to respond. The purpose of the study is to see whether or not the subject will conform to the erroneous opinions of the group. In our study, more than half of the subjects gave the wrong answer at least once just to go along with the group. After the experiment, we asked one subject who did *not* conform what she thought about the experience. She gave advice opposite to the social consensus heuristic: When everyone is doing the same thing, use this as a cue to ask why. This is very good advice for avoiding jumping on bandwagons that aren't worth riding.

❑ If the deal looks too good to be true, it probably is. Before making a purchase, look for these common warning signs of a bad deal: (1) The deal is only good for "today"; (2) the seller offers "free gifts" in return for "minimum" effort; (3) a sale item is suddenly unavailable but a "much better" item happens to be available for "slightly more money" (throwing a lowball); (4) the seller emphasizes the amount of each payment rather than the total amount of the sale; (5) a "repair person" discovers a "dangerous" defect in something you own that must be repaired immediately; (6) you are given little or no time to read a contract; (7) the seller makes you feel guilty for asking questions or asks, "Don't you trust me?"[5]

❑ Always ask yourself: "What are the arguments for the other side?" "What would it take to prove me (or anyone else) wrong?" This will help in avoiding acceptance of a position just because it is agreeable or presented in a pleasing manner. It will also stimulate debate and may result in improving the course of action you eventually adopt.

❑ Teach your children about propaganda. Recall from Chapter 38 that one of the best ways to prevent persuasion is through inoculation. Watch TV with your children and help them develop counterarguments against propaganda. For example, watch advertising with your children and ask such things as: "Do you think that toy can really do that, or is it just TV?" "Why do you think they make the toy look so good?" If need be, take the child to the toy store and compare the toy's real performance with the claims made in the advertising. When violence appears on the TV screen (and it will!) ask: "How do you think the victim felt? Would you like that done to you?"

❑ Support efforts to protect vulnerable groups such as children from exploitative persuasion. For example, you may wish to support efforts to limit the amount and scope of advertising directed toward children (as described in Chapter 38). You may wish to support efforts to limit the amount of TV violence entering the home through "family viewing hours," computer chips that you can use to block certain channels, or letting advertisers who support violent TV programming know that you won't be buying their products.

❑ Avoid being dependent on a single source of information. One of the hallmarks of intense propaganda (of the type found in cults and totalitarian regimes) is centralized communications from a single perspective. As companies in the mass media industry merge, consolidate, and buy each other out, citizens are becoming increasingly dependent on a handful of communications firms to deliver the diversity of opinions needed to sustain a democracy.[6] Public television is a useful alternative to commercial television and encourages the dissemination of shows such as "Sesame Street" and "Mister Rogers' Neighborhood." However, this is no substitute for a return to a quaint, old-fashioned idea: The public airwaves are owned by the public and should serve the public's interest. In distributing broadcast licenses and approving mergers, the government's guiding principle should be "How does this serve the community? How does this insure the dissemination of diverse viewpoints?"—not "How much money can someone make?"

❑ Think of the news as the news and try to separate it in your own mind from entertainment. Don't expect the news media to make every "event" into an entertaining spectacle with the sole purpose of securing ratings. The news media are among the few institutions that have the resources to serve as a watchdog over political and commercial enterprises. If they fail to serve this function, then we do not have the information we need to perform our jobs as citizens.

❑ Use communication style as one of your criteria in making decisions and judgments. For example, we have a friend who is a lifelong Republican; he has voted for every Republican who has run for president since Nixon. However, when the Willie Horton ad ran in the 1988 campaign, our friend declared, "I'll hold my nose and vote for Dukakis. I don't want a president who talks to the American people in this manner." Our friend recognized this ad for what it was—a cheap, mean-spirited play on emotions to get votes, and he wanted nothing to do with it. If we all followed the lead of our friend, then politicians and others would learn that demagoguery doesn't pay.[7]

❑ Support campaign spending reform. Under the current matching funds formula, the American taxpayer foots the bill for much of election-year campaigning—for example, spending more than $170 million to finance a typical presidential campaign. Why pay for propaganda? Instead of giving candidates a blank check to purchase misleading thirty-second spots featuring vivid innuendo and slick images, why not require recipients of federal matching funds to use the money to pay for debates, open forums with the public, press conferences, infomercials that give the viewer a chance to hear the candidate's position in detail, and "talking head" ads such as those used in France? (These are ads in which the candidate talks to the camera without distracting backgrounds such as waving flags or cheering shills, thereby focusing attention on what the candidate says and away from emotion-arousing images.)

❑ Increase your involvement with important issues. We saw in Chapter 3 that we are all prone to propaganda when we process information in a half-mindless state. On the other hand, when we are motivated by the personal relevance of an issue, we think about that issue, scrutinize messages, and seek out more information to help make our decision. The rub is that we often find ourselves in that "tuned-out" state of mind. One solution is to create "involvement devices" to increase the relevance of issues facing our nation. For example, consider something as simple as a tax receipt sent to taxpayers listing how much they paid and how much of their money went to each major budget item. How would this work? Imagine the Jones family, whose income is $34,000.[8] They would typically pay $3,200 in federal tax, $2,600 in Social Security and Medicare taxes, plus state, local, and sales taxes. The Jones family would receive from the IRS a thank-you note and a breakdown of how their money was spent: $1,682 on Social Security and Medicare, $1,102 on defense, $870 on interest on the national debt, $348 on Medicaid. Each of the rest of the budget items cost the Joneses less than $100, including $58 each on items such as unemployment insurance, housing programs, and food stamps and $15 each on items such as federal law enforcement, federal research, student aid, and foreign affairs. Armed with such information, the next time the Jones family sees a multimillion-dollar missile accidentally explode on the TV news they might respond "Hey, that is my thousand bucks on fire" and might become increasingly interested in military procurement procedures. When a politician comes along and says "I'll save tax money by getting rid of welfare cheats and end-ing our involvement in the UN," the Joneses might respond: "Not likely. These are relatively small costs compared to the big-ticket items of Social Security, the military, debt service, and health-care." The point is this: When armed with information that is personally involving, citizens are in a better position to distinguish valid proposals from poppycock.

❑ Demand consumer affairs shows. A good example occurs in the Netherlands, where Astrid Joosten hosts the hit TV show "The Seduction."[9] This talk show brings together advertisers, media critics, and consumers to discuss advertising. The program provides a forum for consumers to complain about ads and for advertisers to respond to their complaints. It also serves as a model for much-needed programming that would take a critical look at the consumer advertising entering our homes.

❑ Write companies asking for proof of advertised claims (as described in Chapter 11). We found that reading through the material we received from companies in support of their advertising claims made us much more sensitive to hollow claims (such as "Coke is it") and made us think about how an advertiser could support the claim (they often couldn't if they wanted to). Perhaps if we all wrote asking for proof, advertisers would realize that the empty promise is not an effective persuasion device.

❑ Support and extend efforts to squelch deceptive advertisements. Deceptive advertising misleads the consumer, harms competitors who must compete against phony claims, and ultimately makes it more difficult for those with legitimate claims to be believed by the consumer. To counter such propaganda, we need to toughen regulations so that advertisers are held accountable for deceptive ads (ones that lie outright) and those that readily induce consumers to draw misleading implications (such as "No other pain-reliever is proven to be more effective"). It is reasonable to expect that the advertiser has a reasonable basis for making a claim, and these reasons should be available on request.[10] In addition, when enacting any consumer protection law we need to make sure there are (1) enough law enforcement agents to enforce it and (2) enough of a penalty to deter would-be criminals.

❑ Support and extend efforts to eliminate misleading labels and other deceptive practices. Action can be taken to eliminate deceptive tactics. For example, the federal government has recently issued guidelines for labels such as "low-calorie" or "low-fat" so that they actually mean something. A simple law requiring a store to stock adequate supplies of advertised sale products can serve to stop lowballing practices that play on false commitments.[11] One area rife with fraud is telemarketing, where fly-by-night companies use high-pressure sales techniques to sell beachfront property in Fresno, California, or worthless gems at inflated prices. Here a number of laws and regulations are needed, including (1) creating internationally available databases for tracking fraudulent telemarketers; (2) requiring full disclosure to the consumer of the owners of the telemarketing firm along with the value of any prizes offered and, in cases where the telemarketer is soliciting for charity, the percentage of the contribution that will actually go to the charity (as opposed to the fund-raiser); (3) revising laws to make it easier for a consumer to take a fraudulent marketer to court;[12] and (4) establishing a registry of consumers who do not wish to be contacted by telemarketers, accompanied by stiff penalties when these wishes are violated. We owe it to ourselves to look for more areas where fraud and deception can be prevented.

❑ Promote the institutions of democracy. We often take for granted the nature of democracy, thinking that is it just "majority rule" or "the freedom to do our own thing." A democracy is a pattern of social relations that encourages deliberative persuasion (not propaganda) and respects the rights and responsibilities of all citizens.[13] The hallmarks of a democracy (as opposed to an autocracy) include the following: (1) Communication is decentralized, with multiple sources of information; (2) authority and power are constrained by a system of checks and balances; (3) agendas and goals are established through discussion, not by leader fiat; (4) there is a reciprocity of influence between leaders and citizens, as opposed to unidirectional influence from elites; (5) group boundaries and roles are flexible, as opposed to there being a rigid social structure; and (6) minority opinion is encouraged as a means of obtaining a better decision, and the rights of those in the minority are protected. We need to keep such characteristics in mind and promote them at every opportunity—when we adopt a social policy, when we interact with our neighbors, when we make decisions with consequences beyond our own self-interest.

❑ Encourage government policies aimed at maintaining a large middle class. It may seem odd that a book on persuasion would recommend enacting policies to ensure the growth of the middle class. However, the seeds of propaganda are often based in dissatisfaction with oneself and with one's life chances. History teaches that propaganda flourishes in times when citizens feel relatively deprived—that is, getting less than they feel they deserve. Those who feel relatively deprived are more likely to scapegoat others (for example, participate in race riots or join militia groups) and to support demagogues.[14] Before Hitler came to power, the German economy was in a shambles; in the American South from 1882 to 1930, as the price of cotton decreased, the lynching of black Americans increased. In contrast, the feeling of participating in the economy that typifies being in the middle class (owning a home or a car, having a bank account, or experiencing the respect that comes from having a good job) is usually accompanied by feelings of responsibility and concern about public issues and thus more scrutiny of persuasive communications.

❑ Finally, one of the most essential actions to take in preventing propaganda is to follow a recommendation from the Bible—to take the plank out of one's own eye before attempting to remove the speck from someone else's. In other words, if we seek to promote positive, ethical persuasion and to eliminate misleading propaganda, then we personally must practice what we preach. We will explore this theme in our next and final chapter.

40

Peitho's Children

Novelists have often portrayed the dark and devious side of persuasion. In the American classic *Elmer Gantry*, Sinclair Lewis tells the story of a hypocritical preacher who delivers spellbinding sermons capable of mesmerizing the faithful and, not inconsequentially, maintaining a tidy income for the Reverend Gantry. In *1984*, the British author George Orwell describes a totalitarian state that successfully employs propaganda techniques to maintain its control over the people. In *A Man of the People*, the African novelist Chinua Achebe chronicles the rise to power of the Honourable M. A. Nanga through rhetoric and policy designed to deceive and fool the masses.

Throughout this book we have seen this dark side of persuasion, whether it be trickery on the used-car lot, misinformation in the mass media, "mind control" in cults, or the propaganda of hate in the Third Reich. In the hands of a demagogue, persuasion can be full of treachery and trickery, appealing primarily to our irrational impulses.

The ancient Greeks present another side of persuasion. During the heyday of democracy in Athens, the Greeks worshiped Peitho, the goddess of persuasion. In Aeschylus' play *Oresteia*, Peitho succeeded in calming the Furies, three avenging spirits of retributive justice whose task it was to punish those who commit crimes. Orestes is on trial for the murder of his mother and her lover, a crime he freely admits he committed. But there is a twist. It is also known that his mother and her lover had killed Orestes' father in order to assume the throne of Mycenae. An Athenian jury must decide if young Orestes is a common murderer or if the homicide is justified. After hearing the arguments, the jury is split and the deciding vote must be cast by Athena, the goddess of wisdom. She votes that Orestes should go free.

The Furies who prosecuted the case are outraged. For them, murder is murder and blood must be atoned by blood. To appease the Furies, Athena offers them a new shrine on the Acropolis and a new name—the Eumenides, or the gracious ones. In return, the Furies must recognize the majesty of Peitho. The message to the Greek audience is clear: Wisdom dictates that persuasion must be used to overcome the baser nature of humankind.

This dual nature of persuasion, as a source of both human destruction and human wisdom, raises a final but crucial question: What should be the nature and role of persuasion in society?[1] For we are not only the recipients of persuasive communications, we are also the sources of such messages. Like it or not, we are all Peitho's children. Sometimes we play the role innocently, recommending a particular restaurant or a certain brand of stereo equipment to a friend. Sometimes it's not so innocuous. Many professions demand a high degree of persuasive skill—not just sales, law, and politics, but also medicine, science, and teaching. Likewise, people who work for political candidates or in support of social causes or charitable organizations depend on their persuasive abilities to attract votes, to garner signatures for petitions, to raise funds, or to spread information. In fact, we can be said to be engaging in attempts at persuasion any time we praise or criticize an object, defend or attack an idea, advocate or oppose a position.

Now that we have discussed how to deliver persuasive messages *effectively*, it would be worthwhile to consider explicitly how to decide *whether or not and how* to do so. The ethical question is a complex one with many gray areas. While this is not the place for an elaborate discussion of moral philosophy, we feel obliged to point out the existence and importance of ethical issues and to suggest a few ways to consider them.

Before doing so, we should note that the "morality" of a persuasive tactic is often based, rightly or wrongly, on its success in accomplishing a goal. For example, an oppressed minority that achieves its goal through a tactic such as a bus boycott is often criticized by the losing majority for its choice of tactics—"I agree with the goal, but not the means" is a common response. Further, history looks kindly on winners and often ignores their excesses. "Successful" traitors, for example, are a rarity: They either fail and are labeled "treacherous" or succeed and are called "patriotic."

One approach is to judge the ethics of a persuasive attempt by assessing its goals; the extreme statement of this viewpoint would be that the end justifies the means. Suppose you are living in Poland in 1942. The Nazis are rounding up Jews and sending them to the death camps; you are safeguarding a Jewish family, hiding them in your cellar. When the Nazis knock at your door asking if there are any Jews inside, you answer that there are not. Few would argue that to lie persuasively in this instance is immoral or unethical; lying is necessary to save the lives of innocent people, and the more convincing you are the more likely you are to save their lives as well as your own and those of your family and loved ones.

When the goals of a persuasive attempt are not so easily defensible, the ethical issues become more problematic. Imagine you are employed as a salesperson at a clothing store selling bluejeans. Your boss suggests that you tell your customers "no jeans have been shown to wear longer than ours." This is technically correct, though it is also true that the jeans you are selling

"Remember, kids, these political debaters are experienced professionals. Do not try this kind of trickery and lying at home."

have not been shown to wear longer than any *other* brand of
jeans. Furthermore, suppose you are paid a sizable commission
for every pair of jeans you sell. Would you feel any hesitation in
using the sales pitch? Would this change if you really *believed* the
jeans were extraordinarily durable and inexpensive? What if you
believed they *weren't*? Finally, if you are reluctant to use this
sales pitch, what message *would* you feel comfortable with? With
this last question, we have broadened our focus from the goals of
the communication to include explicitly a consideration of the
content of the message.

Another perspective on ethics is to judge the actions according to the means employed by the source of the communication.[2] Generally, it can be agreed that one should avoid knowingly dispensing false information, hiding facts, using specious
reasoning, or falsely playing on the emotions. But problems arise
from this approach, too: What about a white lie, for example,
when a person might use deception in order to avoid hurting
someone's feelings unnecessarily?

Evaluating the ethics of a persuasive attempt requires consideration of both the goals and the content of the message. Let's

say you are a staunch opponent of nuclear power, convinced that all nuclear power plants should be shut down immediately. You are on your way to visit a friend, and you feel it is important to convince him to join you in your opposition. In past conversations, you have told him that the waste generated by nuclear plants, which is highly radioactive and currently impossible to dispose of safely, creates a serious and ever increasing threat; he responded that "good old American know-how" will solve the problem in time. You have argued that it is wrong for energy to be controlled and distributed for profit by the centralized, big-business interests necessary to finance nuclear power plants; your friend merely scoffed, chuckling about "the Marxist stuff they keep putting on the tube these days."

So when thinking about your upcoming visit, you admit to yourself that he will probably remain unpersuaded by your two major reasons for opposing nuclear power. Since you believe the threat is such that convincing him of the danger of nuclear power is crucial, you begin to search for additional arguments to present. Recalling that your friend is quite afraid of cancer—his father died of the disease after a long, painful illness—you consider emphasizing the potential carcinogenic effects of radiation emanating from the plants, although you are aware that the risks are undocumented. Knowing that his business relies on a dependable energy supply and that he is concerned about costs, you plan to avoid mentioning the reduction in electricity and increase in costs a shutdown of the nuclear plant in your area would entail.

Just before arriving, you think about whether your attempt to convince him is ethical. You tell yourself your cause is a vital one, you aren't telling any direct falsehoods, and you are merely presenting your arguments in their best possible light. On the other hand, you feel uneasy that you are not sharing all the information as you know it.

The judgment is not an easy one. You may believe strongly enough in an issue to have no qualms about presenting the information in the best way to further your cause, or you might feel uncomfortable giving anything but as complete and neutral an account as you can. Your decision will depend in part on the situation. For example, a trial lawyer, who is expected (and compelled) to advocate a position, might be less constrained by some ethical considerations than a speaker who is thought to be nonpartisan. Someone whose message is preceded or followed by counterarguments might feel free to take more liberties than someone who will speak uncontested. Some people would assert that important causes justify the use of strong persuasion tactics; others would argue the converse—that the more important the topic, the greater the necessity for objectivity.

The issues are complex; there are no simple ethical solutions. This is especially true when we are the ones making the decisions and are not just passive observers and Monday-morning quarterbacks. As Goethe once noted, "Conscience is the virtue of observers and not of agents of action."[3]

At the risk of making the issues even more complex, we would like to suggest another way of evaluating the ethics of persuasion: *The means often determine the ends.* In other words, the choice of persuasion tactics often ends up determining the nature of our beliefs and actions. As the Chinese philosopher Mencius put it, immediate goals may be accomplished with devices that produce long-term evil. Suppose, for example, your friend is convinced by your cancer argument but later finds out that it may not be wholly accurate. Suppose he reads a rather emotional article in a magazine written by a nuclear power enthusiast asserting that (1) the evidence linking radiation leaks to cancer is unsubstantiated and (2) the continued use of fossil fuels and other petrochemicals might destroy the atmosphere and result in greater penetration of harmful, cancer-causing ultraviolet rays from the sun. The article concludes by suggesting that the risk of cancer might actually *increase* if nuclear power is eliminated.

What is your friend likely to think and feel? At best, your persuasive message is for naught; your friend, confronted by two seemingly valid but emotional appeals, does not know who or what to believe. At worst, your friend may feel that you betrayed his emotions; his anger may cause him to reject your message and to henceforth consider you to be a discredited source of information. Perhaps the results would have been different if another type of appeal—one that did not manipulate the emotions—had been used.

The reliance on simplistic persuasion tactics, such as invoking heuristic devices or setting the rationalization trap, carries an implicit danger: If you can successfully use the technique, so can anyone else. The handicraft of one demagogue can be easily undone by the next. The result is a great mass of people who appear fickle and confused. Further, when we realize that we have been cheated and manipulated, we often respond by becoming skeptical and cynical. Historians argue that the widespread knowledge of the misuse of atrocity propaganda by the British and Americans during World War I was one reason—along with pro-isolation sentiments, selective news coverage, and anti-Semitism—that much of the world did not at first believe the truth about Hitler's atrocities.[4] Similarly, contemporary analysts feel that large numbers of Americans do not vote because they believe that all campaign rhetoric is meaningless puffery. To paraphrase an old saw, "Live by propaganda, die by propaganda."

What about the consequences of withholding vital information from your friend, such as the possible negative economic consequences of closing nuclear power plants? Obviously, leaving your friend uninformed about this aspect of nuclear power might backfire as well. The advocate of nuclear power could score big points merely by stating these possibilities. Moreover, the decision not to discuss the economics of energy has another, perhaps more serious consequence: It leaves your friend ignorant.

If using emotional appeals or oversimplified arguments can produce such negative outcomes, why do people use them? Recall that our age of propaganda is message-dense; few citizens have the time, the opportunity, or the capacity to process the vast array of information they receive. Further, as we have seen, news is frequently watched not so much for its information value as for its ability to entertain. This increases the temptation of communicators to manipulate beliefs and opinions not by reason but by appeals to emotions and simplistic thought. Communicators seem to be relying more and more on persuasion devices that make use of prejudices and emotions over fully informed discussion, vivid images over thoughtful discourse, meaningless association over reasoned causal analysis, the propaganda of the demagogue over the persuasion of Peitho.

The consequences for democracy can be dire. As more and more propagandists use simplistic persuasion, the competitive urge to use simpler and simpler persuasion devices increases. As simpler and simpler persuasion devices are used, people become increasingly less informed and sophisticated about civic matters.

As the populace becomes less informed, the propagandist must use even more simplistic persuasion devices. The result is an ignorance spiral—a cynical populace bombarded with more and more thoughtless propaganda that they have less and less skill and inclination to process and ability to understand. Adolf Hitler's belief that the masses are ignorant thus becomes a self-fulfilling prophecy.

We believe that it is possible to avoid these dire consequences. That is why we wrote this book. It is our hope that knowledge about the process of persuasion will allow all of us to detect and resist some of the more obvious forms of trickery and demagoguery. Perhaps, more importantly, it should encourage us to be aware of the consequences of our selection of persuasion devices. After all, an individual's choice of persuasion tactics reveals much about his or her character and ability to think about the issues at hand. By giving close scrutiny to the ways of persuasion, we can promote those techniques that lead to a full and open discussion of the issues at hand while rebuking the antics of the demagogue. In large measure, the responsibility for raising Peitho's children is ours.

REFERENCES ||||||||||||||||||||||

Why We Wrote This Book

1. Walsh, L. E. (1997). *Firewall*. New York: Norton.

2. Statistics about the O. J. trial are from *U.S. News & World Report*, October 16, 1995.

3. Statistics about the Monica Lewinsky saga are from various reports in *Advertising Age* and *Brill's Content*.

1 Our Age of Propaganda

1. Colford, S. W. (1990, March 19). Athlete endorsers fouled by slayings. *Advertising Age*, p. 64.

2. Barrett, L. T. (1990, November 19). Race-baiting wins again. *Time*, p. 43.

3. Statistics are from recent issues of *American Demographics* and *Brill's Content*. Bogart, L. (1995). *Commercial culture*. New York: Oxford University Press; Jacobson, M. F., & Mazur, L. A. (1995). *Marketing madness*. Boulder, CO: Westview; Ries, A., & Trout, J. (1981). *Positioning: The battle for your mind*. New York: Warner; Aaker, D. A., & Myers, J. G. (1987). *Advertising management*. Englewood Cliffs, NJ: Prentice Hall. For a description of the mass media, see Pratkanis, A. R. (1997). The social psychology of mass communications: An American perspective. In D. F. Halpern & A. Voiskounsky (Eds.), *States of mind: American and post-Soviet perspectives on contemporary issues in psychology* (pp. 126–159). New York: Oxford University Press.

4. Holifield, E. B. (1989). *Era of persuasion: American thought and culture, 1521–1680*. Boston: Twayne.

5. Bahne, C. (1990). *The complete guide to Boston's Freedom Trail*. Cambridge, MA: Newtowne.

6. For an excellent history of advertising, see Fox, S. (1984). *The mirror makers*. New York: Morrow.

7. See Adams, H. F. (1916). *Advertising and its mental laws*. New York: Macmillan; Poffenberger, A. T. (1932). *Psychology in advertising*. New York: McGraw-Hill; Scott, W. D. (1917). *The psychology of advertising*. Boston: Small, Maynard, & Co.; Starch, D. (1923). *Principles of advertising*. New York: McGraw-Hill.

8. Creel, G. (1920). *How we advertised America*. New York: Harper & Brothers.

9. For a discussion of the nature of propaganda and persuasion in a democracy, see Pratkanis, A. R., & Turner, M. E. (1996). Persuasion and democracy: Strategies for increasing deliberative participation and enacting social change. *Journal of Social Issues, 52*, 187–205; Sproule, J. M. (1994). *Channels of propaganda*. Bloomington, IN: EDINFO; Sproule, J. M. (1997). *Propaganda and democracy: The American experience of media and mass persuasion*. New York: Cambridge University Press.

10. Marcus, J. (1992). *Mesoamerican writing systems*. Princeton, NJ: Princeton University Press.

11. Of course, only a limited number of Greeks (mostly males who owned property) could be citizens. For excellent discussions of persuasion in the Greek and Roman eras, see Billig, M. (1987). *Arguing and thinking*. New York: Cambridge University Press; Kennedy, G. A. (1963). *The art of persuasion in Greece*. Princeton, NJ: Princeton University Press; Kennedy, G. A. (1972). *The art of rhetoric in the Roman world*. Princeton, NJ: Princeton University Press; Kennedy, G. A. (1980). *Classical rhetoric*. Chapel Hill: University of North Carolina Press; Maccoby, N. (1963). The new science of rhetoric. In W. Schramm (Ed.), *The science of human communication*. New York: Basic Books.

12. Cicero. (1949). *De inventione*. Cambridge, MA: Loeb Classics, p. 3.

13. Ries & Trout (1981), see note 3.

14. See also Cialdini, R. B. (1984). *Influence*. New York: Morrow.

2 Mysterious Influence

1. For excellent histories of Mesmer's influence on American thought, see Fuller, R. C. (1982). *Mesmerism and the American cure of souls*. Philadelphia: University of Pennsylvania Press; Fuller, R. C. (1986). *Americans and the unconscious*. New York: Oxford University Press.

2. See Darnton, R. (1986). *Mesmerism and the end of the Enlightenment in France*. Cambridge, MA: Harvard University Press; Gould, S. J. (1991). *Bully for brontosaurus*. New York: Norton.

3. For a discussion of the facts concerning hypnosis, see Baker, R. A. (1990). *They call it hypnosis*. Buffalo, NY: Prometheus; Spanos, N. P., & Chaves, J. F. (Eds.). (1989). *Hypnosis: The cognitive-behavioral perspective*. Buffalo, NY: Prometheus.

4. Toennies, F. (1971). *On sociology: Pure, applied, and empirical.* Chicago: University of Chicago Press. (Original work published 1887.)

5. For an excellent review of the "magic bullet" theory of the mass media (or what has also been termed the "hypodermic needle" or "transmission belt" theory), see DeFleur, M. L., & Ball-Rokeach, S. (1989). *Theories of mass communication.* White Plains, NY: Longman.

6. Watson, J. B. (1919). *Psychology from the standpoint of a behaviorist.* Philadelphia: Lippincott.

7. Scott, W. D. (1917). *The psychology of advertising.* Boston: Small, Maynard, & Co.

8. Le Bon, G. (1960). *The crowd.* New York: Viking. (Original work published 1895.) For the first presentation of this hypothesis, see Sighele, S. (1891). *La folla delinquente* [*The criminal crowd*]. Turin, Italy: Fratelli Bocca. For a recent discussion, see McPhail, C. (1991). *The myth of the maddening crowd.* New York: Aldine de Gruyter; van Ginneken, J. (1992). *Crowds, psychology, and politics.* Cambridge: Cambridge University Press.

9. Packard, V. (1957). *The hidden persuaders.* New York: MacKay.

10. Dichter, E. (1964). *Handbook of consumer motivations.* New York: McGraw-Hill.

11. Lazarsfeld, P., Berelson, B., & Gaudet, H. (1948). *The people's choice.* New York: Columbia University Press. See also Berelson, B., Lazarsfeld, P., & McPhee, W. (1954). *Voting.* Chicago: University of Chicago Press.

12. Klapper, J. (1960). *The effects of mass communication.* Glencoe, IL: Free Press; McGuire, W. J. (1986). The myth of massive media impact: Savagings and salvagings. In G. Comstock (Ed.), *Public communication and behavior* (Vol. 1, pp. 175–257). San Diego, CA: Academic Press; Schudson, M. (1984). *Advertising, the uneasy persuasion.* New York: Basic Books.

13. Garcia, J., & Koelling, R. A. (1966). Relation of cue to consequence in avoidance learning. *Psychometric Science, 4,* 123–124; Festinger, L., & Carlsmith, J. M. (1959). Cognitive consequences of forced compliance. *Journal of Abnormal and Social Psychology, 58,* 203–210.

14. Marks, J. (1979). *The search for the "Manchurian candidate."* New York: Norton.

15. Politz, A. (1957). "Motivation research" from a research viewpoint. *Public Opinion Quarterly, 20,* 663–667.

16. Hovland, C. I., Lumsdaine, A. A., & Sheffield, F. D. (1949). *Experiments on mass communication.* Princeton, NJ: Princeton University Press; Hovland, C. I., Janis, I. L., & Kelley, H. H. (1953). *Communication and persuasion.* New Haven, CT: Yale University Press; Hovland, C. I. (1957). *The order of presentation in persuasion.* New Haven, CT: Yale University Press; Hovland, C. I., & Janis, I. L. (1959). *Personality and persuasibility.* New Haven, CT: Yale University Press; Hovland, C. I., & Rosenberg, M. J. (1960). *Attitude organization and change.* New Haven, CT: Yale University Press; Sherif, M., & Hovland, C. I. (1961). *Social judgment.* New Haven, CT: Yale University Press. For a review, see McGuire, W. J. (1969). The nature of attitudes and attitude change. In G. Lindzey & E. Aronson (Eds.), *Handbook of social psychology* (2nd ed., Vol. 3, pp. 136–314). Reading, MA: Addison-Wesley.

17. Gerbner, G., Gross, L., Morgan, M., & Signorielli, N. (1982). Living with television: The dynamics of the cultivation process. In J. Byrant & D. Zillman (Eds.), *Perspectives on media effects* (pp. 17–40). Hillsdale, NJ: Erlbaum; Iyengar, S., & Kinder, D. R. (1987). *News that matters.* Chicago: University of Chicago Press.

18. Jones, J. P. (1995). *When ads work: New proof that advertising triggers sales.* New York: Lexington.

19. Zaller, J. (1996). The myth of massive media impact revived: New support for a discredited idea. In D. C. Mutz, P. M. Sniderman, & R. A. Brody (Eds.), *Political persuasion and attitude change* (pp. 17–78). Ann Arbor: University of Michigan Press.

20. See Greenwald, A. G., Brock, T. C., & Ostrom, T. M. (Eds.). (1968). *Psychological foundations of attitudes.* New York: Academic Press; Petty, R. E., & Cacioppo, J. T. (1981). *Attitudes and persuasion: Classic and contemporary approaches.* Dubuque, IA: Brown; Petty, R. E., Ostrom, T. M., & Brock, T. C. (Eds.). (1981). *Cognitive responses in persuasion.* Hillsdale, NJ: Erlbaum; Petty, R. E., & Cacioppo, J. T. (1986). *Communication and persuasion.* New York: Springer-Verlag; Pratkanis, A. R., Breckler, S. J., & Greenwald, A. G. (Eds.). (1989). *Attitude structure and function.* Hillsdale, NJ: Erlbaum.

21. Liddy, G. G. (1980). *Will.* New York: St. Martin's.

22. For more details on these principles, see (especially chapters 4 and 5) Aronson, E. (1999). *Social animal* (8th ed.). New York: Worth.

[3] Mindless Propaganda, Thoughtful Persuasion

1. Burton, P. W. (1981). *Which ad pulled best?* Chicago: Crain; Caples, J. (1974). *Tested advertising methods.* Englewood Cliffs, NJ: Prentice

Hall; Loudon, D. L., & Della Bitta, A. J. (1984). *Consumer behavior.* New York: McGraw-Hill; Howard, D. J. (1990). The influence of verbal responses to common greetings on compliance behavior: The foot-in-the-mouth effect. *Journal of Applied Social Psychology, 20,* 1185–1196; Ogilvy, D. (1983). *Ogilvy on advertising.* New York: Crown.

2. Loudon & Della Bitta (1984), see note 1.

3. Langer, E., Blank, A., & Chanowitz, B. (1978). The mindlessness of ostensibly thoughtful action: The role of "placebic" information in interpersonal interaction. *Journal of Personality and Social Psychology, 36,* 635–642.

4. Preston, I. L. (1994). *The tangled web they weave: Truth, falsity, and advertisers.* Madison: University of Wisconsin Press.

5. Santos, M., Leve, C., & Pratkanis, A. R. (1994). Hey buddy, can you spare 17 cents? Mindful persuasion and the pique technique. *Journal of Applied Social Psychology, 24,* 755–764.

6. Petty, R. E., & Cacioppo, J. T. (1986). The elaboration likelihood model of persuasion. In L. Berkowitz (Ed.), *Advances in experimental social psychology* (Vol. 19, pp. 123–205). New York: Academic Press; Petty, R. E., & Cacioppo, J. T. (1986). *Communication and persuasion: Central and peripheral routes to attitude change.* New York: Springer-Verlag. See also Chaiken, S. (1980). Heuristic versus systematic information processing and the use of source versus message cues in persuasion. *Journal of Personality and Social Psychology, 39,* 752–766; Chaiken, S., Liberman, A., & Eagly, A. (1989). Heuristic versus systematic information processing within and beyond the persuasion context. In J. S. Uleman & J. A. Bargh (Eds.), *Unintended thought* (pp. 212–252). New York: Guilford.

7. Jamieson, K. H. (1992). *Dirty politics.* New York: Oxford University Press.

8. Petty, R. E., Cacioppo, J. T., & Goldman, R. (1981). Personal involvement as a determinant of argument-based persuasion. *Journal of Personality and Social Psychology, 41,* 847–855.

9. Fiske, S. T., & Taylor, S. E. (1991). *Social cognition.* New York: McGraw-Hill.

4 | The Rationalizing Animal

1. Festinger, L., Riecken, H. W., & Schachter, S. (1956). *When prophecy fails.* New York: Harper & Row.

2. Festinger, L. (1957). *A theory of cognitive dissonance.* Stanford, CA: Stanford University Press.

3. Aronson, E. (1969). The theory of cognitive dissonance: A current perspective. In L. Berkowitz (Ed.), *Advances in experimental social psychology* (Vol. 4, pp. 1–34). New York: Academic Press.

4. Pratkanis, A. R., & Turner, M. E. (1999). Groupthink and preparedness for the Loma Prieta earthquake: A social identity maintenance analysis of causes and preventions. In B. Mannix, M. Neale, & R. Wageman (Eds.), *Research on groups and teams: Groups in context* (Vol. 2, pp. 115–136). Greenwich, CT: JAI Press. For a laboratory demonstration, see Turner, M. E., Pratkanis, A. R., Probasco, P., & Leve, C. (1992). Threat, cohesion, and group effectiveness: Testing a social identity maintenance perspective on groupthink. *Journal of Personality and Social Psychology, 63,* 781–796.

5. Cialdini, R. B., & Schroeder, D. (1976). Increasing compliance by legitimizing paltry contributions: When even a penny helps. *Journal of Personality and Social Psychology, 34,* 599–604.

6. Harris, J. (1970). *Hiroshima: A study of science, politics, and the ethics of war.* Menlo Park, CA: Addison-Wesley.

7. For discussions on how to prevent and reduce the harmful effects of collective dissonance reduction, see Turner, M. E., & Pratkanis, A. R. (1994). Social identity maintenance prescriptions for preventing groupthink: Reducing identity protection and enhancing intellectual conflict. *International Journal of Conflict Management, 5,* 254–270; Turner, M. E., & Pratkanis, A. R. (1997). Mitigating groupthink by stimulating constructive conflict. In C. K. W. De Dreu & E. Van de Vliert (Eds.), *Using conflict in organizations* (pp. 53–71). Thousand Oaks, CA: Sage.

5 The Four Stratagems of Influence

1. For an excellent discussion of Lincoln's Gettysburg Address, see Wills, G. (1992). *Lincoln at Gettysburg: Words that remade America.* New York: Simon & Schuster. For a discussion of Abraham Lincoln's life and times, see Bursey, L. G. (1988). Abraham Lincoln. In W. C. Spragens (Ed.), *Popular images of American presidents* (pp. 67–103). New York: Greenwood; Hofstadter, R. (1948). *The American political tradition.* New York: Knopf; O'Reilly, K. (1995). *Nixon's piano: Presidents and racial politics from Washington to Clinton.* New York: Free Press; Tebbel, J., & Watts, S. M. (1985). *The press and the presidency.* New York: Oxford University Press; Zarefsky, D. (1990). *Lincoln, Douglas, and slavery: In the crucible of public debate.* Chicago: University of Chicago Press.

2. Quoted in Colford, P. D. (1993). *The Rush Limbaugh story.* New York: St. Martin's, p. 287. For a discussion of Rush Limbaugh's life

and influence tactics, see Brokaw, T., Fallows, J., Jamieson, K. H., Matalin, M., & Russert, T. (1997). Talk show democracy. *Press/Politics, 2,* 4–12; Colford, P. D. (1993). *The Rush Limbaugh story.* New York: St. Martin's; Franken, A. (1996). *Rush Limbaugh is a big fat idiot.* New York: Delacorte; Laufer, P. (1995). *Inside talk radio.* New York: Birch Lane Press; Limbaugh, R. (1992). *The way things ought to be.* New York: Pocket Books; Limbaugh, R. (1993). *See, I told you so.* New York: Pocket Books; Perkins, R. (1995). *Logic and Mr. Limbaugh.* Chicago: Open Court; Rendall, S., Naureckas, J., & Cohen, J. (1995). *The way things aren't: Rush Limbaugh's reign of error.* New York: New Press; Sturgeon, A. L., Blair, C., & Merriam, J., The Rush Limbaugh Show: A content analysis. Unpublished manuscript, University of California, Santa Cruz.

3. For details of the Ingram incident, see Ofshe, R., & Watters, E. (1994). *Making monsters.* New York: Charles Scribner's Sons; Wright, L. (1994). *Remembering Satan.* New York: Knopf.

4. Aristotle. (1954). *Rhetoric.* In W. Roberts (Trans.), *Aristotle, rhetoric and poetics.* New York: Modern Library.

5. For a fascinating example of the use of the Declaration of Independence to refute slavery, see Douglass, F. (1992). *Frederick Douglass's greatest speeches: The meaning of 4th of July for the Negro.* [Recorded by Fred Morsell]. (Cassette Recording No. TBM CDJ0011). New Canaan, CT: TBM Records. (Originally delivered on July 5, 1852.) Frederick Douglass, an ex-slave, developed many of the themes that later appeared in Lincoln's Gettysburg Address.

6. Quoted in Wills (1992), pp. 38–39, see note 1.

7. Wills (1992), p. 100, see note 1.

8. Quoted in Colford (1993), p. 156, see note 2.

9. For a description of how false memories can be created during therapy and the effect on families and communities, see Gardner, M. (1994). The tragedies of false memories. *Skeptical Inquirer, 18,* 464–470; Goldstein, E. (1994). *Confabulations.* Boca Raton, FL: Upton Books; Johnston, M. (1997). *Spectral evidence: The Ramona case: Incest, memory, and truth on trial in Napa Valley.* Boston: Houghton Mifflin; Loftus, E. F., & Ketcham, K. (1994). *The myth of repressed memories.* New York: St. Martin's; Ofshe & Watters (1994), see note 3; Spanos, N. P. (1997). *Multiple identities and memories: A sociocognitive perspective.* Washington, DC: American Psychological Association; Victor, J. S. (1993). *Satanic panic: The creation of a contemporary legend.* Chicago: Open Court; Wakefield, H., & Underwager, R. (1994). *Return of the furies.* Chicago: Open Court; Wright (1994), see note 3.

10. Bass, E., & Davis, L. (1988). *The courage to heal: A guide to women survivors of child sexual abuse.* New York: Harper & Row; Fredrickson, R. (1992). *Repressed memories.* New York: Fireside/Parkside; Smith, M., & Pazder, L. (1980). *Michelle remembers.* New York: Pocket Books.

11. Quoted in Victor (1993), p. 195, see note 9.

12. Loftus, E. F., & Ketcham, K. (1994), see note 9; Loftus, E. F. (1993). The reality of repressed memories. *American Psychologist, 48,* 518–537; Loftus, E. F., & Loftus, G. R. (1980). On the permanence of stored memories. *American Psychologist, 35,* 409–420.

13. Janes, L. M., & Olson, J. M. (2000). Jeer pressures: The behavioral effects of observing ridicule of others. *Personality and Social Psychology Bulletin, 26,* 474–485.

14. For a discussion of what is appropriate in therapy, see Kramer, J., & Alstad, D. (1993). *The guru papers: Mask of authoritarian power.* Berkeley, CA: North Atlantic Books/Frog Ltd.; Singer, M. T., & Lalich, J. (1996). *Crazy therapies.* San Francisco: Jossey-Bass.

15. Hobden, K. L., & Olson, J. M. (1994). From jest to antipathy: Disparagement humor as a source of dissonance-motivated attitude change. *Basic and Applied Social Psychology, 15,* 239–249; Maio, G. R., Olson, J. M., & Bush, J. E. (1997). Telling jokes that disparage social groups: Effects on the joke teller's stereotypes. *Journal of Applied Social Psychology, 27,* 1986–2000.

16. Quoted in Laufer (1995), p. 245, see note 2.

6 │ Words of Influence

1. Bem, D. (1970). *Beliefs, attitudes, and human affairs.* Belmont, CA: Brooks/Cole.

2. Levin, I. P., & Gaeth, G. J. (1988). How consumers are affected by the frame of attribute information before and after consuming the product. *Journal of Consumer Research, 15,* 374–378.

3. Lee, A. M., & Lee, E. B. (1939). *The fine art of propaganda.* New York: Harcourt, Brace; Institute for Propaganda Analysis. (1937). How to detect propaganda. *Propaganda Analysis, 1,* reprinted in Jackall, R. (1995). *Propaganda.* New York: New York University Press; Werkmeister, W. H. (1948). *An introduction to critical thinking.* Lincoln, NB: Johnsen.

4. Fox, S. (1984). *The mirror makers.* New York: Morrow.

5. For a history of the use of labels in American politics, see Green, D. (1987). *Shaping political consciousness: The language of politics in America from McKinley to Reagan.* Ithaca, NY: Cornell University Press.

6. Lutz, W. (1989). *Doublespeak.* New York: Harper & Row.

7. Bromley, D. G., & Silver, E. D. (1995). The Davidian tradition. In S. A. Wright (Ed.), *Armageddon in Waco* (pp. 43–72). Chicago: University of Chicago Press.

8. Orwell, G. (1949). *1984.* New York: New American Library, p. 246.

9. Allport, G. W. (1954). *The nature of prejudice.* Reading, MA: Addison-Wesley.

10. Bem, S. L., & Bem, D. J. (1973). Does sex-biased job advertising "aid and abet" sex discrimination? *Journal of Applied Social Psychology, 3,* 6–18. For more examples of the effects of sex bias in language, see Henley, N. (1989). Molehill or mountain? What we know and don't know about sex bias in language. In M. Crawford & M. Gentry (Eds.), *Gender and thought* (pp. 59–78). New York: Springer-Verlag.

11. Ries, A., & Trout, J. (1981). *Positioning: The battle for your mind.* New York: Warner.

12. Miller, R. L., Brickman, P., & Bolin, D. (1975). Attribution versus persuasion as a means for modifying behavior. *Journal of Personality and Social Psychology, 31,* 430–441.

13. Miller, Brickman, & Bolin (1975), see note 12.

14. Snyder, M., Tanke, E. D., & Berscheid, E. (1977). Social perceptions and interpersonal behavior: On the self-fulfilling nature of social stereotypes. *Journal of Personality and Social Psychology, 35,* 656–666.

15. Cited in Thomson, O. (1977). *Mass persuasion in history.* Edinburgh: Paul Harris, p. 111.

7 Pictures in Our Heads

1. Lippmann, W. (1922). *Public opinion.* New York: Harcourt, Brace.

2. Evans, W. (1996). Science and reason in film and television. *Skeptical Inquirer, 20,* 45–48, 58; Gerbner, G. (1987). Science on television: How it affects public conceptions. *Issues in Science and Technology, 3,* 109–115; Gerbner, G., Gross, L., Morgan, M., & Signorielli, N. (1986). Living with television: The dynamics of the cultivation process. In J. Bryant & D. Zillman (Eds.), *Perspectives on media effects* (pp. 17–40). Hillsdale, NJ: Erlbaum.

3. Quoted in *Newsweek,* December 6, 1982, p. 40.

4. Haney, C., & Manzolati, J. (1981). Television criminology: Network illusions on criminal justice realities. In E. Aronson (Ed.), *Readings about the social animal* (3rd ed., pp. 125–136). New York: Freeman.

5. See Heath, L. (1984). Impact of newspaper crime reports on fear of crime: Multimethodological investigation. *Journal of Personality and Social Psychology, 47,* 263–276; Linz, D. G., Donnerstein, E., & Penrod, S. (1988). Effects of long-term exposure to violent and sexually degrading depictions of women. *Journal of Personality and Social Psychology, 55,* 758–768; Lavine, H., Sweeney, D., & Wagner, S. H. (1999). Depicting women as sex objects in television advertising: Effects on body dissatisfaction. *Personality and Social Psychology Bulletin, 25,* 1049–1058; Hennigan, K., Heath, L., Wharton, J. D., Del Rosario, M., Cook, T. D., & Calder, B. (1982). Impact of the introduction of television on crime in the United States: Empirical findings and theoretical implications. *Journal of Personality and Social Psychology, 42,* 461–477.

6. Iyengar, S., & Kinder, D. R. (1987). *News that matters.* Chicago: University of Chicago Press.

7. Rogers, E. M., & Dearing, J. W. (1988). Agenda-setting research: Where has it been, where is it going? In J. A. Anderson (Ed.), *Communication yearbook 11* (pp. 555–594). Beverly Hills, CA: Sage. For an excellent review of research on agenda setting, see Dearing, J. W., & Rogers, E. M. (1996). *Agenda-setting.* Thousand Oaks, CA: Sage.

8. McCombs, M. E., & Shaw, D. L. (1972). The agenda setting function of mass media. *Public Opinion Quarterly, 36,* 176–187.

9. Quoted in Dilenschneider, R. L. (1990). *Power and influence.* New York: Prentice Hall.

10. Iyengar, S. (1991). *Is anyone responsible? How television frames political issues.* Chicago: University of Chicago Press. See also Strange, J. J., & Leung, C. C. (1999). How anecdotal accounts in news and fiction can influence judgments of a social problem's urgency, causes, and cures. *Personality and Social Psychology Bulletin, 25,* 436–449.

11. Hart, R. P. (1987). *The sound of leadership.* Chicago: University of Chicago Press.

12. Pratkanis, A. R. (1993). Propaganda and persuasion in the 1992 U.S. presidential election: What are the implications for a democracy? *Current World Leaders, 36,* 341–362.

13. Pfeffer, J. (1981). *Power in organizations.* Cambridge, MA: Ballinger.

14. Cited in Jacobson, M. F., & Mazur, L. A. (1995). *Marketing madness.* Boulder, CO: Westview, p. 15.

15. Cited in Rogers and Dearing (1988), see note 7.

8 Saddam Hussein: The Hitler of Baghdad?

1. For descriptions of metaphors used during the Persian Gulf war of 1991, see Conners, J. L. (1998). Hussein as enemy: The Persian Gulf war in political cartoons. *Press/Politics, 3,* 96–114; Rohrer, T. (1995). The metaphorical logic of (political) rape: The new wor(l)d order. *Metaphor and Symbolic Activity, 10,* 115–137.

2. Gilovich, T. (1981). Seeing the past in the present: The effects of associations to familiar events on judgments and decisions. *Journal of Personality and Social Psychology, 40,* 797–808.

3. For a discussion of metaphors and thought, see Bowers, J. W., & Osborn, M. M. (1966). Attitudinal effects of selected types of concluding metaphors in persuasive speeches. *Speech Monographs, 33,* 147–155; Gibbs, R. W. (1994). *The poetics of mind.* Cambridge: Cambridge University Press; Johnson, J. T., & Taylor, S. E. (1981). The effect of metaphor on political attitudes. *Basic and Applied Social Psychology, 2,* 305–316; Lakoff, G. (1987). *Women, fire, and dangerous things.* Chicago: University of Chicago Press; Lakoff, G., & Johnson, M. (1980). *Metaphors we live by.* Chicago: University of Chicago Press; Mio, J. S. (1996). Metaphor, politics, and persuasion. In J. S. Mio & A. N. Katz (Eds.), *Metaphor: Implications and applications* (pp. 127–146). Mahwah, NJ: Erlbaum.

4. Kennedy, P. (1991, January 24). A declining empire goes to war. *Wall Street Journal.*

5. Corbett, E. P. J. (1990). *Classical rhetoric for the modern student.* New York: Oxford University Press, p. 105.

6. Quoted in *U.S. News & World Report,* May 6, 1991, p. 19.

7. What did Bush win? *Newsweek,* May 13, 1991, p. 27.

8. For another example, see Lyndon Johnson's use of the war metaphor in his "war on poverty." The metaphor was useful for mobilizing the nation and stemming criticism, but it ultimately failed when poverty refused to surrender. See Zarefsky, D. (1986). *President Johnson's war on poverty.* Tuscaloosa: University of Alabama Press.

9 A Questionable Persuasion

1. Kahneman, D., & Tversky, A. (1984). Choices, values, and frames. *American Psychologist, 39,* 341–350.

2. Meyerowitz, B. E., & Chaiken, S. (1987). The effect of message framing on breast self-examination attitudes, intentions, and behavior. *Journal of Personality and Social Psychology, 52,* 500–510. For an

analysis of how message framing works in persuasion, see Smith, S. M., & Petty, R. E. (1996). Message framing and persuasion: A message processing analysis. *Personality and Social Psychology Bulletin, 22,* 257–268.

3. Lockerbie, B., & Borrelli, S. A. (1990). Question wording and public support for Contra aid, 1983–1986. *Public Opinion Quarterly, 54,* 195–208. See also Payne, S. L. (1951). *The art of asking questions.* Princeton, NJ: Princeton University Press. For other examples of how subtle changes in wording can produce dramatic changes in results, see Birnbaum, M. H. (1999). How to show that 9 > 221: Collect judgments in a between-subjects design. *Psychological Methods, 4,* 243–249; Salancik, G. R., & Conway, M. (1975). Attitude inferences from salient and relevant cognitive content about behavior. *Journal of Personality and Social Psychology, 32,* 829–840; Steele, C. M., & Ostrom, T. M. (1974). Perspective mediated attitude change: When is indirect persuasion more effective than direct persuasion? *Journal of Personality and Social Psychology, 29,* 737–741.

4. Mitofsky, W. J. (1999, May). Making sense of the polls. *Brill's Content,* p. 34.

5. Spence, G. (1986). *Trial by fire.* New York: Morrow.

6. Loftus, E. F., & Palmer, J. C. (1974). Reconstruction of automobile destruction: An example of the interaction between language and memory. *Journal of Verbal Learning and Verbal Behavior, 13,* 585–589; Loftus, E. F. (1977). Shifting human color memory. *Memory and Cognition, 5,* 696–699.

7. Institute for Propaganda Analysis. (1937). How to detect propaganda. *Propaganda Analysis, 1,* reprinted in Jackall, R. (1995). *Propaganda.* New York: New York University Press.

8. For an example of how to use rhetorical questions to prompt thought about an issue, see Petty, R. E., Cacioppo, J. T., & Heesacker, M. (1981). The use of rhetorical questions in persuasion: A cognitive response analysis. *Journal of Personality and Social Psychology, 40,* 432–440.

10 The Power of Decoys

1. Pratkanis, A. R., Farquhar, P. H., Silbert, S., & Hearst, J. (1989). Decoys produce contrast effects and alter choice probabilities. Unpublished manuscript, University of California, Santa Cruz. For additional examples, see Huber, J., Payne, J. W., & Puto, C. (1982). Adding asymmetrically dominated alternatives: Violations of regularity

and similarity. *Journal of Consumer Research, 9,* 90–98; Tyszka, T. (1983). Contextual multiattribute decision rules. In L. Sjoberg, T. Tyszka, & J. Wise (Eds.), *Human decision making.* Lund, Sweden: Doxa.

2. Kenrick, D. T., & Gutierres, S. E. (1980). Contrast effects in judgments of attractiveness: When beauty becomes a social problem. *Journal of Personality and Social Psychology, 38,* 131–140.

3. Sedikides, C., Ariely, D., & Olsen, N. (1999). Contextual and procedural determinants of partner selection: Of asymmetric dominance and prominence. *Social Cognition, 17,* 118–139.

11 The Psychology of Factoids

1. Johnson, D. M. (1945). The "phantom anesthetist" of Mattoon: A field study of mass hysteria. *Journal of Abnormal and Social Psychology, 40,* 175–186.

2. Mailer, N. (1973). *Marilyn.* New York: Galahad Books, p. 18.

3. For discussions of the psychology of rumors, see Allport, G. W., & Postman, L. (1947). *The psychology of rumor.* New York: Holt; Cantril, H. (1940). *The invasion from Mars.* New York: Harper & Row; Rosnow, R. L. (1980). Psychology of rumor reconsidered. *Psychological Bulletin, 87,* 578–591; Rosnow, R. L., & Fine, G. A. (1976). *Rumor and gossip.* New York: Elsevier; Shibutani, T. (1966). *Improvised news.* Indianapolis, IN: Bobbs-Merrill; Sifakis, C. (1993). *Hoaxes and scams.* New York: Facts on File.

4. Patterson, R. G. (1998). *The walrus was Paul.* New York: Simon & Schuster; Oxfeld, J. (2000, October). Paul was dead. *Brill's Content,* pp. 108–111, 144; Reeve, A. J. (1994). *Turn me on, dead man: The complete story of the Paul McCartney death hoax.* Ann Arbor, MI: Popular Culture Ink.

5. Bartholomew, R. E., & Howard, G. S. (1998). *UFOs & alien contact.* Amherst, NY: Prometheus; Klass, P. J. (1989). *UFO abductions: A dangerous game.* Amherst, NY: Prometheus; Korff, K. K. (1997). *The Roswell UFO crash: What they don't want you to know.* Amherst, NY: Prometheus.

6. Dezenhall, E. (1999). *Nail 'em.* Amherst, NY: Prometheus.

7. For details, see Dezenhall (1999), note 6.

8. Wegner, D. M., Wenzalaff, R., Kerker, R. M., & Beattie, A. E. (1981). Incrimination through innuendo: Can media questions become public answers? *Journal of Personality and Social Psychology, 40,* 822–832.

9. Rucker, D. D., & Pratkanis, A. R. (2001). Projection as an interpersonal influence tactic: On the effects of the pot calling the kettle black. *Personality and Social Psychology Bulletin.*

10. Webb, C. C., & Chapian, M. (1985). *Forgive me.* Old Tappan, NJ: F. H. Revell.

11. *Falsely accused.* (1999). [Videotape]. New York: A & E for the History Channel.

12. Kassin, S. M., Williams, L. N., & Saunders, C. L. (1990). Dirty tricks of cross-examination: The influence of conjectural evidence on the jury. *Law and Human Behavior, 14,* 373–384; Sue, S., Smith, R. E., & Caldwell, C. (1973). Effects of inadmissible evidence on the decisions of simulated jurors: A moral dilemma. *Journal of Applied Social Psychology, 3,* 345–353; Carroll, J. S., Kerr, N. L., Alfini, J. J., Weaver, F. M., MacCoun, R. J., & Feldman, V. (1986). Free press and fair trial: The role of behavioral research. *Law and Human Behavior, 10,* 187–201.

13. Kapferer, J. N. (1989). A mass poisoning rumor in Europe. *Public Opinion Quarterly, 53,* 467–481.

14. Loh, W. D. (1985). The evidence and trial procedure: The law, social policy, and psychological research. In S. M. Kassin & L. S. Wrightsman (Eds.), *The psychology of evidence and trial procedure* (pp. 13–39). Beverly Hills, CA: Sage.

15. See Francois, W. E. (1978). Mass media law and regulation. Columbus, OH: Grid; Preston, I. L. (1996). *The great American blow-up: Puffery in advertising and selling* (rev. ed.). Madison: University of Wisconsin Press.

12 The Credible Communicator

1. Aristotle. (1954). *Rhetoric.* In W. Roberts (Trans.), *Aristotle, rhetoric and poetics.* New York: Modern Library, p. 25.

2. Hovland, C., & Weiss, W. (1951). The influence of source credibility on communication effectiveness. *Public Opinion Quarterly, 15,* 635–650.

3. Aronson, E., & Golden, B. (1962). The effect of relevant and irrelevant aspects of communicator credibility on opinion change. *Journal of Personality, 30,* 135–146.

4. White, P. H., & Harkins, S. G. (1994). Race of source effects in the elaboration likelihood model. *Journal of Personality and Social Psychology, 67,* 790–807. For additional details, see Petty, R. E., Fleming,

M. A., & White, P. H. (1999). Stigmatized sources and persuasion: Prejudice as a determinant of argument scrutiny. *Journal of Personality and Social Psychology, 76*, 19–34.

5. Pratkanis, A. R. (2001). Propaganda and deliberative persuasion: The implications of Americanized mass media for established and emerging democracies. In W. Wosinski, R. B. Cialdini, J. Reykowski, & D. W. Barrett (Eds.), *The practice of social influence in multiple cultures* (pp. 259–285). Mahwah, NJ: Erlbaum.

6. Walton, D. N. (1997). *Appeal to expert opinion: Arguments from authority.* University Park: Pennsylvania State University Press.

7. Fromm, E. (1997). What I do not like about contemporary society. In *On being human.* New York: Continuum. (Original work published 1972.)

13 Breakfast of Champions, Junk Food for the Self

1. Mills, J., & Aronson, E. (1965). Opinion change as a function of communicator's attractiveness and desire to influence. *Journal of Personality and Social Psychology, 1*, 173–177.

2. Eagly, A., & Chaiken, S. (1975). An attribution analysis of the effect of communicator characteristics on opinion change: The case of communicator attractiveness. *Journal of Personality and Social Psychology, 32*, 136–144.

3. Herbert, B. (1996, August 23). Teen smokers, read this. *New York Times*.

4. Petty, R. E., Cacioppo, J. T., & Schumann, D. (1983). Central and peripheral routes to advertising effectiveness: The moderating role of involvement. *Journal of Consumer Research, 10*, 134–148.

14 How Do You Persuade if Everyone Knows You Are Untrustworthy, Unbelievable, and Disliked?

1. Oliver, R. T. (1971). *Communication and culture in ancient India and China.* Syracuse, NY: Syracuse University Press.

2. Walster (Hatfield), E., Aronson, E., & Abrahams, D. (1966). On increasing the persuasiveness of a low prestige communicator. *Journal of Experimental Social Psychology, 2*, 325–342.

3. Eagly, A., Wood, W., & Chaiken, S. (1978). Causal inferences about communicators and their effect on opinion change. *Journal of Personality and Social Psychology, 36*, 424–435.

4. *Santa Cruz Sentinel*, January 13, 1987, p. A8.

5. Herbert, B. (1996, August 23). Teen smokers, read this. *New York Times*.

6. Oliver (1971), see note 1.

7. Walster (Hatfield), E., & Festinger, L. (1962). The effectiveness of "overheard " persuasive communications. *Journal of Abnormal and Social Psychology, 65*, 395–402.

[15] The Manufacture of Credibility

1. McGinness, J. (1970). *The selling of the president: 1968.* New York: Pocket Books, p. 160.

2. Quoted in *Portraits of American presidents.* (no date). (Version 1.0). Great Bear [CD-ROM].

3. Riechmann, D. (1999, July 23). Praise for Nixon talk was phony, ex-aide recalls. *San Jose Mercury News*, p. 19A.

4. Jamieson, K. H. (1984). *Packaging the presidency.* New York: Oxford University Press.

5. Ansolabehere, S., Behr, R., & Iyengar, S. (1993). *The media game.* New York: Macmillan.

6. Butterfield, S. (1985). *Amway: The cult of free enterprise.* Boston: South End Press.

7. Boorstin, D. J. (1961). *The image: A guide to pseudo-events in America.* New York: Atheneum.

8. Shapiro, R. J. (1994, July 10). Tricks of the trade: How to use the media to your advantage. *San Jose Mercury News*, pp. 1I, 4I. (Reprint of a 1993 article appearing in *Champion* magazine.)

9. Saffir, L. (1993). *Power public relations.* Lincolnwood, IL: NTC Business Books.

10. Ailes, R. (1988). *You are the message.* New York: Doubleday, p. 81.

11. Dilenschneider, R. L. (1990). *Power and influence.* New York: Prentice Hall.

12. Matalin, M., & Carville, J. (1994). *All's fair: Love, war, and running for president.* New York: Simon & Schuster/Random House.

13. Once elected, you can hire an opinion pollster to make sure your image stays strong and positive; for an excellent discussion of how U.S. presidents use opinion polls, see Brace, P., & Hinckley, B. (1992). *Follow the leader.* New York: Basic Books.

16 Prizefighter Slays Eleven with One Look: The Influence of Mass Media Models

1. See *National Examiner,* January 2, 1996, pp. 26–27.

2. Phillips, D. P. (1986). Natural experiments on the effects of mass media violence on fatal aggression: Strengths and weaknesses of a new approach. In L. Berkowitz (Ed.), *Advances in experimental social psychology* (Vol. 19, pp. 207–250). New York: Academic Press.

3. Bandura, A. (1973). *Aggression: A social learning analysis.* Englewood Cliffs, NJ: Prentice Hall.

4. For discussions of the causes of violence and aggression, see Baron, R. A. (1977). *Human aggression.* New York: Plenum; Berkowitz, L. (1993). *Aggression: Its causes, consequences, and control.* New York: McGraw-Hill; Geen, R. G. (1990). *Human aggression.* Pacific Grove, CA: Brooks/Cole.

5. Schneider, C. (1987). *Children's television: The art, the business, and how it works.* Lincolnwood, IL: NTC Business Books.

6. Bryan, J. H., & Test, M. A. (1967). Models and helping: Naturalistic studies in aiding behavior. *Journal of Personality and Social Psychology, 6,* 400–407.

7. Baron, R. A., & Kepner, C. R. (1970). Model's behavior and attraction toward the model as determinants of adult aggresssive behavior. *Journal of Personality and Social Psychology, 14,* 335–344.

8. Bryan, J. H., Redfield, J., & Mader, S. (1971). Words and deeds about altruism and the subsequent reinforcement power of the model. *Child Development, 42,* 1501–1508; Bryan, J. H., & Walbek, N. H. (1970). Preaching and practicing generosity: Children's actions and reactions. *Child Development, 41,* 329–353.

9. Aronson, E. (2000). *Nobody left to hate: Teaching compassion after Columbine.* New York: Worth.

10. For a description of mass media role models and violence, see *National Television Violence Study (1997–1998)* (Vols. 1–3). Thousand Oaks, CA: Sage.

17 Packages

1. Which cereal for breakfast? (1981, February). *Consumer Reports,* pp. 68–75.

2. Comparison based on *Eating to lower your high blood cholesterol.* (1987). NIH Publication No. 87-2920. Washington, DC: U.S.

Department of Health and Human Services. Saturated fats, such as animal fat, and some vegetable fats, such as coconut oil, cocoa butter, palm oil, and hydrogenated oil, have been shown to raise cholesterol levels. Cereal manufacturers sometimes use such fats, especially coconut, palm, and hydrogenated oils, in their products. Some manufacturers are in the process of reformulating their cereals to remove such oils, so check the label before making a final decision.

3. Lempinen, E. W. (1996, May 17). All-natural smokes in a health-conscious market. *San Francisco Chronicle*, pp. 1, A6.

4. Caples, J. (1974). *Tested advertising methods.* Englewood Cliffs, NJ: Prentice Hall; Ogilvy, D. (1983). *Ogilvy on advertising.* New York: Crown; Petty, R. E., & Cacioppo, J. T. (1984). The effects of involvement on responses to argument quantity and quality: Central and peripheral routes to persuasion. *Journal of Personality and Social Psychology, 46,* 69–81.

5. Axsom, D., Yates, S., & Chaiken, S. (1987). Audience response as a heuristic cue in persuasion. *Journal of Personality and Social Psychology, 53,* 30–40.

6. See, for example, Leippe, M. R., Manion, A. P., & Romanczyk, A. (1992). Eyewitness persuasion: How and how well do fact finders judge the accuracy of adults' and children's memory reports. *Journal of Personality and Social Psychology, 63,* 191–197.

7. Cooley, A., Bess, C., & Rubin-Jackson, M. (1995). *Madam foreman: A rush to judgment?* Beverly Hills, CA: Dove, p. 97.

8. Fierman, J. (1991, June 3). The big muddle in green marketing. *Fortune,* pp. 91–101; Hume, S. (1991, January 29). McDonald's. *Advertising Age,* p. 32.

9. Pratkanis, A. R. (1989). The cognitive representation of attitudes. In A. R. Pratkanis, S. J. Breckler, & A. G. Greenwald (Eds.), *Attitude structure and function* (pp. 71–98). Hillsdale, NJ: Erlbaum.

10. For a discussion of when it is appropriate to use heuristics, see Gigerenzer, G., Todd, P. M., & the ABC Research Group. (1999). *Simple heuristics that make us smart.* New York: Oxford University Press.

18 Self-Sell

1. Lewin, K. (1947). Group decision and social change. In T. M. Newcomb & E. L. Hartley (Eds.), *Readings in social psychology* (pp. 330–344). New York: Holt.

2. For a detailed discussion of self-persuasion, see Aronson, E. (1999). The power of self-persuasion. *American Psychologist, 54,* 875–884.

3. Boninger, D. S., Brock, T. S., Cook, T. D., Gruder, C. L., & Romer, D. (1990). Discovery of reliable attitude change persistence resulting from a transmitter tuning set. *Psychological Science, 1,* 268–271.

4. Gregory, W. L., Cialdini, R. B., & Carpenter, K. M. (1982). Self-relevant scenarios as mediators of likelihood estimates and compliance: Does imagining make it so? *Journal of Personality and Social Psychology, 43,* 89–99.

19 Naked Attics and Neighborhood War Heroes: On Vividness in Communication

1. Gonzales, M. H., Aronson, E., & Costanzo, M. (1988). Increasing the effectiveness of energy auditors: A field experiment. *Journal of Applied Social Psychology, 18,* 1049–1066; Aronson, E. (1990). Applying social psychology to prejudice reduction and energy conservation. *Personality and Social Psychology Bulletin, 16,* 118–132.

2. Another condition is when the vivid appeal distracts attention from an argument by being irrelevant to the issues at hand or causes the message recipient to think about issues unrelated or counter to the goal of the communicator. See, for example, Frey, K. P., & Eagly, A. H. (1993). Vividness can undermine the persuasiveness of messages. *Journal of Personality and Social Psychology, 65,* 32–44; Smith, S. M., & Shaffer, D. R. (2000). Vividness can undermine or enhance message processing: The moderating role of vividness congruency. *Personality and Social Psychology Bulletin, 26,* 769–779.

3. Nisbett, R., & Ross, L. (1980). *Human inference: Strategies and shortcomings of social judgment.* Englewood Cliffs, NJ: Prentice Hall. (We also borrowed their definition of vividness used at the beginning of this chapter.) For an experimental demonstration of their example, see Herr, P. M., Kardes, F. R., & Kim, J. (1991). Effects of word-of-mouth and product-attribute information on persuasion: An accessibility-diagnosticity perspective. *Journal of Consumer Research, 17,* 454–462.

4. Jamieson, K. H. (1988). *Eloquence in an electronic age: The transformation of political speechmaking.* Oxford: Oxford University Press.

5. Cited in Nisbett & Ross (1980), see note 3.

6. Carville, J. (1996). *We're right, they're wrong.* New York: Simon & Schuster/Random House.

7. It should be noted that many of the jurors began to see the lawyers' theatrics as cheap tricks that were at best annoying and at worst indicated that they thought the jurors could not be trusted with the facts. This is especially true of the prosecution case, which failed to link their vivid images with a compelling story of how Simpson did it (i.e., a specific timeline for how he moved from Bundy to Rockingham after the murders). Thus, as with the Dukakis tank ad, these vivid images may not have been effective and may even have backfired with the highly involved jurors, although they made for wonderfully entertaining TV. For a description of jurors' reactions, see Cooley, A., Bess, C., & Rubin-Jackson, M. (1995). *Madam Foreman: A rush to judgment?* Beverly Hills, CA: Dove.

8. Spence, G. (1995). *How to argue and win every time.* New York: St. Martin's, p. 130.

9. Ibayan, L. F., & Pratkanis, A. R. (1996). The effects of victim impact statements on jury decision making. Unpublished manuscript, University of California, Santa Cruz.

10. For an alternative perspective on the role played by the mass media in the Vietnam war, see Hallin, D. C. (1989). *The "uncensored war": The media and Vietnam.* Berkeley: University of California Press.

[20] Why Do They Keep Repeating the Same Ads?

1. These examples are found in Fox, S. (1984). *The mirror makers.* New York: Morrow.

2. Zajonc, R. B. (1968). The attitudinal effects of mere exposure. *Journal of Personality and Social Psychology (monograph supplement), 9*, 1–27.

3. Grush, J., McKeough, K., & Ahlering, R. (1978). Extrapolating laboratory exposure research to actual political elections. *Journal of Personality and Social Psychology, 36,* 257–270; Grush, J. E. (1980). Impact of candidate expenditures, regionality, and prior outcomes on the 1976 presidential primaries. *Journal of Personality and Social Psychology, 38,* 337–347.

4. Kinder, D. R., & Sears, D. O. (1985). Public opinion and political action. In G. Lindzey & E. Aronson (Eds.), *Handbook of social psychology* (3rd ed., pp. 659–742). New York: Random House.

5. Quoted in Herzstein, R. E. (1987). *The war that Hitler won.* New York: Paragon House, p. 31.

6. Arkes, H. R., Boehm, L. E., & Xu, G. (1991). Determinants of judged validity. *Journal of Experimental Social Psychology, 27,* 576–605; Bacon, F. T. (1979). Credibility of repeated statements: Memory for trivia. *Journal of Experimental Psychology: Human Learning and Memory, 5,* 241–252; Boehm, L. E. (1994). The validity effect: A search for mediating variables. *Personality and Social Psychology Bulletin, 20,* 285–293; Hasher, L., Goldstein, D., & Toppino, T. (1977). Frequency and the conference of referential validity. *Journal of Verbal Learning and Verbal Behavior, 16,* 107–112; Schwartz, M. (1982). Repetition and rated truth value of statements. *American Journal of Psychology, 95,* 393–407.

7. Described in Harrison, A. A. (1977). Mere exposure. In L. Berkowitz (Ed.), *Advances in experimental social psychology* (Vol. 10, pp. 39–83). New York: Academic Press.

8. Described in Cacioppo, J. T., & Petty, R. E. (1985). Central and peripheral routes to persuasion: The role of message repetition. In A. Mitchell & L. Alwitt (Eds.), *Psychological processes and advertising effects* (pp. 91–111). Hillsdale, NJ: Erlbaum. For a recent extension, see Schumann, D. W., Petty, R. E., & Clemons, D. S. (1990). Predicting the effectiveness of different strategies of advertising variation: A test of the repetition-variation hypotheses. *Journal of Consumer Research, 17,* 192–202.

21 If You Have Nothing to Say—Distract Them

1. In general, researchers have found that a positive mood can result in positive evaluations of an object directly (when we have little motivation to process information) and by making our thoughts more positive (when we are motivated to think). In addition, most of us want to stay in a positive mood. Thus, positive affect produces more message scrutiny when message processing is useful for maintaining the mood and less processing when scrutiny may put us in a less positive mood. For an excellent discussion of positive affect and persuasion, see Petty, R. E., Schumann, D. W., Richman, S. A., & Strathman, A. J. (1993). Positive mood and persuasion: Different roles for affect under high- and low-elaboration conditions. *Journal of Personality and Social Psychology, 64,* 5–20; Wegener, D. T., Petty, R. E., & Smith, S. M. (1995). Positive mood can increase or decrease message scrutiny: The hedonic contingency view of mood and message processing. *Journal of Personality and Social Psychology, 40,* 822–832.

2. Festinger, L., & Maccoby, N. (1964). On resistance to persuasive communications. *Journal of Abnormal and Social Psychology, 68,* 359–366.

3. Osterhouse, R. A., & Brock, T. C. (1970). Distraction increases yielding to propaganda by inhibiting counterarguing. *Journal of Personality and Social Psychology, 15,* 344–358.

4. Ogilvy, D. (1983). *Ogilvy on advertising.* New York: Crown.

5. Petty, R. E., Wells, G. L., & Brock, T. C. (1976). Distraction can enhance and reduce yielding to propaganda: Thought disruption versus effort justification. *Journal of Personality and Social Psychology, 34,* 874–884.

6. Moore, D. L., Hausknecht, D., & Thamodaran, K. (1986). Time compression, response opportunity, and persuasion. *Journal of Consumer Research, 13,* 85–99.

22 If You Want to Gain an Inch, Ask for a Mile—Sometimes!

1. Spence, G. (1995). *How to argue and win every time.* New York: St. Martin's, p. 63. See also Spence, G. (1986). *Trial by fire.* New York: Morrow.

2. Zimbardo, P. (1960). Involvement and communication discrepancy as determinants of opinion conformity. *Journal of Abnormal and Social Psychology, 60,* 86–94.

3. Hovland, C., Harvey, O. J., & Sherif, M. (1957). Assimilation and contrast effects in reaction to communication and attitude change. *Journal of Abnormal and Social Psychology, 55,* 244–252.

4. Aronson, E., Turner, J., & Carlsmith, J. M. (1963). Communication credibility and communication discrepancy as determinants of opinion change. *Journal of Abnormal and Social Psychology, 67,* 31–36.

23 Protagoras' Ideal: One-Sided Puffery versus Two-Sided Debate

1. Herodotus. (1942). *The Persian Wars* (G. Rawlinson, Trans.). New York: Modern Library, p. 499.

2. Aristotle. (1954). *Rhetoric.* In W. Roberts (Trans.), *Aristotle, rhetoric and poetics.* New York: Modern Library, p. 185.

3. Lippmann, W. (1939, August). The indispensable opposition. *The Atlantic,* pp. 186–190.

4. For a discussion of comparative advertising, see Aaker, D., & Myers, J. G. (1986). *Advertising management.* Englewood Cliffs, NJ: Prentice Hall, pp. 305–310.

5. Fox, S. (1984). *The mirror makers.* New York: Morrow.

6. Ries, A., & Trout, J. (1981). *Positioning: The battle for your mind.* New York: Warner.

7. Hovland, C. I., Lumsdaine, A. A., & Sheffield, F. D. (1949). *Experiments on mass communications.* Princeton, NJ: Princeton University Press.

8. Pfau, M., & Kenski, H. C. (1990). *Attack politics.* New York: Praeger. See also Jamieson, K. H. (1992). *Dirty politics.* New York: Oxford University Press.

9. Pratkanis, A. R. (1993). Propaganda and persuasion in the 1992 U.S. presidential election: What are the implications for a democracy? *Current World Leaders, 35,* 341–362.

24 The Fear Appeal

1. Quoted in Faust, C. H., & Johnson, T. H. (1935). *Jonathan Edwards.* New York: American Book, p. 161.

2. Taken from speeches given by Hitler in Munich on April 12, 1922, April 20, 1923, and May 23, 1926, and in Berlin on May 10, 1933. For full text, see Prange, G. W. (Ed.). (1944). *Hitler's words.* Washington, DC: American Council on Public Affairs, especially pp. 71, 251–254; Baynes, N. H. (1942). *The speeches of Adolf Hitler April 22–August 1939.* New York: Oxford University Press, especially p. 59. We thank those who wrote to us pointing out that the quote from Hitler used in our first edition may not actually have been spoken by him (although the anti-Communist and anti-Jewish sentiments were certainly major components of Hitler's rhetoric). Interested readers should see George, J., & Wilcox, L. (1992). *Nazis, Communists, and others on the fringe.* Buffalo, NY: Prometheus.

3. Sapolsky, H. M. (Ed.). (1986). *Consuming fears.* New York: Basic Books.

4. Dolinski, D., & Nawrat, R. (1998). "Fear-then-relief" procedure for producing compliance: Beware when the danger is over. *Journal of Experimental Social Psychology, 34,* 27–50.

5. Leventhal, H. (1970). Findings and theory in the study of fear communications. In L. Berkowitz (Ed.), *Advances in experimental social psychology* (Vol. 5, pp. 119–186). New York: Academic Press.

6. Chu, G. C. (1966). Fear arousal, efficacy and imminency. *Journal of Personality and Social Psychology, 4,* 517–524; Rogers, R. W. (1983). Cognitive and physiological processes in fear appeals and attitude change: A revised theory of protection motivation. In J. T. Cacioppo &

R. E. Petty (Eds.), *Social psychophysiology: A sourcebook* (pp. 153–176). New York: Guilford.

25 | The Granfalloon Technique

1. For reviews and discussion, see Hogg, M. A., & Abrams, D. (1988). *Social identifications.* New York: Routledge; Tajfel, H. (1981). *Human groups and social categories.* Cambridge: Cambridge University Press; Turner, J. C. (1987). *Rediscovering the social group.* New York: Blackwell.

2. Vonnegut, K. (1963). *Cat's cradle.* New York: Dell.

3. For illustrative studies, see Wetherell, M. (1983). Social identification, social influence, and group polarization. Unpublished doctoral dissertation, University of Bristol, Bristol, UK; Abrams, D., Wetherell, M., Cochrane, S., Hogg, M. A., & Turner, J. C. (1990). Knowing what to think by knowing who you are: Self-categorization and the nature of norm formation, conformity, and group polarization. *British Journal of Social Psychology, 29,* 97–119.

4. Cialdini, R. B., Borden, R. J., Thorne, A., Walker, M. R., Freeman, S., & Sloan, L. R. (1976). Basking in reflected glory: Three (football) field studies. *Journal of Personality and Social Psychology, 36,* 463–476.

5. Cialdini, R. B., Finch, J. F., & De Nicholas, M. E. (1990). Strategic self-presentation: The indirect route. In M. J. Cody & M. L. McLaughlin (Eds.), *The psychology of tactical communication* (pp. 194–206). Clevedon, UK: Multilingual Matters; Finch, J. F., & Cialdini, R. B. (1989). Another indirect tactic of (self-) image management: Boosting. *Personality and Social Psychology Bulletin, 15,* 222–232.

6. Miller, D. T., Downs, J. S., & Prentice, D. A. (1998). Minimum conditions for the creation of a unit relationship: The social bond between birthdaymates. *European Journal of Social Psychology, 28,* 475–481.

7. See, for example, Weiss, M. J. (1988). *The clustering of America.* New York: Harper & Row; Mitchell, A. (1983). *The nine American lifestyles.* New York: Warner; Riche, M. F. (1989, July). Psychographics for the 1990s. *American Demographics,* pp. 24–31, 53–55.

8. *Don't fall for a telephone line.* (1997). [Videotape]. Washington, DC: American Association of Retired Persons.

9. Jamieson, K. H. (1988). *Eloquence in an electronic age.* Oxford: Oxford University Press.

10. For descriptions, see Abelman, R., & Neuendorf, K. (1985). How religious is religious television programming? *Journal of*

Communication, 35, 98–110; Hoover, S. M. (1988). *Mass media religion: The social sources of the electronic church.* Beverly Hills, CA: Sage.

11. For a discussion of how pseudoscience—those folks who sell everything from crystals to cancer cures to opportunities to hear the wisdom of a channeled dolphin—creates and uses granfalloons, see Pratkanis, A. R. (1995). How to sell a pseudoscience. *Skeptical Inquirer, 19,* 19–25.

26 Guilt Sells

1. Kassin, S. M., & Keichel, K. L. (1996). The social psychology of false confessions: Compliance, internalization, and confabulation. *Psychological Science, 7,* 125–128.

2. For reviews and discussions of criminal confessions, see Gudjonsson, G. (1992). *The psychology of interrogations, confessions, and testimony.* New York: Wiley; Inbau, F. E., Reid, J. E., & Buckley, J. P. (1986). *Criminal interrogation and confessions.* Baltimore: Williams & Wilkins; Lassiter, G. D., Geers, A. L., Munhall, P. J., Handley, I. M., & Beers, M. J. (in press). Videotaped confessions: Is guilt in the eye of the camera? In M. P. Zanna (Ed.), *Advances in experimental social psychology.* San Diego, CA: Academic Press; Leo, R. A. (1996). Miranda's revenge: Police interrogation as a confidence game. *Law and Society, 30,* 259–288; Rogge, O. J. (1959). *Why men confess.* New York: Nelson; Shuy, R. W. (1998). *The language of confession, interrogation, and deception.* Thousand Oaks, CA: Sage; Wrightsman, L. S., & Kassin, S. M. (1993). *Confessions in the courtroom.* Newbury Park, CA: Sage; Zimbardo, P. G. (1968). Coercion and compliance: The psychology of police confessions. In R. Perruci & M. Pilisuk (Eds.), *The triple revolution: Social problems in depth* (pp. 550–570). Boston: Little, Brown. We should also note that some police interrogation guides strongly recommend against making false statements about possessing incriminating evidence if none has been obtained; see Macdonald, J. M., & Michaud, D. L. (1992). *Criminal interrogation.* Denver, CO: Apache.

3. *I Confess.* (1996). [Videotape]. New York: A & E for the History Channel.

4. Carlsmith, J. M., & Gross, A. E. (1969). Some effects of guilt on compliance. *Journal of Personality and Social Psychology, 11,* 232–239. See also Freedman, J. L., Wallington, S. A., & Bless, E. (1967). Compliance without pressure: The effect of guilt. *Journal of Personality and Social Psychology, 7,* 117–124.

5. Kelln, B. R. C., & Ellard, J. H. (1999). An equity theory analysis of the impact of forgiveness and retribution on transgressor compliance. *Personality and Social Psychology Bulletin, 25,* 864–872.

6. Davis, K., & Jones, E. E. (1960). Changes in interpersonal perception as a means of reducing dissonance. *Journal of Abnormal and Social Psychology, 61,* 402–410. See also Glass, D. (1964). Changes in liking as a means of reducing cognitive discrepancies between self-esteem and aggression. *Journal of Personality, 32,* 531–549.

27 What Is the Influence of One Flower Given?

1. For a history, see Rochford, E. B. (1985). *Hare Krishna in America.* New Brunswick, NJ: Rutgers University Press.

2. Cialdini, R. B. (1984). *Influence.* New York: Morrow.

3. For a discussion of the use of norms in social control, see Cialdini, R. B., Kallgren, C. A., & Reno, R. R. (1991). A focus theory of normative conduct: A theoretical refinement and reevaluation of the role of norms in human behavior. In M. P. Zanna (Ed.), *Advances in experimental social psychology* (Vol. 24, pp. 201–234). San Diego, CA: Academic Press; Kallgren, C. A., Reno, R. R., & Cialdini, R. B. (2000). A focus theory of normative conduct: When norms do and do not affect behavior. *Personality and Social Psychology Bulletin, 26,* 1002–1012.

4. Regan, D. T. (1971). Effects of a favor and liking on compliance. *Journal of Experimental Social Psychology, 7,* 627–639. For another demonstration of the power of the norm of reciprocity, see Cialdini, R. B., Green, B. L., & Rusch, A. J. (1992). When tactical pronouncements of change become real change: The case of reciprocal persuasion. *Journal of Personality and Social Psychology, 63,* 30–40.

5. Cialdini, R. B., & Ascani, K. (1976). Test of a concession procedure for inducing verbal, behavioral, and further compliance with a request to give blood. *Journal of Applied Psychology, 61,* 295–300.

6. Burger, J. M. (1986). Increasing compliance by improving the deal: The that's-not-all technique. *Journal of Personality and Social Psychology, 51,* 277–283.

28 The Committed Heart

1. Freedman, J., & Fraser, S. (1966). Compliance without pressure: The foot-in-the-door technique. *Journal of Personality and Social Psychology, 4,* 195–202.

2. Pliner, P., Hart, H., Kohl, J., & Saari, D. (1974). Compliance without pressure: Some further data on the foot-in-the-door technique. *Journal of Experimental Social Psychology, 10,* 17–22.

3. Greenwald, A. G., Carnot, C. G., Beach, R., & Young, B. (1987). Increasing voting behavior by asking people if they expect to vote. *Journal of Applied Psychology, 72,* 315–318.

4. Cialdini, R. B., Cacioppo, J. T., Bassett, R., & Miller, J. (1978). Low-ball procedure for compliance: Commitment then cost. *Journal of Personality and Social Psychology, 36,* 463–476.

5. McNamara, R. S. (1996). *In retrospect.* New York: Vintage, p. 29.

6. McNamara (1996), pp. 174–175, see note 5.

7. Pentagon papers: The secret war. (1971, June 28). *Time,* p. 12.

8. White, R. (1971, November). Selective inattention. *Psychology Today,* pp. 47–50, 78–84. For an excellent discussion of the social psychology of decision making in the Vietnam war, see White, R. K. (1968). *Nobody wanted war.* Garden City, NY: Doubleday.

9. For a discussion of the ease of commitments, see Salancik, G. R. (1977). Commitment is too easy. *Organizational Dynamics, 6,* 62–80.

29 To Practice What You Preach

1. Aronson, E., Fried, C., & Stone, J. (1991). Overcoming denial and increasing the intention to use condoms through the induction of hypocrisy. *American Journal of Public Health, 81,* 1636–1638; Stone, J., Aronson, E., Crain, A. L., Winslow, M. P., & Fried, C. B. (1994). Inducing hypocrisy as a means of encouraging young adults to use condoms. *Personality and Social Psychology Bulletin, 20,* 116–128.

2. Fried, C. B., & Aronson, E. (1995). Hypocrisy, misattribution, and dissonance reduction. *Personality and Social Psychology Bulletin, 21,* 925–933.

3. Dickerson, C. A., Thibodeau, R., Aronson, E., & Miller, D. (1992). Using cognitive dissonance to encourage water conservation. *Journal of Applied Social Psychology, 22,* 841–854.

4. Franken, A. (1996). *Rush Limbaugh is a big fat idiot.* New York: Delacorte, p. 71.

5. Batson, C. D., Kobrynowicz, D., Dinnerstein, J. L., Kampf, H. C., & Wilson, A. D. (1997). In a very different voice: Unmasking moral hypocrisy. *Journal of Personality and Social Psychology, 72,* 1335–1348; Batson, C. D., Thompson, E. R., Seuferling, G., Whitney, H., &

Strongman, J. A. (1999). Moral hypocrisy: Appearing moral to oneself without being so. *Journal of Personality and Social Psychology, 77,* 525–537.

[30] The Psychology of Scarcity and the Mystique of Phantoms

1. Volokh, A. (1983). *The art of Russian cuisine.* New York: Collier.

2. See Fromkin, H. L., Olson, J. C., Dipboye, R. L., & Barnaby, D. A. (1971). A commodity theory analysis of consumer preferences for scarce products. Paper presented at the annual meeting of the American Psychological Association, Washington, DC; Worchel, S., Lee, J., & Adewole, A. (1975). Effects of supply and demand on ratings of object value. *Journal of Personality and Social Psychology, 32,* 906–914; Knishinsky, A. (1982). The effects of scarcity of material and exclusivity of information on industrial buyer perceived risk in provoking a purchase decision. Unpublished doctoral dissertation, Arizona State University, Tempe. For reviews, see Lynn, M. (1991). Scarcity effects on value: A quantitative review of commodity theory literature. *Psychology & Marketing, 8,* 43–57; Lynn, M. (1992). Scarcity's enhancement of desirability: The role of naive economic theories. *Basic and Applied Social Psychology, 13,* 67–78.

3. Farquhar, P. H., Pratkanis, A. R., & Calvin, D. (1995). Phantom choices: The effects of unavailable alternatives on decision making. Unpublished manuscript, University of California, Santa Cruz.

4. Pratkanis, A. R., & Farquhar, P. H. (1992). A brief history of research on phantom alternatives: Evidence for seven empirical generalizations about phantoms. *Basic and Applied Social Psychology, 13,* 103–122.

5. Mischel, W. (1974). Processes in delay of gratification. In L. Berkowitz (Ed.), *Advances in experimental social psychology* (Vol. 7, pp. 249–292). New York: Academic Press.

6. Holifield, E. B. (1989). *Era of persuasion.* Boston: Twayne, pp. 18–38.

7. Freeman, K., Pratkanis, A. R., & Farquhar, P. H. (1990). Phantoms as psychological motivation: Evidence for compliance and reactance processes. Unpublished manuscript, University of California, Santa Cruz.

8. Snyder, C. R. (1990, August). Scarce experiences and possessions: A source of uniqueness. Paper presented at the annual meeting of the American Psychological Association, Boston; Snyder, C. R., & Fromkin, H. L. (1980). *Uniqueness: The human pursuit of difference.* New York: Plenum.

9. Fromm, E. (1976). *To have or to be?* New York: Harper & Row.

10. Zellinger, D. A., Fromkin, H. L., Speller, D. E., & Kohn, C. A. (1975). A commodity theory analysis of the effects of age restrictions upon pornographic materials. *Journal of Applied Psychology, 60,* 94–99.

11. Farquhar, P. H., & Pratkanis, A. R. (1993). Decision structuring with phantom alternatives. *Management Science, 39,* 1214–1226.

31 Education or Propaganda?

1. For an excellent discussion of the politics of textbooks, see Kahane, H. (1992). *Logic and contemporary rhetoric: The use of reason in everyday life.* Belmont, CA: Wadsworth. To evaluate the portrayal of American minority groups in history books, compare any official textbook with books that describe history from a non-European perspective, such as Templeton, J. W. (1991). *Our roots run deep: The black experience in California, 1500–1900.* San Jose, CA: Electron Access. For example, while many of us know that places such as Virginia and the College of William and Mary were named for British monarchs, we suspect that few Americans realize that California was named for a black queen.

2. Freeman, E. (1937). *Social psychology.* New York: Holt, Rinehart & Winston, especially pp. 263–266; Zimbardo, P. G., Ebbesen, E., & Maslach, C. (1977). *Influencing attitudes and changing behavior.* Reading, MA: Addison-Wesley.

3. For related examples, see Freeman (1937), note 2; Luchins, A. S., & Luchins, E. H. (1978). *Revisiting Wertheimer's seminars* (Vol. 1). Lewisburg, PA: Bucknell University Press, p. 277.

4. Knupfer, N. N., & Hayes, P. (1994). The effects of the Channel One broadcast on students' knowledge of current events. In A. De Vaney (Ed.), *Watching Channel One* (pp. 42–60). Albany: State University of New York Press. For a general discussion of Channel One, see De Vaney, A. (Ed.). (1994). *Watching Channel One.* Albany: State University of New York Press.

5. Vallone, R. P., Ross, L., & Lepper, M. R. (1985). The hostile media phenomenon: Biased perception and perceptions of media bias in coverage of the Beirut massacre. *Journal of Personality and Social Psychology, 49,* 577–585. This is an example of a more general tendency to use one's attitude as a heuristic in problem solving; see Pratkanis, A. R. (1988). The attitude heuristic and selective fact identification. *British Journal of Social Psychology, 27,* 257–263; Pratkanis, A. R., & Greenwald, A. G. (1989). A socio-cognitive model

of attitude structure and function. In L. Berkowitz (Ed.), *Advances in experimental social psychology* (Vol. 22, pp. 245–295). New York: Academic Press.

6. Comstock, G. (1980). *Television in America.* Beverly Hills, CA: Sage.

7. Fallows, J. (1997). *Breaking the news.* New York: Vintage.

8. See Luchins & Luchins (1978), note 3.

9. Maier, N. R. F. (1952). *Principles of human relations.* New York: Wiley; Maier, N. R. F. (1963). *Problem-solving discussions and conferences.* New York: McGraw-Hill.

10. Turner, M. E., & Pratkanis, A. R. (1994). Social identity maintenance prescriptions for preventing groupthink: Reducing identity protection and enhancing intellectual conflict. *International Journal of Conflict Management, 5,* 254–270; Turner, M. E., & Pratkanis, A. R. (1997). Mitigating groupthink by stimulating constructive conflict. In C. K. W. De Dreu & E. Van de Vliert (Eds.), *Using conflict in organizations* (pp. 53–71). Thousand Oaks, CA: Sage; Turner, M. E., & Pratkanis, A. R. (1996). Mitigating the negative consequences of groupthink: Further implications of a social identity maintenance model. Unpublished manuscript, San Jose State University.

32 What Is News?

1. Lippmann, W. (1922). *Public opinion.* New York: Harcourt, Brace.

2. Hale, O. J. (1964). *The captive press in the Third Reich.* Princeton, NJ: Princeton University Press.

3. Benn, D. W. (1989). *Persuasion and Soviet politics.* New York: Blackwell; Mickiewicz, E. (1988). *Split signals.* New York: Oxford University Press; Roxburgh, A. (1987). *Pravda: Inside the Soviet news machine.* New York: Braziller.

4. Steele, R. W. (1985). *Propaganda in an open society: The Roosevelt administration and the media, 1933–1941.* Westport, CT: Greenwood.

5. DeParle, J. (1991, May 6). Keeping the news in step. Are the Pentagon's Gulf War rules here to stay? *New York Times,* p. A9.

6. Fishman, M. (1980). *Manufacturing the news.* Austin: University of Texas Press; Fallows, J. (1997). *Breaking the news.* New York: Vintage; Gans, H. J. (1979). *Deciding what's news.* New York: Vintage; Jamieson, K. H., & Campbell, K. K. (1992). *The interplay of influence.* Belmont, CA: Wadsworth; Kaniss, P. (1991). *Making local news.* Chicago: University of Chicago Press; Nelkin, D. (1987). *Selling*

science. New York: Freeman; Pratkanis, A. R. (1997). The social psychology of mass communications: An American perspective. In D. F. Halpern & A. Voiskounsky (Eds.), *States of mind: American and post-Soviet perspectives on contemporary issues in psychology* (pp. 126–159). New York: Oxford University Press; Tuchman, G. (1978). *Making news*. New York: Free Press.

7. Sigal, L. V. (1973). *Reporters and officials: The organization and politics of newsmaking*. Lexington, MA: Heath.

8. Croteau, D., & Hoynes, W. (1994). *By invitation only*. Monroe, ME: Common Courage.

9. Bagdikian, B. H. (1992). *The media monopoly*. Boston: Beacon. The figures on media monopolies may be out of date before you read them—the mergers keep occurring at a frantic pace. For more information, see Brill, S. (2000, April). The mega threat. *Brill's Content*, pp. 23, 26–27; Rosenwein, R. (2000, January). Why media mergers matter. *Brill's Content*, pp. 92–95.

10. Mark Levy, quoted in *Time*, October 1, 1979, p. 83. See also Bogart, L. (1995). *Commercial culture*. New York: Oxford University Press; Rubin, A. M. (1994). Media uses and effects: A uses-and-gratifications perspective. In J. Bryant & D. Zillman (Eds.), *Media effects*. Hillsdale, NJ: Erlbaum.

11. Ernst, S. W. (1972). Baseball or brickbats: A content analysis of community development. *Journalism Quarterly, 49*, 86–90.

12. Koppel, T., & Gibson, K. (1996). *Nightline*. New York: Random House, p. 230.

13. Mann, P., & Iscoe, I. (1971). Mass behavior and community organization: Reflections on a peaceful demonstration. *American Psychologist, 26*, 108–113. For other examples of how eyewitness reports differ from news accounts, see Dershowitz, A. M. (1996). *Reasonable doubts*. New York: Simon & Schuster; Lang, K., & Lang, G. E. (1968). *Politics & television*. Chicago: Quadrangle Books, especially the chapter entitled "MacArthur Day in Chicago."

14. Gaveling the deadbeats. (1995, July 31). *U.S. News & World Report*, p. 14.

15. For a description of how U.S. presidents control the news, see Maltese, J. A. (1992). *Spin control*. Chapel Hill: University of North Carolina Press.

16. Spence, G. (1995). *How to argue and win every time*. New York: St. Martin's, especially p. 95.

[33] On the Ineffectiveness of Information Campaigns

1. Canon, L. (1964). Self-confidence and selective exposure to information. In L. Festinger (Ed.), *Conflict, decision, and dissonance* (pp. 83–96). Stanford, CA: Stanford University Press. For a review, see Frey, D. (1986). Recent research on selective exposure to information. In L. Berkowitz (Ed.), *Advances in experimental social psychology* (Vol. 19, pp. 41–80). New York: Academic Press.

2. Hyman, H., & Sheatsley, P. B. (1947). Some reasons why information campaigns fail. *Public Opinion Quarterly, 11,* 412–423.

3. Example from Backer, T. E., Rogers, E. M., & Sopory, P. (1992). *Designing health communication campaigns: What works?* Newbury Park, CA: Sage.

4. Schneider, C. (1987). *Children's television: The art, the business, and how it works.* Lincolnwood, IL: NTC Business Books, p. 9.

5. Pratkanis, A. R. (1997). The social psychology of mass communications: An American perspective. In D. F. Halpern & A. Voiskounsky (Eds.), *States of mind: American and post-Soviet perspectives on contemporary issues in psychology* (pp. 126–159). New York: Oxford University Press. For a list of techniques for improving the effectiveness of information campaigns, see Backer, Rogers, & Sopory (1992), note 3, pp. 30–32; Kotler, P., & Roberto, E. L. (1989). *Social marketing.* New York: Free Press.

6. Merton, R. K. (1946). *Mass persuasion: The social psychology of a war bond drive.* New York: Harper & Brothers.

7. Mendelsohn, H. (1973). Some reasons why information campaigns can succeed. *Public Opinion Quarterly, 37,* 50–61.

8. Ball, S., & Bogatz, G. A. (1970). *The first year of Sesame Street.* Princeton, NJ: Educational Testing Service; Bogatz, G. A., & Ball, S. (1972). *The second year of Sesame Street.* Princeton, NJ: Educational Testing Service; Cook, T. D., Appleton, H., Conner, R. F., Shaffer, A., Tabkin, G., & Weber, J. S. (1975). *Sesame Street revisited.* New York: Russell Sage; Liebert, R. M., & Sprafkin, J. (1988). *The early window.* New York: Pergamon; Stein, A. H., & Friedrich, L. K. (1972). *Television content and young children's behavior.* In J. P. Murray, E. A. Rubinstein, & G. A. Comstock (Eds.), *Television and social behavior* (Vol. 2, pp. 202–317). DHEW Publication No. HSM 72-9057. Washington, DC: U.S. Government Printing Office.

9. Entman, R. M. (1989). *Democracy without citizens.* New York: Oxford University Press.

34 Subliminal Sorcery: Who Is Seducing Whom?

1. Cousins, N. (1957, October 5). Smudging the subconscious. *Saturday Review*, p. 20.

2. Key, W. B. (1973). *Subliminal seduction*. Englewood Cliffs, NJ: Signet; Key, W. B. (1976). *Media sexploitation*. Englewood Cliffs, NJ: Signet; Key, W. B. (1980). *The clam-plate orgy*. Englewood Cliffs, NJ: Signet; Key, W. B. (1989). *The age of manipulation*. New York: Holt.

3. Key (1973), p. 1, see note 2.

4. Natale, J. A. (1988, September). Are you open to suggestion? *Psychology Today*, pp. 28–30.

5. Pratkanis, A. R., & Greenwald, A. G. (1988). Recent perspectives on unconscious processing: Still no marketing applications. *Psychology and Marketing, 5*, 339–355. For a description of the history of this research, see Pratkanis, A. R. (1992). The cargo-cult science of subliminal persuasion. *Skeptical Inquirer, 16*, 260–272.

6. For an excellent review of scientific findings on unconscious processes, see Greenwald, A. G. (1992). New look 3: Unconscious cognition reclaimed. *American Psychologist, 47*, 766–779.

7. For example, Hawkins originally reported that subliminal messages could affect physiological drives such as hunger or thirst. However, later he was unable to reproduce this effect. See Hawkins, D. I. (1970). The effects of subliminal stimulation on drive level and brand preference. *Journal of Marketing Research, 7*, 322–326; Beatty, S. E., & Hawkins, D. I. (1989). Subliminal stimulation: Some new data and interpretation. *Journal of Advertising, 18*, 4–8.

8. Moore, T. E. (1982). Subliminal advertising: What you see is what you get. *Journal of Marketing, 46*, 38–47.

9. Haberstroh, J. (1994). *Ice cube sex: The truth about subliminal advertising*. Notre Dame, IN: Cross Roads Books. This book represents one of the best popular efforts to describe and debunk the subliminal affair and is highly recommended to those interested in more information on this topic.

10. "Phone now," said CBC subliminally—but nobody did. (1958, February 10). *Advertising Age*, p. 8.

11. Quoted in Danzig, F. (1962, September 17). Subliminal advertising—Today it's just an historical flashback for researcher Vicary. *Advertising Age*, pp. 73–74. See also Weir, W. (1984, October 15). Another look at subliminal "facts." *Advertising Age*, p. 46.

12. Rogers, S. (1992–1993). How a publicity blitz created the myth of subliminal advertising. *Public Relations Quarterly, 37,* 12–17.

13. See, for example, Gable, M., Wilkens, H. T., Harris, L., & Feinberg, R. (1987). An evaluation of subliminally embedded sexual stimuli in graphics. *Journal of Advertising, 16,* 26–31; George, S. G., & Jennings, L. B. (1975). Effects of subliminal stimuli on consumer behavior: Negative evidence. *Perceptual and Motor Skills, 41,* 847–854.

14. Vokey, J. R., & Read, J. D. (1985). Subliminal messages: Between the devil and the media. *American Psychologist, 40,* 1231–1239.

15. Pratkanis, A. R., Eskenazi, J., & Greenwald, A. G. (1994). What you expect is what you believe (but not necessarily what you get): A test of the effectiveness of subliminal self-help audiotapes. *Basic and Applied Social Psychology, 15,* 251–276.

16. Greenwald, A. G., Spangenberg, E. R., Pratkanis, A. R., & Eskenazi, J. (1991). Double-blind tests of subliminal self-help audiotapes. *Psychological Science, 2,* 119–122.

17. See Pratkanis, Eskenazi, & Greenwald (1994), note 15, pp. 268–269.

18. British Psychological Society. (1992). *Subliminal messages.* Leicester, England. Eich, E., & Hyman, R. (1991). Subliminal self-help. In D. Druckman & R. A. Bjork (Eds.), *In the mind's eye: Enhancing human performance* (pp. 107–119). Washington, DC: National Academy Press.

19. For a description of recent studies claiming subliminal effects, see Epley, N., Savitsky, K., & Kachelski, R. A. (1999). What every skeptic should know about subliminal persuasion. *Skeptical Inquirer, 23*(5), 40–45, 58. It will be interesting to see if the claims made in this research will go the same course as past claims.

20. Zanot, E. J., Pincus, J. D., & Lamp, E. J. (1983). Public perceptions of subliminal advertising. *Journal of Advertising, 12,* 37–45. For more recent poll results, see Haberstroh (1994), note 9.

21. For a description of the trial, see Moore, T. E. (1996). Scientific consensus and expert testimony: Lessons from the Judas Priest trial. *Skeptical Inquirer, 20*(6), 32–38, 60.

22. In Re *Vance and Belknap v. Judas Priest and CBS Records.* 86-5844/86-3939. Second District Court of Nevada. August 24, 1990, p. 31.

35 Persuasion Direct

1. See Baier, M. (1983). *Elements of direct marketing*. New York: McGraw-Hill; Caples, J. (1974). *Tested advertising methods*. Englewood Cliffs, NJ: Prentice Hall; Harper, R. (1986). *Mailing list strategies*. New York: McGraw-Hill; Popeil, R. (1995). *The salesman of the century*. New York: Delacorte; Schumann, D. W., & Thorson, E. (Eds.). (1999). *Advertising and the World Wide Web*. Mahwah, NJ: Erlbaum; Stone, B. (1986). *Successful direct marketing methods*. Lincolnwood, IL: Crain; Wunderman, L. (1997). *Being direct*. New York: Random House; Zeff, R., & Aronson, B. (1999). *Advertising on the Internet*. New York: Wiley.

36 How to Become a Cult Leader

1. Hostetler, J. A. (1974). *Hutterite society*. Baltimore: Johns Hopkins University Press; Redekop, C. (1989). *Mennonite society*. Baltimore: Johns Hopkins University Press; Strayer, J. R., Gatzke, H. W., & Harbison, E. H. (1974). *The mainstream of civilization*. New York: Harcourt Brace Jovanovich.

2. Sifakis, C. (1993). *Hoaxes and scams*. New York: Facts on File.

3. Singer, M. T., & Lalich, J. (1995). *Cults in our midst*. San Francisco: Jossey-Bass. This book is highly recommended to those seeking a more in-depth treatment of cults.

4. See Singer & Lalich (1995), note 3.

5. Examples and details are from Butterfield, S. (1985). *Amway: The cult of free enterprise*. Boston: South End Press; Galanter, M. (1989). *Cults: Faith, healing, and coercion*. New York: Oxford University Press; Hassan, S. (1990). *Combatting cult mind control*. Rochester, VT: Park Street Press; Kanter, R. M. (1972). *Commitment and community: Communes and utopias in sociological perspective*. Cambridge, MA: Harvard University Press; Kaplan, D. E., & Marshall, A. (1996). *The cult at the end of the world*. New York: Crown; Kramer, J., & Alstad, D. (1993). *The guru papers*. Berkeley, CA: North Atlantic Books/Frog Ltd.; Lifton, R. J. (1963). *Thought reform and the psychology of totalism: A study of "brainwashing" in China*. New York: Norton; Osherow, N. (1988). Making sense of the nonsensical: An analysis of Jonestown. In E. Aronson (Ed.), *Readings about the social animal* (pp. 68–86). New York: Freeman; Patrick, T., & Dulack, T. (1976). *Let our children go!* New York: Ballantine; Ritchie, J. (1991). *The secret world of cults*. London: Angus & Robertson; Schein, E. H. (1961). *Coercive*

persuasion. New York: Norton; Stoner, C., & Parke, J. A. (1977). *All God's children.* Radnor, PA: Chilton Book Co.; Tabor, J. D., & Gallagher, E. V. (1995). *Why Waco?* Berkeley: University of California Press; Tobias, M. L., & Lalich, J. (1994). *Captive hearts, captive minds.* Alameda, CA: Hunter House; Weightman, J. M. (1983). *Making sense of the Jonestown suicides.* New York: Mellen. For another example of the use of these tactics, see Pratkanis, A. R. (1995). How to sell a pseudoscience. *Skeptical Inquirer, 19*(4), 19–25.

6. Patrick & Dulack (1976), p. 45, see note 5.

7. For discussions on how to leave destructive cultic groups, see Hassan, S. (2000). *Releasing the bonds: Empowering people to think for themselves.* Somerville, MA: Freedom of Mind Press; Lagone, M. D. (Ed.). (1993). *Recovery from cults.* New York: Norton.

37 Propaganda in the Third Reich: A Case for Uncertainty

1. Hitler, A. (1925). *Mein Kampf.* Boston: Houghton Mifflin, p. 176.

2. Jowett, G. S., & O'Donnell, V. (1986). *Persuasion and propaganda.* Beverly Hills, CA: Sage; Peterson, H. C. (1939). *Propaganda for war: The campaign against American neutrality, 1914–1917.* Norman: University of Oklahoma Press.

3. For excellent discussions of Nazi and World War II propaganda, see Childers, T. (1983). *The Nazi voter.* Chapel Hill: University of North Carolina Press; Doob, L. W. (1950). Goebbels' principles of propaganda. *Public Opinion Quarterly, 14,* 419–422; Hale, O. J. (1964). *The captive press in the Third Reich.* Princeton, NJ: Princeton University Press; Herzstein, R. E. (1978). *The war that Hitler won.* New York: Paragon House; Lipstadt, D. E. (1986). *Beyond belief.* New York: Free Press; Rhodes, A. (1987). *Propaganda: The art of persuasion: World War II.* Secaucus, NJ: Wellfleet; Rutherford, W. (1978). *Hitler's propaganda machine.* London: Bison; Welch, D. (1983). *Nazi propaganda.* Beckenham, UK: Croom Helm; Young, J, W. (1991). *Totalitarian language.* Charlottesville: University of Virginia Press; Zeman, Z. A. B. (1964). *Nazi propaganda.* London: Oxford University Press.

4. Hitler (1925), p. 178, see note 1

5. Hitler (1925), pp. 180–181, see note 1.

6. Bergmeier, H. J. P., & Lotz, R. E. (1997). *Hitler's airwaves: The inside story of Nazi radio broadcasting and propaganda swing.* New Haven, CT: Yale University Press. This analysis of the Nazi use of entertainment as propaganda also contains a CD-ROM with Nazi propaganda through music directed at the Allies.

7. Poliakov, L. (1971). *The Aryan myth*. New York: Barnes & Noble.

8. Corcoran, J. (1995). *Bitter harvest*. New York: Penguin; Dees, M. (1996). *Gathering storm*. New York: HarperCollins; Ezekiel, R. S. (1995). *The racist mind*. New York: Viking.

9. Quoted in Rhodes (1987), p. 13, see note 3.

10. Bronowski, J. (1973). *The ascent of man*. Boston: Little, Brown.

11. Hitler (1925), pp. 182–183, see note 1.

12. Quoted in Rhodes (1987), p. 90, see note 3.

38 Is Forewarned Forearmed? Or How to Really Resist Propaganda

1. Davidson, W. P. (1983). The third-person effect in communication. *Public Opinion Quarterly, 47,* 1–15. For an explication of the psychological processes underlying this effect, see Duck, J. M., Hogg, M. A., & Terry, D. J. (1995). Me, us, and them: Political identification and the third-person effect in the 1993 Australian federal election. *European Journal of Social Psychology, 25,* 195–215; Duck, J. M., Terry, D. J., & Hogg, M. A. (1995). The perceived influence of AIDS advertising: Third-person effects in the context of positive media content. *Basic and Applied Social Psychology, 17,* 305–325; Hoorens, V., & Ruiter, S. (1996). The optimal impact phenomenon: Beyond the third-person effect. *European Journal of Social Psychology, 26,* 599–610.

2. Liebert, R. M., & Sprafkin, J. (1988). *The early window.* New York: Pergamon. See also Macklin, M. C., & Carlson, L. (Eds.). (1999). *Advertising to children.* Thousand Oaks, CA: Sage.

3. Teinowitz, I. (1996, August 26). "Historic" attack on cig marketing. *Advertising Age,* pp. 1, 28.

4. For a review, see Cialdini, R. B., & Petty, R. E. (1981). Anticipatory opinion effects. In R. E. Petty, T. M. Ostrom, & T. C. Brock (Eds.), *Cognitive responses in persuasion* (pp. 217–235). Hillsdale, NJ: Erlbaum.

5. Freedman, J. L., & Sears, D. O. (1965). Warning, distraction, and resistance to influence. *Journal of Personality and Social Psychology, 1,* 262–266.

6. Cialdini, R. B., Levy, A., Herman, C. P., & Evenbeck, S. (1973). Attitudinal politics: The strategy of moderation. *Journal of Personality and Social Psychology, 25,* 100–108; Cialdini, R. B., Levy, A., Herman, C. P., Kozlowski, L. T., & Petty, R. E. (1976). Elastic shifts of opinion:

Determinants of direction and durability. *Journal of Personality and Social Psychology, 34,* 663–672.

7. Watts, W. A., & Holt, L. E. (1979). Persistence of opinion change induced under conditions of forewarning and distraction. *Journal of Personality and Social Psychology, 37,* 778–789.

8. Butterfield, S. (1985). *Amway: The cult of free enterprise.* Boston: South End Press, p. 11.

9. Petty, R. E., & Cacioppo, J. T. (1979). Effect of forewarning of persuasive intent and involvement on cognitive responses and persuasion. *Personality and Social Psychology Bulletin, 5,* 173–176.

10. Williams, K. D., Bourgeois, M. J., & Croyle, R. T. (1993). The effects of stealing thunder in criminal and civil trials. *Law and Human Behavior, 17,* 597–609.

11. Spence, G. (1995). *How to argue and win every time.* New York: St. Martin's, p. 131.

12. Bugliosi, V. (1996). *Outrage: The five reasons why O. J. Simpson got away with murder.* New York: Norton, p. 117.

13. Ross, S. (1988). *Fall from grace.* New York: Ballantine.

14. McGuire, W. J., & Papageorgis, D. (1961). The relative efficacy of various types of prior belief-defense in producing immunity against persuasion. *Journal of Abnormal and Social Psychology, 62,* 327–337. See also McGuire, W. J. (1964). Inducing resistance to change: Some contemporary approaches. In L. Berkowitz (Ed.), *Advances in experimental social psychology* (Vol. 1, pp. 191–229). New York: Academic Press.

15. For a discussion of the use of inoculation in politics, see Pfau, M., & Kenski, H. C. (1990). *Attack politics.* New York: Praeger; Pratkanis, A. R. (1993). Propaganda and persuasion in the 1992 U.S. presidential election: What are the implications for a democracy? *Current World Leaders, 35,* 341–362.

16. McAlister, A., Perry, C., Killen, J., Slinkard, L. A., & Maccoby, N. (1980). Pilot study of smoking, alcohol and drug abuse prevention. *American Journal of Public Health, 70,* 719–721.

17. Pryor, B., & Steinfatt, T. (1978). The effects of initial belief level on inoculation theory and its proposed mechanisms. *Human Communications Research, 4,* 217–230.

[39] What We Can Do to Stop Propaganda in Its Tracks

1. Further discussion of ways to stop propaganda can be found in Anderson, S., & Zimbardo, P. G. (1984). On resisting social influence. *Cultic Studies Journal, 1,* 196–219; Bogart, L. (1995). *Commercial culture.* New York: Oxford University Press; Capaldi, N. (1987). *The art of deception.* Buffalo, NY: Prometheus; Cialdini, R. B. (1984). *Influence.* New York: Morrow; Eiler, A. (1984). *The consumer protection manual.* New York: Facts on File; Gilbert, M. A. (1996). *How to win an argument.* New York: Wiley; Green, M. (1995). *The consumer bible.* New York: Workman; Jacobson, M. F., & Mazur, L. A. (1995). *Marketing madness.* Boulder, CO: Westview; Pratkanis, A. R. (1993). Propaganda and persuasion in the 1992 U.S. presidential election: What are the implications for a democracy? *Current World Leaders, 35,* 341–362; Pratkanis, A. R., & Turner, M. E. (1996). Persuasion and democracy: Strategies for increasing deliberative participation and enacting social change. *Journal of Social Issues, 52,* 187–205; Preston, I. L. (1994). *The tangled web they weave.* Madison: University of Wisconsin Press; Sabato, L. J., & Simpson, G. R. (1996). *Dirty little secrets: The persistence of corruption in American politics.* New York: Random House; Schulte, F. (1995). *Fleeced!* Amherst, NY: Prometheus; Zimbardo, P. G., & Anderson, S. (1993). Understanding mind control: Exotic and mundane mental manipulations. In M. D. Lagone (Ed.), *Recovery from cults* (pp. 104–125). New York: Norton.

2. Sagarin, B. J., Cialdini, R. B., Rice, W. E., & Serna, S. B. (2000). Dispelling the illusion of invulnerability: The motivations and mechanisms of resistance to persuasion. Unpublished manuscript, Northern Illinois University.

3. Quoted in Young, J. W. (1991). *Totalitarian language.* Charlottesville: University of Virginia Press, p. 225.

4. Asch, S. E. (1955). Opinions and social pressure. *Scientific American, 193,* 31–35; Pratkanis, A. R., Horvitz, T., & Gliner, M. (1996). A replication of the Asch line experiment for NBC Dateline. Unpublished data, University of California, Santa Cruz.

5. See Eiler (1984), note 1, for a complete list and excellent advice on consumer issues.

6. Brill, S. (2000, April). The mega threat. *Brill's Content,* pp. 23, 26–27; Rosenwein, R. (2000, January). Why media mergers matter. *Brill's Content,* pp. 92–95.

7. For more ways to stop negative campaigning, see Jamieson, K. H. (1992). *Dirty politics.* New York: Oxford University Press. For a discussion of how to improve media coverage of elections, see Pratkanis, A. R. (2001). Propaganda and deliberative persuasion: The implications of Americanized mass media for established and emerging democracies. In W. Wosinski, R. B. Cialdini, J. Reykowski, & D. W. Barrett (Eds.), *The practice of social influence in multiple cultures* (pp. 259–285). Mahwah, NJ: Erlbaum.

8. These numbers are based on a typical federal budget during the 1990s; the Jones's contribution to each item is merely the percent of the budget for that item applied to the Jones's tax contribution.

9. Suchard, D. (1993, February 15). "The seduction" of TV ads: Popular Dutch talk show focuses on and reviews commercials. *Advertising Age,* I–3, I–22.

10. See Preston (1994), note 1, for an excellent discussion of deception in advertising and what can be done about it.

11. We thank Peter Farquhar and Naveen Goyal for discussions on consumer regulations involving unavailability.

12. See Schulte (1995), note 1, for an excellent discussion of telemarketing fraud.

13. Lewin, K., & Lippitt, R. (1938). An experimental approach to the study of autocracy and democracy: A preliminary note. *Sociometry, 1,* 292–300; Lewin, K., Lippitt, R., & White, R. K. (1939). Patterns of aggressive behavior in experimentally created climates. *Journal of Social Psychology, 10,* 271–299; Pratkanis (2001), see note 7; Pratkanis & Turner (1996), see note 1; White, R. K., & Lippitt, R. (1960). *Autocracy and democracy: An experimental inquiry.* New York: Harper & Brothers.

14. Beck, E. M., & Tolnay, S. E. (1990). The killing fields of the deep South: The market for cotton and the lynching of blacks, 1882–1930. *American Sociological Review, 55,* 526–539; Ezekiel, R. S. (1995). *The racist mind.* New York: Viking; Pettigrew, T. F. (1971). *Racially separate or together?* New York: McGraw-Hill; Pratkanis, A. R., & Turner, M. E. (1999). The significance of affirmative action for the souls of white folk: Further implications of a helping model. *Journal of Social Issues, 55,* 787–815; Senechal, R. (1990). *The sociogenesis of a race riot.* Urbana: University of Illinois Press.

40 Peitho's Children

1. For discussions of the ethics and role of persuasion in society, see Alinsky, S. D. (1971). *Rules for radicals.* New York: Vintage; Entman, R. M. (1989). *Democracy without citizens.* New York: Oxford University Press; Cialdini, R. B. (1996). Social influence and the triple tumor structure of organizational dishonesty. In D. M. Messick & A. E. Tenbrunsel (Eds.), *Codes of conduct* (pp. 44–58). New York: Russell Sage; Fisher, R., Ury, W., & Patton, B. (1991). *Getting to yes.* New York: Penguin; Freire, P. (1968). *Pedagogy of the oppressed.* New York: Seabury; Johannesen, R. L. (1967). *Ethics and persuasion.* New York: Random House; Pratkanis, A. R., & Turner, M. E. (1996). Persuasion and democracy: Strategies for increasing deliberative participation and enacting social change. *Journal of Social Issues, 52,* 187–205; Qualter, T. H. (1962). *Propaganda and psychological warfare.* New York: Random House; Spence, G. (1995). *How to argue and win every time.* New York: St. Martin's; Stone, I. F. (1988). *The trial of Socrates.* Boston: Little, Brown; Zimbardo, P. G. (1972). The tactics and ethics of persuasion. In B. T. King & E. McGinnies (Eds.), *Attitudes, conflict, and social change* (pp. 81–99). New York: Academic Press. For an example of the prosocial use of persuasion, see Pratkanis, A. R., & Turner, M. E. (1994). Nine principles of successful affirmative action: Mr. Branch Rickey, Mr. Jackie Robinson, and the integration of baseball. *Nine: A Journal of Baseball History and Social Policy Perspectives, 3,* 36–65.

2. For an example of one set of rules governing the means of persuasion, see Cialdini (1996), note 1.

3. Quoted in Alinsky (1971), p. 25, see note 1.

4. For an excellent discussion of press coverage of the Holocaust, see Lipstadt, D. E. (1986). *Beyond belief: The American press and the coming of the Holocaust 1933–1945.* New York: Free Press.

INDEX ▪▪▪▪▪▪▪▪▪▪▪▪▪▪▪▪▪▪▪▪

ABOUT THE AUTHORS ||||||||||||||||||||||

ANTHONY PRATKANIS is Professor of Psychology at the University of California, Santa Cruz, where he studies social psychology, social influence, and prejudice reduction. An engaging classroom teacher, he began his career in the business school at Carnegie-Mellon University, where he taught popular courses in advertising and consumer behavior. Dr. Pratkanis's expertise is sought by both public and private enterprises. His testimony on subliminal persuasion at the trial of CBS Records/Judas Priest was instrumental in winning that case for the defense. Currently, he is working with various civic groups and law enforcement agencies on strategies for preventing economic fraud crimes. He has appeared in the mass media more than 200 times, including the "Oprah Winfrey Show," "Dateline NBC," "CBS News," C-Span, and CNN, and his research has been translated into eight languages. A frequent contributor to scientific journals and the popular press on the topics of persuasion and influence, he is a co-editor of *Attitude Structure and Function* and of *Social Psychology*, as well as a past associate editor of the *Journal of Consumer Psychology*. In 1995, he was elected a fellow of the American Psychological Association.

ELLIOT ARONSON is Research Professor of Psychology at the University of California, Santa Cruz, and Visiting Professor of Psychology at Stanford University. He is generally considered to be one of the world's most versatile and distinguished social psychologists. His research on the topics of persuasion, social attraction, prejudice reduction, and cognitive dissonance represents some of the most important and seminal experiments conducted in the field of social psychology. He is the recipient of the American Psychological Association's Distinguished Scientific Career Award. In 1970 he won the American Association for the Advancement of Science prize for distinguished basic research in social psychology. A gifted teacher, he has received numerous teaching awards, including awards from the American Psychological Association, the American Council for the Advancement and Support of Education, the University of California, and the University of Texas. He is the only person in the history of the American Psychological Association to have won all three of its major academic awards: for Distinguished Teaching, for Distinguished Research, and for Distinguished Writing. Dr. Aronson is the author of many books, including *The Jigsaw Classroom, Methods of Research in Social Psychology, The Social Animal,* and *Nobody Left to Hate;* and, for some twenty-five years, he was the co-editor of *The Handbook of Social Psychology.* Inducted in 1992, Aronson is a fellow of the American Academy of Arts and Sciences.